VIRAL MODERNISM

MODERNIST LATITUDES

MODERNIST LATITUDES

Jessica Berman and Paul Saint-Amour, Editors

Modernist Latitudes aims to capture the energy and ferment of modernist studies by continuing to open up the range of forms, locations, temporalities, and theoretical approaches encompassed by the field. The series celebrates the growing latitude ("scope for freedom of action or thought") that this broadening affords scholars of modernism, whether they are investigating little-known works or revisiting canonical ones. Modernist Latitudes will pay particular attention to the texts and contexts of those latitudes (Africa, Latin America, Australia, Asia, Southern Europe, and even the rural United States) that have long been misrecognized as ancillary to the canonical modernisms of the global North.

Barry McCrea, *In the Company of Strangers: Family and Narrative in Dickens, Conan Doyle, Joyce, and Proust*, 2011

Jessica Berman, *Modernist Commitments: Ethics, Politics, and Transnational Modernism*, 2011

Jennifer Scappettone, *Killing the Moonlight: Modernism in Venice*, 2014

Nico Israel, *Spirals: The Whirled Image in Twentieth-Century Literature and Art*, 2015

Carrie Noland, *Voices of Negritude in Modernist Print: Aesthetic Subjectivity, Diaspora, and the Lyric Regime*, 2015

Susan Stanford Friedman, *Planetary Modernisms: Provocations on Modernity Across Time*, 2015

Steven S. Lee, *The Ethnic Avant-Garde: Minority Cultures and World Revolution*, 2015

Thomas S. Davis, *The Extinct Scene: Late Modernism and Everyday Life*, 2016

Carrie J. Preston, *Learning to Kneel: Noh, Modernism, and Journeys in Teaching*, 2016

Gayle Rogers, *Incomparable Empires: Modernism and the Translation of Spanish and American Literature*, 2016

Donal Harris, *On Company Time: American Modernism in the Big Magazines*, 2016

Celia Marshik, *At the Mercy of Their Clothes: Modernism, the Middlebrow, and British Garment Culture*, 2016

Christopher Reed, *Bachelor Japanists: Japanese Aesthetics and Western Masculinities*, 2016

Eric Hayot and Rebecca L. Walkowitz, eds., *A New Vocabulary for Global Modernism*, 2016

Eric Bulson, *Little Magazine, World Form*, 2016

Aarthi Vadde, *Chimeras of Form: Modernist Internationalism Beyond Europe, 1914–2014*, 2016

Ben Conisbee Baer, *Indigenous Vanguards: Education, National Liberation, and the Limits of Modernism*, 2019

Viral Modernism

THE INFLUENZA PANDEMIC AND
INTERWAR LITERATURE

Elizabeth Outka

Columbia University Press
New York

Columbia University Press
Publishers Since 1893
New York   Chichester, West Sussex
cup.columbia.edu
Copyright © 2020 Columbia University Press
All rights reserved

Cataloging-in-Publication Data available from the Library of Congress.
ISBN 978-0-231-18574-5 (cloth)
ISBN 978-0-231-18575-2 (paper)
ISBN 978-0-231-54631-7 (e-book)

LCCN 2019019066

Cover design: Chang Jae Lee
Cover image: A warehouse converted to keep infected people quarantined, 1918;
courtesy of Universal History Archive/UIG/Bridgeman Images

To all my parents

And in memory of
Gertrude, Ada, Marian, Lizzie P,
and Renée

CONTENTS

CONTENTS

ACKNOWLEDGMENTS

I am grateful to many individuals and institutions for their support.

A fellowship from the National Endowment for the Humanities granted me the time and resources I needed to complete this project.

The Imperial War Museum in London houses the most important archive of letters on the pandemic, and their dedicated staff made the many hours I spent in the research room a pleasure. I was also expertly guided by the staff at the Cambridge University Library, which holds the Society of Psychical Research archives; at the Bodleian Library at the University of Oxford; and at the Yale Divinity School Library. The dedicated individuals at the University of Richmond's Boatwright Library, especially Marcia Whitehead, Molly Fair, Lucretia McCulley, and the Interlibrary Loan miracle team (Sam Schuth, Jalesa Taylor, and Travis Smith) provided help at every stage. A special shout-out to Jeannine Keefer, whose image wizardry made the book's illustrations possible.

Many institutions provided me with images and permissions. Special thanks to Trenton Streck-Havill, National Museum of Health and Medicine; Dorothy Lazard and Kate Conn, Oakland Public Library; Holly Reed, U.S. National Archives; Adam Lyon and Kathleen Knies, Museum of History and Industry; Shawn Weldon, Catholic Historical Research Center of the Archdiocese of Philadelphia; James Humble, St. Charles Seminary; Ove

Kvavik, Munchmuseet; Todd Leibowitz, Artists Rights Society; Thomas Haggerty, Bridgeman Images; Tristan Dahn, College of Physicians of Philadelphia; Nicole Courrier, University of Manitoba Archives; Christina Campbell, Sandra Powlette, and Chris Rawlings, British Library; and Martyn Jolly, Australian National University, for speedy advice at a helpful moment. Full credit information may be found with the images.

My home institution, the University of Richmond, awarded me an enhanced sabbatical, which was essential to my work, as well as a subvention to support the book's publication. My deep thanks to my dean, Patrice Rankine, and former dean, Kathleen Skerrett, for their support. The Faculty Research Grants Committee funded summer research and travel to various archives.

As this book was in its final stages, I worked with the Valentine Museum in Richmond on an exhibition that traced the history of diseases in the city, including the 1918–1919 influenza. My gratitude to Meg Hughes, curator of archives; William J. Martin, director of the museum; and the rest of the staff for their encouragement. Thanks, too, to Laura Browder, Rosina D'Angelo, Gertrude Howland, Mary Ann Haske, John Hager, Carol Kennedy, and Gordon and Joan Kerby.

Many colleagues at Richmond have offered support. My chair, Louis Schwartz, cheered the project at every turn. Special thanks to Bert Ashe, Laura Browder, Abigail Cheever, Terry Dolson, Joe Essid, Jan French, Terryl Givens, Libby Gruner, Brian Henry, April and Malcolm Hill, Ray Hilliard, Amy Howard, Lisa Jobe-Shields, Suzanne Jones, Laura Knouse, Lázaro Lima, Tze Loo, Peter Lurie, Joyce MacAllister, Thomas Manganaro, Rob Nelson, Kevin Pelletier, Lidia Radi, Anthony Russell, Nicole Sackley, Monika Siebert, Julietta Singh, Erling Sjovold, Nathan Snaza, David Stevens, Rania Sweis, Emily Tarchokov, Tim Vest, and Eric Yellin.

My incomparable Work-in-Progress group—Amy Howard, Kevin Pelletier, and Monika Siebert—read far more drafts than they should have and offered humor, love, and incisive critiques. The friendship and intellectual energy of Bert Ashe, Abigail Cheever, Libby Gruner, Marie Hawthorne, Peter Lurie, Namita Pandiri Mohideen, Lidia Radi, Anthony Winner, and the Local Saturdays group (led by Kendra Vendetti) sustained me. The Central Virginia British Studies Seminar, led by Christopher Bischof, gave me excellent suggestions for the introduction. A special thanks to Robert Volpicelli for his advice and smart readings.

And thanks to many others who supported both me and the project, including Val Ashe, Sherri Bergman, Amy Byrne, Tam Carlson, Bill Clarkson, Debra Rae Cohen, David Coe, Virginia Cope, Virginia Craighill, Kevin Dettmar, Anne Fernald, Charlie Feigenoff, Fiona Givens, John and Elizabeth Grammer, Mark Gruner, Chuck and Sally Kearney, Stephen Kern, Kirsten Kindler, Clare Kinney, Lisa Kountoupes, Diana Lazarus, Celia Marshik, Kelly Malone, Pamela Macfie, Gayle McKeen, Jennifer Michael, Brendan O'Neill, Uma Outka, Jim Pappas, Ed and Jill Pollard, John Pollard, Mason and Stacy Pollard, Wyatt Prunty, Abuzer Rafey, John Reichman, Sandra Shelley, Vincent Sherry, Ian Tewksbury, Lauryl Tucker, Maya Weber, Jennifer Wicke, Wallis Wheeler, Mark Wollaeger, and Mary and Vince Wood.

My anonymous readers for Columbia University Press offered essential advice for sharpening the manuscript, and I am grateful for their smart readings and suggestions. A very special thanks to Sarah Cole, who gave generously of her time and insight and who was instrumental in suggesting new directions for the manuscript. My terrific editor, Philip Leventhal, shepherded the project through all its stages with skill and patience, and his assistant, Monique Briones, lent her able guidance. Thanks to Michael Haskell, who oversaw the book's production at Columbia; Rob Fellman, who offered outstanding editing; Arc Indexing; and Jordan Ashe. The amazing series editors for Modernist Latitudes, Jessica Berman and Paul Saint-Amour, were early supporters of the project, and I am honored to be part of their distinguished series.

I was fortunate to test many of these ideas during talks at the Modernist Studies Association and the Modern Language Association conferences and during invited talks at Columbia University and the University of Illinois; special thanks to Sam Mitchell and Gordon Hutner for arranging those invitations. Some of the material in the introduction and snippets of other chapters appeared in "'Wood for the Coffins Ran Out': Modernism and the Shadowed Afterlife of the Influenza Pandemic," *Modernism/modernity* 21, no. 4 (2014): 937–60; portions of the Woolf and spiritualism material appeared in "Dead Men, Walking: Actors, Networks, and Actualized Metaphors in *Mrs. Dalloway* and *Raymond*," *NOVEL: A Forum on Fiction* 46, no. 2 (2013): 253–74. I am grateful to both journals for permission to reprint as well as to Faber and Faber Ltd. for permission to quote additional lines from *The Waste Land*, in *Collected Poems: 1909–1962* (London: Faber and Faber, 1963).

I owe a particular debt to several family members. My amazing father and stepmother, Gene and Ann Outka, were incisive interlocutors and cheered the book from its early stages to its final form. The best in-laws anyone could ask for, Elizabeth Pollard and the late Oliver Pollard, Jr., supported me throughout the process. My wonderful mother and stepfather, Carole DeVore and Paul Stuehrenberg, not only offered love and moral support but also braved dusty archives and helped me sort through hundreds of letters at the Imperial War Museum in London. The dedication for my book includes all these parents. Jackie Outka, my brilliant sister, was instrumental in steering me toward several key works, and her generous spirit sustained me through the project. My beloved children, Kate and Tom, spent their high school and college years hearing about the flu, and they nevertheless provided me with constant joy and inspiration. My brother, Paul Outka, a fellow English professor, has been central to this book, bringing his brilliant and always generous critical eye to every page, as well as his humor and unwavering care to every part of my life.

And finally, my deepest gratitude and love go to my husband, partner, and best friend, Trip Pollard. Living with someone who is writing a book is never easy, even if Trip made it seem so, and his intellectual contributions to the project are matched by his love and support from the start to the finish.

Now go get your flu shot.

VIRAL MODERNISM

Chapter One

INTRODUCING THE PANDEMIC

This book investigates a modernist mystery: why does the deadly 1918–1919 influenza pandemic seem to make so few appearances in British, Irish, and American literature of the period? Globally, the pandemic killed between 50 and 100 million people, and the United States suffered more deaths in the pandemic than in World War I, World War II, and the conflicts in Korea, Vietnam, Afghanistan, and Iraq—combined.[1] In Britain, while more died in World War I, a third of the population, or ten million people, caught the flu, and at least 228,000 died, making it, as the historian Mark Honigsbaum observes, "the greatest disease holocaust that Britain ... has ever witnessed."[2] Ireland alone lost 23,000 people, far outstripping the 5,000 deaths from the better-known civic political violence between 1916 and 1923.[3] The pandemic also had profound effects on writers and artists: Guillaume Apollinaire and Gustav Klimt died; D. H. Lawrence, Katherine Anne Porter, the poet H.D., and Edvard Munch barely survived; W. B. Yeats nursed his pregnant wife through her almost fatal brush with the virus; and Nella Larsen "worked seven days a week" nursing patients through the outbreak.[4] Thomas Wolfe lost his brother, T. S. Eliot feared his brain was damaged by his case of the flu, and Virginia Woolf's initial scoffing at the pandemic's danger turned into a profound reflection on illness. Given these effects and the period in which they occurred, it is equally astonishing that the flu is rarely considered in modernist scholarship.[5]

Viral Modernism investigates this conspicuous literary and critical silence, analyzing how our assumptions about modernism, modernity, and the interwar period in Anglo-American culture change when we account for the pandemic's devastation. The era's viral catastrophe has been hidden since its arrival, drowned out by its overwhelming scope, by the broader ways outbreaks of disease are often muted, and by the way the human-inflicted violence of the time consumed cultural and literary attention. Reading for the pandemic offers a case study in how certain types of mass death become less "grievable" (in Judith Butler's formulation) than others, with deaths in the pandemic consistently seen as less important or politically useful.[6] The millions of flu deaths didn't (and don't) count as history in the ways the war casualties did, and *Viral Modernism* examines how and why such erasures happen. When we fail to read for illness in general and the 1918 pandemic in particular, we reify how military conflict has come to define history, we deemphasize illness and pandemics in ways that hide their threat, and we take part in long traditions that align illness with seemingly less valiant, more feminine forms of death. More specifically, this book reveals how the terrain of modernism—and modernist studies—changes when we start seeing the pandemic's effects, altering assumptions about death and sacrifice; shifting enemies, threats, and targets; and changing the calculus of risk and blame between the home front and the front line.

Despite the pandemic's seeming disappearance, its traces are everywhere in the literature and the culture, and this instructive tension lies at the heart of the book. All the reasons for the erasure—from the war's dominance to the invisible quality of this viral threat to the difficulties of representing illness—are intrinsic to the pandemic's literary representations, paradoxically captured in gaps, silences, atmospheres, fragments, and hidden bodies. Recovering the pandemic in the literature requires recognizing these traces and seeing their spectral quality as inherent to a tragedy that fundamentally differed from the war's more obvious manifestations. If we know what to look for, the literature of the era emerges as particularly adept at representing the pandemic's particular qualities and its vast yet hidden presence. The pandemic's very instantiation was often one of atmosphere, of bodily sensations, and of affective shifts, and its threat was literally microscopic. The war, by contrast, was easier to see, with demarcated roles for soldiers and civilians and events that unfolded in a realm accustomed to visibility: male contests of strength and power. Certainly the literature at the time made the war a central focus. Yet this literature (and, as I detail, especially modernist literature) also excelled at representing the pandemic's spectral presence and the changes it produced on the streets, in domestic spaces, within families, and in the body. These realms of experience—the sensory, the atmospheric, and the affective—are often precisely the realms left out of written histories but infused into memories, poems, and novels. While the national governments at the time remained invested in structuring the moment around the war, literature became an outlet for alternative frames, offering places to "see" the private, endlessly repeated horror of a Grim Reaper that stalked silently and stealthily. As we reread texts as familiar as *Mrs. Dalloway* and *The Waste Land* through the lens of the pandemic, metaphors of modernism take on new meanings: fragmentation and disorder emerge as signs of delirium as well as shrapnel; invasions become ones of microbes and not only men; postwar ennui reveals a brooding fear of an invisible enemy.

Establishing the pandemic's importance alters not only the metaphors but also the contours of modernism and how we read it. The pandemic is a hidden force that has been there all along, exerting weight and influence. When we learn to see the effects of this force, a new interpretive landscape emerges. Illness and the body become more central, with iconic texts articulating the rippling and hard-to-capture effects that an invading virus produces within the physical body and in the body politic. The war shifts from the central source of horror and tragedy to a paired event of mass death, its memorialization bringing the war's missing into view while obscuring bodies fallen in the pandemic. New forms of violence—an internal corruption, a miasmic enemy, an invisible weapon, a spreading contagion—become foils to the more visible violence of war. The very avoidance of the pandemic fundamentally shapes the period and thus changes how we read it: the virus becomes the ultimate form of Yeats's "mere anarchy," an invisible power without human agency and outside all control. When we recognize the terror and subsequent evasion that such a threat produced, modernism's indirect qualities emerge as subterranean echoes of the pandemic's horrors and the very ways these horrors go underground.

I structure the book around three clusters of material. Part 1, "Pandemic Realism," establishes a literary pandemic paradigm for the rest of the project. I analyze a group of interwar texts that both defied and represented the silence that surrounds so much of the outbreak: Willa Cather's *One of Ours*, Katherine Anne Porter's *Pale Horse, Pale Rider*, Thomas Wolfe's *Look Homeward, Angel*, and William Maxwell's *They Came Like Swallows*. These part-realist/part-modernist accounts treat the pandemic explicitly, but they also incorporate within their structures the stealthy encroachment of the virus and the reasons for the silence surrounding its emergence and spread. They make visible the miasmic atmosphere the pandemic produced, detailing the hidden suffering it inflicted, and illuminating how its imbrication with the war made it so hard to see. Most of these works are written in the late 1920s and 1930s, revealing how references to the pandemic became more explicit over time. As the pandemic became less of an immediate threat and fears of its return started to recede, authors seemed more willing to resurrect it: to represent its damage directly, to process its meaning, and to assess its lingering effects. Starting with the clearest, most obvious representations of the flu in the interwar era allows us to uncover, in the subsequent sections, the more coded references to the pandemic in works produced in the outbreak's more immediate aftermath.

Part 2, "Pandemic Modernism," uses this new literary frame to reveal the subtle but significant presence of the viral tragedy within iconic modernist texts that are not typically seen in light of the outbreak: *Mrs. Dalloway*, *The Waste Land*, and "The Second Coming." Virginia Woolf, T. S. Eliot, and W. B. Yeats all had intimate encounters with the pandemic, and their works capture the atmospheric dread, the violations of the body, and the radical perceptual shifts a pandemic leaves behind. These texts showcase how central elements of modernist style—from elongated sentences to plotless structures to amorphous characters—provided the ideal form to represent the pandemic's presence and indeed helped shape that very form. The works also reveal how modernism helped fuel the pandemic's erasure, instantiating the gaps and the silences even as it represented them. The authors were, at times, complicit in this erasure, their works revealing the ways that even a lethal mass illness may be present everywhere yet hard to see clearly, especially when bodies are caught in its grip. What emerge are the unprocessed fragments, the sensory and emotional residues left behind. This section argues for a change in our reading practices, becoming both an exercise in and a model for how to read for what is hidden. We are trained in modernism to see the trauma of war but not the trauma of the pandemic. With the history I offer in this introduction and the texts in part 1, we can piece together the fragments and see all the ways the lived experiences of bodies and illnesses infuse these works. Tracing how Woolf, Eliot, and Yeats represent but also obscure experiences that they manifestly had and that were omnipresent in the larger culture becomes in turn a reminder of and a corrective to how marginalized stories may be unseen despite their central presence.

The bleak literary accounts of the pandemic in parts 1 and 2 capture the suffering and the burdens of the outbreak's nihilistic threat. Part 3, "Pandemic Cultures," shifts to responses within popular culture that pushed against the more invisible, miasmic quality of the pandemic by recasting the experience into structured resurrection stories with clear villains and heroes. I investigate how the revival of spiritualism in the 1920s and the creation of pandemic zombie figures placed (in very different ways) the anguish within more concrete and consoling frameworks. I uncover the surprising pandemic links within these prevalent tropes of resurrection, drawing on post-pandemic work by Sir Arthur Conan Doyle, the 1920s obsession with spiritualism, early zombie figures in Abel Gance's film *J'accuse*, and the horror stories of H. P. Lovecraft. These popular manifestations offered audiences a powerful corrective to the burdens of a plotless tragedy caused by an amoral, invisible enemy, granting instead cause-and-effect narratives, a structure of meaning for death, an outlet for the guilt generated by both spreading and surviving contagion, and the image of a body once more alive and healthy—or safely and completely dead.

Throughout these three clusters, I trace two tropes that infuse the works and provide new critical lenses for reading interwar literature and culture. The first trope centers on "miasma" as a central way to recognize and to describe the pandemic's absent presence. The word has old associations with disease, referencing an outdated medical belief that illness came from tainted air. By 1918, germ theory had replaced the miasmic model, but the word still carries an evocative link to a spreading, airborne contagion. The definitions of miasma likewise capture vital features of the pandemic's spectral realities: an unseen, corrupting, and depleting menace; a brooding sense of danger or foreboding; a delirium or hallucinatory reality; and a foglike, obscuring atmosphere. Such elements encompass biological elements of the virus—its airborne and invisible quality, its deliriums and dangers—as well as the way it silently infused itself into bodies and communities. These miasmic qualities were key vehicles for representing the sense of pervasive threat and lingering dread the pandemic left behind. The atmosphere of malaise and enervation that permeates *The Waste Land* and *Mrs. Dalloway*, the delirious and hallucinatory qualities of works from *Pale Horse, Pale Rider* to "The Second Coming," and the emotional grief and contagion fears that saturate works by Thomas Wolfe and William Maxwell all encode a miasmic modernism at the heart of the era.

The miasmic elements of the pandemic's representation have their foil in a second representational strategy: repeated tropes of what I term "viral resurrection" that counter the amorphous characteristics of the outbreak. Images of resurrection in general infuse interwar literature and culture. The interest in the dead returning reflected the extensive grief surrounding the sudden losses of so many, whether in the war or from the flu. Such images drew on and reshaped both pagan and Christian traditions of resurrection, where a sacrificial body is subjected to intense violence that in turn brings redemption. This sacrificial model had been routinely deployed as a way to promote the war and came under vicious denunciation in much of the (anti) war literature. The pandemic, though, eroded the pretense of death as a meaningful sacrifice while at the same time magnifying the loss and thus the desire for some meaning or return. These conditions helped shape recurrent, pandemic-infused tropes of resurrection marked by their links to disease. The "viral" quality of these resurrections worked on multiple levels. Biologically, the virus caused delirium states and later mental-health issues that both in reality and in the literature produced illusions of the dead returning, from Porter's depictions of delirium dreams to Woolf's and Eliot's death-haunted cityscapes to Yeats's visions of a second coming. The millions of disfigured bodies piling up in communities across the globe and insecurely buried filter into repeated literary representations of the returning dead, encompassing Eliot's dug-up corpses and the emergence of zombies in the 1920s. The enervated, living-death state the virus produced in millions of survivors—incomplete resurrections, we might say—infuses the body of Clarissa Dalloway, the voices of *The Waste Land*, and all the pandemic mourners and victims in works like *Look Homeward, Angel* and *Pale Horse, Pale Rider*. The virus's perverse, death-giving fecundity—its ability to replicate exponentially and seemingly forever—are captured in literary images of deathly vitality and in brooding fears of a mass return of the dead. The resurrection images also spoke to the pandemic's position as a spectral trauma to the war, one that lurked at the edge of consciousness and always—quite literally—threatened to return. Despite their illusory and grim nature, though, these images of viral resurrection were at times carefully crafted aesthetic consolations, functioning as ways to make a threat visible, to represent bodies that were not being memorialized, and to make material a degree of loss that often defied representation.

The pandemic fueled an interest in resurrections and living death in part by intensifying anxieties already set in place by the war. Both tragedies led to disrupted funeral rites, both required mass burials, both brought sudden and violent death, both damaged bodies in often grotesque and permanent ways, both caused a widespread sense of living death in survivors, and both left an almost unimaginable number of mourners in their wake. The way these traumas overlapped often makes it difficult to untangle the effects of one from the other.[7] The pandemic, though, did more than simply intensify problems the war had started. The virus was both indiscriminant and delocalized, changing both targets and locations. In 1918, women as well as men were in extreme danger, and the domestic space became as deadly as the front lines.[8] The enemy was no longer visible or from a particular nation, but a silent, nonhuman killer, loyal to no country or creed and able to corrupt the body from within. This adversary could move anywhere and attack anyone. Even those appalled by the war could still argue over the worthiness of the cause, but no such political arguments could structure the grief from the pandemic. It's perhaps no wonder that the anguish went underground.

PANDEMIC FLASHBACK

To uncover this anguish, and to recognize the pandemic, we must learn to read for the symptoms, to diagnose within the literature the pandemic's ghostly presence. In the background section that follows, I offer a sensory and affective history of the pandemic—the forgotten sights, sounds, smells, tastes, sensations, and emotions it produced in victims and witnesses. This history will allow us to see the pandemic's fragmented traces in the literature and the larger culture, traces that reflect flashbacks to the original experience. As trauma research suggests, elements of a traumatic event later become the triggers that lead to flashback; the smell of antiseptic, for example, might trigger in the present the fragmented memories of a past sickroom moment. Flashbacks are often bewildering, conjuring not the complete memory of the past event but pieces of sensory details, emotional states, or bodily sensations associated with it.[9] Literary representations of flashback often reflect the disjointed and confusing elements of a memory's intrusive return, the fragments now seemingly divorced from the initial event.[10] The traumas inflicted by the influenza pandemic produced these gaps and fragmentations, which were further augmented by the delirium it caused, the cultural silencing it engendered, and the unseen quality of the threat. Knowing the original conditions of the pandemic allows us to see the traces and recognize the stories they tell.

To reveal these details, both here and throughout the book, I draw on pandemic histories, newspaper accounts, medical reports, and two remarkable archives. The Collier Archive, held at the Imperial War Museum in London, offers a wealth of firsthand accounts of the pandemic. In the 1970s, the researcher Richard Collier took out advertisements in newspapers across Europe and the United States and received hundreds of detailed letters from people who remembered the pandemic and wrote about their experiences. A second archive, the Pandemic Influenza Storybook, is maintained by the Centers for Disease Control and Prevention (CDC) and is an online collection of firsthand pandemic accounts from the United States. Taken together, these materials reveal the experiential quality of the pandemic and its aftermath.[11]

A Sensory and Affective History

In 1918, much of the world was focused on war, and people everywhere were used to periodic pandemics. While mass outbreaks of disease often spread fear, and while many remembered the severe "Russian" influenza of the 1890s, the arrival of the flu was hardly cause for panic. So when the 1918 strain first emerged, it attracted little attention. The disease came in three waves in 1918 and 1919, with the first wave concentrated in the spring and summer of the first year.[12] This wave was deadly but comparatively mild. Where the outbreak first emerged is unclear; at the time, many people believed it originated in Spain (hence its nickname, "Spanish influenza"), but this belief, perhaps subtly bolstered by an anxious nationalism, likely arose because Spain had less press censorship during the war and thus reported cases earlier.[13] Historians used to believe that ground zero was an army base in Kansas, but some scientists now propose Asia as a possible source, and others find that the location is too difficult to determine.[14] In this early wave, tens of thousands died, including 5,500 British soldiers, but beyond a handful of doctors, few people in these brutal war years paid much attention.[15] The war was so absorbing, and influenza such a common illness, that there was a collective public shrug. As the *Times* noted in 1918, "The man in the street," hearing about Spanish influenza, "cheerfully anticipated its arrival here," and the reporter confidently claimed that "epidemic diseases lose force with each successive visitation."[16] While newspapers in June and July described factory closings and the high number of people stricken, the flu didn't seem remarkably different to most people, and public health systems worldwide were not designed to publicize a problematic wave of influenza. A few doctors, though, were noticing one troubling sign: this flu attacked healthy young adults and killed them in high numbers.

The second wave, however, which came between September and December 1918, killed millions. As one doctor observed, it produced "the most vicious type of Pneumonia that has ever been seen."[17] The war created conditions perfectly designed to spread this strain of flu: millions of men and women in the age range most vulnerable to the virus were living in close quarters and traveling across several continents. In August 1918, outbreaks erupted in three port cities on three continents: Freetown, Sierra Leone; Brest, France; and Boston, Massachusetts.[18] By September, the flu was racing through towns and cities across the globe. Doctors had never seen anything like it. In France, the flu "swept through the lines so suddenly and with such ferocity that it startled even doctors who'd served in Gallipoli and Salonika and [had] witnessed [hospital] wards overflowing with amoebic dysentery and malaria cases."[19] One doctor lamented that watching the men "dropping out like flies" was worse than "any sight they ever had in France after a battle."[20] Hospitals were overwhelmed, and emergency flu wards were hastily established in army camps, schools, and auditoriums (figures 1.1a–c). Bodies piled up, and communities everywhere resorted to mass burials. The third and final wave came between January and May 1919, again causing many deaths, but it was not nearly as vicious as the second wave. And then, after a few isolated outbreaks, it disappeared.

Death rates from the flu were staggering. As the researcher John M. Barry calculates, if the upper estimates of the death tolls are accurate, more than 5 percent of the world's population died in two years, and 8 to 10 percent of the young adults, mainly in the twelve terrible weeks of the second wave. It

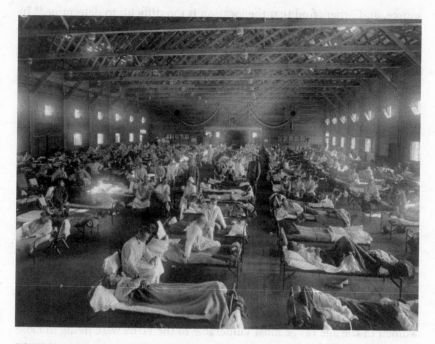

FIGURE 1.1A. Emergency hospital during influenza epidemic, Camp Funston, Kansas, 1918. *Source*: From New Contributed Photographs Collection (NCP 001603), Otis Historical Archives (OHA 250), National Museum of Health and Medicine. Image and permission kindly provided by National Museum of Health and Medicine.

was the deadliest pandemic in history in terms of numbers, though the bubonic plague killed a higher percentage of the much smaller existing population.[21] And it was not just the flu's lethality that made it different; it was the targets. In a typical flu season, casualties are generally among the very old and the very young. This time, the fatalities were also high among healthy men and women between twenty and forty years of age and especially among those between twenty-one and thirty. Scientists were mystified by the anomaly at the time, but research now suggests that a strong immune response, which is more likely in young adults, probably caused the most lethal complications.[22] Those who lived through the pandemic repeatedly recalled how the fittest individuals were targets. One survivor marveled at a "big strong healthy looking chap" who died quickly, and another remembered "the heavy weight boxer of Clifton College" being struck down by the flu.[23] The tragedy of this death toll was deepened by the

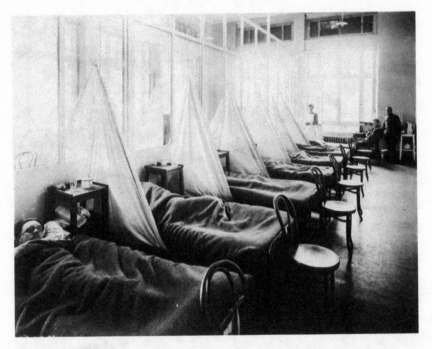

FIGURE 1.1B. Influenza Ward. United States Army Camp Hospital No. 45, Aix-les-Baines, France. *Source:* From the United States National Library of Medicine archives (NLM Unique ID: 101399244; Image ID: A06721). Public domain.

fact that the parents of most young children lay in this age group.[24] Even at the time, many people recognized that the flu was far more devastating than the war. George Newman, the chief medical officer in Britain, noted in his 1920 report on the flu that the pandemic was without a doubt "one of the great historic scourges of our time, a pestilence which affected the well-being of millions of men and women and destroyed more human lives in a few months than did the European war in five years."[25]

The 1918 virus produced an unusual and memorable constellation of symptoms.[26] While it came with the fever, headache, and cough typical of the flu, it also produced more alarming effects that caused many doctors first to assume the outbreak must be some other disease. The virus often penetrated deeply into the lung tissue, producing its deadly form of pneumonia. Doctors reported repeatedly that patients suffered from sudden floods of bleeding from the nose, mouth, or ears; such bleeding could

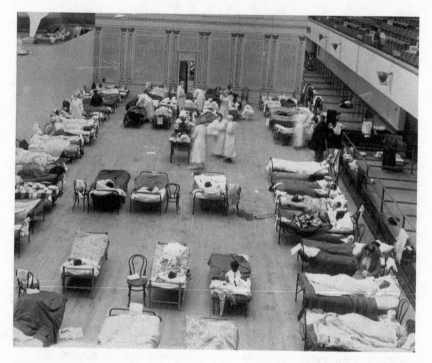

FIGURE 1.1C. Flu ward, Oakland Civic Auditorium, Oakland, California. *Source*: Courtesy Oakland Public Library, Oakland History Room (copl_058).

continue after death, soaking the death wraps. As one survivor remembered, "Blood would shoot out [of orifices] as though kept under high pressure and spray to the end of [the] bed; and this happened about thirty times a day for about 8–9 days until [I] thought [I] could have no blood left."[27] The cough the flu produced was bad enough to rip muscles and rib cartilage, and the body aches could feel like bones breaking. Patients gave off a terrible odor that would be remembered by survivors years later. In the final stages, victims often suffered from *heliotrope cyanosis*, a condition that developed when the lungs became so full of fluid that the body turned purple or blue. The devastation of the lungs, as many doctors observed, was eerily similar to the lungs of soldiers attacked by poison gas.[28]

The virus could also cause short- and long-term mental instability. The high fevers produced delirium, a hallucinatory disorientation that showed up everywhere in the historical and literary accounts of the pandemic. Apart from delirium, the virus also appeared to be a neurotoxin capable of invading the brain and the nervous system; patients who recovered frequently reported depression, mental confusion, and even schizophrenia. Karl Menninger, in a widely cited study published in 1919, examined the dramatic links between psychoses of various kinds and the 1918 virus, and subsequent research has traced similar effects.[29] Research even suggests that the flu, more than the war, was behind the rash of suicides after 1918.[30] One soldier stationed at Blandford Camp in Dorset wrote that the camp had an area they called "suicide wood" because of the many flu victims who went there to kill themselves.[31] Newspapers were full of reports of the violent derangement the flu could produce, with previously peaceful citizens erupting in murderous rages, which I explore at greater length in chapter 4.[32]

The flu's very contagiousness deepened both the physical and the psychological suffering. The virus combined the two traits that epidemiologists dread: it was both lethal and airborne, spreading from person to person through tiny particles that could be inhaled or picked up on bodies or surfaces. At the time, most people understood the basics of contagion and germ theory; while some still believed in the "miasmic" model of disease, they nevertheless rightly perceived the danger to be airborne.[33] And even though scientists thought the flu was caused by a bacteria (viruses were not seen until the advent of the electron microscope, though the term "virus" was still in use at the time as a nonspecific agent of disease), people knew that influenza could be transmitted through breathing in germs and through contact with others.[34] Medical professionals urged patients to stay at home, and, in some areas, masks were widely distributed and used (figures 1.2a–b).[35] The knowledge that a deadly presence infected the very atmosphere created widespread fear—and even after the acute contagious period had passed, the memory of the experience generated a lingering, free-floating anxiety. The virus's contagious quality could also produce particular types of survivor's guilt. Doctors, nurses, and volunteers who sought to alleviate suffering frequently caught the virus and also brought it home.[36] Families, friends, and strangers unknowingly gave it to one another. As we will see, the widespread guilt this innocent killing produced haunted survivors in ways that were hard to address and that were often harder to acknowledge and represent than the regret the violence of war could engender.

In addition to the guilt, the pandemic fueled an atmosphere of paranoia and helplessness. People were often attacked with little warning. Survivors

FIGURE 1.2A. Nurses preparing facemasks during pandemic, Oakland, California. *Source*: Courtesy Oakland Public Library, Oakland History Room (copl_056).

frequently observed that they had felt fine one moment and were violently ill the next. Newspapers in England reported on the high numbers of people who collapsed in the street; in October 1918, for example, the *Times* noted that people were "suddenly affected by the disease in the streets," and by early November, in one twenty-four-hour period alone, "56 people were stricken with sudden illness in the London streets," with 280 similar cases that week.[37] As one letter writer summarized, "people were dropping down dead . . . on the trams, buses, anywhere." In Aberdeen, people "died on the street and children in the playground," and a witness in Stepney recalled that "as long as I live I shall never forget seeing people collapsing in the street."[38] These are just a few of the many accounts. As John Barry notes, "throughout the world reports were common of people who toppled off horses, collapsed on the sidewalk."[39] Death usually came quickly, in a few hours or days, but the disease could also linger and, after the patient had seemed to recover, flare again into pneumonia. The virus could wipe out

FIGURE 1.2B. Policemen wearing facemasks during pandemic, Seattle, Washington. *Source:* Courtesy National Archives (photo no.165-WW-269B-25).

whole families, but it also could inexplicably skip people. Who survived and who did not, who caught the virus and who did not, often seemed mysterious to those who lived through it. As survivors remembered, "It was a phantom, and we didn't know where it was," and "you never knew from day to day who was going to be next on the death list." The author William Maxwell noted that the pandemic taught him that "nobody's safe. Terrible things can happen. To anybody."[40] And these seemingly random strikes were exacerbated by a profound sense of helplessness. There were no cures, though doctors scrambled to find a treatment that might work. Except for caring for the patient's basic needs, doctors, nurses, and caretakers could do little but let the disease take over and run its course.

The flu did not simply unfold behind the closed doors of homes and hospitals; public life was visibly changed. In most communities, the schools, theaters, churches, and factories were all shut down, and many public services simply stopped. Too many people were ill—or taking care of the ill—to keep services running (figures 1.3a–b). One English survivor remembered that in Hambrough Road, Southhall, "so many whole families died that

FIGURE 1.3A. Theater closed during pandemic, Seattle, Washington. *Source*: With kind permission from the Museum of History and Industry, Seattle, Washington.

scores of houses became empty," and another writing about Birmingham recalled that "people were dying like flies[;] in most streets a dozen or more people went down with it and died."[41] In Philadelphia, wagons were pulled through the streets, with priests calling for people to "bring out their dead."[42] People noted the eeriness of the streets, with houses everywhere having their blinds pulled down—the symbol at the time for a death within.[43]

One sensory pandemic memory deserves special mention, as it echoes throughout the literature I discuss: the constant sound of tolling bells that rang for the victims. The lament becomes its own reverberation in both American and European survivor accounts: "The church bells (The 'Dead bells') were almost continuously tolling"; "the bells tolling all the day long";[44] "the church bell would ring every day . . . how awful it sounded";[45] "I could hear the continuous tolling of the death bell; People were dying like flies"; "there was always the ringing of bells"; "The bells tolled incessantly. They had to toll for each dead";[46] "Church bells rang all day long . . . ringing almost around the clock"; "always the bells tolled."[47] The constant

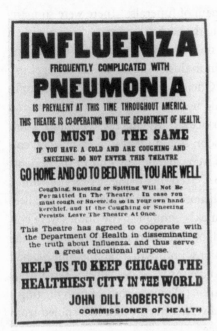

FIGURE 1.3B. Public-health poster, Chicago, Illinois. *Source*: From the United States National Library of Medicine Archives (NLM Unique ID: 101447458; NLM Image ID: A029485).

sound became associated with the oppressive sense of gloom and death. As one army doctor, Gunnar Hegardt, remembered, the bells "constantly tolling" made people "depressed, despondent, fatalistic."[48] In many places, they simply had to stop marking deaths with bells; as E. Bishop noted, "they used to toll the Death Bell in those days [but] had to stop as it was so unnerving."[49] These memories of bells persisted even years later; the survivor Philip Learoyd described a wasteland-like atmosphere he never forgot: "Even today, some fifty-five years later, the sound of a church bell recalls for me the . . . scene of a drab and dreary dormitory with the greyish yellow November gloom."[50] One American documentary on the pandemic is even entitled *We Heard the Bells*.[51]

The pandemic also brought the constant sights and images of bodies, coffins, and funerals. Modernist critics and World War I historians talk of the ever-present bodies in the trenches and their absence at home, but in 1918, bodies were everywhere; in an oft-repeated phrase, they were stacked like "cord wood."[52] At first, the bodies could be treated individually and funerals could be held, but even these services quickly grew overwhelming.

Survivors spoke of the constant stream of funerals: "There were so many died that the funeral processions from the hospital mortuary ... were like a long Lord Majors show";[53] a Baptist minister in Leicester was "conducting the funerals of victims from daylight to dusk ... the funeral corteges followed each other through the town. Often there were more than one coffin in a hearse";[54] the "community could not keep up with the funerals and many were fearful of attending services."[55] Again, these are just a few examples. The pandemic's toll was soon so high that in many places, coffins ran out and individual funerals were abandoned. One of the laments that appears everywhere in survivors' accounts is the scarcity of coffins and the way gravediggers were overwhelmed. As an English witness recalled, "They just could not make coffins quickly enough so the bodies were collected and taken somewhere ... [and] buried in a communal grave."[56] One gravedigger encapsulated the conditions, noting that "at one time we had 500 bodies waiting for burial and no coffins ... so we got the Territorials to help us to dig mass graves."[57] Figure 1.4 shows a group of men digging a similar mass grave in Philadelphia. By 1918, mass death had spilled from the battlefields into the domestic space.

While the pandemic ended by 1920, the aftereffects of the virus lived on in the bodies and lives of its victims. This particular influenza strain could permanently damage the lungs, heart, and nerves and leave the body open to infections.[58] As the scholars Dorothy Ann Pettit and Janice Bailie summarize, the virus "left a train of ailing victims with ... cardiac irregularities, vascular problems, pulmonary tuberculosis, and a host of nervous and paralytic afflictions."[59] Survivor letters confirm a range of long-term repercussions—my sister "went stone deaf"; my throat was "never the same since"—and many reported losing all their hair and its coming back in permanently gray, as if the virus had leached its color.[60] Alongside these serious, long-term consequences was the persistent, lingering enervation the virus left in its wake. One Red Cross official observed in 1919 that "the influenza epidemic not only caused the deaths of some six hundred thousand people [in the United States], but it also left a trail of lowered vitality ... nervous breakdown, and other sequella [sic]."[61] A health commissioner in Ohio noted that after the pandemic, "phrases like 'I'm not feeling right,' 'I don't have my usual pep,' 'I'm all in since I had the flu' have been commonplace."[62]

FIGURE 1.4. Preparing mass graves for pandemic victims, Philadelphia. *Source*: With kind permission from the Catholic Historical Research Center of the Archdiocese of Philadelphia.

Perhaps the pandemic's most persistent legacies, however, were the enduring grief and hardship it left behind. It destroyed families on multiple levels; as one survivor lamented, "My father's death in the flu pandemic affected us economically, emotionally, and socially."[63] Because the virus killed adults in the prime age of parenting, it produced millions of orphans; in New York City alone, "by November 8 [1918] ... 31,000 children from 7,200 families ... had lost one or both of their parents."[64] A medical official in the United States observed that the pandemic "left widows and orphans and dependent old people. It has reduced many of these families to poverty and acute distress. This havoc is wide spread, reaching all parts of the United States and all classes of people."[65] The writer Mary McCarthy, who lost both her parents in the pandemic, noted how the virus robbed her even of family history: "The chain of recollection—the collective memory of a family—ha[d] been broken."[66] And despite the larger cultural silence, the constant refrain in letter after letter from survivors is the pandemic's ongoing, never-forgotten trauma, as these representative passages suggest: Relatives who were forced to put children into orphanages "felt guilty for the rest of their lives"; "[he] never got over the loss or the speed of the situation";[67] "her mother was never the same"; "he never forgot the events of 1918 and it left a great impact [on] him";[68] "I never forgot"; "I for one will never forget it";[69] "the awful feeling of complete prostration ... the feelings of misery and utter helplessness ... [were] something I could never forget";[70] "I was never to forget the sight, and sound, of men becoming delirious and dying and wondering if it would happen to me"; "I will never forget!"[71] These sentiments appear in almost every flu letter, and these memories were offered more than fifty years after the pandemic was over.

THE PANDEMIC'S ABSENT PRESENCE

While the pandemic's role within literature has received little attention, in the past few decades, historians have offered detailed accounts of the pandemic's impacts. Alfred W. Crosby's classic volume *America's Forgotten Pandemic* brought wider awareness of the outbreak in the United States, as did Nancy K. Bristow's *American Pandemic*. With respect to Britain, Honigsbaum's *Living with Enza* and Niall Johnson's *Britain and the 1918–1919 Influenza Pandemic* offer the central accounts. Taking a more global perspective (though still focusing on the United States and Britain), John M.

Barry explores how the pandemic shook the scientific community and modern medicine in his bestseller *The Great Influenza*. And the journalist Laura Spinney's *Pale Rider* examines the broad historical effects of the pandemic, from its effect on the First and Second World Wars to its shaping of Indian independence.[72] Alongside these histories, fears of a new avian flu have inspired more attention to the pandemic than at any time since its arrival. The flu has also made its way into more recent literature; novels from Thomas Mullen's *The Last Town on Earth* to Stephenie Meyer's *Twilight* have helped reintroduce the outbreak to readers (in the latter, the central male character, Edward Cullen, is saved from the 1918 flu only by becoming a vampire).[73] And fans of the BBC series *Downton Abbey* watched a (somewhat sanitized) version of the flu sweep through the family and staff at the end of the second season.

Yet for most of the twentieth century, the pandemic seems to drop off the cultural radar. The pandemic's disappearing act in Britain, Ireland, and the United States did not have a single cause but came from multiple factors coalescing to shape its spectral quality. Before I turn to those specific factors, though, let me extend my earlier discussion of flashback to touch on issues of memory and forgetting within traumatic experiences—and the often controversial status of these issues within trauma studies. Some theorists have argued that a traumatic event exists in a different memory center of the brain, becoming unrepresentable and unspeakable because not fully recorded; others have dismissed this characterization as unsupported by the scientific evidence.[74] While the precise imbrication of trauma, memory, and representation remains contested, central to the definition of post-traumatic stress is that overwhelming experiences that threaten death or injury—such as were experienced throughout the pandemic—may produce disruptions in memory and experience, including flashbacks, avoidance, a sense of disassociation or unreality, and an inability or unwillingness to remember the event yet also intrusive thoughts about it.[75] Traumatic memory is often, by its nature, spectral, ever present but lurking semi-invisibly at the edges of representation. Throughout the literature of the 1920s and 1930s, these elements of traumatic memory play out, as elements of the pandemic become fragmented, silenced, yet obsessively remembered. The effects of trauma, though, do not tell the whole story of why the pandemic is seemingly avoided. The trauma of the war was also famously difficult to represent, yet the war is the dominant event in cultural memory.

The pandemic becomes what I term a spectral trauma in part because of the nature of traumatic memory, but more importantly—and more uniquely—from its historical timing and presentation. Two broad categories account for the silence around the pandemic: how the war overshadowed, blocked, and incorporated the viral outbreak, and the pandemic's particular features and the broader nature of illness itself. While it may seem counterintuitive, we have to understand the ways the pandemic is silenced in order to see how it is represented—and how the silences themselves structure the literary pandemic.

The War's Dominance

OVERSHADOWED

To die in the war was one thing, but to die of influenza was quite another. A death in battle could be seen as courageous (though plenty of soldiers and writers pushed against this idea), but a death from influenza? The flu was a common, everyday illness. And the 1918 strain, despite being remarkably different, was still called influenza. For many, there was something humiliating about dying of the flu in wartime. As Robert Graves recalled after an almost lethal case, "Having come through the war, I refused to die of influenza."[76] Another survivor from London recounts how her father, who believed he had saved his family by his careful nursing, declared that "We came through the Zeppelin Raids [, and] I wasn't going to lose my family now."[77] And getting or paying attention to the flu could feel unpatriotic. One nurse who fell ill in 1918 and who also watched friends die insisted that despite the horrors of Guy's Hospital where she worked, "Our boys ... were in France suffering worse than us."[78] A German doctor working with an overwhelming caseload noted that, despite all the death, "People had more to think about in general than whether or not they would catch the 'Flu.'"[79] The fact that many strong and healthy soldiers survived the war only to be killed by the flu—or returned from war only to find their families dead from the pandemic, which happened frequently—was often too awful, or too humiliating, or too bitterly ironic to contemplate directly.

The war's length also overshadowed the flu's remarkably short tenure. By 1918, the war was in its fifth brutal year, and soldiers and civilians alike had spent those years focused on the battles. Politicians talked mainly of war, newspapers were dominated by war stories, factories produced war materials, those who qualified were in the military, and those who didn't often worked to support the troops. The war could be fought, and by 1918, people were used to fighting it. The flu, however, swept over the globe with extraordinary speed. Compared to the war, the flu was over before anyone had time to process what was happening. The war was well established as the central story, and the flu became an unreal disruption.

The ways the war overshadowed the flu translates into the literature and the culture, both in its absence and in its spectral presence. Writing about the flu could feel disloyal and unpatriotic, a problematic dodge of the more important story, and thus its representations often go underground, reflecting the very ways it seemed subordinate at the time. In Britain, where the war had engulfed public and private life for over four years, this feeling was particularly acute, and it may account for one broad difference between American and British literary treatments of the pandemic: American texts treat the pandemic more directly; in British texts, the war tends to overshadow the pandemic's more hidden but still unmistakable presence.

BLOCKED

The war also served, in both tangible and emotional ways, to block news of the flu and its devastation (though not, of course, to block its spread). First, the war meant that newspapers in countries on both sides of the conflict were censored. British and American governments were eager not to spread panic, and thus news of the flu tended to be minimized, especially in the early months;[80] it was only later that the scope of the tragedy was understood. Articles appeared on the pandemic, but they were both drowned out by the war news and were often set—both visually and in content—as secondary to the war. The war also blocked the flu on a more emotional level. Appearing as it did just at the end of the war, it came when people were beyond ready for a cessation of tragedy. As one flu survivor pointed out, "People were only just recovering from the loss of loved ones in the 1914–1918 war."[81] The mortality rate of the pandemic may have been simply too much to take in. In a 1921 editorial, the London *Times* suggested this saturation and made a prescient prediction about the flu's aftermath: "So vast was the catastrophe [of the flu] and so ubiquitous its prevalence that our minds, surfeited with the horrors of war, refused to realize it. It came and went, a hurricane across the green fields of life, sweeping away our youth in hundreds of thousands and leaving behind it a toll of sickness and infirmity which will not be reckoned in this generation."[82] The language captures the diffuse qualities of the horror—its vastness, its ubiquity, its atmospheric ferocity—that became central to its miasmic representations in the literature.

In a strange reversal, the flu could also block men from war—which in turn further served to block acknowledgment of the flu. In the fall of 1918, flu quarantines prevented many troops from deployment, including writers eager to depart so they could serve in and then write about the war. William Faulkner's training was delayed because of the quarantine, and before he could leave, the Armistice was signed.[83] John Dos Passos fervently wished to join the war and was also prevented by the flu; as he watched men die from the infection at Camp Crane in Pennsylvania, he "considered it ignominious that so many . . . died before ever reaching the war in Europe"; he eventually did depart for the war, but he contracted the flu in November 1918.[84] Rather than a subject in and of itself, the flu felt like something that blocked men's access to the real event, one where men could participate (or so many imagined at first) in valiant adventure. These gendered associations also contributed to the war's dominance and to the way the war became the "real" story in both the literature and the culture. Military conflict has long been the quintessential staging ground for masculinity, while disease suggests weakness and vulnerability—and is often linked to the feminine. The war, with all its male death, became the story, and the pandemic, with its mix of female and male victims who succumbed, a deflating sequel. Writers like Porter and Cather overcame this block by building this very dichotomy into the structure of their stories.

INCORPORATED

The suffering caused by the flu was also incorporated into the outpouring of mourning and remembrance after the war. While they did not overtly acknowledge the flu, the efforts to build war memorials offered a fitting atmosphere for the post-flu era, as pandemic grief was folded into the general postwar mourning. Indeed, in most previous wars, disease had killed more soldiers than battles, so grieving the war dead had always encompassed grieving those dead from illness; in the American Civil War, death rates were two times higher from disease than from battle casualties.[85] Soldiers who died of influenza on the front or in military hospitals are generally included in figures on war casualties so were quite literally incorporated into deaths in battle. As Crosby points out, many people considered the flu to be "simply a subdivision of the war" and found that the best way "to lend dignity to their battles with disease was to subsume them within the war."[86] One Salisbury woman remembered that many Australian soldiers had been sent to the town and died of the flu; in ironic tension with Dos Passos's sense of the ignominiousness of flu deaths, she insisted that these were "brave lads who died for their country—just as much as those that died in the trenches and on the sea."[87] Another survivor observed that the pandemic seemed like "an extension of all the sadness of the casualties of war."[88] Even civilian deaths from the flu were often blamed on and encompassed by the war; many felt that the stark wartime conditions had led to more flu fatalities. As one survivor noted, the flu was made worse "partly from dreadful war," as people had "no food and milk [that] was needed."[89] Newspapers frequently speculated on the connections among the war, the flu, and the weakened state of the populace.[90] This bodily enervation, and the hard-to-untangle atmosphere produced by war and illness, infuses the pandemic literature. Some of the writers, like Porter and Woolf, call attention to the mingled quality of this atmosphere; others, like Eliot and Yeats, seem to reproduce the silent incorporation of the pandemic into the war. The entanglement makes it easy to miss the pandemic as a distinct contributor to a climate that has, until now, seemed a manifestation of postwar grief and enervation. Recovering the flu's particular presence allows us to see the pandemic not as an extension of war but as its own particular threat, with its own effects on bodies and their perceptions.

Representing Illness

The general and literary postwar silence on the flu arose from non-war-related causes as well, some of which stemmed from the broader challenges of representing illness and some from this particular outbreak of disease. Critics like Priscilla Wald and Rita Charon have offered compelling accounts of how illness may be translated into narratives but also of how difficult illness may be to represent.[91] These difficulties were acute during the pandemic, when attempts to identify actors and to form a coherent narrative were consistently frustrated. These very frustrations, though, in turn structured modernist literary strategies that countered—and even incorporated—the challenges.

CHARACTERLESS

Illness and pain are often difficult to characterize—by which I mean both difficult to describe and difficult to turn into tangible characters. Rita Charon observes the often ineffable quality of illness: those listening to stories of disease must "tolerate ambiguity and uncertainty," as "pain, suffering, worry, anguish, and the sense of something not being right are conditions very difficult, if not impossible, to put into words." A serious illness creates a diffuse horror, Charon notes, a sense "that something of value has abandoned [the family], that a deep and nameless sadness has settled in at home," accompanied by "the jarring, jolting, inarticulate presence of dread."[92] The diffuse and hard-to-capture experience of dread is heightened both by the microscopic quality of the threat and by the sense that the body itself is infused with disease, that its borders have been invisibly violated; as Priscilla Wald writes, "microbial indifference to boundaries is a refrain in both scientific and popular writing."[93] These ambiguous and borderless qualities make illness hard to describe, a challenge dramatically compounded when a singular experience of illness is part of a borderless outbreak across the globe.[94]

Illness in general may disrupt the central character in most lives: the self. As Kathlyn Conway, in her work *Beyond Words*, details, "all serious illness and disability share this fundamental characteristic: damage to the body constitutes damage to the self."[95] In minor illnesses, the self can be diminished temporarily, but in more serious cases, "a person's sense of a stable self may be profoundly damaged." As death is approaching, "the total loss of self" may occur.[96] Conway observes how few works capture this shattering of self without quickly moving to portray a self that is healed and whole once more. Given the widespread damage the 1918 virus produced within the body, such a "fix" would have been difficult to portray and helps explain why a character suffering in the pandemic might be challenging—or unappealing—to represent. And the lasting physical and emotional injuries the flu inflicted also tended to be internal (like the harm it did to the heart or lungs) and thus more difficult to perceive. The pandemic literature I analyze pushes against these limitations by representing them, with writers like Porter and Woolf drawing on modernist techniques of fragmentation and porous agency to show bodies and selves shattered by the virus. The diffuse sense of character in *The Waste Land* and the agentless destruction of "The Second Coming" simultaneously represent and encode the characterless horror Charon and Conway describe.

The challenges to agency, along with the "random unfairness" of illness,[97] can lead to frantic attempts to identify other characters—enemies, scapegoats, and heroes—to combat the confusion; the pandemic generally frustrated such attempts. It was hard, first, to characterize a familiar disease like influenza as the enemy it turned out to be. The war provided far more compelling enemies, ones that could be seen and put on posters and placed in stories. The pandemic literature circumvented this difficulty by making the enemy a nameless, shadowy menace without character, one that was difficult to grasp or understand, like the atmosphere of contagion that spreads to every part of Wolfe's *Look Homeward, Angel*. While most people were struck by the agentless quality of the pandemic threat, people at times did envision a materialized enemy: crowded immigrant populations, Jews, and Germans were, in some places, blamed for the outbreak.[98] The flu's very nickname, the "Spanish Flu," potentially carried, in Britain and the United States, a sense of foreign taint. As Wald points out, "it is not unusual for a virus to be described as a foreigner or even an immigrant."[99] H. P. Lovecraft creates monstrous versions of such enemies, shaping early versions of viral zombies that arise directly from a pandemic atmosphere. Recovering how Lovecraft turns a hidden virus into a visible enemy, and the enemy into a foreign threat, not only reveals the pandemic's contributions to the zombie mythos but also suggests the dangers of missing the way large outbreaks may fuel insidious links between disease and foreign "others."

Absent a tangible enemy, illness can also inspire a search for a scapegoat. The random unfairness of illness that Charon notes can lead patients to take blame upon themselves—searching for something they did or didn't do to cause this illness. Assigning blame can be easier than accepting the randomness. Wald has detailed the symbolic role of the carrier figure, or patient zero, who often emerges in disease accounts, a figure who "represented the question of culpability in the absence not only of intention but more fundamentally of self-knowledge."[100] Later accounts of the pandemic have proposed such figures, including one soldier at Fort Riley in Kansas thought to be patient zero (though scientists are now once again unsure).[101] At the time it unfolded, though, the pandemic produced no easy Typhoid Mary figure who could be externalized and scapegoated. Indeed, for most families, the blame was felt everywhere. As one epidemiologist observes about the pandemic, "You can't barrier yourself from being exposed, because the person who looks healthy may be spreading the disease. And that was part of the horror. We can't get away from respiratory diseases of other people because we all have to breathe."[102] The lack of a scapegoat both encouraged the outbreak's erasure and also produced the wide-ranging fear, guilt, and blame that blanket the pandemic literature.

The pandemic also lacked clearly defined and victorious heroes. In later accounts of contagion, such as the ubiquitous mid-twentieth-century narratives that Wald identifies, one of the stock characters is the expert in the field who bravely tracks down the problem and stops it.[103] Part of the comfort of this figure lies in the containment, but part also lies in the human-based control she or he represents: humans can respond to what can seem an indifferent, out-of-control nature. Representations of hero scientists and doctors were intensely appealing in the 1920s, as evident by Paul de Kruif's bestselling 1926 work *Microbe Hunters*.[104] De Kruif chronicles the work of early microbiologists, mostly from the nineteenth century, who track down germs and discover the sources of diseases. His optimistic, gripping style casts scientists as brave heroes who hunt invisible enemies to eradicate them. Understandably, de Kruif ignores the pandemic that had raged just eight years before, an experience directly at odds with his tales of successful scientists; indeed, his microbe hunters served as deeply appealing alternatives to the helplessness of the medical establishment during the pandemic. Certainly medical professionals in the pandemic acted heroically; letter after letter from flu survivors tell of overworked, overwhelmed doctors and nurses who continued to care for patients despite the dangers and the lack of viable treatments. And scientists raced to find a cure. While discoveries during the pandemic led to important advances in public health and medicine, efforts to treat patients during the pandemic remained woefully ineffectual; victories were scarce. The flu was, in general, seen as an embarrassing failure for a medical establishment that had otherwise made astonishing progress in the treatment of diseases, and doctors and nurses were plagued with a sense of helplessness.[105] Notably, Geddes Smith, a journalist who wrote the bestselling *Plague on Us* (1941), continued to cast scientists as conquerors but admitted how influenza represented a stark exception: for these men, "nothing is too small for them, nothing (save influenza, perhaps) too large," and later concedes that "Influenza kept step with the last war. If it came tomorrow we could not stop it."[106] Smith acknowledges but then moves on from the helplessness and the still-present danger posed by influenza, which were at odds with his otherwise upbeat accounts. The pandemic literature addresses this lack of heroes by alternately turning doctors and nurses into terrifying, often ghoulish figures, as Porter, Wolfe, Woolf, and Lovecraft do, or by transforming them, as Arthur Conan Doyle does, into supernatural figures endowed with otherworldly healing powers.

The flu historian John Barry speculates that part of the cultural amnesia surrounding the pandemic is that it involved nonhuman actors and nonhuman violence. "People write about war," he notes. "They write about the Holocaust. They write about horrors that people inflict on people. Apparently they forget the horrors that nature inflicts on people."[107] In some ways, human-based violence is more disturbing but also seemingly more stoppable, with clearer targets for blame. The virus's villainy defied characterization—indeed, it even defied villainy. And yet there is a critical tension to keep in mind in the human versus nonhuman dimensions of the pandemic. On the one hand, the pandemic, as is true for most diseases, absolutely had human causes. The war likely produced the conditions for the virus's origins and certainly produced the conditions for its rapid spread. It reflected multiple failures of multiple public health systems (or lack thereof), and inadequate information on its severity led to more deaths. While largely touted as an equal-opportunity killer, the virus at times hit poorer, more crowded communities more severely.[108] Many critics, medical professionals, and the entire field of biopolitics remind us that disease is not simply a "natural" phenomenon. As Wald observes, "From communicable disease to cancer, disability to drug abuse, health outcomes display the consequences of power and privilege as they register socioeconomic and political inequalities worldwide."[109]

And yet the perception of the pandemic mattered. Compared to the war, it seemed agentless and the result of nonhuman causes. The pandemic in particular and illness in general can function as a specter of something that lies beyond human structures. As Judith Butler observes, "there is a vast domain of life not subject to human regulation and decision, and that to imagine otherwise is to reinstall an unacceptable anthropocentrism at the

heart of the life sciences."[110] The pandemic was, in fact, subject to regulation and human decision, but it was also—and this was, strangely, perhaps
its scarier hidden side—a harbinger of agentless chaos, a reminder that one's
vulnerability can lie outside of all control. This very fear, I argue, both contributes to the pandemic's disappearance from the cultural record and lies
at the heart of the literature I consider. Within the book, I remain attentive
to this tension, to the way human factors were involved in the virus's spread
and to the way it was nevertheless perceived, with some accuracy, as a nonhuman, agentless threat.

PLOTLESS

On multiple levels, the pandemic resisted incorporation into an understandable narrative. As writers from Virginia Woolf to Rita Charon remind us,
illness, in general, is difficult to plot. The medical field may want to "uncover
plot," Charon notes, but "much of what occurs in its realm is, sadly, random and plotless."[111] In her essay "On Being Ill," Woolf muses that "novels,
one would have thought, would have been devoted to influenza" but
acknowledges the problem: "the public would say that a novel devoted to
influenza lacked plot."[112] Charon observes that illness is, in many ways (to
borrow terms from structuralism), a synchronic event, one that lies outside
of time, becoming a "timeless enduring" rather than a diachronic event that
occurs within a temporal sequence. Despite this plotlessness, narrative
frames may bring essential order to illness: by "imposing plots on otherwise chaotic events," narrative allows us "to make *sense* of why things happen" while still, at times, allowing the mystery and uncertainty to be kept.[113]
The pandemic literature embraces this tension: it often eschews clear plots
in ways that reflect the narrative challenges of the outbreak while also developing new strategies to grant some sense of structure.

Priscilla Wald's account of the archetypal "outbreak narratives" that
emerged in the second half of the twentieth century identifies how such stories work to place illness and pandemics within an understandable frame.
"In its scientific, journalistic, and fictional incarnations," Wald writes, the
outbreak narrative "follows a formulaic plot that begins with the identification of an emerging infection, includes discussion of the global networks
throughout which it travels, and chronicles the epidemiological work that
ends with its containment." Such narratives suggest that future outbreaks

might be understandable and even preventable. The outbreak narrative also serves "like the epidemiological map and the electron microscope, [as] a tool for making the invisible appear."[114] Wald traces how this outbreak narrative shapes the idea of contagion in the late nineteenth through the twentieth century. The pandemic, though, does not figure prominently in Wald's analysis, as it lies decidedly outside the formula: identification was obscured by its seemingly familiar form; it appeared to emerge everywhere at once, though its global networks were noted; and it was decidedly not part of a containment narrative. It left as mysteriously as it arrived but was not effectively contained by human efforts.[115] The fear and emotional vertigo this sense of plotlessness produced contributed to the unreality of the experience and helped prevent the pandemic from getting clear purchase within the cultural story. And what little narrative the outbreak did offer would have been more familiar; as Crosby notes, deadly epidemics were more common.[116] The plotlessness inherent to so many modernist works, though, became a ready-made structure for representing illness's non-narrative characteristics. And other efforts, like spiritualism and new tales of protozombies, became ways to impose an understandable structure onto an otherwise unbearable and amorphous story.

MODERNIST STUDIES AND THE PANDEMIC

Reading for the pandemic requires that we reevaluate not only the literature but also some of the assumptions we make in modernist and literary studies about the role of illness, death, mourning, the corpse, and violence. To date, only a handful of literary critics have explored the pandemic's importance on literature directly. Jane Elizabeth Fisher offers the only major book-length study of pandemic literature in her fascinating *Envisioning Disease, Gender, and War: Women's Narratives of the 1918 Influenza Pandemic*.[117] Fisher draws on works from multiple countries across the twentieth century, focusing on how the pandemic could be surprisingly empowering to women. Other critics have written articles exploring specific pandemic works, but what's missing is an in-depth analysis of how the pandemic alters our understanding of Anglophone modernism and the critical conversations that surround it.

The pandemic shifts, for example, assumptions about modernist mourning. Patricia Rae, Tammy Clewell, and other critics have explored how modernism is often marked by a rejection of consolation; rather than being resolved, mourning remains continuous, in part functioning as an ongoing political protest against various aspects of the First World War.[118] The pandemic introduces a different form of anticonsolation and sustained mourning. The pandemic was not a human-caused disaster, though it was certainly aided by the war; it was not started by rival governments or political systems; there wasn't a clear issue to protest or a conceptual framework that might bring mourners together, such as those that marked the war and that have marked other pandemics such as the AIDS/HIV crisis. Mourning for the pandemic also carried a strange unreality, overshadowed by the war and generating few material memorials, shared rituals, or ceremonies. The anguish produced by the death of so many in so short a time, however, did not disappear; instead, mourning became miasmic: everywhere, ongoing, but without a clear form. To understand the pervasive atmosphere of ongoing mourning in modernism, we have to consider the shocks and aftershocks of a vast, nameless grief. Writers like William Maxwell, for example, represent this cloud of unresolved pandemic mourning in ways that reveal its brooding presence in earlier works.

The pandemic also requires a shift in modernist discussions of the corpse. Critics like Allyson Booth have pointed out the divide between dead bodies in war and at home: as the now familiar account goes, the war produced omnipresent bodies on the front lines and in the trenches, where "Trench soldiers . . . inhabited worlds constructed, literally, of corpses"[119]; in Britain and the United States, though, "corpselessness" reigned, as the war dead were not returned home. This eerie absence on the home front of a body to mourn helped produce particular forms of consolation, such as the Tomb of the Unknown Warrior and memorials to the missing. Critics have also explored how modernism's many bodies and corpses, such as those that fill *The Waste Land*, are attempts to address and re-represent these absent bodies.[120] The account of home-front corpselessness—while certainly true in respect to the war dead—becomes more complicated when we remember the flood of flu corpses that deluge the home front just as the Armistice arrives. Unlike the war corpse—omnipresent in one place, absent in another—the flu corpse was simultaneously everywhere and nowhere, unavoidable but seemingly unrepresented. Hidden within modernism's missing and fragmented bodies, its ghostly returns, and its tropes of resurrection are these forgotten dead, memorialized in part by the very way they are buried.

These flu corpses do not simply add another terrible dimension to the war's death tolls. It matters how corpses become corpses. David Sherman brilliantly explores how World War I offers a trenchant example of "how modern states accrue power over the living" through the state's political control of corpses and their representations and how modernist writers like Wilfred Owen and Virginia Woolf worked to expose this control.[121] The sociopolitical uses of corpses, though, depend in part on how they died. As the governments knew, the war dead were potentially politically dangerous but also politically expedient. And the ideological structures that both the state and its citizens could build around a war corpse—it's heroic / it's barbaric / it's a meaningful sacrifice / it's a pointless horrific death caused by corrupt governments—were not structures that could typically work when death came from an invading virus rather than an invading army. Flu corpses presented instead a crisis of representation. Difficult to spin politically or narratively, the flu death was more pointless, less understandable, and less preventable than one from the war. Recovering the impact of these corpses and their ideological structurelessness not only shifts modernism's many bodies; it also reveals how deaths from illness, even when occurring within a highly visible pandemic, carry different literary and cultural weight.

Reading for the pandemic also requires adjustments to recent critical frameworks on modernist representations of violence and anxiety. Sarah Cole's magisterial book *At the Violet Hour*, for example, argues that modernism is "profoundly shaped by the call of violence" in both form and theme, and she examines moments of inflection, "when the body is attacked, violated, or killed" by human-generated violence. What happens, though, if we consider the damage initiated not by humans but by a nonsentient agent? This flu virus caused unmistakable violence to the body, corrupting it from within, destroying organs, and causing bleeding from all orifices. Violence does lie at the nerve center of modernist literature, as Cole argues, but that nerve center also includes a violence generated by illness. Cole's formulation of enchanted and disenchanted violence takes on new resonance with a nonhuman agent. She explores how violence may be read as both "enchanted," offering generative possibilities and a sense of rebirth,

and "disenchanted," producing "the active stripping away of idealizing principles."[122] The flu produced moments of enchanted violence, witnessed in
part by the repeated tropes of resurrection it engendered, though this rebirth
typically was generated less from the violence than as a reaction to its utterly
disenchanted quality. The flu was, in many ways, the ultimate exposure to
disenchanted violence: a violent death resistant to structures of martyrdom,
meaning, purpose, and politics.

Pandemic readings not only change approaches to modernist violence
but shift how we might read what Paul K. Saint-Amour has recently char-
acterized as the interwar era's "anticipatory anxiety," or "pre-traumatic
stress disorder." Saint-Amour, in *Tense Future*, explores how writers like
Virginia Woolf capture the period's climate of apprehension, "the sense that
something terrible, even annihilating, is at hand," and he links this dread
to the new threat of total war. As warfare moved to the air at the end of
World War I, the sense of anticipatory catastrophe became widespread, creating what Saint-Amour terms a "perpetual interwar," a moment charac-
terized by "the real-time experience of remembering a past war while awaiting and theorizing a future one." Writers like James Joyce and Ford Madox
Ford create an "encyclopedic modernism," Saint-Amour argues, that is
detailed and comprehensive without being totalizing.[123] Yet there was that
other source of anticipatory dread in the air, that other totalizing threat with
its own manifestations. The knowledge that an annihilating viral foe might
literally be in the air at any moment, coupled with the haunting memories
of the 1918 flu, led, I argue, not to expressions of an encyclopedic modernism but to a miasmic one. Authors repeatedly describe a diseased and all-
encompassing atmosphere of apprehension that was both metaphorically
representative of the multiple sources of dread in the interwar period but
also a literal and biologic representation of the pandemic's presentation.

Viral Modernism brings a marginalized tragedy to the heart of Anglophone modernism and to these critical debates within the field. I concen-
trate on accounts written or produced by people who were alive during the
pandemic, usually with firsthand experience of its costs, and who lived in
countries directly involved in the war, since the conflict profoundly shaped
the pandemic's literary representations. I focus on the interwar period,
arguing that these twenty-one years reflect a particular grappling with the
aftermath of the two tragedies, before the Second World War's new forms
of mass death and violence took over and again changed the stories it was

possible to tell. Revealing these pandemic representations will, I hope, lead to more explorations of the literary pandemic in other areas and during later times. The pandemic was a global event, and its study invites a new landscape for what Douglas Mao and Rebecca Walkowitz have termed the "transnational turn" in modernist studies.[124] The virus circulated worldwide, becoming a perverse cosmopolitan traveler that crossed national borders as easily as cellular ones, though a nation's experience of this traveler depended on many factors. Places like Nigeria, for example, that were not extensively involved in the war, confronted the pandemic more directly, as Jane Fisher has demonstrated in her exploration of two Nigerian pandemic novels from the 1970s.[125]

Literary scholars investigating the pandemic in the interwar period, though, face a particular challenge: the scarcity of direct literary responses written at the time. And for communities and groups already burdened with systemic discrimination or economic and legal hardships, the difficulties of speaking or writing about an experience that was already hard to convey meant that many voices and experiences are missing from the literary and cultural record. Having found, though, that the pandemic is foundational to literary texts I thought I knew well, in ways I had not seen, I suspect that more pandemic art was produced in the aftermath of the outbreak that scholars, including myself, have not yet considered. The pandemic was global but unfolded in particular ways in different areas, especially those less affected by the war, and thus will have its own literary manifestations and its own ways of—and reasons for—hiding in plain sight. As the pandemic starts to receive attention from literary scholars with expertise across more regions, cultures, and languages, a richer literary history of the pandemic will emerge. This book is one contribution to this effort.

Reframing Modernism

Moving the pandemic to the center of Anglophone modernism requires a radical reframing of our basic assumptions about the period. Judith Butler's work on grievability in *Frames of War* offers an instrumental model for seeing how basic realities may be left out of the historical record—and how such realities may be recovered. Butler's work focuses primarily on war and human-based violence and on the ways conflicts are framed to make certain lives "grievable" and other lives not. Deaths, she argues, count differently, and how we frame conflict shapes the reality we see:

The frame does not simply exhibit reality, but actively participates in a strategy of containment, selectively producing and enforcing what will count as reality. . . . The frame is always throwing something away, always keeping something out, always de-realizing and de-legitimating alternative versions of reality, discarded negatives of the official version. And so, when the frame jettisons certain versions of war, it is busily making a rubbish heap whose animated debris provides the potential resources for resistance. When versions of reality are excluded or jettisoned to a domain of unreality, then specters are produced that haunt the ratified version of reality. . . . In this sense frame seeks to institute an interdiction on mourning: there is no destruction, and there is no loss.[126]

The frames Butler describes are shaped primarily by governments and institutions focused on controlling the discourses surrounding war and conflict; the perceived nongrievability of certain lives can act as a prejustification for violence and war in addition to providing a justification after the fact. We see these discourses at work in numerous ways in World War I, where, in just one example, deaths of both civilians and soldiers of different races and ethnicities were valued—and grieved—unequally by the state. Butler's model, though, offers an important guide for understanding how the war itself acted as a frame for the era in ways that continue to obscure the victims of the pandemic, making those lives, in a sense, less grievable than the lives lost in the war. This process of delegitimization works differently when applied to a pandemic rather than a political conflict. Governments can, as Butler explores, work to define groups of people as ungrievable to rationalize violence and repression that protect other groups deemed more "worthy." The pandemic's dead, though, became ungrievable through a different dichotomy. In the pandemic, the foil was the war: for the war dead to be meaningful, they had to be framed as sacrificial.[127] The pandemic dead were a direct affront to such a model. At the political level, the pandemic's dead needed to be forgotten; they needed to become ungrievable—silenced, left out—to make room for the war's already uncountable dead. The war became, both then and now, "what w[ould] count as reality." The pandemic happened—that is undeniable—but it didn't and doesn't shape our conceptions of the reality of the postwar moment. The pandemic became derealized and delegitimated, one of Butler's "discarded negatives."

Viral Modernism recovers the "specters" that the war's frame has excluded for so long, gathering this "animated debris" as a resource of resistance. Analyzing an experience that is simultaneously widespread and hidden in turn grants a model for recovering other, often intrinsically concealed, stories of illness, revealing as it does the ways so many bodily experiences go unrepresented. Such readings also resonate more broadly with other vast phenomena that are undeniably present, like systemic discrimination or environmental damage, but that are often hidden, obscured by gaps, repressions, silences, and absences. Marianne Hirsch and Leo Spitzer, writing on vulnerability and listening, argue that we must search for such diffuse but powerful experiences, for what they term the dust of the archive, to find narrative possibilities that are hidden in the silences that surround stories. By hearing the "circulating movement and formless opacity" in this dust, they insist, "something beyond the closed narrative stream . . . can be discerned. If, as historians and critics, we permit ourselves to consider this ambient archival dust through the aural resonances and dissonances that stir it into motion, we can disrupt the interpretive limits . . . and reveal dimensions that might otherwise remain unexamined."[128] Reading the letters and stories told by the survivors of the pandemic—and the literary representations that simultaneously revealed and hid these very stories— launch us into new narrative streams, allowing us to hear voices long ignored in part because the viral, dust-like form at the heart of the story was itself invisible and silent.

PART I

Pandemic Realism

Making an Atmosphere Visible

Part 1 establishes a pandemic literary paradigm that offers a new frame and context for reading interwar literature. In this section, I investigate the central works from the Anglo-American interwar period that represent the pandemic overtly and at length: Willa Cather's *One of Ours* (1922), Katherine Anne Porter's *Pale Horse, Pale Rider* (1939), Thomas Wolfe's *Look Homeward, Angel* (1929), and William Maxwell's *They Came Like Swallows* (1937).[1] All four authors lived through the pandemic and saw its devastation, and Porter and Maxwell caught the virus themselves. Together, their novels make visible the pandemic atmosphere, capturing the ways the outbreak entangled with the war and shifted the era's climate of violence, guilt, and loss. At the same time, these works build into their structures all the ways the pandemic became hidden from view, in part by drawing on modernist techniques established by earlier writers.

Most of these direct accounts are written after the more subtle evocations of the pandemic that I explore in part 2. This backward chronology is deliberate. The novels in part 1 grant a detailed literary portrait of the pandemic and its costs, revealing the sensory and affective markers that were all too familiar to those who lived through the era but that were, by their very nature, hard to distinguish in the pandemic's immediate aftermath. As the pandemic grew more distant, the possibility of writing about it more directly seemed to expand. The geographic differences are also notable: all these direct works were written in the United States, which suffered far more in the pandemic than it did in the First World War. The more indirect works in part 2 were written in Britain and Ireland, where the war was more all-consuming; even as the pandemic devastated civilian and military populations, writing about the pandemic directly could seem irrelevant to, or a betrayal of, the countries' central focus.

The overt novels place the pandemic within understandable narratives, expressed through the experiences of defined characters. They thus overcome in part the barriers to representing illness, especially in a time of war, while still incorporating the challenges of this representation into their works. They recreate details of the outbreak, allowing us to see the ways it produced miasmic atmospheres and viral resurrections. They narrate the original traumatic experiences, as well as how the memories of those experiences become fragmented in their aftermath, producing bewildering flashbacks divorced from the full story. These overt works establish the frame we need to see the diffuse elements from the pandemic experience in the works in part 2. Reading the overt works first and establishing the context for the originating conditions allows us to recognize these elements as part of the pandemic era and to trace the fragments back to the precipitating conditions that produced them.

Remarkably, critics have not analyzed these overt pandemic works together—beyond noting that they all concern the outbreak—or explored their differences. I treat them as a specific, interrelated body of texts that establishes three central elements of the literary pandemic. First, they expose the challenges of representation the pandemic produced. They show how the pandemic disrupted lives and expectations, and then they mirror this disruption within their narrative structures. The very existence of these works also suggests how some of the problems the pandemic posed to representation were lifting; by the late 1920s, the virus had shifted to a potential, rather than an imminent threat, and enough time had passed to better understand how the pandemic might fit into the other narrative arcs of the era, especially those from the war. Second, the works expose the miasmic world the virus created, detailing through deathbed scenes, damaged bodies, and depictions of airborne menace how the pandemic blurred distinctions between life and death. They register how fears of contagion, and the ways that contagion produced an amorphous sense of guilt, contributed to this twilight atmosphere. Finally, these authors establish how tropes of viral resurrection capture particular elements of the pandemic's legacy, including the hallucinatory delirium the virus produced, the need for visual markers after so much sudden and unrepresented loss, and the eerie sense that memories of the pandemic were being both buried and relentlessly remembered.

While all the authors address the pandemic's interaction with the war, the works by Cather and Porter analyzed in chapter 2 focus on the ways the two tragedies were entangled. In both stories, the war, at least at first, seems like the central event, while the pandemic encroaches more stealthily. The central pandemic deaths in these stories are those of young soldiers—soldiers whom everyone expected would die for their country in the war. Cather and Porter register the surprise that the enemy had changed and detail how the pandemic usurped the projected death narrative the war had already set in place. Both works nevertheless also exemplify the ways the war repeatedly obscured the pandemic's impact and subsumed its losses—and the surprising gender tensions underlying this war/pandemic dynamic. Chapter 3 turns to works focused on the domestic experience of the pandemic and shifts from pandemic victims to pandemic mourners. Wolfe and Maxwell place the pandemic at the heart of their accounts, moving the war to the background and offering an intimate portrait of the ways the virus literally and emotionally infiltrated individual communities, homes, and bodies. By subordinating the war, these authors narrate how the pandemic dead overtook the war dead and how the casualties extended far beyond young male soldiers.

Chapter Two

UNTANGLING WAR AND PLAGUE

Willa Cather and Katherine Anne Porter

Willa Cather's *One of Ours* (1922) and Katherine Anne Porter's *Pale Horse, Pale Rider* (1939) expose the complicated layers of overlap between the war and the pandemic and the difficulties of representing the pandemic's particular costs amid the war's more public presence. In distinct ways, the two works chronicle how the story of the war—both in history and within the literary accounts—is disrupted by the pandemic's sudden arrival: the role of the male soldier is usurped, enemies and victims are recast, and the setting for danger is relocated. As the passive-voice construction of the last sentence captures, the agent that produced these disruptions was at first hard to acknowledge or see in the subject position. For four long years, the war had been the structuring and precipitating agent—the definer of characters, actions, and setting. Cather and Porter narrate the moment this agency was disrupted and another tragedy moved center stage.

One of Ours is the earliest of the four overt interwar accounts, and while it treats the pandemic directly it also demonstrates, rather than challenges, the way the war narrative engulfed the viral outbreak, especially in the initial years. Cather had less personal exposure to the pandemic's costs than the other authors, and her novel offers an instructive model of how the pandemic was first seen as a distraction from the main story of the war. Cather depicts the arrival of the virus on board a troop ship headed from the United States to France, with the infection killing many soldiers before they even see a battlefield. The episode highlights the transmission routes of the virus as it rapidly spread to different continents through the mass circulation of military personnel. Cather's main character is a young American soldier who views the outbreak as an isolated nuisance, a footnote to the war's exciting possibilities for heroic action and meaningful sacrifice. The question of whether Cather shared his romantic view of the war or sought to expose it has structured much of the critical discussion surrounding the novel.[1] This debate, though, has obscured a different issue. Cather may well arrange her novel to unmask Claude's war illusions, but the pandemic's representation and its structural position within the work reflect a less examined acquiescence to prevailing attitudes toward the pandemic. Cather both spotlights the terrible conditions the outbreak delivered to troop ships—and the very means by which the pandemic is displaced from cultural memory.

Pale Horse, Pale Rider, by contrast, offers a radical rethinking of the pandemic's relationship to the war. Published in 1939 just as the Second World War was starting, it is the latest literary account of the pandemic I consider and one of the most vivid works written by a survivor. Set in Denver at the end of the war and the start of the pandemic, the novella grants equal weight to the two tragedies and offers a nuanced portrayal of their interaction, capturing the bodily dangers, the miasmic realities, the experience of living death, and the haunting sense of viral resurrection and guilt that the contagion produced. Porter deftly switches between modernist and realist techniques to suggest the changes the pandemic brings to the war-laden atmosphere. While critics have long detailed how elements of modernist style—including its broken and elongated sentences, its nonlinear temporal construction, and its often plotless structure—are suited for capturing war traumas, Porter uses these techniques to represent the pandemic's impact and then a more realist approach to describe the war. These shifts showcase the way the war was a familiar, if grim, story by 1918, with particular roles for soldiers and civilians—and then the way the pandemic swept in and disrupted ideas of both narrative and selfhood.

The two works also introduce the ways the pandemic disrupted key gender narratives set in place by the war. In recent years, critics have done important work complicating our understanding of gender and the war, but except for the scholarship of Jane Fisher, the pandemic is generally left out of these discussions.[2] Cather's and Porter's novels reveal, though, how the pandemic upended the war's expected gender roles and stories. As the recent *Gender and the Great War* volume observes, the dominant cultural narrative at the time was one where "war service became proof of manliness" and women, amid many other roles, were still called "to 'keep the home fires burning' and safeguard an image of the tranquil home life for which men made sacrifices of life, limb, and livelihood."[3] The pandemic unsettled these stories on multiple levels. Cather's novel reveals, and in part participates in, a masculine war narrative where influenza robs men of their rightful chance to die in battle. At the same time, the harsh critical reaction to the war parts of the novel and the praise it received for its depiction of illness and domestic life expose the challenges women faced when writing about war versus the pandemic.[4] Porter's work more directly narrates how the pandemic invaded home-front expectations of masculine death and feminine safety, and she places a female body experiencing overwhelming pain— pain that arises from illness rather than war—at the center of the work. The story also suggests the guilt women felt over all the male war deaths and the resulting temptation to see the outbreak as retribution or even a compensating sacrifice women might make—and the utter futility of such a sacrifice. Despite these disruptions, both authors ultimately remain focused on male death: the only main characters who die of influenza in these two novels are soldiers.

CATHER'S PANDEMIC

Willa Cather's own experiences in the war and the pandemic reflected the way the war overshadowed, blocked, and incorporated the viral tragedy. Like many Americans, Cather was focused on the war as it unfolded, alternatively inspired by its gallantry and depressed by its slaughter. She began *One of Ours* as the war drew to a close, her novel in part a tribute to her cousin who had died in the fighting. At the time, she viewed the war as a worthwhile conflict. As she wrote to her cousin's mother on Armistice Day, she believed his death helped make possible "all that this world has gained," the fighting eradicating both monarchies and tyrannies; her cousin, she writes, and the "brave boys. . . . who went so far to fight for an ideal" became "God's Soldiers," with "a glorious part" in "whatever the afterlife may be." The breathy language anticipates the romantic views that her novel's central character has toward the war, an enthusiasm he maintains to his death but that Cather would lose (and indeed would later satirize in her novel). In this same letter, though, she offered a telling aside: "This is not meant to be a letter—I have so many letters to write to friends who have been bereaved by this terrible scourge of Influenza—but I must send you a greeting on this great day when old things are passing away forever."[5] The pandemic is set apart from the war both in punctuation and in thought, terrible yet outside the grander story. In later letters, she continues to position the pandemic as subordinate to the war, remarking that "It's cruel how many boys have died in our training camps here. Before I left Red Cloud we had seven funerals in one week for boys who were sent home from Camp Dodge, Iowa. The rumor is that more of our boys have died [of the flu] in camp at home than have been killed in France."[6] Her tone suggests that these deaths are more senseless, and in a strange way crueler, than those of men in the war who at least had the chance to die for a higher cause.[7]

Even before the fighting started, Cather was primed, as her culture was, to see the war as manly and the pandemic as emasculating. From an early age, Cather strongly identified with male writers and traditional male subjects, declaring that she would not take female writers seriously until they wrote "a story of adventure, a stout sea tale, [or] a manly battle yarn."[8] As the critic Sharon O'Brien has detailed, Cather associated "maleness with the power and autonomy she wanted for herself," finding "in war and combat . . . the apotheosis of masculinity, a temporary refuge from social definitions of feminine identity, linked in her mind with passivity and victimization." Porter saw herself as an inheritor of traits embodied in male family members who were soldiers, even claiming, as O'Brien observes, that "she had been named for her uncle William Boak," who had died in the Civil War, rather than her aunt Wilella, "who had died, unheroically, of diphtheria."[9]

Cather incorporates into her novel the sense that a soldier's death from flu was an abrogation of his expected role. She did, though, work to represent the pandemic accurately in her work, gathering information on the way it unfolded, while still limiting its representation to its military impacts. She drew some of her material from a firsthand account written by an army doctor. After catching a bout of ordinary influenza in 1919, Cather was treated by Dr. Frederick C. Sweeney, who lent Cather his diary describing his grim experiences on a war transport ship during the pandemic.[10] Her novel offers far more details on the pandemic than the diary does, so she likely also gathered information through the many interviews she conducted with returning soldiers; as she notes in a letter, "the sick ones often talked like men in a dream, softly remembering dead lives."[11]

One of Ours thus offers a vivid portrayal of the pandemic but suggests in both form and content how the war remains the dominant narrative. The novel follows the story of Claude Wheeler, a young farmer from Nebraska who enlists in the army and is finally killed in the war. Claude's life—and the novel's narrative arc—gain momentum through the war: caught in a sexless marriage and frustrated by his lack of purpose, Claude finds the war grants meaning and adventure, and he dies with these beliefs largely intact (despite the skepticism of both Cather and other characters). Critics typically focus on the novel's two central sections: the "prewar" part, which concerns Claude's early life and marriage, and the later half on the war, which depicts Claude's experiences in France and in combat. In between these two parts, though, is the account of Claude's journey on a military transport ship, during which a terrible outbreak of influenza erupts. The pandemic episode reflects an instructive dichotomy: On the one hand, it offers a detailed example of the outbreak among the troops, a widespread experience that is ignored by other authors who write about the war. On the other hand, despite the uniqueness and vividness of the scene, it paradoxically reflects the pandemic's erasure on multiple levels. Cather positions the pandemic as part of a broader narrative of waste in the war and as a side episode that literally happened on the way to the main event. Claude, the story's doctor, Cather, and Dr. Sweeney all see the pandemic's horror, but they struggle to incorporate it into any larger story; they all simply move on, the outbreak a strange eruption that seems at once distinct from the war's larger purpose and contained by it. Most critics overlook the episode as well,[12] for without the larger context of the pandemic, it appears (as it did for many at the time) as an isolated if grim side note sandwiched in between the more compelling dichotomy of peace and war. Cather's novel thus reflects the larger cultural dismissal of the pandemic and at the same time exposes how and why the war made this dismissal possible—and, emotionally, even necessary.

Like many actual ships heading to the war during the pandemic, the fictional *Anchises* becomes a floating hospital and morgue almost overnight. Ships provided the perfect conditions for the rapid spread of the virus. As Cather ominously notes as the *Anchises* leaves port, "every inch [of the deck] was covered by a boot. The whole superstructure was coated with brown uniforms; they clung to the boat davits, the winches, the railings and ventilators, like bees in a swarm."[13] The 2,500 men echo the virus itself, coating every surface and clinging to the ventilation system. A few days out, soldiers start to fall ill, with cases rapidly increasing. One soldier "had such an attack of nose-bleed during the night that the sergeant thought he might die before they got it stopped." Soon the hold is crowded with delirious, desperately ill men: "There was almost no ventilation, and the air was fetid with sickness and sweat and vomit." "Medical supplies are wholly inadequate," there are no nurses, and of the three doctors on board, one won't see soldiers, one falls ill, and one is run ragged trying to attend to patients he can do little to help.[14]

The outbreak quickly leads to deaths, and while Cather offers searing accounts of the suffering, the language exposes how the war crowded out the pandemic. One of Claude's men struggles through the end stages of the virus in ways that resemble a death from poison gas:

Big Tannhauser's fever had left him, but so had everything else. He lay in a stupor. His congested eyeballs were rolled back in his head and only the yellowish whites were visible. His mouth was open and his tongue hung out at one side. From the end of the corridor Claude had heard the frightful sounds that came from his throat, sounds like violent vomiting, or the choking rattle of a man in strangulation,— and, indeed, he was being strangled.[15]

The body is distorted in pain, suffocated in bed by an invisible force. The language recalls, perhaps deliberately, Wilfred Owen's famous depiction of a death from poison gas in his poem "Dulce et Decorum Est" (1920). Like Tannhauser, Owen's soldier, with "white eyes writhing in his face," is "guttering, choking, drowning," while "the blood / Come[s] gargling from the froth-corrupted lungs."[16] Though one man is killed from a weaponized, human-inflicted gas and the other from a nonhuman virus, the sensory details are strikingly similar—and doctors were, in fact, startled by the eerie similarities between the lung damage produced by the virus and by poison gas.[17] The overlap, in other words, is not simply Cather's parallel but a biological fact. Both men are soldiers, and it becomes easy to see how an influenza death like Tannhauser's would, in people's memory, blend into— and even be remembered as—a gas death in the war. Cather likewise suggests how the military funerals on board the ship could seem like part of the war effort. The first soldier to die of the flu "was buried at sunrise . . . sewed up in a tarpaulin, with an eighteen pound shell at his feet."[18] The shell suggests a death in battle, the pandemic body sunk by the very ammunition that might have killed it at the front. As the death toll mounts, the men are buried at sea with little fanfare, the funerals becoming as routine as burials at the front.

Cather's account suggests how denial helped fuel the pandemic's disappearance from memory and also how such denial linked to the ways people could ignore the horrors of war. Claude himself holds a romanticized view of the battles to come, convinced the conflict grants him purpose and meaning. Like so many at the time, he misreads his surroundings; as the critic Joshua Doležal notes, he is often "utterly blind to his reality,"[19] and the reality Claude misses encompasses not just the war but the pandemic. Before the voyage, for example, Claude sees a group of ships through idealized glasses: "He knew nothing about ships, but he didn't have to; the shape of those hulls—their strong inevitable lines—told their story, *was* their story; told the whole adventure of man with the sea." Claude understandably misreads these vessels and enters an entirely different story than the one he so confidently expects, a story where ships cut off adventures and quickly deliver men to their deaths. And the denial continues on several fronts once the outbreak begins. The doctor complains about the officers who sequester themselves to play poker: "Either they've got no conscience, or they're not awake to the gravity of the situation." And, in a passage that may reflect Cather's denial as well as Claude's, the soldiers who died "were not very sick. Vigorous, clean-blooded young fellows of nineteen and twenty turned over and died because they had lost their courage, because other people were dying,—because death was in the air."[20] The implication is that death from the virus is a failure of willpower, governed by martial virtues like "courage." Susan Sontag has famously pointed out the dangers of this sort of metaphorizing, when character traits rather than microbes are thought to control illness.[21] Claude cheerfully takes part in such beliefs, assuming, if not verbalizing, that his own continued health is within his power rather than a biological fluke—certainly a less frightening belief than the truth.

Cather in part pushes against this denial in her representation, both by depicting the pandemic at all and by trying to shape the outbreak into an understandable narrative, complete with villains and heroes (traits, as I explored in the introduction, often difficult to incorporate into representations of illness). Claude and the doctor emerge as at least semiheroic figures; the doctor tells Claude that Claude can likely save his ill friend with careful treatment and the constant administration of eggs and orange juice—and his friend lives, ministered to by an upbeat Claude who feels he has found his purpose on the ship and "was enjoying himself all the while."[22] When the villainous chief steward hides the remaining eggs for profit, the doctor and Claude storm into his cabin and threaten to expose him, thereby securing the supplies at least for the one soldier. Claude reads his own escape from infection not as luck but as part of a larger destiny. This narrative shaping is, not surprisingly, missing from Dr. Sweeney's diary, which treats the outbreak as a bewildering anomaly on the way to the war. By creating a greater sense of narrative framing, Cather both obscures the pandemic's plotlessness and also works to represent the outbreak in a way compelling to her reader.

Cather does hint, though, that these pandemic deaths are not only pointless but emasculating, falling outside more compelling martial stories. Tannhauser, Claude thinks, had "only wanted to serve," and he ends up ill and crying for his mother, before being wrapped in a sack and dropped into "a lead-coloured chasm in the sea. There was not even a splash."[23] And once the body enters the waves, the ship "steamed on without him"; a few hours later, he was "already forgotten."[24] Echoing Cather's letter about the soldiers who died in the army camps, Claude will think of these soldiers as having missed the whole purpose of a story defined by masculine sacrifice; they "were never to have any life at all, or even a soldier's death. They were merely waste in a great enterprise," their bodies tossed into an "inhuman kingdom of darkness and unrest." By the novel's end, Cather hints that Claude misreads the war when he imagines it has a greater purpose than these deaths. Nevertheless, Cather encapsulates the haunting sense that flu losses are meaningless, overshadowed, and soon forgotten. And as the doctor in the novel exclaims—echoing the sentiments of many—he plans to "forget this voyage like a bad dream."[25]

Claude is eager to move on to the war, and Cather infuses a sense of mockery into her description of this eagerness that seems aimed at the reader as well. By 1922, readers could expect that novels and poems would be marked by classic iconography of World War I, and Claude has been shaped by the same expectations. As Claude marches with the troops, he reflects that now "They were bound for the big show, and on every hand were reassuring signs: long lines of gaunt, dead trees, charred and torn; big holes gashed out in fields and hillsides . . .; winding depressions in the earth, bodies of wrecked motor-trucks and automobiles lying along the road, and everywhere endless straggling lines of rusty barbed-wire." Claude and the other men are reassured to see the wasted landscape, delighted to have reached the real action. The rest of the novel draws on familiar details of the Great War narrative, with its grim bodies, trenches, and male friendships. For both Cather and Claude, the war takes over and the pandemic is pushed aside. Indeed, Cather deliberately changes the timeline of the pandemic so it happens earlier in the war, allowing the war to continue after the pandemic episode—and deepening the impression that the war subsumed the pandemic.[26] Claude continues to assert the war's dominance, declaring that the war wounded look far worse than the pandemic victims, though the language itself blurs the two together. Visiting the hospital on the day a group of American wounded arrive, Claude observes that "as the men were carried past him, he thought they looked as if they had been sick a long while. . . . The boys who died on board the *Anchises* had never seemed as sick as these did. Their skin was yellow or purple, their eyes were sunken, their lips sore." As we know from pandemic accounts, this description fits flu victims perfectly. Even as Claude insists on the distinction, the ambiguity of which set of bodies Claude's "their" links to suggests the overlap. For his part, Claude wants to forget anyone who didn't die in battle: "To shed bright blood, to wear the red badge of courage,—that was one thing; but to be reduced to this was quite another. Surely the sooner these boys died, the better."[27]

Claude holds this opinion through his own death, which Cather depicts—and which he constructs—as suitably manly. His final moments are set in striking contrast to Tannhauser's death and to Claude's reactions to the men at the army camp: "The blood dripped down his coat, but he felt no weakness. He felt only one thing: that he commanded wonderful men. When David came up with the supports he might find them dead, but he would find them all there. They were there to stay until they were carried out to be buried. They were mortal, but they were unconquerable."[28] Cather occupies a complicated position here. On the one hand, she gives Claude the death that he and many readers would want; Cather herself seems partially to endorse, or at least understand, these desires. On the other, she hints at Claude's overly romanticized views of the war, inviting readers to push against his naïve understanding.[29] In contrast to Claude's death, she had, in Tannhauser's final illness, represented the nonromantic soldier's death that writers like Wilfred Owen had insisted upon. She displaces that death onto the pandemic, though, allowing her to suggest the pointlessness and suffering of war deaths while nevertheless shifting them onto an enfeebling illness outside the main story. Cather creates a narrative that represents pandemic deaths, but the very structure of her novel reflects the culture's wish to turn away, reproducing the dominant template that positioned the pandemic as an emasculating subdivision of the war.

PANDEMIC BODIES IN PAIN: PORTER'S *PALE HORSE, PALE RIDER*

In *Pale Horse, Pale Rider*, Katherine Anne Porter rejects Cather's template, repositioning the pandemic as a tragedy as devastating and important as the war and revealing the ways it upended expectations for both male and female bodies. In 1918, the twenty-eight-year-old Porter only barely survived her bout with influenza. Working as a journalist in Denver for the *Rocky Mountain News*, Porter caught the flu in October. Her friends at the newspaper had prepared her obituary, her family made plans for her funeral, and she was left for dead in the hospital, saved, the story goes, by an experimental injection of strychnine.[30] It took over two decades for her to write about the experience.[31] She sets her story during November 1918 (the height of the second wave) in Denver, though it could be many cities at the time. The story depicts how the pandemic crashes in to the atmosphere of violence and despair that the war casts over the city, infiltrating the bodies of the characters and shifting targets, enemies, and even the nature of guilt. As Porter traces, the pandemic took the constant images of death and war corpses that were in the minds of so many on the home front and brought those images into terrifying material form as the bodies piled up in cities and the atmosphere became, in the words of one character, "as bad as anything can be."[32] Porter divides her story into four parts: a hallucinatory opening that suggests how the pandemic disrupted temporal and spatial realities and the sense of a coherent self; a realist section that depicts life at a city newspaper and the relationship of one of the young reporters—Miranda—and her soldier boyfriend, Adam, who is about to go off to the war;[33] a delirium-infused section describing Miranda's battle with the virus; and a grim return to realism as the Armistice arrives and the plague persists. Throughout the work, the physical body becomes a nexus of shifting threats and new vulnerabilities, endangered by a human-based violence targeting men across the seas, and then suddenly engulfed in pain from a non-sentient entity that delivered a different form of annihilation to men and women alike.

Porter's story begins with a disorienting dream sequence that previews the challenge the virus posed to both narrative and agency. The style mirrors the physical self, the language taking on the traits of the female body depicted:

In sleep she knew she was in her bed, but not the bed she had lain down in a few hours since, and the room was not the same but it was a room she had known somewhere. Her heart was a stone lying upon her breast outside of her; her pulses lagged and paused, and she knew something strange was going to happen, even as the early morning winds were cool through the lattice, the streaks of light were dark blue and the whole house was snoring in its sleep.[34]

Immediately, Porter unsettles both place and time. The ambiguity and confusion of the first sentence suggests that the bed that holds her body, and the room that holds the bed, are both continuous with the ones she laid down in and different—from another place, and another time—seemingly returning the character to a childhood home. The body itself is under threat: her heart is outside her breast, metamorphosed into a stone. Life and death seem strangely mixed: the "she" is alive, but like the prose, her pulses lag and pause, hinting of a coming death. The heart that has been removed from the body and rendered inert indicates death itself. The house, though, seems strangely alive, taking over the body's snores and blurring distinctions between objects and humans. Something strange is not simply going to happen; it already has in the first two sentences.

The opening in part reflects the confused logic of dreams and the war's chaotic elements, but it also thrusts the reader unexpectedly into the layers of confusion the pandemic engendered. Porter takes her contemporary readers back to the sense of dislocation and body estrangement the virus caused and encapsulates some of the iconic features of pandemic death-bed scenes we'll see repeated throughout this study: the hallucinatory experience of delirium, the disruption of place and time, the domestic space as the arena for death, and a twilight atmosphere where life and death blur together. The reader is asked to experience a similar disorientation, unable to find a clear sense of where the body is and where reality might lie; indeed the reality of the experience is captured in its distorted sense of reality. At this point in the story, the pandemic is not mentioned directly—we only get the out-of-context description, a feature that mimics the way the virus appeared seemingly out of nowhere, disorienting a culture already reeling from war. Porter's opening, while referencing the pandemic specifically (given the story that follows), also speaks more broadly to the way illness often seems both plotless and characterless.[35] Here, Porter captures these features in the jumbled narrative, the rambling sentences, the diffuse and hard-to-identify threat, and the seeming disintegration of both self and body.

In the next paragraphs, the still unnamed character grapples with both action and self-definition, caught in a domestic atmosphere blanketed by fear, delirium, and death. The voice switches into the first person, as if the disassociated self of the first paragraph is trying to reassert agency. Her condition, though, threatens the very borders of the self; she wonders frantically, "Do I even walk about in my own skin or is it something I have borrowed to spare my modesty?" In her delirium, she fights to locate not just her self but her outer world, where objects have become strangely animate and hidden: "Where are my things?" she asks; "Things have a will of their own in this place and hide where they like." The confusion and paranoia are exacerbated by the way death blankets the home; as the speaker laments, "Too many have died in this bed already, there are far too many ancestral bones."[36] She knows the "lank greenish stranger" who has taken family members in the past is stalking the house, for "I saw him pass the window in the evening." And grief over all this death threatens to overwhelm her as she thinks of the people she has lost: "What else besides them did I have in the world? Nothing." In part, the speaker references a general sense of loss that might accrue in any household, but in emphasizing the way death stalks the domestic space, the "too many" deaths, the piling up of bones, and the sweeping feelings of grief, Porter echoes both how the pandemic brought mass death home—and how the loss was often unnamed and thus experienced as an unspecified presence of grief and fear. The speaker attempts to fight against this nothingness, desperate to go riding in the early morning because then, "trees are trees . . . stones are stones set in shades known to be grass, there are no false shapes or surmises."[37] She longs for a defined landscape without the uncertainty of her miasmic surroundings. Without yet naming the threat, Porter instead registers the pandemic's atmosphere and how illness may shatter a sense of reality and selfhood.

The speaker then embarks on a horse ride with a personified Death, the figure simultaneously encapsulating the desire to identify and externalize the threat the virus posed and the reality that this threat could not easily be defined. In part, the "stranger" seems a material presence. He is "Death and the Devil," and his horse is gray, "with tarnished nose and ears." The description mirrors the virus's twin weapons of lethality (the rider) and contagion (the tarnished horse). The rider has a physical presence, for he "sw[i]ng[s] into his saddle" and rides beside her "easily, lightly, his reins loose in his half-closed hand, straight and elegant in dark shabby garments that flapped upon his bones; his pale face smiled in an evil trance." The figure is familiar to the speaker; she knows she has "seen this fellow before. . . . He is no stranger to me," and his tarnished horse and shabby clothes suggest he has been around a long time.[38] Such a figure is likely no stranger to the reader either; Porter draws on classic iconography of the Grim Reaper, with his pale face, flapping garments, and bones, and she also references the fourth horseman of the apocalypse, identified in Revelation 6:7–8 as "Death," who rides a "pale horse" and destroys through "sword, famine and plague."[39] Porter evokes in this imagery the old-fashioned quality of the pandemic threat—it seemed at the time like an archaic form of death, like "something out of the Middle Ages,"[40] as one character later remarks. In making this threat visible and palpable, Porter also grants the virus a degree of characterization, even if it's a ste-reotyped one, placing the speaker into a brief narrative where she may out-race death. While Porter may offer a visual enemy, she also hints at the more frightening reality that this "new" danger was invisible, nonhuman, and eerily purposeless. The speaker finds she cannot quite "place him" after all, and the prose slips back to the third person, as if her agency has again been lost; the figure regards her "without meaning, the blank still stare of mindless malice that makes no threats and can bide its time."[41] The pale rider becomes a fantasy of embodiment—and an embodiment of the meaninglessness and pointlessness of the pandemic's form of death.

The opening's confusing, hallucinatory prose and temporal and spatial dislocations mimic the ways the pandemic unsettled the more familiar frameworks of war, plunging communities into a chaotic new reality. In her next section, Porter leaves this mode and delivers her readers and the (now named) Miranda back to the grim but established plotline of war. Shifting to a realist, linear mode, Porter recreates the home front's pre-pandemic landscape: the war dominates people's thoughts and actions, shaping the perceptions of vulnerable (male) bodies, the guilt of noncombatants, and the well-worn narratives and roles available at the time, both at the level of the story and in the lives of everyday citizens. The war, her style suggests, is what seemed real, despite all the propaganda and cant that swirled around its justification. Porter may depict these perceptions of the war—as that's the way it was often experienced at the time—but unlike Cather, she thoroughly rejects the corresponding move to relegate the pandemic to a subordinate position in her own story. Instead, by establishing this pre-pandemic landscape, Porter can showcase two forms of "real": the war, and how the pandemic then subtly—and suddenly—changed bodies, guilt, and the sense of reality itself.

Pale Horse, Pale Rider's second section introduces the constant specter of war violence that hung over bodies, especially male ones, even on the home front. The language and thoughts of the characters are haunted with threats of dismemberment and bodies that are in pieces, violence associated with the brutal new weaponry on the front. Miranda notes, for example, "two pairs of legs dangling [] on either side of her typewriter," seemingly unconnected to the two bodies of the men to whom they belong, who are trying to threaten Miranda into buying war bonds. Miranda tries not to respond angrily, telling herself, "Keep your head." Her editor, frustrated with interruptions like these men, demands a colleague take another visitor out to the alley to "saw his head off *by hand*," a threat repeated several times. A coworker of Miranda's, who cannot enlist because of health issues, muses regretfully that he could already have been to the trenches and returned "with a leg off by now."[42] All these examples suggest the actual threats to the male body posed by the war, though the home front is still what Allyson Booth has termed "corpseless."[43] The threats are made more manifest when Miranda visits a military hospital full of wounded men. Miranda knows the hospital hides the more seriously injured, allowing only "a selected presentable lot" to be shown. She finds an "unfriendly bitter" soldier "lying on his back, his right leg in a cast and pulley." Injured in the war, he also suggests the emotional damage that engulfs even the bodies of noncombatants like Miranda. He wants none of her ministrations, and she flees, thinking how her own thoughts and fears have taken physical form: "It is like turning a corner absorbed in your painful thoughts and meeting your state of mind embodied, face to face. . . . My own feelings about this whole thing, made flesh."[44] Porter establishes the ways the war literally and figuratively threatens male bodies, and male and female minds, before the pandemic arrives.

At first, the body of Miranda's boyfriend, Adam, seems the antithesis of these images of damage. Right after Miranda's visit to the soldier in the hospital, Porter introduces the strong and whole Adam, who looks "like a fine healthy apple" and whose name suggests he represents men more generally (though in the biblical context of Eden, his resemblance to an apple is ominous). Adam is infused with an aura of masculine strength; he tells Miranda "he had never had a pain in his life that he could remember," and he is described as "tall and heavily muscled." He has the "best tailor" make his uniforms, and he wears "stout polished well-made boots [that] set[] themselves down firmly" as he walks.[45] Throughout the story, though, Miranda and Adam remain acutely aware of what must be coming for Adam's body, haunted by the kind of pre–traumatic stress disorder Paul K. Saint-Amour links to the constant threat of totalizing war.[46] His uniform unites the contradictory sense of health and vulnerability: he is "infinitely buttoned, strapped, harnessed into a uniform as tough and unyielding in cut as a strait jacket, though the cloth was fine and supple."[47] The language implies that he is both protected by his uniform and trapped in a strait jacket, his fate already preordained: if not death, then possibly madness. Despite his clean uniform, Adam knows the "before" picture is ending; in the trenches, he says, "you mostly crawl about on your stomach here and there among the debris . . . they make it sound awfully messy." Miranda knows that he is "committed without any knowledge or act of his own to death."[48] He may be "pure" and "flawless" but those are only the requirements for his fated role. His face may be "smooth and fine and golden," but it becomes "set in a blind melancholy, a look of pained suspense and disillusion."[49] Depicted here is the haunting sense at the time that the healthy male body held a palimpsestic double, a shadowed body slated for death, dismemberment, or madness. The tone is one of revelation, uncovering the future body from the apparent present one. Yet Porter also reveals something even more hidden. Her carefully depicted representation of how the threat of war dominated the sense of male bodies also helps establish how blindsided people were when the threat suddenly shifted and bodies faced a danger no one had anticipated. Ironically, what will ultimately kill Adam is not shrapnel but a virus.

Alongside the threat the war posed to male bodies, Porter also describes the pre-pandemic atmosphere of guilt and danger experienced by women, an atmosphere that shifts to a new register once the pandemic arrives. Miranda and her coworkers (especially the female ones) are frequently bullied by salesmen selling war bonds. They threaten her job, question her patriotism, and demand she give part of her meager salary to the war effort. Miranda wants to tell them "to hell with this filthy war,"[50] and she recognizes their huckster quality, but she and her female colleagues are still burdened by guilt and fear, wondering if, indeed, they could sacrifice more to buy the bonds. Miranda's most intense guilt, though, is reserved for Adam. She knows he is the "sacrificial lamb," and she rails against the knowledge, feeling (and indeed being) powerless to protect him and the other men from the war.[51] Her own body seems indirectly threatened by the war as well, as the stress, poor diet, and sleeplessness it engenders robs her of energy. Bodies are so under siege, she sees no point in caring for hers; she and Adam smoke constantly: as he declares, it doesn't "matter so much if you're going to war," and Miranda counters that "it matters even less if you're staying at home knitting socks." When Adam points out she can't knit, she confesses soberly, "I do worse . . . I write pieces advising other young women to knit and roll bandages and do without sugar and help with the war."[52] For Miranda and other noncombatants, guilt is pervasive, accruing from not being part of the war effort—and from being part of the war effort. The very binaries (men vs. women, civilian vs. soldier, part of the war effort or not) that produced this guilt also enhanced the shock when the flu-victim category emerged and disrupted these divisions. Everyone was part of the pandemic "effort."

Throughout this section, Porter exposes the constant propaganda surrounding the war, but at the same time, she establishes that there are ready-made stories and characters that shape its meaning, however farcical they may be. While bond salesmen may use the patter of road-show promoters to further their cause, they effectively cast Miranda as a callous noncombatant, shamelessly standing by while "our American boys are fighting and dying in Belleau Wood"[53] against the evil Boche. Later in the story, when

Adam and Miranda attend a show she must review, another bond sales-
man frames the war into a narrative of heroes, villains, and sacrifice so
familiar that Porter suggests it no longer needs connecting words: "These
vile Huns—glorious Belleau Wood—our keyword is Sacrifice—Martyred
Belgium—give till it hurts . . . atrocities, innocent babes hoisted on Boche
bayonets" and ending with how the war will mean "a safe world forever and
ever." Miranda angrily points out how false this narrative is and how it hides
other, less palatable stories about the economic underpinnings of war: "Coal,
oil, iron, gold, international finance, why don't you tell us about them, you
little liar?"[54] Both the clichéd narratives and the oppositional ones, though,
are available—Miranda may reject the dominant narrative, but she can push
back with a different story of her own. The war, Porter suggests, was something that could be placed into a framework with clear characters and
meanings, however shoddy and untrue that framework might be—and
other stories could in turn counter the prevailing one. The performance
ends with the audience singing war songs, and Miranda and Adam to their
surprise join in enthusiastically, if "shamefacedly,"[55] caught up in a heady
mix of collective grief and comforting deceptions.

The flu slowly begins to infiltrate this narrative (both in Porter's story
and in the actual historical timeline), at first incorporated into the realist
prose and then, as the infection takes over Miranda's body, gradually presented in the fragmented, delirious style of the opening, as if the virus is
permeating the language. In the second half of the novella, Porter begins
to trace how the war and the pandemic tangle together—overlapping each
other and augmenting each other's pain—and how the war at first obscures
the pandemic. Porter then documents, though, the profound shifts the pandemic introduces, including the ways those shifts are hard to see given the
layers of entanglement. The war narratives and roles she introduced in the
previous section are disrupted as the nature of enemies, victims, threats,
guilt, vulnerable bodies, and violence change. These changes fuel the representational challenges we will see throughout this study, challenges Porter registers even as she works to overcome them.

In the first stages of the pandemic's introduction, influenza appears as a
confusing anomaly. The pandemic first arrives through funerals that quite
literally block the paths of the characters. Adam and Miranda walk together
through the city, and "at the first corner they waited for a funeral to pass";[56]
a bit later, "they paused at another corner . . . and hardly glanced at a funeral

procession approaching," and then again, "they stood while a funeral passed, and this time they watched it in silence." While the cause of the funerals is not yet named, Adam tells Miranda that "this funny new disease" has hit the army as well; the soldiers, he says, "are dying like flies." Miranda notes that "It seems to be a plague . . . something out of the Middle Ages. Did you ever see so many funerals, ever?"[57] Porter captures the paradoxical mix of omnipresence and avoidance the pandemic introduced: it's everywhere, and yet it's unnamed and either ignored or watched in silence. It's a "new" disease—and thus hard to understand—and also an old-fashioned one that's not supposed to be part of the story they feel is unfolding. Porter acknowledges the temptation, in the face of this mystery, to fold it into the familiar framework of war. When Miranda goes to the office, her colleagues are mocking this temptation, laughing at the rumors about the still unnamed illness: "They say . . . that it is really caused by germs brought by a German ship to Boston, a camouflaged ship, naturally, it didn't come in under its own colors. Isn't that ridiculous?" And, in a related theory, "they think the germs were sprayed over the city—it started in Boston, you know—and somebody reported seeing a strange, thick, greasy-looking cloud float up out of Boston Harbor and spread slowly all over that end of town."[58] Such rumors were in fact in circulation at the time, a way to incorporate the pandemic into the war and to identify a clear enemy—in this case, the Germans—to blame for its arrival and circulation.[59] The stories also illuminate the sense of paranoia infusing the atmosphere much like the virus itself, as well as the sense of uneasy bewilderment about its genesis.

As the virus infiltrates Miranda's body, she starts to realize that a different danger has entered the narrative, one that thrusts women and other noncombatants into roles previously held by soldiers. At first, Miranda attributes her exhaustion to the war: when she tries to identify "the insidious career" of her current headache, "it seemed reasonable to suppose it had started with the war."[60] She gradually realizes that "There's something terribly wrong," and she tells Adam, "I feel too rotten. It can't just be the weather, and the war."[61] As Miranda grows sicker, her thoughts become more broken and scattered, as the new physical and emotional pain from the virus mixes with the preexisting conditions of the war: "I have pains in my chest and my head and my heart and they're real. I am in pain all over, and you are in such danger as I can't bear to think about, and why can we not save each other?"[62] An annihilating and real pain has entered the female body, and the ambiguous "you"—which could accurately describe both her and Adam—reflects the shifting dangers that few could think about. Miranda has, in effect, entered into Adam's role earlier in the story: her body is now vulnerable—and also in immediate rather than potential danger (and Adam is now under threat from both the virus and the war). Adam, likewise, takes on a noncombatant role: he brings Miranda back to her apartment and becomes her temporary nurse, changing the more familiar gender positions Miranda enacts earlier in the story when bringing supplies to injured soldiers. Adam, though, is as powerless to save Miranda as she was to shield him from the war. And Miranda knows she now shares Adam's foreshortened fate; they are both marked for death, and the two talk about what they might have done had their ends not already been decided. The home front, too, is changing its meaning. As Adam tells Miranda in one of her brief moments of lucidity, "It's as bad as anything can be . . . all the theaters and nearly all the shops and restaurants are closed, and the streets have been full of funerals all day and ambulances all night."[63] The pandemic can no longer be ignored.

The pandemic does more, though, than just bring noncombatants into similar dangers to soldiers; it represents, Porter suggests, a distinctly new threat, one that posed additional dangers when people failed to acknowledge its differences from the war. Rather than the external weaponry that the couple imagines will damage Adam from the outside, this threat is infused into the air, passing freely into the body and out again; the very nature of contagion means that the danger is everywhere. Sources for possible transmission abound in the story: Adam's army camp, Miranda's office, the restaurants, dance halls, theaters, and hospitals. But like so many at the time, they are so focused on the threat the war poses to Adam's body that they ignore the far more immediate threat that surrounds them both. As Adam nurses Miranda, he washes her face, kisses her, cleans her vomit, touches her chin and head and mouth and hands, and shares her cigarette. While actual flu viruses would not be seen until the introduction of the electron microscope in the 1930s, in 1918 people were well acquainted with how influenza was transmitted, emphasized by Miranda's hysterical landlady, who insists Miranda leave immediately as "this is a plague," and she's "got a houseful of people to think about!"[64] Aware of the danger, Adam fails to engage in even a modicum of protective maneuvers. Porter suggests here the grave costs of seeing only through a war lens and of not adjusting quickly enough to a new narrative and a different enemy. She also acknowledges, though, the reasons these new elements are hard to read. There may be a cause-and-effect story—catching the virus leads to illness—but given the proliferating and invisible routes of transmission, the trajectory is hopelessly muddled. The enemy and its actions lie outside the more understandable narrative told about the war earlier in the story, with its well-defined roles and masculine narrative thrust. And the new threat in turn produces a delirium that further unsettles narrative, disrupting both spatial and temporal realities. As Miranda feverishly realizes, "There were no longer any multiple planes of living, no tough filaments of memory and hope. . . . There was only this one moment and it was a dream of time."[65]

Caught in her flu delirium, Miranda has a vision that exemplifies the pain of this new enemy and the particular forms of guilt it introduces. In her vision, Miranda finds herself in a terrifying forest, where arrows sing in "inhuman concealed voices":

She saw Adam transfixed by a flight of these singing arrows that struck him in the heart and passed shrilly cutting their path through the leaves. Adam fell straight back before her eyes, and rose again unwounded and alive; another flight of arrows loosed from the invisible bow struck him again and he fell, and yet he was there before her untouched in a perpetual death and resurrection. She threw herself before him, angrily and selfishly she interposed between him and the track of the arrow, crying, No, no . . . It's my turn now, why must you always be the one to die? and the arrows struck her cleanly through the heart and through his body and he lay dead, and she still lived, and . . . every branch and leaf and blade of grass had its own terrible accusing voice.[66]

Like the virus and its weapons, the enemy shooting these arrows from the "invisible bow" is concealed and inhuman. The ammunition, though—in this case, the arrows—is materialized, as if the flu microbes have taken on visible form. The arrows make no visible mark, striking Adam but leaving him "unwounded" and "untouched," the damage produced not that of artillery, or indeed of normal arrows, but of an internal and unseen invader. In choosing the image of arrows, Porter references an older form of death and an outdated form of weaponry, notably different than any used in the war. As with the figure of the Grim Reaper, the choice highlights the way flu deaths could seem old-fashioned, a throwback from an earlier story out of place within the new modes of warfare. The critic Jane Fisher argues convincingly that Miranda's dream recalls the figure of St. Sebastian, both the patron saint of plague victims and a saint who met his death by arrows (as he is so often depicted in the iconography), a link that further places the flu as a throwback.[67] The pandemic, Porter suggests, didn't fit the modern narrative—which helps explain why it gets ignored historically and why so many modernist writers shied away from the pandemic to focus on the newer means of death found in the trenches. By drawing on older iconography, though, both here and in the figure of the pale rider, Porter highlights how the very modernity of the moment was defined by a shocking return of a medieval-style plague.

Alongside the archaic references, the dream encapsulates the classic features of viral resurrection that arise repeatedly in the remaining works I investigate. In part, Porter holds up for mockery the trope of a redemptive, sacrificial violence pushed by the war propagandists earlier in the story. The cycle of death and resurrection speaks not to renewal or hope but to a sense of perpetual pain and death brought not only by the war but also by the way the pandemic exponentially expanded the killing and—in its widened geographic scope and targets—made the act of dying itself seem perpetual. The pandemic entrenched the sense of a cyclical narrative, "a perpetual death and resurrection" that never moves to victory, as the war finally does. This decidedly secular resurrection brings no salvation. Indeed, resurrection in the dream only allows for more death, like the virus's own proliferating yet lethal fecundity.

Miranda's anguish over her inability to stop this viral resurrection speaks both to new sources of survivor's guilt and to larger cultural attempts to bring female flu deaths into sacrificial structures. The dream echoes a repeated cry—would we call it wistful? haunted? angry?—in the flu letters: perhaps this new threat to women was rough justice, a fate-fueled balancing for all the male casualties. As one survivor explained, many people felt that "Nature decimated the women to balance out, as it were, the huge numbers of young men who fell in the war. It was a quite remarkable but an established fact."[68] Another eyewitness who worked as a nurse in the flu wards wrote that death "snatched away the blooming youthfulness of these girls in such a cruel way, it seemed to me as if this might be the work of an inscrutable Fate in balancing out the loss of the young soldiers carried off by the war."[69] Yet another survivor echoed these sentiments, lamenting all the women who had died, especially those who were pregnant, and declaring that "It seems as if 'nature' wanted to re-dress the balance for the deaths of thousands of young men in the trenches."[70] Porter weaves such sentiments into Miranda's dream, suggesting Miranda's strong desire to participate in this balancing. Indeed, Miranda hungers to take Adam's place and wishes her death would not just even the score but become itself a sacrificial gesture, one that might keep Adam safe. Her hunger suggests the guilt women felt over all the male death in the war and the frustrations at feeling useless, complicit, and outside the main event—and the way the pandemic offered a false sense that a rebalancing might be possible. It is her turn, Miranda cries, but the arrows do not kill her. The pandemic did not grant such a bargain.

Instead, the dream gives voice to the guilt-ridden sense (and biological truth) that you could unwittingly give the fatal virus to a loved one, as Miranda may have done: the arrows have passed through her and hit Adam. As we've seen, though, the transmission routes were clear generally but not specifically; Adam could well have passed the virus to Miranda or contracted it at his camp.[71] Miranda can only watch, powerless to stop the arrows or to save Adam. It is these very qualities—the unwitting spread, the inability to protect another, the invisible exchange, and the unclear paths of transmission—that produced a sense of nameless, haunting, and hard-to-represent guilt. She is left alive, and her guilt manifests in nature: "every branch and leaf and blade of grass" speaks in "its own terrible accusing voice."[72] The dream landscape accentuates how the accusation comes from everywhere—even the grass seems to speak it—and yet maintains its diffuse and nameless quality.

After Miranda is moved from her apartment to the hospital, her delirium grows along with her guilt, trapping her in an ever-expanding nightmare of perpetual accusation and terror that is nevertheless eerily silent and unseen. From her bed, Miranda watches as in "whiteness and silence" two "speechless" figures wrap up "another speechless man in white" and vanish with him, "wordless and white." Once they leave, Miranda feels that "a pallid white fog rose in their wake insinuatingly and floated before Miranda's eyes, a fog in which was concealed all terror and all weariness, all the wrung faces and twisted backs and broken feet of abused, outraged living things, all the shapes of their confused pain and their estranged hearts."[73] In these visions, Porter suggests the hidden, obscure quality of the pandemic deaths and how the terror and bodily suffering were concealed (the pallid fog) and also mixed with the pain of bodies broken by the war. Cutting through this fog—yet still obscured—is the guilt and terror of the (former) noncombatants. Moving from the mist are "two executioners" who drag "the misshapen figure of an old man" who tries to resist his "fate": "In a high weeping voice he was trying to explain to them that the crime of which he was accused did not merit the punishment he was about to receive. . . .'Before God I am not guilty,'" he cries out.[74] Miranda is likewise stalked by a nameless guilt: "The wrong she had done followed her and haunted her dream: this wrong took vague shapes of horror she could not recognize or name, though her heart cringed at sight of them."[75] Miranda and the older man— representing two groups who, during the war, were for the most part shielded from danger in Britain and the United States—are now targeted by the flu, and their delirium reflects their sense that they are being punished for crimes they cannot identify by enemies they cannot see—as, in a strange way, they are. Porter overcomes the difficulties of representing this nebulous guilt by making its obscurity central to her depiction. She also captures how guilt became a climate without clear referents, a climate that infused the iconic modernist works I analyze in part 2.

Porter represents how the flu's plotless and characterless qualities meant that people incorporated its dangers into more familiar images of war. In her delirium, Miranda transforms her doctor into a figure who might have marched out of the war propaganda narratives earlier in the story:

Across the field came Dr. Hildesheim, his face a skull beneath his German helmet, carrying a naked infant writhing on the point of his bayonet, and a huge stone pot marked Poison in Gothic letters. He stopped before the well that Miranda remembered in a pasture on her father's farm . . . and into its pure depths he threw the child and the poison, and the violated water sank back soundlessly into the earth.[76]

The symbols here are obvious and direct: the enemy is identified, the crime is monstrous, and its effects clear, disastrous, and widespread. War imagery, Porter suggests, was easily at hand to frame the pandemic experience. The flu struck so quickly, no one had time to build an original set of imagery around it. As Susan Sontag points out, while an elaborate (and damaging) set of metaphors were built up around diseases like tuberculosis and cancer, "diseases understood to be simply epidemic [are] less useful as metaphors, as evidenced by the near-total historical amnesia about the influenza pandemic of 1918–1919."[77] And yet, within this war imagery, Porter hints of a threat that enters the domestic space, poisoning the water like a silent, spreading contagion. The dream pushes against and reflects the amnesia Sontag describes, revealing how the virus became enfolded into the ready-made metaphors of the war—and how, through that very process, it sank "soundlessly into the earth" while still diffusing its poison.

As the virus multiplies and death approaches for Miranda, language reaches a further crisis of representation. In both content and form, Porter's hallucinatory prose displays how the virus disrupts the body along with borders, time, and space.[78] As Miranda imagines staring into a pit of oblivion, she thinks, "there it is, there it is at last, it is very simple; and soft carefully shaped words like oblivion and eternity are curtains hung before nothing at all. I shall not know when it happens, I shall not feel or remember." Porter shifts to the ambiguous "it," trying to describe something that words obscure and the body cannot record. All the images Miranda creates to give the moment substance cannot finally represent it: "Granite walls, whirlpools, stars are things. None of them is death, nor the image of it. Death is death . . . and for the dead it has no attributes. Silenced she sank easily through deeps under deeps of darkness until she lay like a stone at the farthest bottom of life, knowing herself to be blind, deaf, speechless, no longer aware of the members of her own body." For Miranda, everything falls away—the mind and "all ties of blood and the desires of the heart."[79] While Porter's description (such as it is) of death and oblivion applies to the war and any death, Porter nevertheless delineates the peculiar namelessness and silence surrounding the pandemic. Death is hard enough to imagine, but without a visible cause and no larger structure of meaning to construct around it, memory and language may fail.

The images of viral resurrection I explore become, paradoxically, ways to depict this lack of representation and to counter the intangible qualities of the pandemic through a returned material presence. In her second dream of resurrection, Miranda is transported from the terrifying sense of oblivion and nothingness in the previous passage to a visually rich landscape, encompassing both a seashore and a meadow. Moving toward her she sees "a great company of human beings . . . all the living she had known," and Miranda is filled with a sense of happiness and peace.[80] Porter experienced a similar "beatific vision" during her bout with the flu, a near-death experience that pushed against the dissolution brought by illness.[81] As if to remind her readers, though, of the real conditions of the pandemic and its representational challenges, Porter quickly plunges Miranda into a reverse resurrection: "Miranda felt without warning a vague tremor of apprehension, some small flick of distrust in her joy . . . something, somebody, was missing, she had lost something. . . . Where are the dead? We have forgotten the dead, oh, the dead, where are they?"[82] In the questions and in Miranda's vague sense that something is missing, Porter in part evokes the countless dead and missing in the war and the haunting sense that people might soon forget the sacrifices; for precisely this reason, war memorials were built to remember the dead and the missing. Porter also, though, powerfully registers the unmarked pandemic losses, her language depicting how they are in fact missing twice over: not only are the flu dead literally missing, the very fact of their loss was being forgotten. It is a resurrection without any bodies.

Porter brings the reader back to this loss, transporting Miranda from the beautiful landscape to a cold wasteland of stone, where she is overwhelmed by pain and the "sickening smell of rotting flesh and pus" that comes from her own body.[83] The pain the virus inflicts is so intense that Miranda longs for death; resurrection turns into an ever-renewing punishment, as she looks with agony on the doctor and nurse who are trying to save her. Porter works to depict Miranda's suffering (and her own remembered suffering), and at the same time she offers a vivid picture of how physical pain challenges this very depiction. Miranda cries out to the doctor, "let me go," but her pain cannot be articulated and only comes out as the "incoherent sounds of animal suffering."[84] As Elaine Scarry so cogently details in *The Body in Pain*, pain unmakes language: "physical pain does not simply resist language but actively destroys it, bringing about an immediate reversion to a state anterior to language, to the sounds and cries a human being makes before language is learned." Porter captures this linguistic destruction, turning Miranda's voice into sounds, yet also pushes against this destruction through what Scarry would term the material making of her story.[85] In other words, by carefully detailing the unmaking of language that Miranda's pain produces—a pain experienced by millions of others—Porter creates a way to remake the language, transferring the pain into the physical form of the novella.

Porter's depiction of influenza pain, though, also offers an important addition to Scarry's work that in turn suggests additional distinctions between the war and the pandemic. What might be the differences between pain caused by illness and that caused by human-inflicted violence? While the physical sensations of pain within the body may be identical, whatever the cause, Scarry carefully details the particular issues pain presents in torture and war, exploring the ways pain is inflicted and then hidden, translated away from the suffering body to appalling political ends. While she mentions pain from illness and to a greater extent from accidents, her focus remains, quite understandably, on the ethical implications of pain from torture and war. In war, injured bodies may be used, among other things, to "lend the aura of material reality to the winning construct." The pain of torture may internally be the same as other pain, she argues, but this pain is then appropriated, externalized to an outside enemy and translated into regime legitimization. She does note, though, that "perhaps only in the prolonged and searing pain caused by accident or by disease . . . is there the same brutal senselessness as in torture."[86] Both Porter and Cather detail such brutal senselessness and the strange way the war could obscure it. Read together, they suggest a pain that was widespread, prolonged, and indeed searing; it was purposeless; it could not easily be appropriated for political ends; no consent was given (as it is, Scarry argues, in certain forms of war); the inflicting agent could not be visualized.

I make no case for which type of pain—that inflicted by humans or a virus—would be harder to handle, only that the attention paid to each type of pain, and to male versus female bodies, was, and is, different. Porter brings attention to a body in agonizing pain from the virus, pain as widespread as the number of pandemic victims, whether they survived or not. Even in a story set during the war, she focuses on a female body, and she takes the pain seriously and not as a sign of fragility or feminine weakness. She thus brings center stage a pervasive experience and the new threat paradigm of 1918. At the same time, she highlights how literary and cultural accounts left these suffering bodies out of a history that remains focused on the bodies of male soldiers injured or killed in battles (which were also being systematically hidden and forgotten—but not to the same degree). And no zero-sum calculus is implied here: paying attention to the pain of the pandemic body or to the pain of illness more generally does not involve a choice to take bodies in pain from the war or military conflict less seriously. The pain has different causes and remedies and requires different actions. But Porter reminds us how easy it is to forget these pandemic bodies precisely because their pain arrived alongside a war that had visible enemies, central male characters, and political ends.

In the novella's final section, Miranda rises out of her delirium just as the war ends. Lying in her hospital bed, Miranda hears "Bells scream[ing] all off key" and horns and whistles blending "shrilly with cries of human distress . . . shrieking like a mob in revolt." Miranda in one way mistakes these sounds; she hears screams and anguish, but the nurse tells her that "they're celebrating,"[87] the noise signaling the Armistice and the end of the war—it's the happy conclusion to the war's bleak narrative. Miranda also interprets these noises correctly, however; the war may be done, but not only will its pain and discord linger, but the pandemic carries on, a bitter reminder that the suffering is far from over. As we will see, pandemic accounts frequently reference similar meetings of the Armistice and the pandemic: stories abound of people hearing the bells marking the end of the war from a hospital or sickbed. Funeral cortèges for the pandemic dead would run into (sometimes literally) Armistice celebrations, as they did at the funeral of Guillaume Apollinaire, which I discuss in chapter 7. Victory parades themselves led to steep rises in influenza deaths, the crowds providing the perfect conditions for transmission. Everyone had waited for so long for the war to be over, but the pandemic disrupted the ending, changing the sense of elation for many. And in another detail repeated throughout pandemic accounts, the sound of bells came to be associated with the constant tolling for the pandemic dead. Porter captures all this in Miranda's reading of the bells as a sign of continued distress and suffering.

Despite her return to the "real" world, Miranda feels caught in a state of living death, and she struggles for definition both in her body and in the world. Echoing the sense from the opening that she has borrowed even her skin, she asks, "Can this be my face?" "Are these my own hands?" The body, she feels, "is a curious monster, no place to live in, how could anyone feel at home there?" The virus has alienated her from her self, making her wish for death. She struggles to articulate her experience but finds she feels like "an alien who does not like the country in which he finds himself, does not understand the language nor wish to learn it, does not mean to live there and yet is helpless, unable to leave it at his will."[88] Illness creates this helplessness—the body has been taken over—as well as this alienation and inarticulate despair. Even her surroundings participate in the bleak ambiguity: in this "dull world to which she was condemned . . . the sharp planes [were] melted and formless, all objects and beings meaningless, ah, dead and withered things that believed themselves alive!"[89] The pandemic alters Miranda's sense of her own body and the world, robbing her of agency and creating a climate of living death and meaningless struggle. Porter reminds us that not all resurrections are welcome. To continue living after the war and the pandemic, with all their losses, was in many ways a punishment.[90] Forced to continue, Miranda finally submits to efforts to reconstitute her body, to "pull her inseparable rack of bones and wasted flesh to its feet, to put in order her disordered mind."[91] Like Porter herself, whose own case left her, as she wrote, "crippled from phlebitis in my left leg, and bald as an egg,"[92] Miranda must resurrect herself, declaring, "Lazarus, come forth."[93] As the critic Caroline Hovanec writes, Miranda must "reconstruct[] herself from artificial, rearticulated parts . . . in order that, as she phrases it, 'no one need pity this corpse.' "[94] Reconstructing the body becomes a laborious task both for women and for men in the post-1918 moment, one that Porter suggests arose as much from the virus as it did from the war.

By the end of the story, the pandemic's disruption of war narratives reaches its final form. As Miranda gets ready to leave the hospital, she learns Adam has died of the flu in an army camp. The moment is not climactic; she finds out from a letter written by a stranger some weeks before. Despite their earlier certainty that he would be the sacrificial lamb and die in the war, and their assumption that they *knew* the story they were in, even though they didn't want to be in it, Adam dies instead in an unnarrated story. In the novella's concluding moments, Porter offers a final moment of viral resurrection, one that indicates not renewal but the bleak threshold world of the post-pandemic moment and the frustrated sense of narrative stasis that it engendered:

Miranda wondered again at the time and trouble the living took to be helpful to the dead. But not quite dead now, she reassured herself, one foot in either world now; soon I shall cross back and be at home again. The light will seem real and I shall be glad when I hear that someone I know has escaped from death. . . .

At once he was there beside her, invisible but urgently present, a ghost but more alive than she was, the last intolerable cheat of her heart; for knowing it was false she still clung to the lie, the unpardonable lie of her bitter desire. She . . . stood up trembling, trying by the mere act of her will to bring him to sight before her. If I could call you up from the grave I would, she said, if I could see your ghost I would say, I believe . . . "I believe," she said aloud. "Oh, let me see you once more." The room was silent, empty, the shade was gone from it, struck away by the sudden violence of her rising and speaking aloud. She came to herself as if out of sleep. Oh, no, that is not the way, I must never do that, she warned herself. . . .

No more war, no more plague, only the dazed silence that follows the ceasing of the heavy guns; noiseless houses with the shades drawn, empty streets, the dead cold light of tomorrow.[95]

The passage echoes the delirium of the previous sections, blending reality, memory, dreams, and nightmares. Death permeates, even after the "ceasing of the heavy guns," emerging in the domestic spaces, in the noiseless houses and empty streets. The virus continues to haunt the present, quite literally living on in Miranda's body, which remains weakened by its presence. Miranda occupies a twilight space, and her ambiguous language suggests that while she has determined to live—to enter the cheerful narrative where surviving is the desired outcome—she also longs to die. Her living death suggests the strange sense of corpsefulness and corpselessness that broods over the passage. The dead are present, here in the almost actualized vision of the dead Adam and in Miranda's own corpselike presence, and yet also missing, leaving rooms "silent, empty." The resurrection vision captures both states and highlights the way the pandemic was everywhere and nowhere at once, indeed "invisible but urgently present." Adam, the novella's central flu death, seems in part more alive than Miranda feels, but his ghostly status also reflects the terrible loss and absence the pandemic brought that was in turn covered over. Indeed, brooding over the whole passage is a sense of emptiness (the room "empty," the shade "gone," the "empty streets") and of silence ("The room was silent," "the dazed silence," the "noiseless house"), suggesting the massive death count and the way this tragedy threatened to stay unvoiced.

Miranda remains infused with survivor's guilt and also what we might term survivor's envy. Porter hints at the zero-sum calculation Miranda feels—the more alive she becomes, the more dead Adam seems; the shade disappears, "struck away by the sudden violence of her rising and speaking aloud," as if her life (her rising) has dispelled his. Buried within this phrase is the tangled sense that Adam has been sacrificed for her, that her life has meant his death, and that she may well have been the delivery system for this new form of sudden violence. Yet this guilt also reveals the scarier possibility: the sacrificial model is a lie. Adam's death is meaningless; it protected no one and had no higher cause. This knowledge, combined with the overwhelming grief and guilt and her own bodily weakness, means that Miranda, like so many, longs for death and envies Adam. At the same time, she longs for the dead's return, to believe in some kind of material continuity after so much loss, and to counter her own sense that the virus had dissolved her body and made it immaterial. She cannot bring the lost bodies back, though, by "a mere act of her will," caught instead in the emptiness and vulnerability the flu delivered.

Porter would later describe how her own flu experience created a division from which she never recovered. In an interview from 1963, she recounts that her bout with the flu "simply divided my life, cut across it like that. So that everything before that was just getting ready, and after that I was in some strange way altered, ready. It took me a long time to go out and live in the world again. I was really 'alienated,' in the pure sense."[96] Her life is separated, divided in two in language that echoes the literal fragmentation of the body in the war and the sense of bodily disintegration in the pandemic. Time is likewise bifurcated and for Porter never again rejoined into wholeness. The war is commonly assumed to be such a watershed moment, both for individuals and the culture, something that split time into a before and after. The pandemic, as Porter describes both here and in her story, was precisely such a moment, but one where the cause of the divide, and the fact of the divide, always threatened to slide out of sight.

One of Ours and Pale Horse, Pale Rider showcase the narrative challenges the virus produced and the many ways the war tangled with the pandemic both in the historical accounts and in the literature. Porter's novella is far more attentive to and self-reflexive about how the two tragedies interacted, investigating the impact not simply of the pandemic's historical timing but also of the virus's particular threat to individual bodies. While Cather replicates rather than interrogates the pandemic's subordinate position to the war, in the process she provides an instructive example of how the stories and myths surrounding the war drowned out the less appealing narrative drive of the pandemic. The two works initiate our rereading of the interwar period, illuminating stories and tensions that have largely disappeared from our conceptions of the era.

These tensions shape the narrative structures of both works, and these very structures highlight the larger set of gender dynamics the pandemic produced not only within the two stories but for the authors themselves. Of the four overt pandemic accounts I explore, it's both surprising and not surprising that it's the two women writers who narrate most clearly the collision of the war with the pandemic, while it's the two male writers who focus on the pandemic's domestic effects. The war-pandemic collision maps precisely the places where the gender issues grow most complicated and introduces the gendered reasons the pandemic is so difficult to see. In *One of Ours*, it's not just Claude who has a hard time taking the pandemic seriously—it's Cather, and her culture, and a whole generation of critics. Cather chooses to uphold the cultural frame and insist on the war's centrality; Porter works to adjust the frame's borders to expose the new guilt and narrative disruptions the relationship produces. Both works highlight, though, how writing about the war or the pandemic, for women, was often a challenging endeavor. On the one hand, war as a topic presented predictable roadblocks: Miranda is relegated to "feminine" topics in her columns, and Cather herself faced a vicious sexist backlash for daring to write about military subjects at all. On the other hand, writing about illness, or paying attention to it, was also thorny territory for women not simply because of all the representational challenges but because it could seem like the expected topic for a woman writer. Many male reviewers of *One of Ours*, for example, praised the novel's first half, concerning Claude's domestic life in Nebraska and the pandemic episode, but excoriated the treatment of war in the book's second half, which H. L. Mencken declared "drops precipitately to the level of a serial in the *Ladies' Home Journal*."[97] In review after review, the underlying message is that Cather is fine when she sticks with what she "knows"—family and domestic life and illness, all suitable topics—but strays into forbidden territory when she writes of war. This very attitude suggests the double bind for women in 1922: don't write about war, which is the only real story to be told, and if you write about illness, that's a woman's story.[98] By 1939, Porter can explore—and resist—this bind, though she doesn't write about the war directly—and the central flu death is that of a soldier. These works not only reveal the gender tensions the pandemic introduced; they remind us that when we assume the pandemic is a tangential event to the war, we may participate, however unwittingly, in sexist assumptions about what counts as history.

Chapter Three

DOMESTIC PANDEMIC

Thomas Wolfe and William Maxwell

The pandemic changed public life—closing schools, churches, and businesses and filling hospitals to overflowing—but much of its anguish happened privately and within the domestic space, unphotographed and unrecorded. Thomas Wolfe and William Maxwell crafted novels that made this private atmosphere visible, recording the impact on individual families struck by the virus. In contrast to Porter and Cather, Wolfe and Maxwell focus on the domestic trauma, and in their works the pandemic dominates the war; the virus is immediate and personal, the war positioned as a more distant tragedy. Both writers still wrestle with ways to represent the virus's amorphous presentation and the climate of mourning it left in its wake, drawing on images of viral resurrection to suggest the endless yet spectral quality of these losses. They offer vivid portraits of physical suffering, but they emphasize the hard-to-define emotional costs, tracing how the pandemic's sudden and unexpected strikes could break families beyond repair. While each author portrays the grief of a single family, the very individuality of these portraits suggests the levels of private wreckage repeating across the world.

Wolfe's novel *Look Homeward, Angel* (1929) demonstrates how the angel of death indeed looked homeward during the pandemic. Wolfe traces the miasmic atmosphere that illness may bring, one that seems to infect all parts of the novel, even before the pandemic arrives. Illness and the suffering flu body become the central points of reference, to which war corpses might be compared, rather than the reverse. Like Porter, Wolfe plays with both modernist and realist styles, but instead of using them to contrast the war and the pandemic, he instead uses them to contrast different temporal moments in the pandemic's narrative. Maxwell's novel *They Came Like Swallows* (1937) likewise focuses on the domestic pandemic, but he presents a death that was ubiquitous in the historical pandemic and missing from the other three direct accounts: the death of a woman. The featured deaths in Cather, Porter, and even Wolfe are all young men who either are soldiers or of military age. In portraying the death of a pregnant mother, Maxwell makes visible the victim most likely to die in the outbreak and at the same time highlights the way such figures are missing in the other accounts.[1] Both Wolfe and Maxwell, though, stay focused on the domestic space, and they carefully develop their pre-pandemic narratives first. When the pandemic arrives, it becomes the defining, disrupting, centralized event, its costs revealed by the shattering of the earlier world it displaces.

DEATH COMES HOME

Wolfe's sprawling autobiographical novel *Look Homeward, Angel* paints a vivid picture of the grim realities of this influenza. The work represents some of the repeating elements of the pandemic experience: the sensory overload the virus's ravages produce, the horror that a new form of mass death could invade the domestic space, and the drum beat of denial that runs through the experience. Alongside these elements, Wolfe foregrounds the virus's intimate invasion of both body and community, showcasing how the pandemic represented striking yet paradoxical shifts in scale: on the one hand, unlike the visible vastness of the war, the battle now unfolds on a tiny landscape, within an individual body and a particular family unit. On the other hand, like the virus, this local scene replicates exponentially, even if not always experienced as such, expanding and spreading everywhere.

This expansion dovetails with what we might term Wolfe's taxonomy of viral resurrection in the novel. Wolfe's resurrections are viral in two distinct ways: they are states produced *by* the virus, and they also display characteristics *of* viruses and infectious diseases more generally. In the first category, Wolfe depicts the grim state of living death experienced physically by the dying and emotionally by the mourners, states of unfinished or incomplete resurrections that seem perpetual and are fueled by both delirium and grief. Porter captures a parallel state, but in the body of a survivor (who was also a mourner). In the second category, Wolfe's resurrections encode viral characteristics. Wolfe evokes, for example, how a general atmosphere of living death infuses the air like contagion. His repeated images of resurrection further suggest, in their spectral nature, the unseen traits of this danger, while at the same time they push against—and by the end, even make material—the pandemic's losses and its erasure from history.

Wolfe based his novel on his own firsthand experiences in the pandemic. In October 1918, while he was at college in North Carolina, he received an urgent telegram from his family: his brother, Ben, was sick, and Thomas should return home to Asheville. By the time Wolfe arrived, Ben's influenza case had moved into double pneumonia.[2] He eventually drowned in the fluids that had flooded his lungs. Wolfe had been close to his brother, and his death was devastating. One of Wolfe's biographers, Richard S. Kennedy, notes that Ben's death was "the greatest grief of his early life."[3] The critic Paula Gallant Eckard writes that Ben's death in the pandemic, along with the earlier death of Ben's twin, who died of typhoid fever at the age of twelve, "had an enormous impact on the writer and his family."[4] Wolfe wrote to his sister in 1929 that Ben's death "affected me more than any other event in my life."[5] He felt keenly that Ben had been taken too soon; as he told the scholar Norman H. Pearson, in language that suggests both the real Ben and the fictional Ben in *Look Homeward, Angel*, "the death of Ben is a tragedy because Ben is a young man, little more than a boy, who has missed, has never found, has never gotten in life, any of the things he longed for and that he should have had."[6] Ben's death reverberated into every aspect of Wolfe's fiction. It was, he told his mother, part of "why I think I'm going to be an artist. The things that really mattered sunk in and left their mark."[7]

In particular, Ben's death inspired an obsession with the idea of returning from the dead; Wolfe's fiction is haunted with ghosts and spirits and infused with the longing for the dead to come back. Wolfe would later describe the writing of *Look Homeward, Angel* as a kind of ghostly possession: "The book took hold of me and possessed me. In a way, I think it shaped itself."[8] In an article on the pervasiveness of loss and ghosts in Wolfe's work, Gérald Préher argues that Wolfe "kept trying to bring [his brothers] back to life in his fiction," an attempt that both succeeded—for most of *Look Homeward, Angel*, Ben is transformed into a "live" character, and he returns from the dead at the end of the story—and was constantly frustrated. Wolfe, Préher notes, was caught on the threshold between life and death, "stranded in a kind of no-man's-land, a borderland where past and present, death and life, constantly intermingle and cannot be really told apart."[9] Like the spiritualists I explore in the final chapter, Wolfe seeks to make this threshold more tangible and more controllable, to bring the dead back in ways that might be seen and felt.

Throughout his novel, Wolfe creates an atmosphere of mortality emblematic of the pandemic climate. The novel, set in the fictional town of Altamont, traces the fortunes of the Gant family and in particular follows the early life of Eugene Gant, largely considered Wolfe's surrogate in the novel. Drawing on Wolfe's experiences living with his family in Asheville, the novel leads to the terrible death of Eugene's brother Ben in the pandemic. Well before Ben's death, however, Wolfe infuses his novel with elegiac musings on mortality and loss, creating a seemingly naturalized environment of both infection and mourning that appears—in a temporally fluid way— both to produce the pandemic and extend retrospectively from it. Ben's death reverberates forward and backward in time, foreshadowed by the death of his twin from typhoid early in the novel, by his run-ins with the town's undertaker, and by the narrator's clear knowledge of Ben's eventual fate that broods over the entire work. And the novel's very setting is saturated in illness; as Eckard points out, Asheville (the town on which Altamont is based) was at the time a popular rest retreat for people suffering from tuberculosis,[10] so the area was already associated with illness and death, even before the pandemic hits. As Eugene feels, Altamont is "like a city of the dead."[11] Eugene's father is an engraver of tombstones and graveyard statuary, his work deepening the sense of death and remembrance that blankets the novel and the era. In imagery he later evokes in Ben's illness, Eugene fears being buried alive in the town, imagining the horror of "waking life-in-death, his slow, frustrated efforts to push away the smothering flood of earth" like a "drowning swimmer claws the air."[12] Wolfe suggests a world always on the brink of dissolution, not from the war but from the pandemic, with Ben's influenza death the larger symbol for the senseless loss of so many young adults.

The death-infused atmosphere inspires Wolfe's and Eugene's constant musings on the afterlife and rebirth. Wolfe's repeated lament, "O lost, and by the wind grieved, ghost, come back again," blows through the novel both early and late, a call for his lost brother to return. The "ghost" here could be many things—Eugene's youth, a vision of beauty he cannot quite recapture, the past more generally, and so on.[13] But the lament itself captures the pandemic's climate of loss, the grief brought on a pathogenic wind, and the intense desire that the dead might return. And Wolfe includes the idea of invisible presences in other ways too. Throughout the novel, Ben talks repeatedly to his "Angel," having a seemingly one-sided conversation with this mysterious presence. Even when Ben is still alive, Eugene imagines him with the dead; as Eugene thinks of how the dead might awaken with the spring, he seems to include Ben in their number: "all of the men who had died were making their strange and lovely return in blossom and flower. Ben walked along the streets of the tobacco town looking like asphodel. It was strange to find a ghost there in that place."[14] For Wolfe, the pandemic's living-death atmosphere almost seems to infect the past, making Ben a walking ghost before he has even died. Like Porter's Adam—and so many men of military age at the time—Ben seems marked for death, his live body in the present always also suggesting a shadowed dead one. Unlike Porter, though, Wolfe does not link this deathly double to the war, which he largely ignores. Ben is shadowed by disease, and Wolfe makes visible here what was true but still hidden: everyone in Altamont is, in fact, now potentially marked for death from the coming virus.

The novel's central flu scenes offer searing images of a living corpse and deathly animations. Although foreshadowed for hundreds of pages, the pandemic formally enters the novel near its end. Like Wolfe, Eugene is at college when the second wave of the pandemic hits in October 1918. His mother tells him in a letter that they are experiencing a "siege" of flu at home: "Every one has had it, and you never know who's going to be next." Like many observers, she notes one of the haunting aspects of this particular strain: "It seems to get the big strong ones first," killing "a fine healthy man in the prime of life."[15] Eugene is summoned home a few weeks later, with news that Ben has fallen ill. He returns to find an atmosphere of dread and denial. His mother at first declares that Ben may recover, despite the "terror in her heart" and the "bright knives of fear" in her eyes: "I don't believe he's half as bad off as he looks. . . . I believe there's going to be a change for the better." When Eugene's sister tries to assert that Ben is near death, the mother ignores her and instructs Eugene that when he goes to see Ben, "don't make out as if you knew he was sick" and just "make a big joke of it all" and declare "there's nothing wrong." Faced with the horror of his brother's illness, though, Eugene too embraces denial. As his mother breaks down, he tells her, " 'It's all right! It's all right! It's all right!'—knowing that it was not, could never be, all right."[16] Wolfe represents here how the virus's ravages were often too much to face, creating an understandable disavowal mixed with a bitter awareness. While denial is a familiar feature in illnesses and in the aftermath of deaths from any cause, the pandemic created the perfect conditions for its perpetuation, combining a familiar disease in a radically new form, an invisible and fast-moving enemy, and a populace already burdened by mass deaths in the war. The denial in turn contributed to the brooding but diffuse sense that death and waste had become a domestic climate, one reflected (as we'll see) in works like *The Waste Land* and *Mrs. Dalloway*.

After the denial, Eugene must confront the ravished but still animate pandemic body, trapped in a perverse living-death version of viral resurrection:

Ben's long thin body lay three-quarters covered by the bedding; its gaunt outline was bitterly twisted below the covers, in an attitude of struggle and torture. It seemed not to belong to him, it was somehow distorted and detached as if it belonged to a beheaded criminal. And the sallow yellow of his face had turned gray; out of this granite tint of death, lit by two red flags of fever, the stiff black furze of a three-day beard was growing. The beard was somehow horrible; it recalled the corrupt vitality of hair, which can grow from a rotting corpse. And Ben's thin lips were lifted, in a constant grimace of torture and strangulation, above his white somehow dead-looking teeth, as inch by inch he gasped a thread of air into his lungs.

And the sound of this gasping—loud, hoarse, rapid, unbelievable, filling the room, and orchestrating every moment in it—gave to the scene its final note of horror.[17]

This death echoes scenes across literature by authors from Dostoevsky to Coetzee, but it's also emblematic of the bodies this virus produced and the larger climate of death that the pandemic and the war had together created. Ben, brutally caught in the world of the living, bears the marks of many deaths—starvation ("its gaunt outline"), dismemberment (the body seems detached from its head), disease (obviously), torture, suffocation, and strangulation. Wolfe creates a body that represents the war dead as well, a corpse that might be found in the trenches, dead from shells or poison gas or starvation or drowning. Yet part of the deathbed horror is the way all this violence and violation unfolds internally. Ben strangles with no rope, suffocates from no gas, drowns without water, bleeds from no wounds, burns without fire, and dies from no weapons. There's no one to blame, really (though the family members blame one another), and the way that the body is seemingly doing all this to itself makes the death both harder to grasp and potentially more horrifying. The scene also presents a striking reversal to how war deaths and flu deaths were generally portrayed in the larger culture: rather than the war body symbolically (and in most cases, silently) subsuming the flu body, as we saw with Cather, here the flu body takes precedence, becoming the larger signifier for death in the post-1918 moment. In the United States, far more people would have witnessed such a flu death than witnessed a death in the war. There's a way, too, that this flu body exposes a truth about the war body: the stark meaninglessness of this flu death reveals a parallel meaninglessness of war death, stripped of all its illusory framing. Such emptiness shapes a sense of viral resurrection, one that comes without salvation, and where vitality becomes "corrupt," a mockery of life where hair grows "from a rotting corpse."

Wolfe captures many of the pandemic's sensory details in this scene. Visually, Ben's body is "distorted" and unfamiliar, his skin by turns sallow, gray, granite, red, and black. The bedding suggests his struggle and restless turning. Haunting the room are also the terrible sounds of his gasping breaths, a macabre bass line that gives the scene "its final note of horror." Ben's touch likewise reflects his illness; he seizes Eugene's wrists "fiercely in the hot white circle of his hands." The atmosphere is rank, the next day dawning with "a drear reek of murk and fog," suggesting the smell of the sickroom and the shadowy quality of this attacker. And in a macabre perversion of taste, Eugene feels "choked" by the "ugliness and discomfort of the death," and he accuses his family of "feeding with its terrible hunger for death on Ben's strangulation."[18] At the same time, though, that Wolfe depicts with careful detail this deathbed horror, he suggests how it simultaneously shuts down the senses. When he first enters the sickroom, "for a moment Eugene could see nothing, for dizziness and fear," and when Ben speaks to him, "The boy stood white and dumb for a moment," seeming to lose his identity along with his voice.[19] I trace a similar sensory overload, coupled with sensory deprivation, in Eliot's *The Waste Land*, one that echoes the pandemic's aftermath.

Wolfe exposes how a state of living death applied not just to flu victims but to its mourners. Eugene finds that he approaches Ben's room "with a shriveled heart and limbs which had gone cold and bloodless." Wolfe describes Eugene's mother, Eliza, as part of this walking dead after she leaves Ben's side: "her feet were numb and dead. Her white face had an ashen tinge, and her dull eyes had grown bright and staring"; "her dead white face had a curious carven look," like one of her husband's grave statuaries.[20] Eugene's father shares this corpselike existence; he "was dead. Gant was living, death-in-life ... a corpse lit by infrequent flares of consciousness."[21] And in a gothic touch, even the medical professionals who are trained to sustain life are described in deathly terms: Ben's doctor has a "long yellow skull's-head" and the nurse a "death's-head" with "a cold lust for the miseries of sickness and death."[22] Such figures—the medical life-bringers-turned-death-bringers—recur throughout the pandemic literature, from Miranda's horrifying image of her doctor to the grisly pandemic doctors of H. P. Lovecraft; they suggest both the ways medical professionals could bring death by (unwittingly) infecting patients and the suspicion engendered by ineffectual treatments.

By emphasizing the in-between-ness of all these bodies, however—already half corpses yet struggling still for life—Wolfe embodies (almost literally) how this moment was haunted not just by the dead but by *dying*, the process of dying, repeated and imagined everywhere in these brutal years. And even the living—the ones who would not yet be allowed to die—were still part of the process. Wolfe draws out the deathbed scene, highlighting how long the family seems to live with Ben's dying. And in another experience endemic to this virus, described by Cather as well, they are essentially watching Ben as he drowns. He lies gasping for days, trying to "force air down into his strangled and cemented lungs." As the doctor tells them, when asked if there's anything left to do, "He's drowning! Drowning!"[23] They cannot save him but still must watch. Wolfe captures the agony of witnessing a loved one die—a common experience and yet one dramatically intensified in a moment when such deaths are repeated in millions of homes.

The flu's delirium produced one final version of death-in-life. Like Miranda and other sufferers, Ben grows delirious as the disease advances.

He experiences fits of rage, regresses to childlike behavior, and finally starts to hum "snatches of popular songs," mainly sentimental songs from the war.[24] In a moment, he moves from fear to seriousness to anger to confusion to thoughts of beauty. Wolfe evokes the atmosphere of delirium but for the most part describes it through realist techniques. Other writers, as we saw with Porter and will see with Woolf, Eliot, and Yeats, reflected these hallucinatory elements—the rapid changes of mood, the fragments of songs, the broken syntax, the temporal jumps—in disrupted sentence structures, allowing the language to become, in a sense, delirious and recording the strange slippage between one world and the next.

The atmosphere in Wolfe's death scenes, however, retrospectively suggests the pandemic's contributions to the alienation and bleakness that infuse the earlier modernist works. Wolfe describes the family as "trying to escape from the tragic net of frustration and loss in which they were caught."[25] In motions that recall characters from Stephen Dedalus to many of the voices in *The Waste Land*, Eugene "paced restlessly up and down the hall or prowled through the house a-search for some entrance he had never found." He feels he is "caught, he [is] strangling, in the web of futility" surrounding Ben's death.[26] These feelings arise from non-pandemic-related causes too, but Wolfe suggests how the pandemic's lingering effects had contributed to a pervasive atmosphere of early-twentieth-century futility. Eugene's entrapment and strangulation, coupled with Ben's scene of drowning, become dark pandemic twins to Wilfred Owen's quintessential modernist depiction of death, one Cather, too, had evoked:

> I saw him drowning
> In all my dreams before my helpless sight,
> He plunges at me, guttering, choking, drowning.[27]

Owen's brutal description of a death from poison gas in "Dulce et Decorum Est" links to Ben's death not simply in imagery and experience but also in aftermath, in the way both Owen and Wolfe are caught in traumatic repetition, witnessing in memory a senseless death they must continually see but are helpless to stop. Wolfe recovers a critical contributor to modernist futility, one easy to miss in part because the very characteristics of this viral shaper echoed, and then were subsumed by, more publicized war deaths. In terms of literary influence, Wolfe, like Cather, is indebted to Owen's earlier model, but his depiction should also shift the way we read Owen and his historical moment.[28] Owen demands his readers see the vicious, degraded quality of death in modern warfare; Wolfe reveals the hidden deaths that were unfolding at the same time. Wolfe doesn't need to expose any false cant of meaningful sacrifice, as Owen must; he needs to expose the deaths themselves and their haunting parallels to those from poison gas.

At Ben's final moment of death, Wolfe suggests a viral resurrection with more comforting features, one that he will bring into startling and puzzling material form at the end of the novel. Ben's body appears dead, growing "rigid," but then things take a surprising turn:

But suddenly, marvelously, as if his resurrection and rebirth had come upon him, Ben drew upon the air in a long and powerful respiration; his gray eyes opened. Filled with a terrible vision of all life in the one moment, he seemed to rise forward bodilessly from his pillows without support—a flame, a light, a glory—joined at length in death to the dark spirit who had brooded upon each footstep of his lonely adventure on earth; and, casting the fierce sword of his glance with utter and final comprehension upon the room haunted with its gray pageantry of cheap loves and dull consciences and on all those uncertain mummers of waste and confusion fading now from the bright window of his eyes, he passed instantly, scornful and unafraid, as he had lived, into the shades of death.[29]

Ben seems ineffable as he passes—a flame, a light, a glory—a beautiful counter to the more sinister formlessness of the virus itself and its dissolution of the body. However uncertain, Wolfe offers a vision of resurrection that imagines an escape from a bleak landscape of "cheap loves and dull consciences" that is filled with waste and uncertainty. The virus had, fundamentally, helped produce this landscape, becoming a silent part of its enveloping emotional content of confusion and enervation. In death, though, Ben pushes against the dull bleakness, gaining at the end a fierce certainty and lack of fear unavailable to his living family. In creating this dichotomy, Wolfe uses the pandemic context to represent a key modernist trope; it is not simply the bleak environment of waste that evokes modernism but also the contradiction, the waste coupled with the hungering after a sense of resurrection or a forgotten aesthetic realm of beauty just out of reach, a hunger we find in Eliot's *The Waste Land*, in Miranda's vision of paradise, and in Clarissa's and Septimus's ecstatic musings in *Mrs. Dalloway*. Certainly the war fueled the desolation and a hunger for lost loved ones, but Wolfe here follows the virus to its hunting grounds, evoking a domestic space literally infected with death and the corresponding desire for an escape we find repeated everywhere in these years. If we forget the pandemic's presence in this dichotomy of waste and resurrection, we miss the way various modes of living death in the interwar period reflected a physical—and not simply an emotional or metaphoric—reality for flu victims.

Wolfe brings Ben back a second time in a dramatic scene that ends the novel and that speaks to the pandemic's recurring presence. The scene begins with Eugene standing in the deserted public square of his town that "lay under blazing moonlight" as the clock strikes 3:15 a.m. "Troubled and a little afraid," he walks to his father's funeral statuary shop that overlooks the square, the stone angels seemingly "frozen, in the moonlight."[30] On the porch—appropriately, the literal threshold between the store's death wares and the public square—he finds his brother Ben leaning on the railing and smoking. In disbelief, he asks Ben repeatedly if it's really him and if he's a ghost. Ben declares that he is not dead and that he is not a ghost, and he laughs and agrees when Eugene thinks he must be going crazy. When Eugene maintains that Ben is dead, that he must be dead, that he "saw [him] die," their subsequent conversation unsettles Eugene's realities and the divisions between the two:

> His voice rose to a scream, "Don't you remember? I tell you, you are dead, Ben."
> "Fool," said Ben fiercely. "I am not dead."
> There was a silence.
> "Then," said Eugene very slowly, "which of us is the ghost, I wonder?"
> Ben did not answer.[31]

Wolfe imagines a threshold world that works both ways. In a welcome if eerie contrast to the family's oppressive sense that they are partially dead in the aftermath of Ben's illness, the threshold here allows the living to come to the dead. Wolfe does not suggest this return is part of Eugene's deranged imagination; this is no flu delirium, and the scene is not presented as a dream or a hallucination inspired by Eugene's grief. For Eugene, Ben has returned, with no explanation—and none is forthcoming; Ben does not seem angelic or spirit-like—he is a material Ben. And Wolfe deliberately leaves the reality of the experience ambiguous. When Eugene asks if he is "imagining all this" and if they are "talking together, or not," Ben scoffs and says, "How should I know?"[32] The moment opens up a fictional space that ironically seems more real—and more alive—than the death-soaked atmosphere of the rest of the book. Wolfe reifies Ben, and in doing so he grants a live material presence to the pandemic itself. He also, though, grants an aesthetic consolation, a secular resurrection that—at least for a moment— replaces loss with presence and the seemingly real return of a loved one.

The scene has been cited by many as the most modernist section of the novel, with critics frequently comparing it to various moments in Joyce's work. Richard S. Kennedy, for example, links the jumbled style of the final scene to Stephen Dedalus's walk on the beach in the Proteus chapter of *Ulysses*.[33] Jimmie Carol Still Durr argues that the language in the final chapter suggests a unique "stream of consciousness" style.[34] Vernon Hyles finds that the scene parallels the Circe chapter of *Ulysses*, with both authors creating a strange blend of reality and dreams that captures elements of the unconscious.[35] What these critics miss, though, is how these modernist elements are used by Wolfe to depict the pandemic-specific elements of the scene; Wolfe's repeated use of thresholds and blurred boundaries captures the grim realization that mass death had invaded the domestic space, infiltrating into the heart of American towns. His surreal blend of reality and dreams recalls the flu's delirium but also the sense of haunting loss and the desire that this loss might be erased by the dead's return. Wolfe insists on the concrete realness of the scene; Ben seems to have returned, as solid and as material as when he left, not an angel or a perfected being but very much himself. At the same time, though, the scene itself is surreal and takes on an apocalyptic atmosphere as it unfolds. Eugene's grief and confusion appear to blur temporal boundaries and disrupt his thoughts, creating a modernist moment that extends from the flu's overwhelming presence.

After the initial meeting, Eugene's experience grows more hallucinatory, combining a sense of temporal disruption with visions of legions of dead. In a moment that echoes the spirit photographers I explore in chapter 7, Eugene sees "the silver space" of the square "printed with the thousand forms of himself and Ben," a viral reproduction that here suggests life rather than death. As he watches, versions of himself and Ben at different moments in time move through the square, "the great lost legion of himself—the thousand forms that came, that passed, that wove and shifted in unending change." Likewise, he sees forms of "deathless Ben" cross the square, bringing back "the lost years, the forgotten days"; it is, he muses, "the army of himself and Ben."[36] As these shapes vanish, his visions grow more apocalyptic, the sense of resurrection bleaker. He sees "fabulous lost cities," with "the billion living of the earth, the thousand billion dead: seas were withered, deserts flooded, mountains drowned." Like Porter's Miranda, he searches for "the happy land," only to be told by Ben that it doesn't exist. Eugene maintains that he will continue to look for some kind of arcadia, even as "he saw that he had left the million bones of cities . . . [and] he was alone with Ben, and their feet were planted on darkness."[37] Wolfe brings the pandemic into a narrative of apocalyptic terror, in which the multiplying and disappearing versions of Ben and Eugene become the countless dead and a deadly form of viral replication. The world has drowned, the cities are bones, and search as they might, Eugene and Ben are trapped in a bleak vision of end times that, like the vision I trace in Yeats's "The Second Coming," promises scant redemption or escape.

Embedded in this scene is a final remarkable moment that encompasses the horror and the surreal quality of the pandemic's domestic version of mass death. Standing on the porch with the resurrected Ben, Eugene sees through the window of his father's shop that the angel statues have started to move in the eerie light, "walking to and fro like huge wound dolls of stone," with marble cherubim flying about and the stone lambs grazing on the floor. Eugene is astonished, asking if Ben sees it, and Ben essentially shrugs, saying, "They have a right to, haven't they?" Eugene, somewhat ambiguously, cries out, "Not here! Not here! . . . It's not right, here! My God, this is the Square! There's the fountain! There's the City Hall!" As the bank tower clock rings out (a sound, as we've seen, intimately tied to pandemic memories), Eugene continues to insist, "But not here! Not here, Ben. . . . There is a place where all things happen! But not here, Ben! . . . Not here, Ben! It is not right!"[38] Eugene is in part insisting that surreal experiences like funereal statues moving should not happen in the stolid reality of the town, but he also gives voice to the frantic sense that deaths like Ben's, happening on such a scale, should not have entered the home front, should not have come to the ordinary town, that surely some space could have remained safe in the terrible years during and after the war. As Wolfe has shown, though, the landscape is replete with angels, ghosts, bones, and legions of the dead.

CONTAGION GUILT AND PARENTAL LOSS

William Maxwell's autobiographical novel *They Came Like Swallows* narrates a pandemic death from the viewpoint of three members of the same family who are both survivors and mourners. While Wolfe narrates the pandemic from the viewpoint of a single narrator, Maxwell's use of multiple perspectives reveals how the virus broke the structure of the family alongside its individual members. Maxwell drew heavily on his own grim experience during the outbreak, when his whole family caught the flu. At the time, the newspapers in Illinois where they lived had been reporting that the pandemic had started to wane, and the family thought it was safe to go to a postwar celebration (though, as Maxwell makes clear in his novel, how and where the virus was transmitted was always hauntingly uncertain). Maxwell and his brother both came down with the virus, as did his parents, who had taken a train to a nearby medical facility in hopes of a safer delivery for their third child. After giving birth to another boy, Maxwell's mother died from the flu. The biographer Barbara Burkhardt cites this death as "the defining event of Maxwell's life and, later, of his literature"; the family broke up, and, as Maxwell recalled, "the shine went out of everything."[39] Maxwell translates this experience into his novel, and in doing so, he makes visible three widespread elements of the pandemic that were particular to young families and that are largely missing from the other accounts. On the broadest level, Maxwell's novel suggests the devastating cost of parental loss during the pandemic. As I detail in the introduction, in New York City alone, by the first week of November 1918, 31,000 children were orphaned or lost a parent.[40] Maxwell offers a vivid portrait of the suffering behind these numbers. The novel also captures how, in families made up entirely of noncombatants (often families with younger children), the pandemic could become the dominant tragedy, with the war a background event that might even offer comfort. Finally, the novel presents how the insidious contagion guilt the pandemic produced could be particularly damaging for children and spouses who felt responsible for a parent's death.

Like Wolfe, Maxwell subordinates the war to the pandemic, but he also shows the way the war structured family life before the outbreak, its normalized presence a foil for the pandemic's sudden appearance. In ways large and small, the family's life is shaped by the war, with references peppered throughout the story: the mother "cut[s] bandages for the Red Cross";[41] the youngest child, Bunny, hears the "terrible shriek" of the bells and whistles signaling the Armistice; the older boy, Robert, goes off to see the end-of-war parades; an estranged uncle is in the army; and suspicions lurk about German neighbors and servants.[42] The war further structures the imaginative play of both boys, and tensions between them parallel the two sides of the war: Robert reads *The Boy Allies in Bulgaria* (a Central Power) while Bunny reads about boy allies in Belgium (an Allied Power); Bunny builds a model Belgian village in a back room, which he tries to protect, but Robert dismantles it to construct an airfield. Robert's toy soldiers are also a constant source of both pleasure and conflict. When Bunny breaks them, Robert attempts to piece them back together—his own amputated leg (lost in an earlier accident) aligning him both to the toy soldiers and to real ones. He falls sick with influenza before he can finish, a parallel to the way the flu hit an already damaged population.

Despite the mild conflict suggested by the war references, both boys find the war offers intriguing stories and appealing visuals that are broken (like Robert's soldiers) by the pandemic's arrival. Bunny is upset when the war ends, for "he was *interested* in the war. . . . He liked the flags, the speeches, and the Liberty Loan Drives. He liked the quiet and satisfying excitement of tracing battle lines across a map with red and green pins." He wants to continue to help with war efforts, "doing everything as he had been doing it. He wanted the men in uniform to go right on marching, and the women to go right on knitting sweaters and socks. . . . There was no telling what things would be like, without the war."[43] For Bunny, the war could be mapped; people at home could contribute, and soldiers could fight—and it could all take place far away. Right after he has this thought, the dizziness that had seemed outside him all day descends "and became an intimate part of him," and he falls dangerously ill with the flu. The virus replaces the war's more appealing stories and roles—where the threat remains at a safe distance—with a chaotic personal invasion. Robert likewise enjoys the parades and the bands at the war's end, and he and a friend wish it could be like that every day, for then " 'Things wouldn't be so dead.' 'Things wouldn't be nearly so dead' ";[44] he arrives home from a celebration to find his brother ill, and his own illness and his mother's death quickly follow.

For these boys, the war provides a more understandable structure and a more exciting narrative, and Maxwell suggests such war framing is childish, a kind of infantile masculinity that imagines destruction as adventure. The flu punctures this fantasy, introducing a different form of tragedy that disrupts the war narrative and also suggesting that the pandemic's brutal truths are actually a more accurate representation of the war. Robert senses the shift when Bunny is sick, realizing that "something was happening in town, all around him. Not an open excitement like the day the Armistice was signed, with fire engines and whistles and noise and people riding around in the hearse. But a quiet thing that he couldn't see or hear; that was downstairs in Bunny's room, and on Tenth Street where Arthur Cook [dead from the flu] lived, and in more places than that."[45] Maxwell registers how the war's noisy, visible, and public fanfare (especially at its ending) could appealingly but problematically counter the vast uncertainty and quiet menace the virus brought as it snuck into homes.

Maxwell highlights these differences in parallel newspaper accounts read aloud by the father. Early in the novel, the father reads about the new "Spanish influenza," and the account emphasizes the ambiguity that surrounds the outbreak: "What is Spanish influenza? . . . Is it something new? . . . Does it come from Spain? . . . The disease now occurring in this country and called 'Spanish influenza' resembles a very contagious kind of 'cold.' "[46] The ellipses (which are in the original) and questions indicate the wide gaps in knowledge. The reporter goes on to note that while the illness can cause "a feeling of severe sickness," in most cases, the patient rapidly recovers, unless complications arise. It is "not known" if this outbreak is "identical with the epidemic of earlier years," and its origins remain uncertain, with hints of a foreign connection (Spain? The Orient? The German eastern front?); misinformation and uncertainty permeate the account.[47] By contrast, the report he reads on the war later in the novel is full of concrete facts, describing concrete things: the number of boats, guns, airplanes, wagons, and prisoners that the Germans must surrender; the key players in the battles; the specifications of the Armistice terms, and the like.[48] The father is so intent on reading the war account—and annoyed when others are not listening—that the parents miss at first that Bunny has become ill, a microcosm of how war news drowned out the growing pandemic threat. The war news is appealing, being solid, far away, and about the war's end; the pandemic is nebulous, close at hand, and just beginning. Indeed, when the father reads the influenza accounts, the mother finally asks him to stop and read about something more distant, the "floods in China, or the Kaiser"; she quips, "Already I've begun to have fever, pains, and depression."[49]

When the virus arrives in the home, Maxwell depicts aspects of the illness that are now familiar from the Porter, Cather, and Wolfe accounts: The two brothers experience delirium, fever, and nightmares, though in general they suffer through a milder form of the outbreak than we've seen elsewhere. The father flashes back to the "terrible last hour of [his wife's] breathing," though her deathbed scene is not narrated directly.[50] All the survivors are weakened physically, with the father, through a combination of fatigue and grief, looking "grey," "lifeless," and like a "poor fellow" who "is done for."[51] Bells constantly ring throughout the novel.

The depiction of the actual illness, though, is not as striking as the vivid picture of contagion guilt that Maxwell paints, one that suggests the self-blame the pandemic could generate. These elements took a different form than in previous outbreaks; Nancy Tomes, in *The Gospel of Germs*, has outlined how in the decades surrounding 1900, new fears of invisible microbes prompted campaigns of purity and cleanliness within American homes. And scholars like Allan Conrad Christensen, in *Nineteenth-Century Narratives of Contagion*, have detailed the biological—but also the moral, political, and religious ends that metaphors of contagion have encompassed.[52] For the most part, though, the influenza pandemic happened so quickly that it did not seem to produce such metaphors, though Tomes notes that the outbreak "reinforced anxieties about contagion and the need for personal vigilance to escape it."[53] As Porter suggests, and as Maxwell details, the pandemic's contagious qualities could, however, produce a disabling guilt, especially as the virus was often passed among family members.

In detailing this guilt, Maxwell first introduces snapshots of possible avenues of transmission: A classmate Bunny had played with falls ill, and when he tries to tell his mother, he repeatedly gets silenced. After hearing about his friend, his mother sends him to the store, where the storekeeper is sneezing and discussing the pandemic. The mother berates her oldest son for having so many handkerchiefs that his pockets are bulging, an ominous reminder of contamination—and Robert then goes off to the crowded war parades. Schools and churches are closed, and train travel is discouraged. When Bunny falls ill, the doctor demands that the mother stay out of the room, recommending that they "tie her down" if she won't stay away, especially given her pregnant state;[54] the mother enters Bunny's room anyway. The parents take a train to a hospital in the hopes of having a safer birth but expose themselves to crowds in the process. As we saw with Porter, though, the precise avenue of transmission cannot be mapped, creating the perfect conditions for a wide-ranging but undefined guilt.

Maxwell reveals how this guilt, and the blame and helplessness it produces, damages the family, breaking the sense that they can protect one another from harm and introducing the terrifying possibility that they caused the harm themselves. The mother first feels responsible for Bunny's illness: "If I'd only had sense enough. . . . If I'd only taken Bunny out of school when the epidemic first started," which the father dismisses with a fatalistic "If things are going to happen . . . they happen. There's no use trying to forestall them."[55] Later, though, he is haunted by the sense that he might have prevented his wife's illness. After her death, he keeps circling back to a moment at the station when he chose the train car they boarded: "I was trying to get seats for us before the others got on. If I'd stepped back and let the others get on first, I'd have seen the interurban draw up alongside that train. . . . The interurban had a parlor car that was almost empty. It would have been ever so much better to take that. . . . That way we wouldn't have exposed ourselves."[56] He can't stop returning to this "what if" moment, to the troubling possibility that a different choice might have saved her: "the same idea occurred to him over and over—he might be able to change what had already happened" "if he could only go back." His own illness, he feels, meant that "he could not make people do the things he wanted them to" at the hospital.[57] Maxwell suggests an endless feedback loop of guilt, fueled by the hidden paths of transmission and a compelling but illusionary narrative of personal responsibility that is continually thwarted by the reality of powerlessness.

Perhaps the most damaging guilt, though, is experienced by the older son, Robert, who also blames himself for the mother's death. During Bunny's illness, he had to chase a swallow out of the sickroom, and while he was distracted, his mother came to sit with Bunny, despite being forbidden from the room. He is plagued by the sense that if he had been paying more attention, his mother would not have died. The bird in the cuckoo clock— one that keeps ringing throughout the novel—"reminded him of how he let his mother into the room where Bunny was—a thing he would rather have forgotten. When that escaped from his mind, he was still aware vaguely that there was something he *had* been worrying about."[58] With imagery suggestive of flashback, the language evokes how contagion guilt could live in the mind as a constant low-lying presence that, at times, like the popping of the cuckoo out of the clock, could break into awareness. He tries to push it aside, but he knows "if anything happened to his mother, it would be *his* fault." His aunt finally notices his despair and reassures him that the virus attacked three days after exposure—so his mother could not have been exposed through his actions. The aunt acknowledges to the father, though, that "each of us has his private nightmare. Robert isn't the only one," and she shares her own guilt that her sister was a far better person than she was—as the father thinks again about the train.[59] While guilt, blame, and helplessness are common features of mourning, Maxwell foregrounds how the pervasiveness of the virus, the severity of the threat, and the uncertainty of exposure fueled a guilt that, like the virus itself, was everywhere yet difficult to acknowledge.

Alongside the contagion guilt, Maxwell highlights the impalpable loss of structure and meaning the death of a parent leaves in its wake, creating a deep sense of unreality. At the start of the novel, Bunny recognizes that his mother is the enabling framework of his world: "If his mother were not there to protect him . . . what would he do? Whatever would become of him in a world where there was neither warmth nor comfort nor love?"; "if his mother was not there . . . nothing was real to Bunny—or alive."[60] Here, Maxwell suggests the collateral damage a death in the pandemic could cause, producing a challenge to both agency and reality that are independent of the challenges to both that the virus already produced in the ill victim. And Bunny's fears that he will be lost without his mother are realized through the novel's form; while the first part of the novel is narrated from Bunny's point of view, after the mother dies, the father takes over the narration, and Bunny's voice and presence fades from the story. Like Bunny, though, the father finds that with the mother's death, all structure has collapsed, and he awaits "the final and complete disintegration of his house."[61] Meaning, language, and even his sense of his physical surroundings threaten to dissolve. He wanders out into the snow at night, wondering "to what purpose?" and "hearing the words, he lost their meaning and all connection with what had gone before." He tries to get his bearings, feeling "there was no way possible for him to get out";[62] he sees a wagon in the distance and, his reality disrupted by grief, he thinks his wife has come to take him with her. In the novel's final moments, he acknowledges directly the mother's reality-building role. As he stares down at her body in her casket in the living room, he knows

it was Elizabeth who had determined the shape that his life should take, from the very first moment that he saw her. And she had altered that shape daily by the sound of her voice, and by her hair, and by her eyes which were so large and dark. And by her wisdom and by her love.

"You won't forget your mother, will you, Robert?" he said. And with wonder clinging to him (for it had been a revelation: neither he nor anyone else had known that his life was going to be like this) he moved away from the coffin.[63]

Embedded in this ending is both the implication that the shape of life has been changed, alongside the paradoxical impulse not to forget and to move away, stunned at the unexpectedness and unpredictability of this loss. Maxwell echoed these very sentiments about his own mother's death. As he recalled, "It happened too suddenly, with no warning, and we none of us could believe it or bear it. . . . The nightmare went on and on . . . the beautiful, imaginative, protected world of my childhood was swept away."[64] Like Porter, Maxwell finds that the pandemic bifurcated his life and unmade his world.

Maxwell uses two moments of viral resurrection that highlight how central the mother's role had been and how damaging her loss would be. Robert, caught in a delirium nightmare, believes his mother has come to his room on the night she dies at the hospital. She comforts him, telling him he must be having a "very bad dream," and like Miranda, he feels he is lying over a pit. He thinks he won't drop into it if she stays but feels "There was too great a distance between them," and she leaves his room.[65] The next morning, he finds she has died. The father later experiences a nondelirious version of this visitation when he moves to rebuke Bunny for making a wreath out of his mother's funeral flowers: "As James started forward he could have sworn, almost, that he felt a slight pressure on his arm. And he turned, in spite of himself—in spite of the fact that he knew positively no one was there."[66] Both moments are brief glimpses of the mother's essential role within this family, comforting a dangerously ill Robert and protecting Bunny from the overly harsh attentions of his father. They suggest in part a comforting presence and a not uncommon experience for many after the death of a loved one. They also, though, paint a subtle but profound picture of how much is lost when a parent dies, including all the small, unrecorded gestures a parent may offer a child. Maxwell resurrects here the hard-to-capture elements of the pandemic's damage, suggesting the depths of parental losses that at the time were unusually concentrated and widespread. And while the returns in part register the continued force of the mother's vital presence, the ghostly visitations finally underscore her absence. On a broader level, the moments of resurrection highlight the victims missing in the other accounts. In an atmosphere dominated by war, young women were not supposed to die; as one character exclaims, "It doesn't seem possible. . . . I say it just doesn't seem possible! She was so young."[67] Unexpected, and drowned out by the flood of male deaths, the deaths of women in the pandemic are largely obscured, yet—as Maxwell's story suggests—they are still present, the impact of the loss still returning to haunt the living. Just as the family cannot avoid the mother's body stretched out in the coffin in the living room, Maxwell reminds his readers that the virus came for women too.

Wolfe and Maxwell register the shock and bewilderment that ensued when an annihilating force entered the domestic space, representing this shock as an individual tragedy that kept repeating, like Eugene's multiplying avatars. Read outside the frame of the larger pandemic—as such deaths were often experienced at the time by both readers and mourners—these accounts might appear simply as two especially poignant literary examples of a death by illness. Why are these accounts any different than, say, Virginia Woolf's vivid portrayal of Rachel Vinrace's fatal illness at the end of *The Voyage Out* (1915) or any number of deaths in the novels of Charles Dickens? Certainly, the deaths can be read alongside such examples, but we also misread them when we do. The deaths Wolfe and Maxwell portray only *appear* to be single stories, but they are in fact representations of millions of others at the time, and they must be read in this context, as narrating a moment when such individual tragedies became epidemic. The very singularity of these stories compared to the known statistics of the deaths hint at the millions of stories we do not have, the legions of silenced voices where the experience was too damaging to make the telling possible.

By placing a pandemic death as the defining event and subordinating the war, these novels help shape a new frame for the interwar period, one that redefines which deaths "count" and returns us to Judith Butler's ideas on grievability. Accounts of war and violence, Butler observes, can "instrumentaliz[e] certain versions of reality" and "de-legitim[ize] alternative versions of reality," allowing governments for political ends to position some lives as grievable and others as acceptable losses.[68] Wolfe's and Maxwell's novels demonstrate how the war itself became a frame, obscuring the pandemic's domestic casualties. They reconfigure this frame, highlighting not the loss of soldiers (even if from the virus) but the loss of everyday citizens. By showcasing the pandemic's agonizing deaths and the terrible grief that followed, they make these deaths once again grievable. The pandemic becomes the defining reality to which war losses might be compared, a "stable" benchmark that (ironically) reveals the instability, the unbearable contextless quality, and the surreal nature of the pandemic and its losses. At the same time these works bring these losses into the frame, they should also alert us to the many losses not represented in the Anglo-American interwar pandemic literature, such as those experienced by recent immigrants or people of color. Just as we should not take the paucity of overt pandemic literature as a sign that the pandemic didn't matter, we need to use the literature we do have to remember how many voices remain unrepresented.

All four writers I have analyzed in part 1 lived in a country less consumed by the war and, except for Cather, wrote at a later moment than the authors in part 2. In shaping their pandemic representations, these writers certainly borrowed techniques and images from the modernists I consider next: Porter's desolate dream landscape recalls Eliot's *The Waste Land*, the death-saturated atmosphere of Wolfe and Porter evoke both Eliot's poem and Woolf's *Mrs. Dalloway*, Wolfe's apocalyptic vision carries resonances of Yeats's "The Second Coming," and Maxwell's evocative portrait of a devastating maternal loss echoes *To the Lighthouse*. Another study could be written about this trajectory and this influence, but it is not my central aim here. Porter, Cather, Wolfe, and Maxwell return us to the 1918 atmosphere, detailing the sights and psychological impacts and tensions of the moment;

the pandemic produced most of the same conditions in Britain and Ireland as it did in the United States, even if it was represented differently. The works in part 1 reestablish the conditions from which the works in part 2 emerged, allowing us to recognize the pandemic's traces at a moment and in a place where the story remained more fragmented and hidden.

PART II
Pandemic Modernism

Part 2 turns to three iconic modernist works: Virginia Woolf's *Mrs. Dalloway* (1925), T. S. Eliot's *The Waste Land* (1922), and W. B. Yeats's "The Second Coming" (1919). Each writer had an intense personal encounter with the pandemic virus, and each text maps a particular pandemic landscape. In shifting to these works, I move from direct and clearly intentional treatments of the flu to the more subtle ways the pandemic weaves its way into earlier modernist texts and into the canon. Cather, Porter, Maxwell, and Wolfe, writing in the United States where the war was less present, mostly at a later moment in time, and generally in less experimental forms, offer us clearer linear narratives, the kinds of stories that can be told after a traumatic event has been pieced back together and placed in temporal sequence. What the modernist works examined in part 2 suggest are the more immediate traumatic fragments—the sensory and emotional pieces that have yet to be formed into a coherent story. Fragmented symptoms appear without a clear context, the atmosphere of vulnerability is unmoored from particular causes, and the pandemic itself remains largely unnamed, capturing a time before it had developed into a discrete event with more understandable contours. The pandemic literary paradigm established in part 1 provides a set of diagnostic tools for reading this atmosphere, an atmosphere that shapes a modernist pandemic model with its own language and stylistic features. Just as we bring our knowledge of trench conditions to read the rats and alleys in *The Waste Land*, we can bring the literary pandemic lens to these works to see what has been hidden in plain sight.

Modernist literary techniques emerge as aesthetic tools suited both to representing a hard-to-depict viral threat and to obscuring it. The experimental structures and fragmented qualities of the language could parallel the delirium and confusion of the virus's acute phase. The more unsettled temporal frames—the past's repeated intrusions into the present, the chronological circling—are ideal for representing the virus's disorientations, as well as its lingering presence in the body. As these authors pushed away from linear narratives or traditional poetic forms, they move to more fluid structures that in turn can capture the disruptions of plot that illness may produce. Modernist shifts at the level of character—the borderless qualities of identity, the radical subjectivity of perception—are likewise suited for representing bodies infiltrated at the cellular level and the sense of dissolution this infiltration could produce. At the same time, all the modernist indirection, ambiguity, and fragmentation made the pandemic's presence and effects easier to obscure, in ways that continue to conceal this viral tragedy.

The tension between representing and hiding is well expressed by the elements of viral resurrection that haunt these works, which, like the later texts, are full of ghosts, delirium visions, the walking dead, flashbacks, and a sense of deadly vitality. Christian and pagan tropes of sacrificial resurrection are routinely evoked and emptied of their traditional meanings. Critics have detailed how the war fueled these images of deadly returns, as it did. Viewed through the pandemic lens, though, they emerge as representations of this spectral trauma, evoking the symptoms of delirium, a haunting fear of contagion, a way to make such losses visible and yet to encode their elusiveness, and a way to grant at least an aesthetic structure and meaning to an otherwise anarchic loss.

In making these connections, I am not proposing a cause-and-effect model; these elements of modernist style are already in place before the pandemic arrives, though the outbreak did shape them into new forms. I also do not claim Woolf, Eliot, and Yeats were always making intentional choices to represent the outbreak—the pandemic was an experience that even as it was unquestionably unfolding was hard to register or believe was real; the pandemic's very nature means its representation will not always be deliberate or clear. I argue instead for a critical recognition of a symbiotic atmosphere of influence; the pandemic is an essential presence in the style and structure of these works, and they in turn help define and confront the experience of the pandemic in its immediate aftermath. Collectively, these works shape the sense of global menace, of a coming apocalypse or waste land that involves a form of mass death tied to—but distinct from—the more visible violence of the war. Adjusting our framework to include the shadowy landscape of pandemic suffering requires a parallel retooling of modernist scholarship on violence and the body. And at a broader level, the very act of tracing how we have overlooked the literary pandemic helps train us to see the larger ways illness is obscured and the many other gaps, silences, and untold stories waiting to be recognized.

I begin with *Mrs. Dalloway*, the latest of the three works and, in many ways, the most traditionally chronological. Of all the pandemic literature I investigate, Woolf's novel grants the most extensive mapping of the virus's long-term aftereffects on bodies, teasing out the hard-to-see interchanges between physical health and perception. The novel not only tracks the virus across time; it investigates the cumulative, composite blows the war and pandemic together have on the societal and individual body. By contrast, *The Waste Land*—closer to the pandemic by three years—presents a more diffuse atmosphere of global and individual breakdown, with no direct mention of the viral tragedy. Instead, the poem is marked by often bewildering temporal leaps, capturing both the immediacy of illness, with symptoms randomly erupting in the poem with little interpretive framework, as well as a seemingly endless aftermath of bone-deep enervation. The poem incorporates not only a general modernist malaise but the particular postviral experience of Eliot, his wife, and millions of pandemic survivors. From Eliot's pandemic sensory graveyard, I move to Yeats's "The Second Coming," by far the most violent and apocalyptic literary portrait of the post-1918 moment I consider and the only one of the works analyzed in this book that was completed during the pandemic. Yeats composes his poem in the immediate aftermath of his pregnant wife's near-fatal attack; the poem captures the raw, chaotic quality of the experience, depicting at once an epic, universal cataclysm that also unfolds internally as a bodily cataclysm. The language suggests political conflict but also introduces a new form of Yeatsean violence, an illness-based anarchy that encompasses both the societal and the corporeal.

Chapter Four

ON SEEING ILLNESS

Virginia Woolf's *Mrs. Dalloway*

Like many people during the pandemic, Virginia Woolf initially treated the outbreak as a side note to the larger story of the war. In July 1918, as the first wave struck, she records in her diary that influenza "rages all over the place" and indeed "has come next door" to infect their neighbor, but she does not seem unduly alarmed.[1] The next week, she reports "a funeral next door; dead of influenza," but she embeds the news in a sentence where she also remarks on the rain. During the second wave, in October 1918, she describes how Lytton Strachey is fleeing London to avoid the disease, and she writes dismissively and parenthetically about the outbreak: "(we are, by the way, in the midst of a plague unmatched since the Black Death, according to the Times, who seem to tremble lest it may seize upon Lord Northcliffe, & thus precipitate us into peace)." While Woolf knows about the flu's spread—it is "raging," and the *Times* is quite accurately comparing it to the plague—she suggests the hysteria is misplaced. She sees it (as, she says, does the *Times*) through the lens of the war: the *Times* is trembling, she mocks, because they fear it might lead to a premature peace. As for many, Woolf finds the impulse to move on after these grim years is strong. By December 1918, Woolf observes both that "influenza seems to be over" and that "as for public news, the war already seems an unimportant incident."[2]

Her diary tone, though, hints of bravado and denial. Woolf had good reasons to be wary of influenza—even the ordinary strains. Her mother had died years before after complications from a severe case, and Woolf was plagued with influenza in the years surrounding the pandemic.[3] Despite telling a friend in 1915 that "influenza germs have no power over me," she contracted the virus repeatedly.[4] In April 1916, she is told by her doctor after a bad case to be careful for two weeks.[5] In February and March 1918, just as the pandemic strain was emerging in Kansas, she again catches influenza, reporting in her diary that "I was kept in bed 8 days" with influenza, "divorced from my pen; a whole current of life cut off";[6] as she wrote her sister, her doctor lectured her continually about the connections between "influenza and the nervous system which I had to hear every day from [Dr.] Fergusson."[7] She also contracted influenza at the end of 1919, and this version was likely part of the pandemic strain. She complained to her sister that her doctor "won't let her get up" and confided that her heart has been affected: "I thought I was probably dying, but Fergusson says its only the nerves of the heart go wrong after influenza."[8] She suffered through another case of influenza in early 1922 and could not work for over a month. Her heart once more seemed affected; Dr. Fergusson told her her pulse rate was troubling, and a heart disease specialist predicted she would not live long.[9] Additional bouts of influenza hit in 1923 and 1925. Overlapping and interspersed with these attacks were headaches, mental health challenges, faints, possibly rheumatic fever, and a constant stream of tooth extractions in the hopes that they would reduce the constant infections.[10] As she understandably and understatedly noted to a friend in 1920, "I don't like influenza."[11]

After all her personal experience with influenza, and despite her initial shrug at the pandemic outbreak, by 1926, she had published two profound meditations on illness that spoke to the pandemic's aftermath: her novel *Mrs. Dalloway* and her nonfiction essay "On Being Ill." In her essay, she questions directly why literature has been so silent on the impact of illness: "one would have thought," she writes, that "novels . . . would have been devoted to influenza."[12] In *Mrs. Dalloway*, she had, in fact, centered a novel on influenza, though it is rarely read as such,[13] crafting innovative ways to write about illness that embody the pandemic's effects as well as exposing (paradoxically) the way it hides in plain sight. She remaps London through the eyes of illness, and she shows how language and our perceptions of reality are shaped by disease. While Woolf focuses at the level of individual sufferers and mourners, the pervasiveness of illness in the work echoes the widespread quality of the outbreak. Reading through the lens of pandemic illness—as indeed her characters do—demands in turn a new critical framework for approaching the novel. This chapter proposes that framework.

I begin the chapter by analyzing the reasons Woolf offers in "On Being Ill" for why illness is so rarely a topic of literature. I then investigate the strategies Woolf uses in *Mrs. Dalloway* to overcome the representational challenges illness poses, offering two pandemic readings of the novel. I first explore Clarissa Dalloway as a pandemic survivor; critics have long read the shell-shocked Septimus Smith as the central survivor in the novel, a victim of the war's unprecedented trauma. I reframe the novel as in fact structured around two survivors and two cataclysmic threats, one human, one viral. Clarissa showcases a stage of the pandemic not fully addressed in the other literature I've considered: the lingering physical and psychological damage the virus could inflict even months and years after the attack. Woolf offers a vivid picture of the post-pandemic body and how that body's experiences shape what it sees, painting a pandemic reality that also speaks profoundly to the perspective illness may offer more generally. In a series of encoded moments that draw on images of bells, mourners, sickrooms, and contagion, the novel makes material the way illness reverberates into the outer world and in turn how the body's vulnerability leaves it open to incursions from its surroundings.

Clarissa is the more obvious influenza survivor—she is recovering from her bout with the illness, as the narrator reminds us many times—but in my second pandemic reading, I analyze Septimus as a surprising composite figure of the early twentieth century's two great tragedies. The war, as we know, left lasting physical and mental scars on bodies. The 1918 virus, through other means, not only did long-term damage to the body's systems; it could also produce profound psychological damage (as Woolf and her doctors knew well). This damage was not simply from the trauma of the near-death experience (which is largely the trauma Clarissa seems affected by) but from neurological effects ranging from delirium to psychosis. In Septimus, Woolf registers all this damage, granting a more immediate picture of the suffering involved in multiple traumas and the surreal and unsettling perspective they grant to London. As a composite of both a war and influenza body, Septimus also reflects the inextricable interplay between physical and mental health. Woolf develops through Septimus what I term the hallucinatory-delirium mode, one that echoes through the overt accounts, and one that I trace in Eliot and Yeats as well. This mode blends mental and physical suffering and allows Woolf to place the body's experience as the basis for both language and perception. It becomes a way to create a novel and a language devoted to influenza—and to all that influenza represented at the time both for Woolf and the larger culture.

REVEALING ILLNESS IN "ON BEING ILL"

Woolf published "On Being Ill" in 1926 in T. S. Eliot's journal *New Criterion*. She wrote the essay following the parade of influenza encounters I have described—as well as other illnesses—and during another lengthy sojourn in the sickroom after she had fainted at one of her sister's parties.[14] Meandering through a dizzying set of literary allusions and temporal leaps from the ice age to the end of the world, at its core the essay considers why illness is so consistently ignored in literature despite how radically sickness can alter one's perspective. She explores various reasons for the silence, making the case that the view from the sickroom can offer a wealth of new vistas and considering what would be necessary for representing illness accurately. Her argument that illness has been silenced in literature, though, doesn't apply to her works. She had treated illness directly and powerfully in her first novel, *The Voyage Out* (1915), and, as we will see, more subtly in *Mrs. Dalloway*. And as Susan Sontag reminds us, illness has long been a topic of literature, from tuberculosis to cancer.[15] What, then, does Woolf claim is missing? She suggests that the perspective of the ill body—and the way this perspective shapes what the world looks like—is glaringly absent and that illness is difficult to describe or incorporate into plot. These are, indeed, the very elements of illness Woolf had woven into *Mrs. Dalloway*. Her essay essentially offers a primer for reading her experimental novel.[16]

Even as she writes about the hidden qualities of illness in literature (and represents these qualities in her novel), Woolf deftly hides and reveals the biggest outbreak of illness since the plague. She talks repeatedly about influenza but not specifically about the devastating strain that had so recently overwhelmed the world. Influenza and indeed all the diseases she mentions are treated at the level of individual suffering, not as collective public tragedies. In places in the essay, her tone toward influenza seems flippant, recalling attitudes at the start of the pandemic, including hers. And yet, if we read the essay in the context of the previous chapters, the pandemic emerges everywhere: in the relationship Woolf draws between illness and war, in the reasons she offers for the repression of illness, in the challenges illness poses to representation, in the collective "we" of the essay and the delirious quality of its prose, and in the very aesthetic consolation that Woolf offers to counter the costs of illness. All these elements speak directly to the pandemic's impact, scope, and suffering, yet the pandemic's hidden quality at the same time enacts within the essay the very process of erasure that Woolf is discussing.

From the opening of the essay, Woolf draws a subtle parallel between war and disease, and she questions why illness receives so little attention:

Considering how common illness is, how tremendous the spiritual change that it brings, how astonishing, when the lights of health go down, the undiscovered countries that are then disclosed, what wastes and deserts of the soul a slight attack of influenza brings to light, what precipices and lawns sprinkled with bright flowers a little rise of temperature reveals, what ancient and obdurate oaks are uprooted in us in the act of sickness, how we go down into the pit of death and feel the waters of annihilation close above our heads and wake thinking to find ourselves in the presence of angels . . . when we think of this and infinitely more, as we are so frequently forced to think of it, it becomes strange indeed that illness has not taken its place with love, battle, and jealousy among the prime themes of literature.[17]

In detailing the vast impact of illness and its puzzling erasure, Woolf constructs a parallel between the devastation of illness and war, subtly equating the two cataclysmic events of the preceding years. The language is laced with an apocalyptic tone often tied to the Great War, harnessed here to describe illness. Influenza (even a slight case) reveals "wastes and deserts," producing a pathogenic no-man's-land, with uprooted trees, pits of death, precipices, and waters of annihilation. The "bright flowers" on the lawn recall the ubiquitous poppies (see "In Flanders Field"); the "lights of health" going down recall both the famous comment attributed to Sir Edward Grey at the start of the war, "The lamps are going out all over Europe,"[18] and also Woolf's own statement in her diary of 1917 that "the dipping down of the electric lights" before an air raid is "in future our warning."[19] As the essay continues, Woolf returns to battle imagery for illness, noting "those great wars which [the body] wages by itself . . . against the assault of fever."[20] By appropriating familiar tropes of the First World War and using them to describe illness, Woolf not only reminds us of the devastation illness may bring but also (intentionally or not) sets up a parallel (in terms of seriousness) between the Great War and the influenza pandemic. And while the language here and in the rest of the essay focuses on the individual's encounter with illness, Woolf continually implies the broad nature of the experience she traces: the commonness of illness and the "countries" it reveals. The collective voice—the "us" and "we" who speak throughout the essay—further suggests that she is evoking a widespread experience. Illness by its nature is a combination of general experiences—universal symptoms that define a particular disease—and also an utterly individual occurrence within a particular body.

At the same time, though, that she sets up a comparative link between illness and the war, her tone is flippant and dismissive, belying the gravity of the images. The vast changes she traces come from merely a "slight attack" of influenza and "a little rise" in temperature, and the sight of angels is revealed to be the prosaic dentist saying "rinse the mouth" (a reference to her own experience of getting her teeth extracted after her repeated bouts of influenza).[21] When she goes on to call for novels on influenza and "epic poems to typhoid," she continues this tone despite how grimly she viewed both diseases; her brother Thoby had died of typhoid in 1906.[22] Like her diary entries and letters regarding the pandemic, the tone suggests bravado, a wish, shared by the larger culture, to keep the grimness and seriousness of the topic at bay, to push against the knowledge even as she describes it. Indeed, much of the rest of the essay explores how difficult it is to find the right language to talk about illness at all, deeply engaging the representational challenges I trace throughout this study.

Woolf considers various reasons for the literary silence surrounding illness that echo the reasons for the pandemic's disappearance; these reasons in turn suggest the subtle differences between the tragedy of the war and the tragedy of the pandemic, despite the similarities in devastation and seriousness. First, Woolf suggests the private quality of illness and then offers three vague requirements to break the silence: "Those great wars which [the body] wages by itself, with the mind a slave to it, in the solitude of the bedroom against the assault of fever or the oncome of melancholia, are neglected. Nor is the reason far to seek. To look these things squarely in the face would need the courage of a lion tamer; a robust philosophy; a reason rooted in the bowels of the earth."[23] Woolf explicitly links the body's struggles to the great war(s), one fought, though, not in groups or against nations but individually, in solitude. Even a pandemic—by definition, a mass outbreak of illness—is made up of individual sufferers who, while all fighting a common enemy, are also fighting one specific to that body and completely internal to that body. The mind, Woolf says, is a "slave" to the body, trapped within and subject to the body's torments—and thus not entirely distinguishable. The body and mind might fight each other, but they are within the same territory, the battle hidden and the characters obscured. To break this silence and face "these things"—the entrapment, the isolation, the great wars, the assaults—would require a new body-centered vision: we would need, first, to possess the courage to face bodies that are wild, unpredictable, and dangerous (the lions); we would need, second, to have a "robust" philosophy, not the ivory-tower mentality she references in an earlier passage that ignores the body but one that would combine the cerebral life suggested by "philosophy" with the vitality of a healthy body. Finally, pushing against the way illness rips us up by the roots (like the earlier oak), we would need to root our reason in the body or in materiality more generally—in the very bowels of the earth.

Seeing illness, then, requires a new paradigm, a way of seeing the world through the body and acknowledging that the mind's perceptions are inextricably tangled with that body. Woolf attempted precisely this vision in *Mrs. Dalloway.* Here, though, she suggests all the elements that make representing this perspective so difficult: the body's unpredictable nature, its powerlessness, its isolation, and the knowledge that in this war, there are only solitary soldiers against encroaching, intangible enemies. Creating this body-centered vision faces familiar narrative and linguistic challenges:

More practically speaking, the public would say a novel devoted to influenza lacked plot; they would complain that there was no love in it. . . . Finally, among the drawbacks of illness as a matter for literature there is the poverty of the language. English . . . has no words for the shiver and the headache . . . language at once runs dry. There is nothing ready made for [the sufferer]. He is forced to coin words himself, and, taking his pain in one hand, and a lump of pure sound in the other . . . so to crush them together that a brand new word in the end drops out.[24]

Woolf might be describing her own early critics here, and her own achievements, as well as much of what we've observed about the pandemic. The pandemic did not lend itself to plot: the deaths did not fit into a story of love or heroism, and the tragedy seemed meaningless. On a more individual level, the experience of illness could seem unstructured, as Woolf indeed captures in the free-floating, mildly delirious quality of her essay and her jumps from topic to topic. Anticipating Elaine Scarry's observation that bodily pain breaks language into inarticulate sounds, Woolf describes how illness requires new words, ones created from a violent crushing together of pain and pure sound.[25]

Woolf also hints of a language issue that was specific to the pandemic and that contributes to its silencing even within her essay: the very word "influenza." As she notes, the phrase "I am in bed with influenza" doesn't begin to convey "the great experience; how the world has changed its shape." In addition to suggesting the depth of experience beneath an ordinary outbreak, the comment captures how the word "influenza" hid the pandemic experience on both the general and the individual level. Globally, the seriousness of the outbreak was missed, again and again, because "influenza" signified a familiar disease, the word failing to convey the carnage the pandemic produced that had, indeed, changed the shape of the world. On an individual level, Woolf describes how singular the experience is in ways that cannot be conveyed: "The experience," Woolf writes, "cannot be imparted and, as is always the way with these dumb things, [the ill person's] own suffering serves but to wake memories in his friends' minds of *their* influenzas, *their* aches and pains which went unwept last February, and now cry out, desperately, clamorously, for the divine relief of sympathy."[26] Woolf offers a picture of collective yet particular pain. Not only can the experience not be conveyed more universally, but it only serves to remind others that their pain wasn't appreciated, deepening both the universality of the experience and its paradoxical but accompanying isolation. Woolf's description embodies the landscape of vast, pandemic-level suffering, of desperate and clamorous voices calling out to be heard.

Woolf goes on to suggest the overwhelming grief of 1918, when the pandemic arrived—in the words of the London *Times*—after "our minds [were] surfeited with the horrors of war" and could not process the "catastrophe" of the flu.[27] When stricken with influenza, Woolf says,

sympathy we cannot have. Wisest Fate says no. If her children, weighted as they already are with sorrow, were to take on them that burden too, adding in imagination other pains to their own, buildings would cease to rise, roads would peter out into grassy tracks; there would be an end of music and of painting; one great sigh alone would rise to Heaven, and the only attitudes for men and women would be those of horror and despair.[28]

Woolf subtly suggests that after the war, sympathy for catastrophic illness was too much to expect. It would overburden and cripple the imagination, end creative endeavors, and leave only horror and despair. The culture had to turn away, Woolf hints, had to set aside pandemic illness in order to continue.

As many critics point out, though, "On Being Ill" is centrally concerned with the surprising benefits of illness—or at least, the wealth of visions that the view from the sickroom can afford. Jane Fisher, one of the few critics who links the essay and *Mrs. Dalloway* to the pandemic, explores at length the way the pandemic, despite its horrors, can offer women in particular unexpected freedoms and new creative energy, something Woolf certainly suggests about illness in her essay.[29] Illness, writes Woolf, can grant the invalid a kind of honesty, and the powers of observations change in the sickroom, producing what Hermione Lee has termed a "recumbent literature."[30] The sky, for example, becomes a "gigantic cinema," changing its shape and color incessantly; light, sounds, colors are experienced differently. Flowers, poems, and plays may all be seen with new eyes. Even words "seem to possess a mystic quality" in the sickroom.[31] Woolf uses the very novelty of this viewpoint to push against the silencing of illness, and in *Mrs. Dalloway*, she demonstrates the visions granted by illness through her portraits of both Clarissa and Septimus.

One of these visions in particular suggests a new aesthetics of consolation for the pandemic, one focused not around the creative spaces opened by illness but on Woolf's own creative reshaping of the pandemic. Both in her essay and in *Mrs. Dalloway*, she transforms one of the outbreak's central horrors—that it revealed an utterly indifferent nature, a violence so disenchanted as to defy meaning itself—into one of illness's comforting insights. As the invalid stares up at the sky, she or he can see that nature is both "divinely beautiful" and "divinely heartless," that it will go on well after we are gone: "It is only the recumbent who know what, after all, Nature is at no pains to conceal—that she in the end will conquer; the heat will leave the world" and all life will be wiped out. Nature's very "indifference" is what's "comforting";[32] in this vision, individual bodily suffering and the agonies of real and metaphoric hearts are replaced by something that is beautiful *because* it is heartless. Illness, Woolf suggests, allows the sufferer to see annihilation in this wider, more reassuring context. Rather than focusing on the destructive, uncaring, and nonhuman qualities of a virus infecting the individual body (and its hearts), the ill can see a conquering Nature that grants beauty now and victory "in the end" by excising the sufferer. Woolf translates Nature's indifference and its possibilities for pandemic-level annihilation from a horrifying spectacle to a special vision granted to the ill. She makes related, if somewhat bleaker moves in *Mrs. Dalloway*, granting voice to pandemic victims and suggesting ways to reimagine illness, even as she underscores the suffering.

REFRAMING *MRS. DALLOWAY*: TWO TRAGEDIES, TWO SURVIVORS

Frame 1: Septimus and War. Scholars have typically seen the war as the framing tragedy of *Mrs. Dalloway*, with the veteran Septimus Smith the key survivor and victim. War pervades the novel, occupying the thoughts of the characters, structuring the plot, and directing key elements of the critical conversation. Casualties from the battles punctuate the text (Mrs. Foxcroft's "nice boy"; Lady Bexborough's son, "John, her favourite," both "killed"),[33] and London seems saturated in flashbacks (the airplane, the backfiring car) that foreshadow future conflicts. Septimus is the epicenter of the war's presence, bringing the madness of battle and its lingering damage into central London. In creating her character, Woolf drew in part on her interactions with the war poet Siegfried Sassoon, who had survived the Western Front and remained haunted by his experiences.[34] Woolf depicts in Septimus a brutal portrait of the damage that war inflicted, from the romantic delusions that compelled men into battles for which they were unprepared, to the constant terror of injury and death that persisted long after the fighting, to the ensuing grief, guilt, and trauma that could tip them into madness. And by surrounding Septimus with noncombatants who primarily seem interested in forgetting the war, Woolf makes him both a central focus of the novel and an isolated, marginalized figure who stands out. Critics have exhaustively explored such features—what Sandra M. Gilbert and Susan Gubar have termed the "war-haunted" qualities of the novel—considering Septimus as a shell-shock victim, uncovering how violence infuses the text, and revealing the novel's battle-saturated atmosphere.[35]

Frame 2: Clarissa and the Pandemic. War, though, is not the primary frame for death in the novel, and Septimus is not the only survivor. Clarissa Dalloway is an obvious foil for Septimus—age to his youth, upper to his middle class, a society hostess to his social isolation, a civilian to his veteran status, and a woman rather than a man. But she is also a foil in another sense: She is a survivor of the other cataclysmic tragedy of the early twentieth century, a more hidden victim set against the better known and more public status of a surviving soldier. Clarissa has come close to dying from influenza, and her body still registers the virus's lingering damage. At the start of the novel, she is seen by Scrope Purvis pausing on a London street corner; she is pale, "Very white since her illness," her heart possibly compromised, "affected, they said, by influenza."[36] As the novel takes place in 1923, Clarissa could have been recovering from a more recent outbreak, but any reference to influenza in 1925—especially one with continued serious side effects—would have evoked the pandemic. Woolf was still plagued by heart issues from her own bouts with influenza during and after the pandemic. The pandemic link is easy to overlook for the same reasons the outbreak was initially dismissed: influenza is a familiar illness, and its unusual virulence was unexpected.

In Clarissa, Woolf grants a portrait of a *post*-pandemic survivor, focusing not on the pandemic's initial outbreak or the immediacy of the illness's acute phase but on the lingering aftermath. She creates, in effect, the body-centered vision (and a pandemic-centered one) she describes in "On Being Ill," showing how Clarissa's thoughts and her perceptions of London are shaped by her body and the continued effects of her illness. Woolf captures the way these effects start to become part of a naturalized environment, the precipitating cause gradually dissipating from memory. Clarissa's role as a pandemic survivor comes into sharper focus when viewed through the overt portrayals I explored in part 1. Like many of the characters in those accounts, Clarissa is caught in a state of living death, her body weakened, and her own agency diffuse. While at times she revels in the life and energy of the London day, her body is exhausted, and thoughts of death are never far from her mind. "Since her illness," she thinks, echoing Purvis, "she had turned almost white," as if she had died and become a ghost already, her sense of herself as a walking corpse anticipating Porter's Miranda, Wolfe's Ben, the father in Maxwell's novel, and so many other survivors.[37]

Woolf suggests that the bodily sense of living death had its architectural parallel in the sickroom. Connected to the life of the outside world through its windows and through the lights, sounds, and glimpses of sky that filter in, the sickroom is nevertheless a place of lurking death.[38] Such rooms mirror the liminal state of the ill body within them, one that is also on the threshold of life and death; the perspective of the space overlaps with the perspective of the body. The sickroom also occupies a strange twilight presence in memory: by its nature a space set apart, and thus easier to forget or ignore, its presence in memory at the time was also extraordinarily widespread. Infection rates during the pandemic were substantially higher than the death rates—in Britain, one-third of the population caught the flu—which suggests that memories of sickrooms, both isolated and crowded ones, were as pervasive as the lingering weakness and sense of living death the virus left behind.[39] Woolf chronicles this common experience, revealing how influenza remains a haunting presence, its sickroom fears experienced as flashback and its persistent physical effects shaping bodies and the material spaces they inhabit.

Clarissa's obligatory return to her room in the middle of the day, as her husband and her doctor mandate, reflects these architectural/body overlaps. Her corpselike body arrives at a house "cool as a vault." As she laboriously climbs the stairs to her room, she feels stretched, "suddenly shrivelled, aged, breastless . . . out of her body and brain which now failed." Her room in the attic, where her husband "insisted, after her illness, that she must sleep undisturbed," holds a twin-sized, coffin-like bed: "the sheet was stretched and the bed narrow"; Clarissa feels isolated, mounting "up into the tower alone" while others are "blackberrying in the sun." The door is shut, and the views are distant, and, like the sickroom that Woolf's describes in "On Being Ill," "the sounds came thin and chill."[40] The sickroom and body map on to each other, both caught between life and death. Clarissa's illness shapes how she sees and experiences this room, and conversely, the room shaped how she experienced her illness and now shapes how she experiences its aftermath. Embedded here is the way a traumatic memory might work: a temporal moment—the acute stage of her illness—remains spatially mapped onto her body and the room where the moment took place.

Clarissa's return to the sickroom also registers how influenza eroded both agency and narrative structure. While she may buy the flowers herself, Clarissa's days remain dictated by her illness (and her spouse). The isolation of her room suggests her exclusion from broader narratives of companionship or sexual unfolding—her bed holds only her; she feels aged and breastless: "It was all over for her." Her illness seems to have robbed her not only of agency and story but of her very body. Clarissa knows how invisible she is, how much this suffering remains concealed; she finds that "this body, with all its capacities, seemed nothing—nothing at all. She had the oddest sense of being herself invisible, unseen; unknown." In this portrait, Woolf references broader issues surrounding aging, but she maps them onto the way illness in particular is gendered and so often coded in terms of female weakness and dependency. Clarissa had just imagined, for example, the chronically ill Evelyn Whitbread in terms similar to the ones she uses for herself, as a "dried-up little woman." Lady Bruton, known for "talking like a man," is constantly exasperated by women who "got in their husbands' way" by needing "to be taken to the seaside in the middle of the session to recover from influenza,"[41] and Clarissa later feels she must hide her illness from Lady Bruton. Woolf registers this gendered quality but also brings illness out of isolation and hiding, representing in Clarissa the continued physical suffering of millions of flu victims.

The bodily impacts of influenza extend to Clarissa's emotions, with the lines between physical and mental health blurring in ways I consider at length with Septimus. Clarissa describes how she feels tormented by a specter since her influenza. Her language hints at mental instability, and Woolf suggests how such instability may both materialize a threat and affect the body. Clarissa notes her irrational hatred of her daughter's tutor, Miss Kilman, which she admits is fueled by many things, having grown larger than Miss Kilman herself: the hatred "had become one of those spectres with which one battles in the night; one of those spectres who stand astride us and suck up half our life-blood." These sorts of visitations have grown worse after her bout with influenza, becoming monsters and brutes that seem to prey upon her:

It rasped her, though, to have stirring about in her this brutal monster! . . . never to be content quite, or quite secure, for at any moment the brute would be stirring, this hatred, which, especially since her illness, had power to make her feel scraped, hurt in her spine; gave her physical pain, and made all pleasure in beauty, in friendship, in being well, in being loved and making her home delightful rock, quiver, and bend as if indeed there were a monster grubbing at the roots.[42]

Woolf describes the experience of hatred, fear, and insecurity that surely could come from many sources for Clarissa. But her language also offers a vivid picture of the dread and anxiety stemming from influenza, the sense that Clarissa could never again be secure "since her illness," that this shadowy monster might return at any time, a fear that was, as we've seen, pervasive after the pandemic. The specter endangered pleasure, beauty, friendship, health, and love; it rocked and bent the home itself, the foundational "roots" that Woolf notes illness may rip up in "On Being Ill." Woolf captures too how the pandemic's damage and the threat of its return lurked somewhat obscurely in the consciousness; the fear here is linked to the virus yet is also becoming suppressed, returning in nightmarish but shadowed terms as a specter or a monster. This monster, though, is not simply metaphorical: it has the power to scrape her spine, give her physical pain, distort her very reality, "as if indeed there were a monster." It embodies the effects of influenza on Clarissa's body, registering the potent mix of the inextricable physical and mental costs of illness. This specter is out for blood, anticipating the pandemic zombies I explore in the final chapter.

Woolf reveals how this post-pandemic suffering and sickroom perspective extends out into the streets, shaping the city in ways that are easy to miss when reading through a postwar lens. Woolf exposes how the tragedy continued to reverberate—and continued to be drowned out by the war and by the ineffable qualities of the virus. She repeatedly links, for example, the ringing of bells with Clarissa's influenza: "One feels even in the midst of the traffic, or waking at night, Clarissa was positive, a particular hush, or solemnity; an indescribable pause, a suspense (but that might be her heart, affected, they said, by influenza) before Big Ben strikes. There! Out it boomed. First a warning, musical; then the hour, irrevocable."[43] The language first suggests a silence—a hush or a pause or a suspense— something "indescribable" at any rate that extends both temporally and spatially: present both day and night, in public and at home. When sound arrives, it is ominous, first a warning, then an irrevocable tolling. The silence and the sound together connect to the fluttering heartbeat, raising the fear—or is it the anticipation?—that the heart might pause altogether. The language evokes symptoms and their diagnosis, the physician and patient listening for the heartbeat ("There!"). The passage links to the pandemic in both overt and subtle ways. Clarissa's influenza appears in a parenthetical aside, buried within a passage about a silence that stretches across time and space. The language suggests the pandemic's spectral presence, paradoxically hidden and silenced and yet omnipresent—and indeed manifesting within a kind of physical negation, in a pause of the damaged heart. A bell's tolling is a quintessential literary trope of death and time passing, elements Woolf is certainly gesturing to, but the ringing of bells, as I explore in the introduction and part 1, had special resonance in the post-pandemic moment. The letters from flu survivors repeatedly cite the burden of the ringing bells, which seemed to toll constantly during the pandemic.

Woolf registers in these bells not only actual sounds in the pandemic but also a sense of how grief and fear reverberate, like sound waves and the virus, through the bodies of the populace, becoming almost material. Once acknowledged, though, these emotions are pushed aside, and Clarissa moves to an ecstatic celebration of the London day and a declaration that "the War was over"—except for the mothers who continued to grieve for their sons.[44] Woolf suggests in this passage how even the war is starting to be evaded, and this evasion indeed further covers over the pandemic's lingering presence that nevertheless vibrates through bodies and permeates the atmosphere.

Later in the novel, Woolf creates another link between bells and Clarissa's influenza that this time highlights the position of a pandemic mourner, one who must witness the weakness and suffering of a loved one while coping with both denial and shock at a sudden death. The moment occurs in a thought monologue of Peter Walsh. Walking through the streets of London, Peter hears the bells of St. Margaret start to ring; he links the sound to a memory of Clarissa coming down the stairs, which grants him a surge of intense happiness. As he struggles to identify the place and time of the memory, though, thoughts of Clarissa's illness overtake him:

But what room? What moment? And why had he been so profoundly happy when the clock was striking? Then, as the sound of St. Margaret's languished, he thought, She has been ill, and the sound expressed languor and suffering. It was her heart, he remembered; and the sudden loudness of the final stroke tolled for death that surprised in the midst of life, Clarissa falling where she stood, in her drawing room. No! No! he cried. She is not dead![45]

As in the previous passage, influenza shows up in the pause—the silence, with its languishing quality, recalling for Peter Clarissa's illness, in an instant replacing his happiness with despair. The languor and suffering suggest both the condition of the flu victim and the grief of the loved one who watches. All at once, though, death arrives, both "sudden" and a "surprise[]," the bell's "final stroke" a death knell as he imagines Clarissa collapsing in her home. Like many mourners, he denies the death (paralleling characters from Wolfe, Porter, and Maxwell), but in Peter's case, he is right. Clarissa, though weakened, remains alive. While the passage incorporates the sense of bewildered denial perpetuated by the pandemic's unexpected strikes, Peter's fear also reflects the way the threat of sudden death had shifted into the domestic space, striking a woman at home in her drawing room. The possibility of such death is, obviously, present at all moments, but Peter's reaction offers a microcosm of how the pandemic's presence, here suggested by Clarissa's damaged heart, had produced a flood of such domestic shocks.

The damaged bodies that linger in Clarissa's London extend well beyond her own. On Clarissa's walk through the city, Woolf brings the reader to a broader literary tableau of death and grief, one that offers two representative corpses that haunted the cityscape at the time. As she walks down the street to buy the flowers for her party, Clarissa pauses to read a book in a store window display, a book open to a song about death from William Shakespeare's *Cymbeline*:

What was she trying to recover? What image of white dawn in the country, as she read in the book spread open:

Fear no more the heat o' the sun

Nor the furious winter's rages

This late age of the world's experience had bred in them all, all men and women, a well of tears.[46]

The imbedded quotation, which Clarissa will repeat to herself throughout the day, is apt on many levels. A funeral lament, it is sung over the bodies of two characters in Shakespeare's play: one decapitated in a fight, and one, Imogen, allegedly dead from illness—a fitting dichotomy for the two tragedies Woolf explores.[47] Imogen, however, is in fact in a living-death state brought on by a potion, so the comforting thought that she is now beyond the ravages of heat and cold will prove untrue. Like Clarissa and so many survivors, she will need to endure. Clarissa's ambiguous question about what she is trying to recover suggests not only her own (at least partial) recovery but a vague sense that something is missing that must be recovered—and that there is something that needs to be re-covered. Woolf offers an answer in the two bodies, a reminder of both tragedies but also a visual representation that they occurred side by side and that death encompassed women as well as men. And as the final line suggests, what is breeding out of this landscape is a grief and a danger that covers "all, all men and women," regardless of gender; this is not simply a postwar atmosphere but an atmosphere where death has come in many forms and where the sense of death has—like a contagion—blanketed the city itself.

A parallel scene offers a broader sickroom perspective and a heightened sense of the virus's spectral presence in the bodies, streets, and domestic spaces of the city. Woolf captures a moment repeated many times during the pandemic: the experience of hearing the street celebrations for Armistice while suffering from the virus or nursing those who were. Katherine Anne Porter's Miranda, in *Pale Horse, Pale Rider*, hears the end-of-war bells for Armistice from her hospital bed, and flu survivors frequently offer accounts of similar moments. One English survivor, for example, recalled being semiconscious from the virus, and "the first thing I remember was hearing the church bells of St. Andrew and St. Mary . . . ringing" to signal the end of the war.[48] Such moments held a discordant quality, the celebratory atmosphere contrasting sharply with the ongoing agonies of the sickroom.[49] In Woolf's depiction, the moment becomes both less overt than what Porter describes yet more universal, broadly suggesting the jarring crash of a public, spectacle-like military celebration with the private experience of illness and death. The moment occurs when Clarissa's daughter, Elizabeth—who has just been contemplating becoming a doctor, for "she liked people who were ill"[50]—is walking near St. Paul's:

The noise was tremendous; and suddenly there were trumpets . . . blaring, rattling about in the uproar; military music; as if people were marching; yet had they been dying—had some woman breathed her last and whoever was watching, opening the window of the room where she had just brought off that act of supreme dignity, looking down on Fleet Street, that uproar, that military music would have come triumphing up to him, consolatory, indifferent.

It was not conscious. There was no recognition in it of one's fortune, or fate, and for that very reason even to those dazed with watching for the last shivers of consciousness on the faces of the dying, consoling . . . this voice, pouring endlessly, year in year out, would take whatever it might be; this vow; this van; this life; this procession, would wrap them all about and carry them on, as in the rough stream of a glacier the ice holds a splinter of bone, a blue petal, some oak trees, and rolls them on.[51]

In the time scheme of the novel, this moment takes place in June 1923 (or perhaps simply in the narrator's mind, or Elizabeth's), but the juxtaposition of the military music, with people marching to loud trumpets and blaring sounds, while up in a sickroom a man watches a woman die (in another reversal of the typical gender roles in the war), recalls the repeated moments when the end of the war met the height of the flu. The military celebration is public, noisy, out on the streets; the sickroom is isolated, private, quiet, and personal, a more subtle version of the dichotomy William Maxwell traces between the war parades and the domestic stage for the flu. The woman's death is honored—it is a dignified death—yet the language hints that it is also ignored, in the conditional "had" of the first sentence, as if to blur the reality of the death. The noise or voice from outside is indifferent to the suffering within the sickroom. This very impersonal quality, though, is consoling, suggesting a welcome oblivion to personal tragedy, an unconscious juggernaut that takes an oak as easily as a petal, a splinter of bone along with a vow and a van, and rolls on. The indifference here links to the comforting indifference of nature Woolf notes in "On Being Ill" as one of the special realizations that illness may bestow. The atmosphere also parallels the quiet bewilderment and surrender we see in the overt pandemic accounts—there's little attempt to figure out an answer, to puzzle through the bitter contradictions inherent in the Armistice celebrations alone, and then also in the juxtaposition of those celebrations to the countless sick and dying from the pandemic. What could one say? The experience seems beyond reconciliation. Woolf creates a record of the juxtaposition and the sense of being overwhelmed by the "rough stream" of these contradictions. Woven in to her account are also suggestions of why the flu becomes hidden in cultural memory. The quietness of the woman's death in the room above, achieved, at least, with "supreme dignity," has little chance of being heard and remembered in the noisy and public commotion below. Woolf records the silence surrounding this death while nevertheless making it visible within her own cultural narrative.

The various ways influenza continues to reverberate in Clarissa's body and within the city suggest how, as Woolf writes in "On Being Ill," an attack of influenza may make "the world . . . change[] its shape."[52] In the essay, she hints that this shape change may grant new ways of seeing the world that are beneficial. Implicit within this claim is the idea that the imagination—or artistic responses—may also transform the way we see illness. In *Mrs. Dalloway*, Woolf experiments with the ways this might happen, offering moments when contagion in particular is reimagined in ways that grant representation and at times consolation. In several passages of the novel, Woolf crafts metaphors that suggest an invisible presence blanketing the public spaces of London. The ambiguity of the images suggests a potentially positive force—something that connects rather than simply infects—an imaginative re-creation of infection that transforms it into something less threatening. Woolf's repeated metaphors also offer potentially helpful ways to visualize an invisible threat, to reflect in language the ineffable ways an entity living in one body may transfer into another, changing those bodies in profound but largely unrepresented ways. Naturally, these metaphors speak to many experiences, but Woolf's language encodes some of the representational difficulties that the flu (and illness in general) presented and finds a way to represent them anyway. For example, she describes the invisible force that extends from the car of perhaps the queen or the prime minister (no one is sure) in Bond Street, leaving "a slight ripple which flowed through glove shops and hat shops. . . . Something so trifling in single instances that no mathematical instrument . . . could register the vibration; yet in its fulness rather formidable and in its common appeal emotional; for in all the hat shops and tailors' shops strangers looked at each other and thought of the dead."[53] Woolf is certainly speaking of the war here and of the way a sense of blind, undefined nationalism can fuel its cause, but she also constructs an image that speaks to the way a virus might move—and be remembered: silently, trifling in these small expressions and unable to be detected, but formidable and finally flooding everywhere, bringing death to everyone's mind.

In a related metaphor, Woolf's image of the webs that connect people to one another suggests a more material presence for contagion. The image captures the odd overlap and blending of personalities that can happen when people have gathered together; it also speaks to the way infection moves. Richard Dalloway and Hugh Whitbread walk away from Lady Bruton, and as

they went further and further from her, being attached to her by a thin thread (since they had lunched with her) which would stretch and stretch, get thinner and thinner as they walked across London; as if one's friends were attached to one's body, after lunching with them, by a thin thread, which (as she dozed there) became hazy with the sound of bells, striking the hour or ringing to service, as a single spider's thread is blotted with rain-drops, and, burdened, sags down. So she slept.[54]

These threads that connect people even as they walk away offer a powerful image of a contagion passing from person to person (and moving across London). This image mingles, then, with the figure of the sleeper and with the sense of the bells that themselves recall the pandemic and reflect the invisible forces that can move across a city. The troubling sense that these webs may be "blotted" and "burdened" with raindrops hints both at an ominous connection and one that threatens to sever connection itself. In "On Being Ill," Woolf had drawn on similar imagery to describe how the Victorian family worked: "It was a web, a net, spreading wide and enmeshing every sort of cousin and dependant, and old retainer."[55] In both passages, the web serves as a metaphor for how people influence one another and suggests a creative reenvisioning of how contagion might move.

Clarissa brings such imagery into her musings on the afterlife in ways that imaginatively transform the pandemic's vaporous presence into something more positive. As we've seen with the authors in part 1, tropes of resurrection could both counter and evoke the pandemic's representational challenges, and Woolf draws on similar imagery to represent and recast the flu's invisible threat and its challenge to bodily agency. Indeed, in "On Being Ill," Woolf muses on how illness makes "even the recumbent" think about "the universal hope—Heaven, Immortality."[56] As Clarissa wanders down Bond Street, she finds that her memories of illness and near-death turn her thoughts to the afterlife. Unlike the moment when she climbs the stairs to her attic room, thinking grimly of her shriveled body's invisibility, here she imagines her dissolving body in a more positive light:

Did it matter then, she asked herself, walking towards Bond Street, did it matter that she must inevitably cease completely; all this must go on without her; did she resent it; or did it not become consoling to believe that death ended absolutely? but that somehow in the streets of London, on the ebb and flow of things, here, there, she survived, Peter survived, lived in each other, she being part, she was positive, of the trees at home; . . . part of people she had never met; being laid out like a mist between the people she knew best, who lifted her on their branches as she had seen the trees lift the mist, but it spread ever so far, her life, herself.[57]

Clarissa at first finds comfort in imagining that death ends her self completely, wondering if death might come as a welcome relief (a thought, as we've seen, on many minds at the time). And yet, she goes on to imagine a diffuse kind of survival, one based in blending and continuity, as if particles of the self might continue on in the very streets of London. She envisions precisely how the pandemic virus moved, attaching itself to objects, drifting through the air like mist and becoming part of the body, only to spread to new bodies (both strangers and friends) and find new life there. The language transforms contagion, recasting it as a kind of immortality for the self, an anti-flu miasma that connects rather than infects. She animates the dead and reinvents the mode of living death, with the emphasis on the living. The quintessentially Woolfian sentence structure supports this vision, tying different clauses together with a semicolon, the punctuation mark, we might say, of living death, hinting at a sense of ending yet also of continuity and connection.

Repositioning Clarissa as a pandemic survivor subtly shifts the terrain of both *Mrs. Dalloway* and the era. Within the novel, the body's often quiet and private battles with illness maintain their hidden qualities while simultaneously emerging as central to this cultural moment—representing one half of the era's two cataclysms. When we see Clarissa's experience as both singular and widespread, as both particular to her and representative of millions of suffering bodies, we can recover the way the aftermath of a pandemic outbreak registers differently than a war, changing everything yet lying apart from the more structured, visible histories left by more public battles. Mass illness leaves separate traces and represents an alternative history, one experienced as an individual bodily cataclysm that unfolds—privately—everywhere. Woolf's modernist prose grants a new and dexterous way to register this history, tracing how the body's sensations slide into words and perceptions, how emotions shift the body's responses, how the spectral presence of an almost lethal illness alters the very way one walks down a street. In these techniques, Woolf creates the aesthetic superstructure the moment demanded, one capable of registering the subterranean interplay of illness and the body and of capturing a historical event so pervasive that it disappeared even as it continued to shape perception, alter time, and change the very terrain of the city.

REFRAMING SEPTIMUS: TWO TRAGEDIES, NO SURVIVORS

Frame 3: Having positioned Clarissa and Septimus as representative survivors of two separate tragedies, I now adjust the frame again to consider how these two events also collided within individual bodies. In Septimus, Woolf depicts a war veteran, but she also embodies a key element of the post-1918 world, subtly representing the cumulative blows the previous years had delivered worldwide. While for most of this study I emphasize the distinctions between the war and the pandemic, the physical and psychological impacts of these two events did not fall neatly onto separate populations. Soldiers were infected at extraordinary rates in the pandemic, and, as Porter and Cather remind us, the trauma of one became entangled with the trauma of the other. Septimus suggests a physical embodiment of these intersecting traumas, his own body a hidden history of the accumulating costs of war, of illness, and of the psychological impacts they both produced. Alongside his shell shock, Septimus experiences extreme versions of Clarissa's sickroom memories, ones that echo passages from "On Being Ill" and Woolf's personal knowledge of influenza and of the overlaps among different physical states. His haunting sense of being a walking corpse and of seeing his friend Evans return from the dead arise from his war experiences, and they also echo the delirious visions of physical and mental illness more generally, experiences the pandemic produced everywhere. Septimus unites the bodily costs of these years, costs that in turn highlight how physical and psychological illness may blur together and shape perception. Before turning to Septimus directly, I introduce the surprising overlaps between mental health and the pandemic.

The Pandemic and Mental Health

The shell shock and mental anguish the First World War inflicted is well documented in both the criticism and fiction about the war. What's less well known, however, is how this particular influenza virus could cause an astonishing range of psychological damage, from delirium (which one might expect) to psychoses (which one might not). Even before the pandemic, doctors had observed the high incidence of nervous system disorders that the ordinary influenza virus could produce; as Sir William Osler noted in the then well-known 1915 edition of *Principles and Practice of Medicine*, "almost every form of disease of the nervous system may follow influenza," and doctors frequently cited this remark when reporting on the psychiatric issues produced by the 1918 pandemic.[58] Edwin O. Jordan wrote in a 1927 survey, *Epidemic Influenza*, that Osler's observations had certainly "been substantiated in the [pandemic] outbreak." From fever delirium to full-blown psychoses, Jordan observed, "there is no doubt that the neuropsychiatric effect of influenza are profound and varied."[59] One of Virginia Woolf's early doctors (whom she brutally satirized in *Mrs. Dalloway*), Sir George Savage, noted in 1919 that influenza could "originate any form of insanity" and was the infectious disease "most likely to be followed by mental disorder."[60] Woolf's doctor at the time of the pandemic warned her repeatedly about the damage to the nervous system the virus could do, as I quoted at the chapter's opening. "There would appear," summarized London scientists in 1934, "to be no doubt that influenza exerts a profound influence on the nervous system."[61]

The types of psychiatric disorders after influenza varied. One of the most frequently cited studies was by Karl A. Menninger. In 1919, Menninger published the results of his research into the link between mental health and the pandemic influenza in patients at the Boston Psychopathic Hospital. He found that the disorders fell into four groups: delirium, dementia praecox (what doctors would now call schizophrenia), other psychoses, and unclassified, with dementia praecox being the most common type. As Menninger observed, though, the hospital likely saw fewer delirium patients, as these individuals rarely ended up at the psychopathic hospital. In all the categories, he noted that "delusions and hallucinations are the most common symptoms," affecting all the dementia praecox and delirium cases and "two-thirds of the remaining cases." One "representative" patient, he writes,

"suddenly became excited and rushed from her bed into the street, scream-
ing," and seemed "bewildered, deluded and hallucinated." Some of the
patients had symptoms before contracting influenza or had family members with disorders, though others did not; Menninger concluded that "the
influenza acts in two ways: as an inciting factor for a process not previously
manifest; and as an exciting factor for rendering visible a previously latent
or semilatent process." While Menninger reported that "depression is traditionally the postinfluenzal symptom *par excellence*," it was less dominant
for the patients he observed.[62] Other doctors, though, were reporting high
rates of depression following this flu.[63] Suicide rates also appeared to
increase after the virus had struck; in a more recent statistical case study,
I. M. Wasserman concluded that while the war in the United States "did
not influence suicide; the Great Influenza Epidemic caused it to increase."[64]
Current researchers have proposed links between influenza—in particular
the H1N1 strain that produced the 1918 pandemic and the 2009 swine flu
outbreak—to various psychiatric issues, including schizophrenia, depression, suicidal tendencies, and mania, with some of these disorders found
in the offspring of women who contracted the flu while pregnant. [65] And
in 1918 and 1919, cases of post-influenza mental health issues were not isolated; John Barry confirms in *The Great Influenza* that the psychiatric
impacts reported from the flu stretched throughout Europe and America
and included psychoses, depression, and hallucinatory delirium.[66]

Case studies and individual accounts of the pandemic are full of examples of the flu causing violent derangement, hallucinations, and suicidal
depression. In stories of violent reactions, for example, the London *Times*
of 1918 noted (surprisingly sympathetically) that Leonard Sitch, head baker
in Stowmarket, Suffolk, and a well-respected citizen, became violent after
contracting the flu, stabbing and smashing the heads of his wife and two
children during his illness before hanging himself.[67] The article made clear
in its subheading that the violence was attributable to "An Attack of Influenza," casting the virus, rather than the baker, as the perpetrator. Another
witness to the violence was W. F. Eaton, who noted that during his time at
Loxworth Hospital Liverpool patients were dying as "fast as they came in,"
and "They were in such a state some almost mad they had to strap them to
their bed" because "they put razors on the broom handles and chased people."[68] One survivor from Virginia tells how her father, in a flu-induced
delirium, had grabbed her, thinking she was "a wild cat . . . attacking his

family," and was about to throw her in the fire when the mother intervened just in time.[69] A doctor from Berlin recalled that "It was necessary to tie [flu victims] to their beds to prevent them from hurting themselves as they threw themselves about."[70] The violence represented by these cases reflects a strange, literal agency, as the nonhuman destruction the flu wreaked within the body transfers into—and produces—a human-based violence in the world. I investigate at length the difference among such forms of violence in chapter 6.

Survivors also routinely reported on the delirium the flu could produce. Dorothy E. Jack recalled "having a very high temperature and we were all delirious, having terrible nightmares."[71] Eric Newell, who was at a boys' school in Canterbury, noted that when dorms had to be turned into hospital wards, he was relieved to get a bed next to a "sane" boy, as "all the beds seemed to be occupied by boys in various stages of delirium."[72] Hilda Toone, who recalled the hellish sights in the pandemic, when it "was nothing to see piles of coffins and people being buried in the hundreds," reported that "Delirium prevailed and comas."[73] And the hallucinations that could arise during these episodes included virus-induced images of resurrection. A. M. Spark, for example, remembered that during her case, "in delirium, I always saw my brother in his uniform at the foot of my bed. He was an officer in the Gordon Highlanders and had been killed, in active service, in July 1917."[74] As I detailed in chapter 2, Katherine Anne Porter's *Pale Horse, Pale Rider* offers a long, hallucinatory section on the delirium the main character experiences during her bout with the flu, believing she sees her boyfriend— who dies in the pandemic—shot with arrows and then rising repeatedly, "in a perpetual death and resurrection."[75] Such hallucinations involving soldiers suggest in part the intertwined quality of the war and the pandemic and also the complicated layers of survivor's guilt that the war could produce in those suffering in the influenza outbreak.

The high rates of depression and suicide after the pandemic are likewise confirmed in the personal stories of survivors. Frederick Bebbington, who was in the RAF and stationed at Blandford Camp in Dorset, writes, "I remember the huge number of men down with, and who died of flu[;] a small wood below the camp was called 'suicide wood' because of the number of men, who had flu, committing suicide there. The flu seemed to leave people with distracted minds."[76] Philip Learoyd recalled the grim atmosphere at his school, where so many were dangerously ill; the atmosphere, he said, "reduced the inevitable post-influenza depression to almost suicidal depths."[77] E. Philips Cole remembered two nurses ended up "in a mental home" after their bouts with the illness.[78] And sometimes it was difficult to distinguish between the depression that inevitably follows so many deaths and the depression left by the virus; Marie Svenningsen recalled how one woman who caught the flu and whose sister died in the pandemic "turned mad, and spent several years just looking out of one specific window in her home."[79]

One well-known pandemic survivor, Edvard Munch, captured in paint the mental devastation of this strain of influenza. Munch, who lost a close friend in the pandemic, only barely made it through his own case.[80] He created two paintings as he recovered that make visible the hallucinatory and depressive states the pandemic could produce. Munch, already subject to mental health issues, first offered the haunting *Self-Portrait with Spanish Flu* (figure 4.1). A seated, hollow-eyed figure turns toward the viewer, a bed extending across the horizontal plane of the canvas, almost like an extension of the subject. The face recalls Munch's famous images of *The Scream*: the eyes are circles, the face angular yet distended, and the mouth a round O. This open mouth, though, gives the impression not of someone in mid-scream but of someone too exhausted to yell or even to close his mouth. The figure is wrapped in dark, featureless blankets, and one critic, James C. Harris, observes that the blanket on the bed looks crumpled and "suggests his tossing and turning in bed"; both the walls and the subject's face are alight with red in the original painting, evoking a feverous burning. [81] As with Clarissa, the sickroom reflects the body's anguish, with Munch's experimental techniques capturing the bodily experiences of this flu in both the figure and the room. Hints of delirium abound: shapes seem indistinct, depths are flattened out, and a hallucinatory atmosphere broods over the painting. The face is only suggested, its features blurred and the figure blended into the surroundings, indicating the loss of agency that attends this illness. The subject seems to embody a viral, living-death resurrection, the figure corpselike yet also alive. In a second painting, *Self-Portrait After the Flu* (figure 4.2), Munch offers another figure of living death, but one suggesting the flu's depressive aftermath. The hallucinatory atmosphere fades: the figure and the objects are more distinct and less abstract, as if the painter's eyes have come more fully into focus. The delirium, though, gives way to enervation. The figure stares hauntingly at the viewer, his eyes rimmed

FIGURE 4.1. Edvard Munch, *Self-Portrait with the Spanish Flu*, oil on canvas, 1919, National Museum of Art, Architecture and Design, Oslo, Norway. *Source*: Jacques Lathion, © National Museum of Art, Architecture and Design (NG.M.01867; PE0495), Oslo, Norway. © 2018 Artists Rights Society (ARS), New York. Creative Commons License: cc-by-nc, Nasjonalmuseet/Lathion, Jacques, non-commercial.

in shadow and his red, mottled, swollen skin suggesting that the fever lingers. The anguished animation and pain of the earlier face is replaced by the eerie stillness and hopelessness of the second; the fire is out. The figure is dressed in black, a marked contrast to the light behind him, as if the room has recovered more fully than he has.

FIGURE 4.2. Edvard Munch, *Self-Portrait After Spanish Influenza*, oil on canvas, 1919, Munchmuseet, Oslo, Norway. *Source:* © Munchmuseet CC BY 4.0 Munchmuseet. https://creativecommons.org /licenses/by/4.0/. © 2018 Artists Rights Society (ARS), New York.

In Woolf's own life, influenza blurred with mental health issues on various levels. Her first serious mental breakdown occurred after her mother's death from complications including influenza, and her own frequent bouts of influenza often overlapped with anxiety and depression, helping forge an association between the two.[82] As we've seen, Woolf noted in 1918 that her doctor lectured her "every day" about the connections between "influenza and the nervous system."[83] After Fergusson and her other doctors concluded her encounters with influenza had weakened her heart, Woolf wrote that her "eccentric pulse had passed the limits of reason & was in fact insane," the pulse taking sentient form and blending physical and mental illness.[84] Woolf's constant high temperatures, labeled "influenza" by her doctors, caused her to have three teeth removed in 1922 in the hopes that it might eradicate pockets of infection; pushed by Dr. George Savage, the treatment was, as Hermione Lee notes in her biography of Woolf, "also a recommended treatment for 'insanity.'"[85] After a later bout of influenza, Woolf observed that "influenza has a special poison for what is called the nervous system," requiring her to take to her bed and "lie still."[86] While these influenza attacks were mostly outside the pandemic, they nevertheless forged a connection between influenza and mental health issues that dovetailed with a defining feature of the pandemic. More generally, throughout Woolf's life, physical illness coincided with psychological disruptions; as Lee observes, for Woolf, "severe physical symptoms signaled and accompanied phases of agitation or depression."[87]

A Composite Septimus

The psychological impacts of influenza that I summarize above fell on bodies already worn down by the mental health issues the war produced, from shell shock to grief to survivor's guilt. And the flu's physical impacts fell on bodies physically weakened by combat and wartime scarcity. Even before the war and the pandemic, many bodies, like Woolf's own, were already struggling with health issues of many kinds. Conveying the post-1918 landscape required not simply representing the war's costs, or shell shock, or even the pandemic and the wider suffering of disease, but the experiential reality of these cumulative and intersecting blows.[88] Septimus is both soldier and mourner, both survivor and patient; he is psychologically damaged from the war but also in ways that echo the sickroom experiences of the flu victims described earlier and of Clarissa and Woolf herself. Septimus embodies the multiple traumas of the moment, his body and his perceptions a swirling mix of the violence of war and illness, of the overlapping mental and physical damage each tragedy inflicted, and the way mental and physical illness are so often inextricably linked.

In conveying Septimus's experience, Woolf draws on what I term a hallucinatory-delirium mode, a mode that also infuses the works of Eliot and Yeats that I discuss in the following chapters. The mode suggests the mingled realities of the war and the pandemic and the way these experiences could fragment and distort perception. It simultaneously speaks to multiple times and traumas: to the immediate, often hallucinatory experiences of combat and to the acute stages of flu delirium as well as to the longer-term psychological distortions both the war and the pandemic could produce. At the same time that Woolf showcases the delusional qualities of these visions, she also suggests how they arise from actual bodily experiences in both illness and war and how these delusions are experienced as real by the sufferer. Like Clarissa, though in more dramatic form, Septimus reveals the ways these accumulating bodily experiences shape perception and reality, granting some benefits but also extracting enormous costs.

Septimus's everyday experiences reflect this blend of bodily traumas, fusing war memories, sickroom perspectives, and mental and physical sensations. As he sits on a bench in Regent's Park, his reality is grounded in the hallucinatory-delirium mode:

He lay resting, waiting. . . . He lay very high, on the back of the world. The earth thrilled beneath him. Red flowers grew through his flesh. . . . Music began clanging against the rocks up here. It is a motor horn down in the street, he muttered; but up here it cannoned from rock to rock, divided, met in shocks of sound which rose in smooth columns . . . and became an anthem, an anthem twined round now by a shepherd boy's piping. . . .

But he himself remained high on his rock, like a drowned sailor on a rock.[89]

Septimus feels outside the world, yet sounds filter to him, turning car horns into music, which morphs into columns, and then into an anthem and a boy's piping. His sense of his body is hallucinatory, with flowers growing through flesh, an image that reads as metaphoric to the reader but that is experienced as real by Septimus. The language hints of war and mourning: the cannon sounds; the red, poppy-like flowers; the anthems. It also parallels the sickroom perspective Woolf outlines in "On Being Ill":

"I am in bed with influenza,"—but what does that convey of the great experience; . . . the tools of business grown remote; the sounds of festival become romantic like a merry-go-round heard across far fields; the friends have changed, some putting on a strange beauty, others deformed to the squatness of toads, while the whole landscape of life lies remote and fair, like the shore seen from a ship far out at sea, and he is now exalted on a peak and needs no help from man or God, and now grovels supine on the floor glad of a kick from a housemaid.[90]

In both passages, the subjects undergo the radical shifts in distance and place Woolf finds indicative of the sickroom, with reality telescoping from exalted peaks to floors and park benches. Sounds from the outer world drift into the subjects' minds. The parallels between the passages—and their perspectives—position Septimus as a shell-shocked soldier and as a figure who suggests broader experiences of illness, both mental and physical, and the ways all these experiences combine to shape the experience of reality. His bodily sensations position him in multiple times and places, his perception reflecting both the immediacy of delirium and the hallucinatory aftermath of traumatic experience. There's also a change in intensity between the two passages that speaks to Septimus's position as a composite sufferer. In the essay passage, Woolf hints at delirium in the deforming friends and the shifting sense of place and emotions, though both descriptions could be taken metaphorically. In the novel passage, the metaphors become literal, as the reader is thrust into Septimus's reality: for him, flowers grow through flesh, sounds transform into shape, and his body occupies multiple planes. The world has changed, remade through trauma and illness, showcasing what happens to the body, the mind, and language both in the midst of catastrophic breakdown and in the aftermath of traumatic experience.

As the passage continues, Septimus embodies another melding indicative of the hallucinatory-delirium mode, one we have seen throughout this study: the widespread sense of living death experienced by soldiers but also by Woolf in the aftermath of her flu, and by Clarissa, by Porter's Miranda, by Maxwell's father character, and by Wolfe's Ben and his family. Septimus sees himself as "a drowned sailor on a rock. I leant over the edge of the boat and fell down, he thought. I went under the sea. I have been dead, and yet am now alive, but let me rest still; he begged." On multiple levels, the description is both delusional and experiential. On the one hand, Septimus unites the acute phases of delirium, the sense of being subsumed or drowned (the "pit of death" and the "waters of annihilation" Woolf describes in "On Being Ill,"), as well as the enervated aftermath of the post-1918 moment, when bodies seemed caught in a threshold world of life and death. On the other hand, the drowning imagery is not simply hallucinatory or metaphoric. It hints of actual threats to the body present in both tragedies: in the war, sailors drowned at sea, and massive rains—or floods of dirt from explosions—could drown soldiers in the trenches; in the flu, as we've seen repeatedly, victims drowned in fluids in their beds. He also fears that he and the world might "burst into flames," that "the flesh was melted off the world," and that "his body was macerated until only the nerve fibres were left."[91] These fears are again both hallucinatory and experiential, making visible the body's pain and actual threats to those bodies: the real chance in the war that your world would burst into flames and your flesh would be melted, and the real chance in the pandemic that a burning fever would dissolve the self—with the intertwined senses of delirium and mental disruption these experiences also produced. Woolf may not have had either the pandemic or the war in her mind as she wrote, but Septimus nevertheless channels a subterranean bodily history, one where actual bodily threats, like drowning and burning, meld into (and even produce) a hallucinatory-delirium reality.

One of Septimus's most startling delusions is his repeated sense that his friend Evans, who was killed in the war, has returned. These moments of imagined resurrection suggest shell shock but also the vast landscape of accumulating grief, guilt, delusion, and trauma that the combined blows of these years produced. Septimus's visions of Evans also allow us to see how war resurrections melded into viral ones. In both tragedies, such visions could seem real and could take place along what we might term a resurrection continuum: on the one end, intrusive thoughts of the dead could invade present thoughts; a shade closer to reality, repeated nightmares and dreams of the dead could haunt or tantalize survivors; and at the far end of the spectrum, delirium and hallucinations could make it seem that the dead had actually returned. As has been well documented, the war's mental afflictions created constant experiences of this very continuum. W. H. R. Rivers, one of the central doctors treating shell shock, for example, detailed the patients' relentless and vivid nightmares of the dead returning, often with mangled bodies; after treatment, these dreams could morph into the dead returning with comfort for the sufferer and with bodies repaired.[92] Siegfried Sassoon and Wilfred Owen, both treated by Rivers, wove such experiences into their poetry. Sassoon, in "Repression of War Experience," depicts the intrusive-thought end of the spectrum, as a returned soldier sits at twilight trying desperately to keep his thoughts from war but constantly pulled to the sensory reminders of battle and the "crowds of ghosts among the trees."[93] Wilfred Owen offers the other end of the spectrum in "Mental Cases," a poem where soldiers driven insane by the carnage see the dead forever; in a perverse kind of resurrection, the dead who return are nothing but bones and flesh and blood.[94] Such accounts were common, as the critic Jay Winter has detailed.[95] Since Woolf likely based Septimus in part on Sassoon, she may well have had such experiences in mind.

As we have seen, imagined resurrections were intrinsic to the pandemic experience and within pandemic literature as well. In part, the viral resurrections I explored in Porter, Wolfe, and Maxwell and in the accounts of delirious flu victims seeing visions of the dead speak to particular elements of the pandemic experience: the delirium of the acute phase or the mental instability of the aftermath, the pervasive sense of contagion guilt, the fear the virus might return, and so on. While distinct, these viral resurrections also combined with an existing war environment and share broader characteristics of the experiences described by Rivers, Owen, and Sassoon, including the hallucinatory reality and the haunting sense that bodies were everywhere. The pandemic, in other words, introduced new burdens but also intensified existing ones. Woolf already establishes through Clarissa how the lurking dead—and the living dead—in London suggest influenza victims as well as war victims, reflecting a legion of ghosts hidden not just by being dead (or almost dead) but by being forgotten and ignored. Septimus's visions of Evans speak to war traumas, and they also suggest this broader environment and the mental health issues the traumas of the era produced. The profound grief and guilt that help trigger Septimus's vision of his friend resonate across the tragedies, a way both to find consolation and to make material and visible the loss. Such visions hint of repeating, overlapping narratives unfolding everywhere: mourners who were also survivors, haunted by the dead and struggling both physically and mentally.

A representative moment of Evans's return grants an illustration of these cumulative blows. Septimus is sitting in Regent's Park when he sees Evans approach; language, illness, hallucination, and Evans seem to meld into a physical, material form:

The word "time" split its husk; poured its riches over him; and from his lips fell like shells, like shavings from a plane, without his making them, hard, white, imperishable words, and flew to attach themselves to their places in an ode to Time; an immortal ode to Time. He sang. Evans answered from behind the tree. The dead were in Thessaly, Evans sang, among the orchids. There they waited till the War was over, and now the dead, now Evans himself—

"For God's sake don't come!" Septimus cried out. For he could not look upon the dead.

But the branches parted. A man in grey was actually walking towards them. It was Evans! But no mud was on him; no wounds; he was not changed.[96]

Suggestions of war are woven throughout the passage: words fall "like shells," the word "plane" hints at war planes, and Septimus is surprised to see Evans with "no mud" and "no wounds" when he was killed in the war; the scene echoes the soldier's experiences in both Owen's and Sassoon's poems. And yet, the passage narrates other burdens and stories too. It evokes Woolf's own confrontation with mental illness unconnected to the war; in the midst of one hallucinatory episode, she thought she heard birds speaking in Greek outside her window, suggested here by Evans's singing and the reference to Thessaly.[97] Septimus's language resembles a fever delirium and the extended mental instability the pandemic virus could produce on top of the war's damage. And the terrible fear that the dead were waiting until the war was over and were now coming into London narrates how such inchoate fears were literally realized with the pandemic's arrival. Overwhelmed, Septimus transforms into a universal figure, "the giant mourner," overseeing how "the millions lamented."[98]

Septimus's suicide scene, which contains the last vision of the resurrected Evans, brings together the intersecting, accumulating layers of mental and physical disruptions. At first, Septimus embodies the sickroom invalid that Woolf describes in her essay. He lies "on the sofa in the sitting-room," watching the patterns of light outside the window.[99] Septimus's senses are heightened to the beauty of the light and trees, and sounds from outside filter into the room, reaching him as from a distant shore. Despite the enhanced perspective his illness allows (and as Woolf describes in "On Being Ill"), Septimus struggles to hold on to reality—to see as they are the objects and the other person (Rezia) who occupy the space with him. He drifts in and out of this reality, at times noting the various objects and enjoying their solidity and their constancy. And yet, he also drifts into hallucinatory visions suggesting delirium and flashback. The experience is one of both unreality and material reality—and of the mind's inextricable incorporation within the body. He struggles to stay in the present, but his knowledge that his vision can warp at any moment haunts him. Woolf's tableau—where an ill individual lies on a sofa, looking at a woman sewing—echoes out in memory to millions of homes where individuals had struggled to recover from both war and plague, working, as Septimus does, to parse the reality from the distortions:

He shaded his eyes so that he might see only a little of her face at a time, first the chin, then the nose, then the forehead, in case it were deformed, or had some terrible mark on it. But no, there she was, perfectly natural, sewing . . . there was nothing terrible about it, he assured himself . . . for what was frightening or disgusting in her as she sat there in broad daylight, sewing? . . . Why then rage and prophesy? Why fly scourged and outcast? . . . Miracles, revelations, agonies, loneliness, falling through the sea, down, down into the flames, all were burnt out.[100]

Septimus fears Rezia's face will morph into something terrifying, the language suggesting both delirium and traumatic flashback. His fears reflect the literal experiences of those who witnessed the war's atrocities and the virus's ravages. The war routinely deformed faces and left terrible marks, and it routinely sent men to fiery deaths; the pandemic altered women's and men's bodies grotesquely, turning the skin purple and inflicting burning fevers. As Woolf notes in "On Being Ill," illness may distort faces, allowing some to put on "a strange beauty" and "others [to] deform[] to the squatness of toads," and while she in part means a metaphoric shift in vision, she also suggests the visual distortions brought by illness.[101] In Septimus's vision of Rezia, Woolf encodes these elements and the way a past reality can superimpose itself on a present moment. In the war and the pandemic, one's worst nightmares could come true.

The scene is again haunted by Evans, evoking the way the war's memory overlays London, even far from the battlefield, and, in his presence in the sitting room (and in the park and in the street), the way the dead spread during the pandemic from the front lines into the city and the domestic space. Like so many people in the wake of such mass death, Septimus is struck by a sense that the threshold between the living and the dead seems both porous and inviolable. In the scene, he imagines this threshold as a kind of screen, behind which he can hear singing. As Rezia recalls, Septimus feels "that man, his friend who was killed, Evans, had come, he said. He was singing behind the screen."[102] Later, though, he feels utterly isolated, and the visions seem to desert him:

He was alone, exposed on this bleak eminence, stretched out—but not on a hill-top; not on a crag; on Mrs. Filmer's sitting-room sofa. As for the visions, the faces, the voices of the dead, where were they? There was a screen in front of him, with black bulrushes and blue swallows. Where he had once seen mountains, where he had seen faces, where he had seen beauty, there was a screen.

"Evans!" he cried. There was no answer. A mouse had squeaked, or a curtain rustled. Those were the voices of the dead.[103]

Woolf narrates the experience of both patient and mourner. She captures the sense of loss and the entangled qualities of grief: the longing for the dead to live on; the fear that believing in the dead's return might simply be a delusion; the tantalizing advantages—and widened perspective—even hallucinations may bring; and the struggle to, and impossibility of, seeing through the screen or veil between the living and the dead. Septimus's experiences were literally resonant with many who suffered from hallucinations in the wake of the war and the pandemic and emotionally resonant with those struggling with grief in the aftermath of so much loss.

The costs of these experiences are reflected in Septimus's suicide, an act that speaks both to the high numbers of war and pandemic survivors who killed themselves and to the profound inadequacies of medicine at the time. As Woolf and Septimus experienced firsthand, doctors were woefully unable to treat mental health issues, the common "rest cure" enforced by Woolf's doctors and proposed by Septimus's often exacerbating symptoms rather than relieving them. Indeed, Septimus is triggered to leap out of the window by the sudden arrival of one of his doctors. As critics observe, Woolf's portrayal of the doctors in *Mrs. Dalloway* is notable for its sweeping denunciation.[104] The viciousness reflects her own experiences with doctors, who were largely unable to help her and who often made her conditions worse. Her critique also reflects common experiences with the medical establishment at the time: its failures to find effective or humane tools for treating PTSD and other mental health issues arising from the war and the pandemic and its inability to find effective treatment during one of the worst plagues in history. Negative portrayals of the medical establishment are, in fact, defining features of pandemic accounts: Thomas Wolfe depicts the doctor and nurse as ghoulish figures; Porter's Miranda in *Pale Horse, Pale Rider* sees hers as nightmarish creatures in her delirium and as controlling figures in her recovery; Cather portrays most of the doctors on board the ship as callous; and H. P. Lovecraft, as I investigate in chapter 7, turns doctors into the monstrous sources of the pandemic's horror. Woolf positions her doctor figures as power hungry, controlling, and worse than useless, revealing the devastating consequences of their inadequacy in Septimus's final leap.

Reading Septimus as a composite figure highlights the intersecting layers of mental anguish these years produce. Not only does he make visible the war's damage; he also makes visible the often hidden burdens of mental health issues, of illness both in the pandemic and more broadly, and the ways all these issues accumulate within bodies and shape perception and the reality of this London day. Septimus allows the era's relentless and overlapping bodily traumas to come back into focus. He becomes a network in motion, not simply an amalgamation of traumas but a dynamic representation of the intersections and amplifications those traumas produced. When we leave the pandemic out of this equation, we leave out an experience widely endured at the time, and we risk making cataclysmic illness a tangential event rather than a powerful structural force contributing its own gravity and effects.

TRAUMAS AND SURVIVORS

At the end of *Mrs. Dalloway*, Clarissa's party—like Septimus—gathers together the era's different traumatic elements. Metaphoric guests include death, living death, guilt, mental and physical illness, and a temptation to forget. It is the only moment in the novel when the two survivors "meet." Septimus is present only in ghost form, but the story of his suicide makes Clarissa aware of him for the first time; "in the middle of my party" she thinks, "here's death." The phrase echoes how death had rippled through homes, first from afar—through the news of war—and then from within the home, erupting in the midst of Armistice celebrations. Clarissa dwells on, and with, Septimus for much of the party, as if the two survivors have united. Clarissa continues to perceive her world through her body and now through his as well. She contemplates the physical details of his suicide: "Always her body went through it first," she thinks, as she imagines his injuries as if they are happening to her.[105] Her body and her thoughts vacillate between exhilaration and fatigue, cycling through life and death and their combination. As she dwells on her own weakness and coming end,

Septimus's suicide, her status as a survivor, her guilt, and the uselessness of the doctors to help with any of this, she becomes her own composite figure, encapsulating the post-1918 atmosphere and the lingering impacts of both tragedies. She becomes, too, the prime witness—the one person who seems to remember what has happened amid the seeming indifference and forgetfulness of the other partygoers.

In one representative moment, Clarissa confronts her own frailty and the atmosphere of death that surrounds her as she watches through a window the old lady in the house next door. She thinks how odd it is that her party goes on while "that old woman, quite quietly, go[es] to bed. She pulled the blind now. The clock began striking. The young man had killed himself."[106] The description offers the final encapsulation of the combined toll of these years. Woolf draws on multiple images of death, from the clock striking, to the suicide, to the pulled-down blinds, that resonate with the web of imagery I've explored.[107] The blinds also hint of the covering over of all this death and a forgetting of how close death remains.

Like so many survivors, Clarissa feels conflicted about her status. Woolf depicts in Clarissa the paradoxical sense of astonishment, guilt, and joy at being alive at all in 1923, coupled with the hard-to-pinpoint atmospheric sense that death and the dead are ever close, intertwined with the living. Learning of Septimus's suicidal leap, Clarissa views it with admiration, even envy, and also with the guilty mind of the survivor: "Somehow it was her disaster—her disgrace. It was her punishment to see sink and disappear here a man, there a woman, in this profound darkness, and she forced to stand here in her evening dress."[108] Clarissa mourns the deaths not simply of soldiers but of women and men—the legions of people who had disappeared in the preceding years. She represents a vivid image of the startled and lonely survivor, suggesting the costs of remaining alive when so many had already sunk into death.

Reading *Mrs. Dalloway* and "On Being Ill" through the pandemic brings to light the profoundly body-centered vision Woolf constructs and the wide-ranging but often subterranean impact of illness. Woolf grants a new map of post-1918 London, its people and air and store windows and parks replete with the lingering sensory and affective details of a viral invasion. She positions the war as part of this atmosphere, its trauma woven into a web of illness and pain. Woolf constructs, in effect, an alternative history that could register bodies and their experiences, that could, in other words, contain the realms where illness makes its impact. The novel captures a threat that targeted everyone and that was rendered invisible not simply because the agent was, or because illness isolates, but because illness suggested a weakness and vulnerability profoundly at odds with the war's dominant narrative.[109] Woolf moves a new story into the frame and finds a language to depict the subtle bodily instantiations of this story, bringing mental and physical health issues into visibility. Even as she captures layers of experience not often represented, she builds within the language all the reasons for—and ways of—burying this experience. Woolf adapts her style to her subject, crafting a sentence structure capacious enough to travel from the body to the outer world, a narrative perspective that could move as nimbly among bodies as a virus, a plot defined less by linear timelines and more by temporal and experiential fluidity, and a structure that could express the delirious, hallucinatory reality that infused the culture.

Chapter Five

A WASTELAND OF INFLUENZA

T. S. Eliot's *The Waste Land*

In the years surrounding the writing and publication of *The Waste Land*, influenza was a constant presence for T. S. Eliot and his wife, Vivien. The couple caught the virus in December 1918, when the second wave of the pandemic raged over England. Eliot's attack was comparatively mild, though in a letter to his mother on December 8, 1918, he writes that it left him "so very weak afterwards."[1] Vivien then caught it and was much sicker; the virus, Eliot wrote, "affected her nerves so that she can hardly sleep at all." [2] Vivien described their influenza encounter in a letter to Charlotte Eliot a week later, noting that while Eliot's case was not serious, it still "left him very weak," and he was "worrying himself about his mind not acting as it used to do."[3] Given the strain on Eliot and his marriage at the time, the causes for this disruption extended beyond the flu, but as another letter from the same period suggests, the term "influenza" encompassed the larger atmosphere: Eliot writes of the "long epidemic of domestic influenza"[4] they have just weathered in 1918, the language registering the actual illness and the illness of his domestic arrangements.

As for Virginia Woolf, the Eliots' influenza attack both preceded and followed a cloud of physical and mental health issues, culminating in Eliot's nervous breakdown in 1921. The pandemic's second wave also corresponded with other deaths for Eliot; his aunt died in December 1918 and his father shortly after, of a heart attack in January 1919. [5] Several months after his

1918 episode, Eliot wrote to his brother Henry that "There has been a great deal of pneumonic influenza about and if one of us got it he would have to go to a hospital." His own health remained precarious; as he told Henry, "I have simply had a sort of collapse; I slept almost continuously for two days, and now I am up, I feel very weak and easily exhausted."[6] Eliot confided in his mother later that "We were afraid it might be influenza at first, but it appears to have been only exhaustion."[7] The Eliots' servant contracted pneumonia in February 1919 (the most common complication of the flu), and Vivien helped nurse her through it. Vivien continued to be ill as well, along with her mother.[8] And in the months leading up to his nervous breakdown, during which he worked on *The Waste Land*, Eliot linked influenza, dryness, and the landscape in ways that resonate within his poem: in his "London Letter" in the *Dial* in July 1921, he reports a "hot rainless spring" and "A new form of influenza . . . which leaves extreme dryness and a bitter taste in the mouth."[9]

The atmosphere of influenza and illness described by the Eliots in their letters was a microcosm of the broader, and now familiar, pandemic climate. The sense of enervation, fragmentation, and vulnerable bodies are, of course, iconic elements of *The Waste Land*, though they have not been seen through a pandemic lens. As perhaps *the* quintessential modernist poem of the twentieth century, the work—with all its corpses, bones, and malaise—has been subject to wide-ranging critical attention. Critics read the poem as arising from the ashes of the First World War; as a response to Europe's, and specifically Eastern Europe's, disintegration; and as an expression of Eliot's own personal struggles with his marriage and his sexuality, among many other readings.[10] Famously, the writer John Peter advanced a controversial reading of the poem as an ode to Eliot's suppressed desire for his friend Jean Verdenal, killed at Gallipoli in the First World War (a reading Eliot fought against).[11] Scholars have explored Eliot's acknowledged debts to the anthropological work of J. G. Frazer and Jessie Weston and to the myths of the Fisher King; investigated Eliot's use of Buddhism, ecocritical perspectives, and popular culture; analyzed his many literary references, and much more.[12] Despite this wealth of readings, critics have missed the poem's viral context.

Eliot never mentions the pandemic directly in *The Waste Land*, but in this respect, it's worth considering how scholars have approached the role of the war in the poem. Scholars most often link all the death, bodies, rats, and so on to the war and to European unrest—to, in other words, the costs imposed by human-based violence. Eliot pushed against this reading, declaring testily that the poem was "only the relief of a personal and wholly insignificant grouse against life";[13] indeed, there's only one tangential reference to the war (Lil's husband getting "demobbed").[14] Critics have rightly pushed against Eliot's claim, arguing that the poem captures the gestalt of the postwar moment. As Samuel Hynes observes, the lack of direct war references doesn't negate the poem's links to the war: "It isn't that the poem describes the war; Eliot simply picked up the fragments that existed in post-war consciousnesses, and made a poem out of them, a poem that his contemporaries founds haunting, even when they didn't understand it, because they shared its fragments."[15]

Part of the poem's power, I argue, is that Eliot did the same thing for post-pandemic consciousnesses, channeling a set of experiences and fragments that were haunting the culture but were difficult to represent. He may or may not have been channeling pandemic experiences intentionally—as he may or may not have been channeling the war intentionally—but he grants a voice to widespread experiences that by their nature were inchoate and elusive. Indeed, Eliot strove in his poem not to mention any particular event directly, and he famously excoriated the war poets for including the war in their work, as the critic Ezekiel Black has detailed.[16] Poetry, Eliot wrote in the poem "A Note on War Poetry," should be an "abstract conception / Of private experience at its greatest intensity / Becoming universal"—not, in other words, about a particular event.[17] As Eliot observes in "Tradition and the Individual Talent," poetry should instead seek to capture and distill a range of experiences that would otherwise be missed. Poetry, he writes, is "a new thing resulting from the concentration, of a very great number of experiences which to the practical and active person would not seem to be experiences at all."[18] The poet, then, needs to give voice to what is hard to see, to take a vast number of experiences and weave them into verse. Approached from this frame, and with a detailed knowledge of the pandemic atmosphere, *The Waste Land* emerges as a powerful record of the pandemic's enduring emotional and physical costs, as well as a record of the denial that surrounded it even as the culture remained mired in the guilt, suffering, and fear it produced. Indeed, Eliot's aim to capture ordinary experiences that would otherwise be missed was ideally suited for the elusive bodily and mental sensations the virus generated. His desire, too, to stay apart from his subject—the impersonality he strove for and the universal statement he wished to make—dovetailed with the larger culture's desire to push against the pandemic's memories.

I divide my pandemic reading of *The Waste Land* into two sections. In "Outbreak," I read the poem as a record of the sensory experiences of acute infection, including the reality-bending delirium, the fever, the dehydration, and the threat of drowning. I move, in "Aftermath," to the ways the poem evocatively captures three widespread experiences that came in the pandemic's wake: death, reflected in the bones, corpses, rats, and insecure burials; viral resurrections, including perpetual states of living death and barren tropes of sacrificial renewal; and finally, the arrival of silence and the breakdown of communication in the face of so much suffering. Throughout my reading, I remain attentive to the many influences that shape these elements, including the war, and I do not propose that the pandemic is the key to all mythologies, to borrow George Eliot's phrase.[19] I do, however, argue that the miasmic residue of the pandemic experience infuses every part of the poem, in ways we have been missing all along.

OUTBREAK

In an oft-cited observation, Michael Levenson points out that the opening of *The Waste Land* is told from a corpse's point of view, granting a beneath-the-ground perspective from inside a dead body.[20] Buried within the poem is a parallel perspective: what reality looks like from within bodies suffering from acute illness. Eliot develops his own hallucinatory-delirium mode, one that parallels conditions we have seen in the pandemic accounts explored so far. On the broadest level, the poem's well-known fragmentation, its multiple voices, and its constant leaps from topic to topic suggest what we might term a delirium logic, a comprehensive vision of reality from within a fever dream. More specifically, various moments seem to slip into particular bodies or perhaps memories. The disintegrating language at the end of "The Fire Sermon," for example, suggests the viewpoint of someone trapped in a feverish hallucination:

Burning burning burning burning
O Lord Thou pluckest me out
O Lord Thou pluckest

burning[21]

Eliot's footnotes on these lines cite the allusions to Augustine's *Confessions* and to the Buddha's Fire-Sermon; both works caution against bodily passion, so the references here—and the sensations expressed—are in ironic juxtaposition to the sterility and lack of passion in so much of the poem. These allusions, though, don't explain the confusion of the lines or their incomplete quality. Seen through the lens of the pandemic, the lines embody the experiential reality of a delirium brought on by a high fever, a bodily experience that would have been painfully familiar to contemporary readers. As one survivor remembered, in broken language that reflected Eliot's own fears about his flu case, "Fever every bone aches in your body . . . you surely don't think straight for weeks afterwards."[22] Such agitated bodies are evoked in the repetition of "burning," a delirious tossing back and forth—the gerund form reflecting the ongoing quality of this experience. After the frenzy of the first line, the speaker seems to run out of breath and energy, not making it to the end of the third line before falling silent and then muttering a final, and seemingly weaker, "burning." Such moments are later fleshed out in Porter's and Wolfe's depiction of flu deliriums and burning fevers; here, we have just the sensory fragments. Eliot's lines ironically make logical sense, though, when seen within a delirium context, evoking the splintering of thought illness could produce.

Many parts of the poem speak in this same delusionary jumble of language. The poem's fragmentation—what Samuel Hynes calls "its formal principle"—has often been linked to the war; as Hynes argues, the fragmentation reflects "the visual reality of the Western Front [that] had imposed itself on language," the broken language "an expression of the war's impact on consciousness."[23] And yet, the fragmentation also speaks to an experience Eliot actually had, suggesting the virus's impact on consciousness and the physical and spiritual costs of the pandemic. In "A Game of Chess," we get a glimpse of a sickroom scene that parallels similar moments I explored with Virginia Woolf, where threats encroach and the room's hush and isolation overlaps with ambient sounds that trickle in:

> staring forms
> Leaned out, leaning, hushing the room enclosed.
> Footsteps shuffled on the stair.
> Under the firelight, under the brush, her hair

Spread out in fiery points
Glowed into words, then would be savagely still.[24]

The reader is thrust inside a hallucinatory dreamscape, a visual and auditory jumble where eerie forms seem to stare from corners and noises mix with the hush (or, potentially, attempts to hush). The sound of footsteps filter in, and the visuals suggest a confusion of senses: the hair is under both firelight and a brush, it spreads out in fiery points, it turns into words and then freezes, savagely. As with Septimus, bodily sensations turn into language. Indeed, the "burning" lines I just explored seem like the logical extension of this sickroom atmosphere, the fever rising and the language disintegrating further.

In the poem's final section, the hallucinatory quality intensifies in a corresponding moment concerning hair:

A woman drew her long black hair out tight
And fiddled whisper music on those strings
And bats with baby faces in the violet light
Whistled, and beat their wings
And crawled head downward down a blackened wall
And upside down in air were towers
Tolling reminiscent bells, that kept the hours
And voices singing out of empty cisterns and exhausted wells.

In this decayed hole among the mountains
In the faint moonlight the grass is singing[25]

Hair turns into fiddle strings, which turn into sound. The eerie forms from the previous passage have morphed into bats with baby faces crawling down walls. The sufferer's world has turned upside down, and the ambient sounds have grown more ominous and distorted: whispered music, whistling bats, tolling bells, voices from empty cisterns and wells, and singing grass. Porter uses similar imagery in *Pale Horse, Pale Rider*, within her depiction of Miranda's flu delirium: she sees the nurse's hands as "white tarantulas" and her doctor throwing a naked baby into a well. Like Eliot's singing grasses, Miranda thinks she hears nature speaking: "the wood whistled and sang and shouted, every branch and leaf and blade of grass had its own terrible accusing voice." She finds herself searching for the dead in the waste land, leaving her "alone in a strange stony place of bitter cold, picking her way along a steep path," with "pain running through her veins like heavy fire."[26] Porter, in effect, makes the same connection I am making here, her "waste land" reference linking Eliot's poem to the buried sensory details of the flu's delirium.

Additional hallucinatory moments capture a pervasive bodily experience in the pandemic: the burning thirst that accompanies high fevers. As noted earlier, Eliot linked thirst to influenza, noting in the *Dial* letter from 1921 that "A new form of influenza [had appeared] . . . which leaves extreme dryness and a bitter taste in the mouth."[27] In the poem's final section, the sufferer's desperate thirst mingles with delirium:

> If there were water we should stop and drink
> Amongst the rock one cannot stop or think
> Sweat is dry and feet are in the sand
> If there were only water amongst the rock
> Dead mountain mouth of carious teeth that cannot spit[28]

The language portrays a wandering in a desert as well as a more metaphoric spiritual crisis, but it also embodies a pandemic perspective, manifesting confused thinking, bodily distortion (the feet are in sand, the body seems already dead, sweat is dry), helplessness, and overwhelming thirst. In the "hair" passage just discussed, the voices singing from "empty cisterns and exhausted wells" suggest a similar hallucinatory dryness.[29] A few lines later, the speaker becomes even more drained, the language paring down as exhaustion takes over:

> If there were water
> And no rock
> If there were rock
> And also water
> And water
> . . . .
> Not the cicada
> And dry grass singing
> But sound of water over a rock

. . . .
Drip drop drip drop drop drop drop
But there is no water[30]

The language is feverish, the speaker jumping between broken thoughts and circling back to a sense of thirst, the delirium in fact underlying the modernist fragmentation. Such thirst and such brokenness, as critics have noted since the poem's publication, speak to a larger spiritual thirst, the aftermath of war, and a broken Western culture. But the language also links to literal thirst and a language broken by fever and reduced to sounds. Eliot's poem serves as a memorial to *bodily* states, not just spiritual or psychological ones, a record of suffering and confusion translated into language in both its form and its content.

Amid the hallucinatory thirst, Eliot depicts an opposite state that paradoxically accompanied the dryness and dehydration of the pandemic: the threat of drowning. In the first section, the medium Madame Sosostris ominously intones, "Fear death by water" and sees "the drowned Phoenician Sailor" in the tarot cards, a body we find again in part 4, "Death by Water," which offers us Phlebas's corpse, "who was once handsome and tall as you," drifting in the current.[31] The sailor, seemingly within the most death-targeted age group for both the war and the pandemic, echoes not simply the many soldiers who were lost at sea or who drowned when trenches filled with water or the air with poison gas but also the central cause of death in the pandemic: when fluid flooded the lungs, as one medical researcher summarized, "the body effectively drowned itself."[32] Eliot himself had a morbid fear of drowning during these years.[33] The language speaks to the universality of the threat: the accusatory voice reminds the reader that such a death might claim "you" even at the prime of life—and even if you were not a soldier. And yet, the tone in the section is not one of overt fear or horror. Sarah Cole points to the section as one depicting an "enchanted violence," the tone more "dreamlike" and meditative than the grimmer bodies and death depicted elsewhere in the poem; the section even suggests, Cole argues, a poetic consolation for death and suffering, the corpse transformed into a thing of beauty.[34] In keeping with this perspective, we can read "Death by Water" as a positive, dreamlike delirium, like the one we saw in Ben's singing in *Look Homeward, Angel*, or in Septimus's visions of peaceful waves, or in Woolf's visions of the sky in "On Being Ill." Phlebas can leave behind "the cry of gulls," rocked by the current in a stream of backward-moving time (from "age" to "youth").[35] The language is sleepy, as if the speaker is drifting off amid the visions. The vision, though, pulls out of Phlebas's perspective at the end, moving from the sufferer to the observer. Much as Eliot calls out readers at the end of the first section, reminding them that they are complicit in what is happening in the poem ("You! hypocrite lecteur!—mon semblable,—mon frère!"), here the speaker warns, "O you who turn the wheel and look to windward, / Consider Phlebas, who was once handsome and tall as you."[36] This vision of Phlebas, the speaker suggests, might turn into a reality for any reader. In all these images of delirium—both the nightmarish and the more placid visions—Eliot speaks to a different type of bodily violation than what the war produced, granting space to the quiet but no less devastating violence that illness brings to the body, one where agency is hidden and the effects are both internal and diffuse.

The ominous warning to look "windward" for your own coming death is part of a larger pattern of imagery that Eliot uses throughout the poem, one that speaks evocatively to a broader pandemic atmosphere that runs parallel to the individual one I have just explored. The poem builds repeated images that suggest a miasmic, contagion-like threat. Like Thomas Wolfe's constant refrain about a grievous wind, Eliot fills his poem with ominous, powerful—yet by their nature, invisible—forces, all consistently linked to death. The city in "The Burial of the Dead" is caught "Under the brown fog" through which the living dead move, exhaling.[37] The air in "A Game of Chess" is saturated in the "unstoppered" and lurking "Strange synthetic perfumes" that "drowned the sense in odours," scents that are "stirred by the air / That freshened from the window."[38] In the same section, in the frantic questioning between the (maybe) married couple, one speaker asks what the noise is, to which is offered the silent reply, "The wind under the door." The follow-up question of "What is the wind doing?" is answered as "Nothing again nothing."[39] There's more than a hint of delirium here—the person may well be talking to themselves—as well as anxiety, but there's also logic within the paranoia: at the time, it was not paranoid to think of the air as dangerous, to suspect the wind might represent danger, to wonder what it might be doing—it was nothing, again and again, but no less dangerous because of that. In "The Fire Sermon," the city remains "Under the brown fog," and "The wind / Crosses the brown land, unheard."[40] The speaker hears "a cold blast" at his back, bringing "The rattle of the bones."

Later a "Southwest wind / Carried down stream / The peal of bells," the tolling sound another threatening, invisible presence, which I will discuss further on.[41] Finally, in "What the Thunder Said," we find "only the wind's home" in the empty, abandoned chapel with its "tumbled graves." And while "a damp gust" brings rain to the dry land, whether it revives or drowns is unclear.[42] Eliot builds a pathogenic atmosphere of wind, fog, and air, the images capturing contagion and the power of the threat alongside its ineffability and diffuseness. Whether he intended the images to function in this way is immaterial; he channels the atmosphere at the time, taking the characterless quality of illness I explored in the introduction and finding a way to represent it that embodies—and turns into art—the very lack of agency that helped make the pandemic so difficult to represent. The pandemic's remnants have always been present here, but like the outbreak's absent presence in cultural memory, they have hidden in full view.

The poem also reverberates with the constant tolling of bells, a sound that offers both another image of an invisible force spreading through the atmosphere and penetrating bodies as well as a more literal echo of the bells that rang continuously for the pandemic dead. Such sounds—and the atmosphere they helped produce—echo throughout Eliot's poem. In "The Burial of the Dead" section, the speaker, seeing the living dead flow over London Bridge, notes that they file down the street "To where Saint Mary Woolnoth kept the hours / With a dead sound on the final stroke of nine"; the death-announcing function of the bells mingles with and even supplants their timekeeping function.[43] Bells ring again in the middle of the poem, "The peal of bells" echoing down the Thames River, and again in the final section: the towers "Tolling reminiscent bells, that kept the hours" blend with the fever dreams of "bats with baby faces" and "voices singing out of empty cisterns."[44] Eliot reevokes the death atmosphere that had become a multisensory experience, reproducing here the sounds that arose not on the battlefields but in the very air of the city and its domestic spaces.

AFTERMATH

Option 1: Death

The Waste Land not only captures elements of the pandemic's acute phase at both the individual and collective level; its atmosphere is also saturated

with the two most common outcomes of the outbreak: death, and an enervated living death (which I address in the next section). The poem is,
famously, full of dead bodies—the opening corpse, the drowned sailor
Phlebas—as well as scattered bones: the alley "Where the dead men lost
their bones"; "The rattle of the bones"; "White bodies naked on the low
damp ground / And bones cast in a little low dry garret."[45] The water "Picked
[Phlebas's] bones in whispers"; the empty chapel holds "Dry bones."[46] And
death extends everywhere, from a "dead land" to a "dead tree" to a "dead
sound."[47] These bodies and bones of course suggest the war dead, as critics
note. David Sherman, for example, argues the poem is a "burial ground"
that nevertheless attempts to push against the modernized and deritual-
ized treatment of corpses "in the wake of mass war."[48] Paul Fussell links the
poem's dead to the lost soldiers, and Sarah Cole notes how "the imagery of
war underlie[s] the poem," including its "ubiquitous dead" and the "burial
phobias."[49] The lurking, somewhat hidden quality of these bodies in the
poem also suggests the haunting absence of war corpses at the home front,
though they were ever present in memory and in memorials.[50] All these
bodies and bones—and their strange absence/presence—signify differently
when the pandemic dead are considered. The poem's bodies and bones flip
their meaning, suggesting the material reality of the civilian corpses that
had flooded cities and homes, where the dead body was far from absent
in 1918.

The confluence of rats and dead bodies provide a telling example of the
differences we might see when reading through the lens of the pandemic
rather than the war. In "A Game of Chess," one of the 'speakers' thinks "we
are in rats' alley / Where the dead men lost their bones."[51] In a parallel passage in "The Fire Sermon," a rat creeps "softly through the vegetation /
Dragging its slimy belly," while the speaker sees (or imagines) "White bodies naked on the low damp ground / And bones cast in a little low dry
garret, / Rattled by the rat's foot only."[52] These images again echo the war;
rats were a constant, haunting presence at the front, eating the dead and
evoking horror for the soldiers.[53] The "alley" links to the trenches, as does
the damp ground and the dead bodies. And yet, the pandemic dead are also
buried in these images. Rats are the perennial symbol of disease, for centuries incorrectly blamed for the bubonic plague, to which the influenza
pandemic was often compared, both in symptoms and in casualties.[54] These
rats and bodies seem, after all, to be in London—or at least not at the

battlefront—recalling how the pandemic shifted the location of both bodies and danger. Embedded here, also, are parallel images of war and plague: the bodies in the low damp ground (the trenches), next to the bones in the low dry garret (the home front). The garret bones are hidden, though, forgotten and still except for the movement supplied by the rat's foot. Eliot's poem replicates the grim reality of spreading death and its intimacy, tucked into garrets and domestic spaces, leaving a trail of bones behind.

Eliot's images of pervasive death and bones echo images and accounts from the era. One drawing, "The Spanish Flu," by the Austrian artist Alfred Kubin, depicts the stark bones of a Grim Reaper figure (figure 5.1). Beneath a turbulent, ominous sky, a leering skeleton with a scythe appears to mow down a heap of bodies, all twisted in agony. A no-man's-land stretches behind him, with low, blasted looking scrub brush and wooden plank paths stretching to no destination. A townscape can be seen in the distance, and the one tower with an orthodox cross on the top is overshadowed by the skeletal hand of the reaper. The drawing reflects the repeated reports during the pandemic of the heaps of bodies that overwhelmed hospitals, towns, and cities; as the flu historian John Barry notes, "the most terrifying aspect of the epidemic was the piling up of bodies. Undertakers, themselves sick, were overwhelmed. They had no place to put bodies."[55] Eliot offers in his poem a place to put them and a record of how death and bones overtook the landscape.

Endemic to these images of bodies and bones is the eerie sense of insecure or disrupted burial. As is well known, the war produced pervasive problems with unburied bodies,[56] but the pandemic produced its own acute burial problems closer to home. Legitimate fears of contagion, combined with the numbers of bodies, meant mass graves, scarce coffins, and disrupted funerals, as I detail in the introduction. The photographs in figure 5.2 show piles of flu corpses juxtaposed to a mass grave being dug to hold them. Eliot's line about "bodies naked on the low damp ground" takes on new resonance when set beside such images.[57] The line also recalls a harrowing moment from one of the most well-known plague narratives, Daniel Defoe's *A Journal of the Plague Year*, which I address at greater length in the next chapter. Defoe's description of a mass grave, with bodes being dumped from a wagon to fall "quite naked among the rest," all "huddled together in the common Grave," suggests that such scenes were familiar pandemic sights.[58]

FIGURE 5.1. Alfred Kubin, *The Spanish Flu* (*Die Spanische Krankheit*), ink on paper, c. 1920, private collection. *Source:* © Eberhard Spangenbert/Artists Rights Society (ARS), New York/VG Bild-Kunst, Bonn. Image provided by Bridgeman Images.

The poem captures this insecurity at the end of "The Burial of the Dead" section. The section's title suggests a perverse recasting of the traditional Anglican funeral service, a move that in itself reflects the disruption of mourning practices. In the speaker's well-known confrontation with "Stetson," Eliot underscores the widespread anxiety about burial:

FIGURE 5.2. Digging mass graves for influenza victims, Philadelphia. *Source*: The image is used by kind permission of the College of Physicians of Philadelphia. Copyright 2018 by the College of Physicians of Philadelphia.

There I saw one I knew, and stopped him, crying, "Stetson!
"You who were with me in the ships at Mylae!
"That corpse you planted last year in your garden,
"Has it begun to sprout? Will it bloom this year?
"Or has the sudden frost disturbed its bed?

"Oh keep the Dog far hence, that's friend to men,
"Or with his nails he'll dig it up again!"[59]

In a tone of unhinged pleasantry sharply at odds with the subject, the speaker suggests a parodic resurrection. The corpse planted last year remains buried but capable of return, threatening to sprout and bloom, threatening to rise from its bed, disturbed. Such an image of a body insecurely buried speaks on both a literal and figurative level to the postpandemic moment. With coffins scarce and gravediggers overwhelmed, bodies were in fact buried in backyards—though the second wave's arrival in the winter months meant that the ground was often too frozen to dig graves, and bodies piled up for burial; "sudden frost" could in fact disturb the bed. There are echoes here of the war, but this is a domestic burial, one that takes place after a war (if we assume the First Punic War given the Mylae reference); indeed, part of the haunting quality of this image is the closeness of the body to the domestic space and the breezy over-the-garden-wall-chat quality of the exchange. Within this pleasantry are the ominous questions over whether this corpse might spread—sprouting and blooming again—speaking to the virus's deathly fecundity, to its infectious quality, and to its repeated returns. On a more figurative level, we might see in this corpse the efforts in 1922 to bury the body psychologically, to forget the flu and return to normal conversations (that nevertheless carry the traces of the tragedy and the perversity of a desire to assume normality). The corpse as memory and as body is hidden but remains near, just outside in the garden, capable of being dug up despite precautions. On a broader level, no one knew, in 1922, whether the flu would come back, as virulent as ever; more corpses were always possible. Eliot records the desire to push the dead away, to bury grief and move on, and at the same time he insists that the memory of these bodies should—and will—always return.

Option 2: Viral Resurrection

Amid all the death and bones, *The Waste Land* serves as a foundational wellspring of viral resurrections. In addition to the viral threat embedded in the return of Stetson's corpse, Eliot's poem showcases different elements of viral resurrection, from the images of deathly vitality that open the poem, to the spreading crowds of the walking dead, to the parade of bodies caught in a miasma of living death, to the scattered, failed tropes of classical and Christian models of resurrection. I've traced such states across the flu accounts, from the anguished limbo experienced by both victims and mourners to the hallucinatory visions of the walking dead. While the deathly vitality of Eliot's poem links to these examples, to the war, and to a general sense of cultural disintegration, it also does more. What's different about Eliot's version is how structurally foundational viral resurrection becomes. It's not just bodies that are affected—though they certainly are—but the city, the landscape, the vegetation, emotions, thoughts, minds, language, words, and even the poem. And these elements are not simply caught in a twilight existence; they embody this state. Viral resurrection becomes a contagion that has spread everywhere even before the poem begins—we don't see the spread, and there's really no outside viewpoint where we might imagine another state—it just becomes part of everything.

Eliot and his wife both personally felt caught in a perpetual living death in the pandemic/post-pandemic moment. The seemingly endless cycles of illness, recovery, fatigue, and failure wore Eliot down until his nervous collapse. In the 1918 letter when he complains of the "long epidemic of domestic influenza" they have just weathered, he goes on to explain the "red tape" he faced in getting into the navy and how these failed attempts, combined "with several disappointments during the summer, and still (as a result of this plus peace plus influenza) feel very tired, and [am] not writing at present."[60] The war, influenza, his failures, and the flurry of peace blend to create a cloud of exhaustion. This atmosphere persisted in the coming years. Eliot wrote Lytton Strachey in February 1920 that London remains "extraordinarily difficult," for "One bleeds to death very slowly here."[61] Later, Eliot dates his sense of living death as having started just after the war had, and grown worse. Writing to John Middleton Murry in April 1925, Eliot confesses that "In the last ten years—gradually, but deliberately—I have made myself into a *machine*. . . . I don't know what it will do to me—and to V.[ivien]—should I come alive again. I have deliberately killed my senses—I have deliberately died—in order to go on with the outward form of living—This I did in 1915. What will happen if I live again?"[62] He retrospectively imagines that he turned his body into a machine midway through the war and then augmented the transformation in the ensuing years. The move suggests an emotional coldness, but it also offers a fantasy protection from the war (he has become the deadly technology) and also from illness (machines can't catch biological viruses). Eliot translates this experience of life-in-death—and the agony it both represents and seems to cause—into every section of the poem.

In the poem's epigraph, Eliot anchors his work in a haunting story of living death from Petronius Arbiter's *Satyricon*. The speaker in the work, at a lavish banquet where stories and boasts are exchanged, tells the tale of meeting the Sibyl. The Sibyl had, according to myth, been given a wish by Apollo and had requested a long life while neglecting to ask for eternal youth. The speaker in Arbiter's tale (and Eliot's epigraph) claims to have met the Sibyl after her withered but still living body had been enclosed in a jar for safekeeping:

> For I once saw with my own eyes the Cumean Sibyl hanging in a jar,
>   and when the boys asked her, "Sibyl, what do you want?" she answered,
>   "I want to die."[63]

The Sibyl is quite literally encapsulated in living death, stuck in a jar like a medical specimen, technically alive but blocked from any meaningful existence. She is a fitting figure for this cultural moment, forced to go on living despite being overwhelmed by physical (and emotional) suffering. She recalls Eliot's enervation and captures the bodily states of many pandemic figures, from Miranda's longing for death in the aftermath of her illness, to the anguished need to continue living despite feeling like walking corpses that Thomas Wolfe describes, to Virginia Woolf's exhausted Clarissa Dalloway. And in selecting a nonmilitary, female figure, Eliot nods to the widespread sense of this living death, tying it to a figure who was herself associated with plague—or its prevention. The Sibylline Books of prophecy offered instructions on the proper rituals to prevent calamities; the ancient Roman historian Livy (Titus Livius) speaks of how the Romans consulted her books repeatedly in times of plague in hopes they might ward off disease.[64] Like so many of the cultural signs of renewal that Eliot evokes in the poem (April, Christian and pagan resurrections, etc.), only to show how they have become empty shells in the modern age, the figure of Sibyl hints at a previous power, at the possibility of renewal or defense from plague that in the current world has become hopelessly ineffectual. Her central prophetic power is now to announce the suspended death-in-life quality of the poem and the larger culture.

From this cry for death, the poem moves to perverse images of deadly fecundity. As I noted earlier, Levenson observes that the first speaker appears to be a corpse, delivering its message from underground.[65] Yet this corpse is not quite dead, though, like Sibyl, it might long to be. The speaking corpse offers a dense set of death-and-life pairs: "Lilacs" and "dead land"; "dull roots" and "spring rain"; "little life" and "dried tubers," with the phrases also functioning as rough death-in-life pairings: "dead" and "land," "little" and "life," "dried" and "tubers."[66] These blends are not simply mingled states of being; embedded here and everywhere is the process itself, the agonized uncertain *movement* between life and death. Such movement seems perpetual, captured in the word "burial" from the title of the section. "Burial" is a "deverbal" noun, a word that describes not a person, place, or thing but a process. The format makes burial something ongoing, an action that never finally buries. This sense of perpetual process is built into the gerunds as well: "breeding," "mixing," "stirring," "covering," and "feeding."[67] Such words imply ongoing life, sustenance, and protection, but what they sustain seems to be death. The paradox of the images captures the deadly fertility of the flu virus. It killed as it bred and mixed and fed; it multiplied, and death flourished.[68] Buried in the first stanza, walled in by words, earth, and snow, we find "forgetful"[69] at the center, a hushing away of the living death that's here, a sense that it might be better to forget. These lines echo the anguished thoughts of survivors and mourners, thinking of bodies imperfectly buried and lost and absent but not finally put to rest because traditional burials had for so many been disrupted. One can also hear the physical and mental exhaustion of the still semiliving, "bleed[ing] to death very slowly," with all the frailties and injuries still present, haunted by the thought that it might have been better not to have survived after all. And as war deaths bled into flu deaths, the experience of living death became a perpetual state without resolution.

The rest of the poem is full of direct and indirect references to living death, lending the poem what the *Times Literary Supplement* identified in 1922 as its "purgatorial quality."[70] So many voices in the poem seem stranded, not able to reach the two poles (death or life) definitively, instead shuttling between them without ever reaching either extreme. This state affects not only the possible former soldiers in the poem but seemingly everyone, everywhere, as if, indeed, there is an invisible, deathly force that has sapped bodies of life within cities and domestic spaces. As the narrator remarks,

A crowd flowed over London Bridge, so many,
I had not thought death had undone so many.
Sighs, short and infrequent, were exhaled,
And each man fixed his eyes before his feet.
Flowed up the hill and down King William Street[71]

The state of living death infuses the crowd and the landscape: the individual members barely seem to be breathing, and these walking dead flow over and into bridges and hills and streets. The all-encompassing quality of this atmosphere, with "so many" undone by death in any number of ways, captures a moment when death seemed to come from everywhere, for everyone, turning even the living into ghosts of their former selves. This process of living death resembles less an explosive violence or a visible threat and more the lingering aftermath of a not-quite-fatal struggle with a hidden enemy.

Amid the masses of walking dead are voices of individual sufferers, caught in a state of perpetual, viral resurrection. In the burial section, for example, the speaker laments "I could not / Speak, and my eyes failed, I was neither / Living nor dead, and I knew nothing."[72] Here, the speaker combines the experience with a sense of silence and miscommunication. The enjambment of the first two lines offers a sense of stuttering midsentence, as the speaker tries to put into words something hard to grasp. In the next section, other voices echo these lines in the frantic yet deanimated exchange:

> "Do
> "You know nothing? Do you see nothing? Do you remember
> "Nothing?"
> I remember
> Those are pearls that were his eyes.
> "Are you alive, or not? Is there nothing in your head?"[73]

The silent speaker in the middle, who might even be a ghost or hallucination, thinks of death and bones and rats and nothing, punctuated by fragments of culture; the frantic question of whether he is alive or not seems legitimate. In the last section, another voice puts the situation more definitively, gesturing to individual and collective experiences and multiple forms of dying:

After the torchlight red on sweaty faces
After the frosty silence in the gardens
After the agony in stony places
The shouting and the crying
Prison and palace and reverberation
Of thunder of spring over distant mountains
He who was living is now dead
We who were living are now dying
With a little patience[74]

These lines in part reference the betrayal and death of Jesus,[75] but we can see hints not simply of a postwar atmosphere but also a post-pandemic one—the sense of emptiness and silence, the memories of red, sweaty faces of feverish or exhausted soldiers and civilians, the echoes of no-man's-land but also of frosty gardens and Stetson's corpse. Like a mininarrative of the war's mass deaths blurring into the pandemic's, these images of death and agony seem to spread through the world from battlegrounds to gardens, becoming part of the weather—invisible, essentialized, and reverberating. And what is left "after" all this cataclysm is the living death at the end of the passage, with its hint that just a little more patience might bring the relief of actual death. Persistent is the sense of an ongoing experience, the sense that what is agonizing is not so much the state but the process of it, the dying and the living, not the being dead or alive. The language registers the slow violence of bodies damaged and weakened but not killed outright—an experience endemic to mass illness and now naturalized and divorced from its origins.

Alongside living-death resurrections, Eliot also rifles through key Western tropes of resurrection and sacrificial violence and, in particular, the Holy Grail/Fisher King legends and Christian accounts of Jesus's return. While plentiful, the critical discussion of these elements in the poem has ignored how the threats to the kingdom at the heart of these stories—what precipitates the need for renewal and resurrection—has always included illness and in particular pandemic illness. Sickness in these original models may be read as a sign of punishment, something that might be redeemed or averted by virtuous action. What happens, Eliot seems to ask, when we translate these stories into the modern age? And what happens when we consider how the pandemic might shape and disrupt a sacrificial model of resurrection?

As even an introductory reader of Eliot's poem learns, *The Waste Land* plays with the grail quest and the legend of the Fisher King, drawing on the works of Jessie L. Weston and Sir James Frazer. Weston's *From Ritual to Romance* provided, Eliot writes in his footnotes, "not only the title, but the plan and a good deal of the incidental symbolism of the poem." In her work, Weston explored the grail-quest tradition and its links to older pagan rituals. "The main object of the Quest," she wrote, "is the restoration to health and vigour of a King suffering from infirmity caused by wounds, sickness, or old age . . . and whose infirmity, for some mysterious and unexplained reason, reacts disastrously upon his kingdom."[76] Readers have noted the ways the poem reflects such infirmity; the characters and the land itself suffer from physical and mental war wounds, spiritual sickness, and depleted bodies. Yet in the poem's evocation of illness and its grim aftermath, it also registers the actual infirmity that spread across the land. The pandemic was a moment, in fact, when the myth was realized, when a recombined virus in a single, originating body made an entire world sick; it seemed "mysterious"; it seemed "unexplained"; it indeed reacted disastrously upon the kingdom. The knight is supposed to find the grail and restore the king and the kingdom, though not surprisingly, a heroic cure is unavailable in the poem, as it was unavailable in reality, however desperately wanted. The poem creates a record, not just a trope, offering historically accurate descriptions of the pandemic's impact.

Eliot also draws on—and reimagines in a post-pandemic moment—the models of sacrifice James Frazer describes in *The Golden Bough*. Frazer looked closely at traditions that required the death of a "Divine King"; the king needed to die while he was still young and healthy to ensure the world's renewal, capturing a sense of a sacrifice for larger gain that permeates the Christian tradition as well. The idea of a figure "who annually died and rose again from the dead" paralleled and helped ensure, the belief went, the renewal of life and nature.[77] As I've touched on, this rhetoric of sacrifice underscored much of the rhetoric surrounding war: young, healthy men would be sacrificed to renew the land (something Rupert Brooke's famous poem "The Soldier" seems to take literally, as he imagines his body renewing the land and bringing England to foreign shores).[78] Much of the war literature questioned the idea that the sacrifices of young men in war would bring renewal, and Eliot's poem, much less directly, offers little sense of war as producing meaningful sacrifice. Embedded in the poem, though, is the way the pandemic far more brutally exposed the sacrificial model of death, producing—in a bitter irony that would be too obvious in a work of fiction—the death of millions of young healthy men and women without any sense that such loss would bring renewal and with no ability to frame the deaths as part of a larger calculus of gain.[79] Such exposure, not surprisingly, was hushed up, but Eliot's refusal to place the poem's deaths within a clear frame of resurrection, while still acknowledging the desire for one, reflects the pandemic's aftermath as surely and brutally as it does the war's.

Alongside these pagan models, Eliot specifically evokes and then rejects Christian traditions of resurrection too, placing them in the category of delirious illusions. As the critic Barry Spurr observes, Christian resurrection is "a concept . . . denied repeatedly throughout *The Waste Land*."[80] While the service for "The Burial of the Dead" in the Book of Common Prayer consoles through a promise of the afterlife, Eliot's rewrite of the service imagines resurrection either as grisly moments where flu and war bodies make literal returns or as hallucinatory visions of—and by—the walking dead. In the one moment in the poem when Jesus appears to make a shadowy appearance, the episode reads like a fever dream. Eliot references the biblical story of the road to Emmaus, when a postcrucifixion Jesus appears to a few of his disciples as a hooded figure. In Eliot's version, the speaker telling the story seems delusional, repeating questions and unclear on whether there are two or three people on the road. The speaker cannot make out the gender of the mysterious figure "wrapt in a brown mantle, hooded" who seems to appear ahead of him.[81] While the links to the Emmaus episode are clear, Eliot observes in his notes that he was also referencing the hallucinatory experiences recounted by Sir Ernest Shackleton, writing of his expedition to the Antarctic, where the explorer had described his delusion that another person was present beyond their group.[82] The resurrection story transforms from a comforting narrative into a delirious rant, with Jesus more a Grim Reaper figure (the hooded stranger) with uncertain aims. The story becomes one of ambiguous characters, amorphous threats, and unanswered questions, where the sense of a meaningful sacrificial death—which lies at the heart of the Christian story—is lost. Instead, the episode becomes delusion, the ravings of a speaker pushed beyond physical and emotional limits, a story that encapsulates the sensations and affective climate of the post-1918 moment.

Option 3: Silence, Forgetting, and Their Afterlife

Alongside all the ways *The Waste Land* registers the pandemic, from the symptoms of the virus to its aftermath of death and enervation, it also works as a testament to its erasure. Critics have frequently pointed out the poem's multiple references to silence and the difficulties of communication; indeed, such difficulties became a defining feature of modernism, in part through Eliot's defining poem.[83] The problems with speaking and communicating have been traced to the war, among other causes, but the poem is poignantly a showcase—and a resistance, and an example, and a representation—of the silence that surrounded the pandemic and the ways it became unspeakable and forgotten. The reasons for the perfect storm of silence that I outline in my introduction are folded into the poem's language, the work at once revealing and participating in the ways the outbreak so often remains unseen and unspoken. The qualities that prevented the culture—and even Eliot—from seeing the pandemic directly are part of what, in turn, have prevented us from seeing the pandemic's impact and scope. Woven into what follows are the two broad reasons for the silence from the introduction— the war's dominance over the pandemic and the difficulties of representation that illness presents—and an investigation of how Eliot's work grants voice to that silence.

Ironically, the war's very inexpressibility overshadowed and blocked the pandemic's corresponding challenges to representation. The war famously produced a crisis of language. How could the horrors of modern warfare possibly be captured in literature? One critic terms this "a primary creed in war literature," found "from rough diary notes to canonical poetry: the inexpressibility of war experience."[84] Ezekiel Black concurs, observing that "neither Eliot nor the war poets could voice their reaction to the Great War; more specifically, *The Waste Land* and trench poetry struggle with the ineffability of the age"[85] and use a variety of techniques and images to convey this difficulty. Black explores the poets' uses of prosopopeia (when a writer speaks for someone who cannot speak), as well as images of mouthlessness, muteness, blindness, paralysis, deafness, and the institutional impacts of censorship and bureaucracy during the war, all to express the sense that the war is inexpressible. Despite these challenges, the war's presence in the poem has been seen since its publication, trained as we are to read its presence within the gaps and silences. It's the other even more hidden and inexpressible trauma that we need to remember to see, one expressed in—and obscured by—all these images of erasure and voicelessness.

The Waste Land offers a miasmic atmosphere of failed vision, unseen deaths, silence, and failed communication. The poem begins with a double burial, the "forgetful snow" "covering / Earth," which in turn covers the dead.[86] The repeated line from The Tempest, "Those are pearls that were his eyes," suggests vision is opaque and also references a (supposed) drowning death in The Tempest that is not seen.[87] A voice in "The Burial of the Dead" proclaims "my eyes failed," while the frantic voice in "The Game of Chess" demands of her nonlistener, "Do you see nothing?" and a Cupid "hid[es] his eyes behind his wing."[88] Fogs and shadows abound. The two quasi-prophetic voices in the poem have vision issues: Madame Sosostris is "forbidden to see" whatever the "one-eyed merchant" "carries on his back," and Tireseas is blind.[89] This consistent failure to see coincides with breakdowns of hearing and speech. "I could not / Speak" says a voice in the opening section, and the frantic voice in the next demands " 'Speak to me. Why do you never speak? Speak.' " Even the singer can "speak not loud or long."[90] The recurring image of Philomel, brutally prevented from speaking when her tongue is cut out, leaves only the "Jug jug jug" to convey the horror of her traumatic tale.[91] The Waste Land as a whole is full of failed, one-sided conversations, from the couple in "The Game of Chess," to the pub scene, to the encounter with the typist and the young man carbuncular, to the voices throughout that seem to speak into a void. And silence pervades the poem: there is "no sound of water"; sounds are "dead"; rooms are "hush[ed]; the wind is "unheard"; a "frosty silence" reigns.[92] A sense of forgetfulness broods over the poem. The poem paradoxically gives voice to silence and erasure, recreating the climate in which the pandemic and its suffering became overlooked, unspoken, and unheard. The language hints of a shadow, something that has been forgotten or not dealt with; memories and bodies are lost to silence. Whether Eliot meant to, he captures the cultural position of the pandemic, brooding just below the surface but struggling to be heard amid all the noises of modern life and modern warfare.

Afterlife: When the pandemic is left out of critical discussions of The Waste Land, we miss a whole realm of ordinary—or at least widespread—experience. The poem registers the body's story in a way we have missed, since that story itself is hidden on so many levels. The poem's language and structure speak to the body's infection, delirium, fatigue, and suffering; its anxiety and terror and disrupted consciousness. It captures the elusiveness not just of the enemy but of a bodily experience and the shape that experience gave to thoughts and perspectives. Reading the poem through this lens grants more than additional context. It reveals how an experience may be everywhere, changing perceptions, language, memories, and the body, yet remain encoded, diffuse, and out of sight, part of a seemingly naturalized climate. The poem allows us to recognize these elements as constitutive qualities of an illness that has reached pandemic levels, granting a memorial to the unmemorialized.

The pandemic lens also invites a shift in how we see one of the poem's defining features—its ubiquitous fragments—so often imagined as the aftermath of a bomb, with the explosions of World War I leaving behind these bits of cultural shrapnel. These fragments should also be seen as the aftermath of a proliferating viral catastrophe—both in the body and in the air—the results of which fragment thoughts, memories, communities, bodies, stories, structures, and minds. The poem's many voices, another defining feature of the poem, emerge as a way to capture a difficult-to-balance quality of pandemic suffering: it was both an individual experience—a conflict fought within the body—and a global tragedy. The voices speak to the individual quality, but their numbers and their overlap, and the way a cacophony of contemporary voices blend with the crowd of allusions, register the collective quality of a global outbreak. To read *The Waste Land* in its full context, we must hear what these voices tell us about the silencing of illness and the pandemic's ghostly but widespread afterlife.

Chapter Six

APOCALYPTIC PANDEMIC

W. B. Yeats's "The Second Coming"

In November 1918, at the height of the pandemic's deadly second wave, W. B. Yeats watched helplessly as his pregnant wife, George, struggled to fight off the virus at their rented house in Dublin. Outside, the pandemic was sweeping through the city. The countryside where Yeats thought of taking George offered no escape, already overrun with funerals and bodies. Before it was over, the flu would infect between 600,000 and 800,000 people in Ireland and kill far more than were lost in the internal political violence that was also consuming the country.[1] While coming close to death, George ended up surviving the virus, unlike so many pregnant women at the time.[2] Just a few weeks later, during his wife's recovery, Yeats wrote arguably his most famous poem, "The Second Coming," one widely read as channeling the zeitgeist of its turbulent moment. The poem is the only work I've considered so far that was not only completed while the pandemic was still unfolding but written directly after witnessing a near-fatal case. Perhaps for this reason, the poem offers a different pandemic landscape, one that plunges the reader into the immediacy of a nightmarish present. While Woolf and Eliot offer flashes of symptoms and the authors in part 1 detail particular cases, they also grant some sense of the body's aftermath. Yeats, though, brings us into a violent cataclysm as it unfolds, one that telescopes between an internal, bodily apocalypse and the vast societal breakdown wreaked by a pandemic-level event.

"The Second Coming" is rarely considered through a pandemic lens. This neglect arises in part from the familiar suspects I trace throughout this study—the ways the war's violence became what counted as context, the ways illness is hard to represent, and so on. More specifically to Yeats, though, the pandemic is hard to see because the parameters of critical discussions surrounding the poet and violence are set entirely around the violence that humans inflict on one another.[3] Scholars routinely place violence at the center of his work—as Michael Wood summarizes, "Yeats is a poet almost everyone associates with violence"—and this association centers on politically based conflict, especially on clashes within Ireland and Europe.[4] This focus is appropriate because such violence is the type that primarily *did* occupy the poet. In his work, Yeats narrates political violence from recent outbreaks (for example, "Easter 1916," "Nineteen Hundred and Nineteen") to those of the distant past ("Leda and the Swan"). He depicts specific violent acts (like the shooting of Ellen Quinn in "Nineteen") as well as mythological ones (the rape of Leda). He at times makes the agents and victims of the violence visible (the swan, the soldiers, the mother, Leda) and at times makes the violence more hidden or deemphasized ("Easter 1916"). The violence generated by humans is central to all these works, and thus it is no surprise that "The Second Coming" is typically read in this context as well. Critics repeatedly cite a trio of historical events that fuel the poem's apocalyptic atmosphere: the First World War, the Russian Revolution, and the violence in Ireland, specifically acts committed by the Black and Tans. Both Yeats and his wife later noted most of these influences.[5]

The focus on the poem's political violence has obscured, however, the distinct viral violence that was unfolding at the same time, both within Yeats's home and in the streets of Dublin. When we consider "The Second Coming" in light of the pandemic—and also in relationship to Yeats's other work and other accounts of plagues—an illness-based destruction emerges as a powerful, overlooked force in the pantheon of Yeatsean violence. Encoded within the poem are the two landscapes on which such violence unfolds: on the body and on society. On one level, the poem captures the individual destruction inflicted by an invisible agent, capable of producing a reality-shattering delirium; on another level, it depicts the society-wide breakdown produced by a lethal, global outbreak in the aftermath of world war. When we account for illness-based violence, we grant a critical pandemic context to the poem, but we also do more. The violence at the heart of lethal illness becomes visible, the pandemic emerges as the cataclysmic force it was, and our readings of Yeatsean violence shift, as viral- and human-generated destruction emerge as instructive foils for each other.

I read the poem first as the internal perspective of a body caught in a violent delirium. For both the reader and the speaker(s) within the poem, the source of the destruction is either hidden or mysterious, even while the violence seeps into every line. The miasmic atmosphere I've traced in other works is present, but here infused with a catastrophic immediacy. The depiction differs from Yeats's portrayals of political conflict; to illuminate the distinctions, I place the "The Second Coming" in conversation with a cluster of his major poems on violence, teasing out how reading for nonhuman threats changes how we assess violence across his works. In the last half of the chapter, I move to the second terrain of illness-based violence: the broad unraveling of the social fabric wrought by pandemics. I put Yeats's poem in dialogue with two iconic literary plague narratives, Giovanni Boccaccio's *The Decameron* and Daniel Defoe's *A Journal of the Plague Year*, as well as with accounts of conditions unfolding in Ireland and Dublin during the 1918 pandemic. Read within these contexts, "The Second Coming" emerges as a concentrated, twenty-two-line version of pandemic-level violence and the dissolving order it brings. Yeats reenvisions common Christian tropes for framing societal breakdown, drawing on apocalyptic imagery and imagining a violent resurrection that threatens destruction rather than salvation. In the face of all this internal and external violence, though, Yeats shapes his poem into a possible antidote, granting, to borrow a phrase from the poet A. R. Ammons, "one place to dwell."[6]

A word on intention before I begin: Yeats may well have had the pandemic and its deadly threat to his wife and unborn child in mind as he wrote the poem and thus deliberately crafted his language to reflect the experience. Alternatively, the pandemic's presence might have been less deliberate, a product of his recent experience but not something he consciously wove into the language, given how little time he had had to process the event. Yeats spent much of the 1910s and 1920s focused not only on politics but also on developing his mystical, world-structuring theories of historical epochs, and George spent those years helping him do it. Both of them saw George's role as that of support figure, a conduit (literally) for Yeats's spiritual guides, and neither of them were used to considering George at the center of a critical event or illness as historically important. Yeats did not need to consciously write the pandemic into his poem for its effects to be registered, though; indeed, the poem suggests how hard such an experience was to see clearly. The poem evokes the immediacy of a traumatic event as it unfolds: the emotions and fragments of thought, the hallucinatory reality, the bewildering, overwhelming sense of cataclysm. It doesn't mention the pandemic or the war or indeed any historical event directly. The nature of a traumatic event, as Yeats had just seen, is precisely one of emotional and sensory immediacy without a clear frame for what is happening. When we add a traumatic experience that by its nature is a vast, spreading, unseen contagion that produces as it unfolds a reality-altering delirium in its victims, we have an event where a clear representation not only becomes difficult but would fail to capture the way it was experienced at the time. Yeats's poem brings the reader into this confusion and terror in ways that reproduce, even in how it does not name, the experience of a viral trauma. If we limit our readings of the poem's threats to the political violence Yeats later cited, we miss a vast realm of experience that was hard to see, even for the poet. Like the automatic writing the couple practiced, "The Second Coming" channels the pandemic experience as well as its suppression, capturing a violence and a threat the poet had just witnessed. If he did not process the violence directly and pushed aside its memory once it passed, as so many did, the poem nevertheless registers this experience profoundly.

TAKE ONE: A DOMESTIC APOCALYPSE

"The Second Coming" evokes the individual sickroom in surprising ways, capturing the Yeatses' particular struggle and also the more general bodily violence the virus inflicted on its victims. George would have been about six months pregnant when she came down with influenza on November 18, 1918.[7] Pneumonia developed, and she quickly became seriously ill, requiring both a day and night nurse. Ann Saddlemyer, George's biographer, offers one of the few full accounts of the illness, noting, "It was not long before [Yeats] feared that George was dying";[8] Yeats wrote in a letter to Lady Gregory on November 26 that "Poor George is very ill. . . . I am very anxious."[9] He was right to be; as the historian John Barry observes, "Those most vulnerable of all to influenza, those most likely of the most likely to die, were pregnant women," with death rates ranging between 23 and 71 percent.[10]

In all my research on the pandemic, I have rarely come across a story about a pregnant woman who caught the virus and survived; unlike William Maxwell's mother, George was one of the lucky ones. By November 29, Yeats could report that she was somewhat better and sleeping without drugs—though "She sleeps constantly now or half sleeps & is of course very week [*sic*]" and might soon be able to go to the country.[11] Lady Gregory wrote to say that the country was far from safe, with Gort full of "hearses and funerals" from pandemic deaths.[12] By December 10, George was well enough to be moved to a nearby house, but by Christmas, Saddlemyer reports, she "was still in a highly nervous condition and [Yeats] was not much better," with nightmares so severe that the spiritual "guides" that advised the couple through George's automatic writing were giving advice on how to cure them.[13]

As George lay "gasping for breath upstairs," the horror of the experience was deepened for Yeats by a dramatic confrontation with Maud Gonne.[14] Gonne, a beautiful Irish revolutionary and Yeats's famous muse, to whom he'd proposed several times, owned the house where the couple was staying. She had been imprisoned in London but released because of poor health, and she snuck back into Ireland disguised as a Red Cross nurse. Gonne was ill with pulmonary tuberculosis and was racing to escape the authorities. She arrived at the house and demanded entry and was astonished when Yeats angrily denied her. As the fighting continued, the doctor intervened, declaring that the noise and disruption were life-threatening to George. Gonne left but sent outraged letters to Yeats in the aftermath. While they later reconciled, "things were never quite the same again between them."[15] These intense experiences—his wife feverish and plagued by nightmares, she and their unborn child near death, and a woman central to his life and poetry outraged, ill, and raving—weave their way into "The Second Coming," alongside additional sensory details that other pandemic victims would have recognized.

From one perspective, the poem reads as a fever dream or a delirious nightmare seen from within a dangerously ill body, a mode that parallels the hallucinatory experiences we saw in Woolf, Eliot, and Porter. The sense of restless tossing, a "turning and turning," infuses the poem's opening, the meter itself echoing a relentless repeated motion.[16] The turning evokes Yeats's concept of the gyres but also, far more concretely, suggests the restless agitation of fever.[17] The speaker in both stanzas of the poem seems to be raving and disjointed, declaring, famously, that "Things fall apart; the centre cannot hold" before shouting out about "some revelation" and "The Second Coming!"[18] And then all at once, a hallucination abruptly "troubles" the speaker's "sight": "a shape with lion body and the head of a man," moving across a nameless desert before "darkness drops again."[19] The end of the poem conjures not a vision of war but precisely the kind of nightmare a deadly ill, delirious, pregnant woman might have: "twenty centuries of stony sleep" are "vexed to nightmare by a rocking cradle," before an ambiguous "rough beast" is born.[20] Indeed, the section reads like a pregnancy-centered horror flick, complete with the rocking cradle and demon spawn. And it's hardly far-fetched to think that George's personal experiences are woven into the poem right beside Yeats's larger theories about history's two-thousand-year cycles; images from the poem had already been shaped by George's earlier automatic writing, as several scholars have argued. The critic Simona Vannini, for example, notes that George "was instrumental in the genesis of 'The Second Coming' by contributing to the elaboration of Yeats's philosophical system and by suggesting symbols and images that reappeared in the final version of the poem."[21] Both Yeats and his wife reported that they often dreamed compatible or connected dreams, with the visions from one spilling over (it seemed to them) to the other.[22] The poem's language offers a linguistic representation of such a connection, a shared nightmare, as it were, shaping the poet's thoughts.

At the same time, the poem also captures the perspective of a bedside observer, a witness from outside the ill body gripped by terror, dread, and bleakness over what unfolds. Much of the language fits the grim conclusions of someone watching a loved one inch closer to death: the gyre widens, communication between partners breaks down, things fall apart, innocence drowns. In the second stanza, an "I" emerges as the hallucinatory vision unfolds, creating the sense of a shared thought conversation between a delirious voice and an observing one:

> Surely some revelation is at hand;
> Surely the Second Coming is at hand.
> The Second Coming! Hardly are those words out
> When a vast image out of *Spiritus Mundi*
> Troubles my sight[23]

The first lines extend the sense of delirium—the speaker repeats words and phrases, the tone is agitated, the speaker shouts the third line. There's a tonal shift, though, after the shout. The phrase about the words being hardly "out" hints at a new presence different from the one who has just spoken. The tone modulates to a calmer register—the speaker, now identified as a "my," is "trouble[d]" by a vision, not quite the intense raving of the earlier lines. The whole poem may be read as voiced by a single speaker, moving among moods and visions, but the shifts also reflect the very process by which the couple so often worked, with George channeling spirit voices that in turn conjured Yeats's visions.[24] The stanza hints at this relationship and the seeming overlap of consciousness between the two, but here the exchange is translated into a nightmarish setting that recalls a sickbed vigil. For this second observer, the "rough beast" appears as a pitiless coming threat, one that grants a paradoxically ambiguous certainty: "now I know," the speaker states, that all this "stony sleep" produced a nightmare from a "rocking cradle."[25] The language links to Yeats's larger cosmic vision and at the same time powerfully evokes the emotional resonance of this particular (potential) deathbed: a sense of endlessness, of a deathly sleep, of a nightmare of an empty cradle. And what, the speaker asks at the end, will be born of this moment—death? More violence? Certainly not, it would seem, a child or a savior.

The forms of violence embedded in the language of this scene suggest the distinct qualities of the flu's threat. If we think of violence as typically having both characters and plot—the victims, the perpetrators, and the unfolding of the act itself—"The Second Coming" presents a story where perpetrators and acts are obscured. As critics have observed, Yeats carefully revised the threats within the poem, editing the language to make the dangers more ambiguous. These changes stripped the violence of its human agency in ways that register the pandemic. The detailed scholarship (started by Jon Stallworthy and Curtis B. Bradford and carried on by many others)[26] on the revisions suggests that Yeats played with different versions, originally highlighting specific events and people. At first, for example, his rough drafts included references to murders and to individuals associated with revolutions, like Marie Antoinette and Edmund Burke:

Marie Antoin ette has
Most [?brutally] [?died], and ~~no~~
Burke ~~has spoken [?to the]~~ has [?cried][27]

The tyrant has the anarch in his pay
And murderer to follow murderer[28]

~~While~~ the mob fawns upon the murderer[?s]
And
~~While~~ the judge ~~nod~~ nods before his empty dock,
And there no Burke to cry aloud no Pit[29]

Yeats includes specific victims of political violence, along with possible perpetrators—the tyrant, the anarch, the murderer, the mob. No recourse is present—the judge nods, Burke and Pit are absent. References to Germany and Russia, present in other drafts, also disappear in the final poem. All these elements clearly evoke Yeats's typical focus on human-based violence. In the final version of the poem, though, this language disappears. As Vannini convincingly argues, the "destructive energy" in the poem became impersonal, losing references to specific political events, countries, or people: the "human and non-human, historical and natural agents finally concurred to produce an apocalyptic, universal scenario of 'great cataclysm' that was both geological and cosmological"[30]—and, as I argue, biological.

In making his revisions, Yeats not only made the poem broader and more universally allusive, but within this very broadening, he creates a form that better captures the elusive quality of the pandemic's violence. The perpetrator of the destruction is unclear and, even when more materially present, is no longer human; in the first stanza, Yeats hides the threat in a series of phrases in the passive voice: "Mere anarchy is loosed," "The blood-dimmed tide is loosed," "The ceremony of innocence is drowned."[31] The threat comes from nowhere and everywhere at once, a seemingly agentless force that brings destruction. The one semipolitical word, "anarchy," signals broad chaos and is notably different than the draft's "anarch," which implies a human perpetrator. The language instead conjures a hostile, miasmic omniscience, a viral-like threat with broad destructive powers. When a villain does seem to arise, it remains ambiguous: it is "a vast image" appearing "somewhere in sands," "A shape" that disappears while "darkness drops again." Even the concrete image of the sphinx-like beast holds a neutral and nonhuman quality: his gaze is "blank and pitiless as the sun,"[32] like a virus (or pathogenic god) that moves without intent, emotion, or agency. We end with a question as to "what rough beast" this might be.[33] The characteristics of this threat—its ambiguity, its vastness, its blankness, its purposeless destruction—suggest the broader climate of the time and also encapsulate the form and terror of a vast, pitiless, global contagion. These very qualities made the threat hard to visualize or locate. When the *Times* tries to explain the pandemic in 1921, for example, the writer speaks of the difficulty of grasping it, resorting to a destructive weather metaphor: "So vast was the catastrophe [of the flu] and so ubiquitous its prevalence that our minds, surfeited with the horrors of war, refused to realize it. It came and went, a hurricane across the green fields of life."[34] The poem channels this sense of vast catastrophe and ubiquitous threat that so many nevertheless refuse to "realize."

Yeats's changes also made the possible victims of this violence—and the type of suffering they face—more resonant with the pandemic. When the speaker declares that "the ceremony of innocence is drowned,"[35] he or she evokes what the virus did to mothers and their babies; as we've seen, flu victims drowned in their beds from the fluids that accumulated in their lungs, as George came close to doing. The "blood-dimmed tide" also echoes ominously.[36] The idea of a tide so infused with blood as to dim the water—one where the cause of this blood is hidden and its effects are loosed upon the world—suggests both the larger threat of a worldwide virus and the dramatic hemorrhaging this flu produced; as John Barry summarizes, "when the virus turned violent, blood was everywhere," "pouring from the . . . nose, mouth, even from the ears or around the eyes."[37] For Yeats's readers in 1920, the "blood-dimmed tide" recalled a violence that snuck into bodies and violently corrupted what it found.

A PARTICULAR FORM OF VIOLENCE

I've focused on the way "The Second Coming" evokes a viral-like threat and suggests a body experiencing an illness-based violence. Before turning to the way the poem registers the repercussions of such violence on the broader society, I pause here to highlight the distinctions and continuities between the violence within "The Second Coming" and the violence in other poems. I turn to specific moments in three of the most famous poems of Yeatsean violence: "Easter 1916," "Nineteen Hundred and Nineteen," and "Leda and the Swan."[38] In the first poem, written before the pandemic, Yeats ponders an explicitly political violence, mulling over whether the sacrifice of the Irish revolutionaries executed by England might in the end be worthwhile, though he has his doubts. The tone of the poem is markedly different from "The Second Coming," and some of this difference arises not from the type of violence depicted but from the stage it has reached. "The Second Coming" occurs within a still unfolding destruction, the poem's present-tense structure capturing the body's suffering and terror as it happens. "Easter 1916," a poem largely in the past tense, takes place in the aftermath of violence, the speaker sorrowful but also thoughtful, calm, and reflective. The tonal difference also suggests the forms of violence each poem explores. Sarah Cole describes the violence within "Easter 1916" as in part "enchanted," capable of generative possibilities.[39] The violence represented by the revolutionaries might still be placed within a structure of meaning—their actions might well grant more rights, eventually, to Ireland. While Yeats notes that "Too long a sacrifice / Can make a stone of the heart,"[40] gripping the revolutionaries in a single-minded pursuit where their humanity is potentially jeopardized, the violence they represent remains within a sacrificial structure capable of bringing gain. The additional violence suggested in the poem—the execution of the revolutionaries by the English state—is mentioned only by implication, and even this violence might be mitigated. "England," the speaker muses, "may keep faith."[41] By contrast, part of the terror of "The Second Coming" is how outside the sacrificial structure the violence seems to be, how purposeless and fruitless this "mere anarchy" is.[42] As I investigate in the next section, Yeats may evoke a Second Coming model and explain the anarchy through his elaborate theories on historical epochs, but the atmosphere of violence remains frighteningly unstructured, produced by an unseen force and potentially increasing with the arrival of something inhuman. By 1919, Yeats had grown increasingly disillusioned with political violence, but "The Second Coming" registers a violence without meaning or even a visible enemy.

The representations of the perpetrators are also markedly different in the two poems and highlight the distinctions between human- and illness-based violence. In "Easter 1916," Yeats identifies in concise but vivid detail the individual revolutionaries, who are both instigators of a violence that carries a "terrible beauty" and also its victims.[43] He notes specific strengths among the group—poetic talent, daring, courage, sweetness, horsemanship—and acknowledges weaknesses. The other perpetrator—England—is named but largely left out; the omission does not seem to be because the threat is too hard to define but because Yeats seeks to put the revolutionaries center stage. England is not the main character in the story he tells. The violence takes place elsewhere, its eruption over before the poem begins. "The Second Coming," though, hides the perpetrators in all the ways I have described, marking a sense of widespread political upheaval but also suggesting a new conveyer of violence in the very lack of identification he offers.

By the time Yeats starts "Nineteen Hundred and Nineteen" in 1921—after his experiences in the pandemic and after the conflicts in Ireland and in Europe had reached bloody new heights—his views on the generative possibilities of political violence had shifted. Perhaps the most studied poem in the canon of Yeatsean violence, "Nineteen Hundred and Nineteen" offers both an instructive overlap with "The Second Coming" and a revealingly different image of violence. In many ways, the two works serve as companion poems, two representations of the cataclysmic events of that historical moment. If we read "The Second Coming" as a poem that speaks in important ways about illness-based violence within a larger atmosphere of war, we can read "Nineteen Hundred and Nineteen" as a poem primarily about human-inspired destruction within a larger atmosphere of nightmarish delirium and miasmic threat.

The climate of "Nineteen Hundred and Nineteen" in part seems equally fitting for the aftermath of both types of violence. From the loss evoked in the first line, "Many ingenious lovely things are gone," to the bass line of lament, enervation, and despair that runs through the poem, Yeats narrates a grim moment.[44] The structures set in place against chaos—laws, productive work, aesthetic invention—are all deemed worthless and hopelessly naïve. "No work can stand," the speaker declares, even if "health, wealth [and] peace of mind" were sacrificed.[45] All efforts are in vain, and the great, the wise, and the good should all be mocked—and then, we can "mock mockers."[46] The dream that a cure might be found for humankind and all its violence is, the speaker says, itself a sign of madness:

O but we dreamed to mend
Whatever mischief seemed

To afflict mankind, but now
That winds of winter blow
Learn that we were crack-pated when we dreamed.[47]

The language speaks to Yeats's own dashed hopes to effect productive change through his poetry and his other aesthetic projects and to the larger expectations at the start of the twentieth century that advances in technology, medicine, and diplomacy might mend both bodies and nations. All these efforts are revealed as a mad dream, the hopes blown away by the "winds of winter," an image that registers both the storms of political violence and the terrible winter of the pandemic's second wave. A ferocious wind blows throughout the poem, one more overtly violent than the contagion-like wind of *The Waste Land*; the speaker describes the "levelling wind," the "wind shriek[ing]," a "sudden blast of dusty wind," and "the labyrinth of the wind," all fitting images for a time of "mere anarchy" and destructive, invisible forces raging around an unprotected populace.[48]

Unlike "The Second Coming," though, the later poem is crowded with human agents and references to military violence. There are rogues and rascals and great armies; cannons, guardsmen, and a drunken soldiery; incendiaries, bigots, and mockers. The many violent actions that are referenced are human initiated: bribing, threatening, murdering, burning, breaking, trafficking. By contrast, the violent actions within "The Second Coming" are markedly free of human agency. Anarchy and blood are "loosed" upon the world, the drowning comes from no agency that is seen. The beast moves and lurches; birds turn and reel; a cradle vexes—but despite the poem's atmosphere of intense violence and horror, the source is far less tangible than the perpetrators within "Nineteen."

Two passages in particular suggest the atmospheric overlap between the two poems and the distinctions between the violence they depict. In the first, the speaker describes an act of horrific violence against another mother and her unborn child:

Now days are dragon-ridden, the nightmare
Rides upon sleep: a drunken soldiery
Can leave the mother, murdered at her door,
To crawl in her own blood, and go scot-free;
The night can sweat with terror[49]

Yeats narrates a specific story of violence: the infamous English Black and Tans had shot the pregnant Ellen Quinn as she sat on the front lawn of her house, holding another child.[50] Like "The Second Coming," the language hints of hallucinatory altered states—the dragons, the nightmare, the sleep, the drunkenness, the terror and sweat. The violence—one that takes place within the domestic space and not on the battlefield—is senseless and goes unpunished. This violence, though, is human based: the villains and victims are clear, the violence committed is murder, the blood is "her own," and while the soldiers go free, they are at least generally identified and visible. None of these differences mitigate the horror, but they do suggest two different representations of violence faced by two representative mothers: one fighting a hidden enemy that produced a "blood-dimmed tide" across the globe and one a victim of visible violence produced by ongoing political conflict. Both turned 1919 into a hallucinatory nightmare when nights and bodies "can sweat with terror."

The second passage that evokes a similar atmosphere yet a different violence is the last section of the poem. Critics frequently note the overlap between the ending of "Nineteenth" and "The Second Coming."[51] The tone is apocalyptic, with hints of the hallucinatory-delirium mode:

> Violence upon the roads: violence of horses;
> ....
> All break and vanish, and evil gathers head:
> ....
> A sudden blast of dusty wind and after
> Thunder of feet, tumult of images,
> Their purpose in the labyrinth of the wind;
> ....
> But now wind drops, dust settles; thereupon
> There lurches past, his great eyes without thought
> Under the shadow of stupid straw-pale locks,
> That insolent fiend Robert Artisson
> To whom the love-lorn Lady Kyteler brought
> Bronzed peacock feathers, red combs of her cocks.[52]

On the one hand, the imagery links back to "The Second Coming" on multiple levels. The atmosphere is one of turmoil and confusion. The horses evoke the four horsemen of the apocalypse, bringing both war and pestilence. Confusion reigns, and the wind suggests both an invisible threat and a purposeless one. The fiend at the end recalls the hallucinatory vision of the rough beast, one slouching and one lurching, both seemingly senseless. Amid these similarities, though, the threat here is far more human; the lines I've omitted all suggest human violence—military horses on parade, a reference to Herodias's daughters (one of them Salome, who asked for John the Baptist's head), and women being groped. The coming threat seems almost comically ordinary, like a regency romance villain (that insolent fiend Robert!), though Yeats's footnote tells us he is a fourteenth-century evil spirit.[53] The critic Michael Ragussis reads this ending as antiapocalyptic, producing no escape and bringing no knowledge, and Wood finds that the ending signals a modern deflation.[54] To some extent, this ending is the logical extension of the futility of human endeavor Yeats notes earlier and the senselessness of the human-based violence depicted. Rob Dugget observes that here is "a sacrifice utterly devoid of heroism," with "no heroes" and, even at the very end, "no clear villains" either.[55] We end with decadence and human(ish) figures that promise nothing good, but they are a more deflated and more visible threat than the ominous, undefined, and nonhuman terror of the beast. From another perspective, though, this ending fits the pandemic as well: a purposeless coda to the political violence that preceded it, its ordinary name (influenza, Robert) hiding the scope of the danger.

If "Nineteen Hundred and Nineteen" is a companion poem that suggests both an overlap with, and the distinctiveness of, the violence within "The Second Coming," Yeats's later poem "Leda and the Swan" is in many ways a negative-print image of "The Second Coming." Written several years after the pandemic, "Leda" narrates a violent rape that—in Yeats's schematics of history—takes place at the other end of the gyre, in an epoch before the birth of Christ rather than at the bloody end of the Christian era.[56] Instead of a monstrous birth, the poem details a moment of conception, what Yeats called a "violent annunciation,"[57] that begins with "A sudden blow."[58] Both the agent of the violence and its victim are clear. The rapist, Zeus in the form of a swan, has a distinct if overwhelming body, with wings, webs, bill, breast, loins, blood, and beak. The survivor of this violence, Leda, likewise has an identifiable physical presence, with nape, thighs, breast, and fingers. Leda's specific mental and physical suffering is represented: she staggers, she is beaten and caught, she is helpless, she is terrified. The rape, committed by a swan, is not technically an instance of human-based violence, but in as much as Zeus represents a humanlike god with agency and political power, the violence fits within Yeats's depictions of specifically agented, human-initiated acts. The poem offers no passive-voice constructions where the agents of violence are unseen. The intent of the poem's perpetrator is brutally obvious, the swan far from an ambiguous rough beast with uncertain aims.

The narratives of violence within the "Leda" poem have a corresponding brutal clarity and are positioned within larger frameworks. The swan beats, catches, holds, masters, and drops Leda, and the rape itself leads to war and its human-based violence, engendering "The broken wall, the burning roof and tower / And Agamemnon dead."[59] Yeats places the rape within a (mythical) historical arc, one that—in giving birth to Helen of Troy—is a precipitating cause for the Trojan War. This rape suggests the start of a literary arc as well, engendering those two classic narratives of human-based violence, The Iliad and The Aeneid. As many scholars point out, Leda's rape may also be read as a representation of Ireland's colonization, further framing it within an explicitly political narrative.[60] Whether this violence may be generative in other ways—whether Leda will be able to "put on his knowledge with his power"—remains a (deeply problematic) question.[61]

Despite the clarity of both character and action in this representation of human-initiated violence, in his turn to myth, Yeats creates a far more stylized and performative violence than we see in the other poems, one that, indeed, serves as a counter to the other depictions. In its escape into classical models, the poem seems at a distance from both the grim realities of the Irish and European conflicts as well as from the immediacy of the amorphous violence of "The Second Coming." In "Leda," the image of blood translates into power: the "brute blood of the air" masters Leda even as it suggests the violence committed.[62] The image is a far less immediate and disturbing representation than the "blood-dimmed tide" or Ellen Quinn's spilled blood. Indeed, there's a way that the circumscribed nature of this violent act, with one perpetrator and one victim, and its specificity (a single act, though it ripples out to produce greater conflict) helps counter the more widespread violence in both "Nineteen" and "The Second Coming" and, to a lesser extent, in "Easter 1916." The poem's nonfatal attack, controlled within the poem's formal sonnet structure, becomes an odd kind of shelter from the larger atmosphere of both human and nonhuman violence that infuses the other poems.

Despite shared qualities with the other works, "The Second Coming" stands as distinct in the nonhuman agency it suggests. "Easter 1916," "Nineteen Hundred and Nineteen," and "Leda and the Swan" may each offer different takes on violence, but they all concern specific people and acts, a specific history, and a human-initiated destruction, all seen from the vantage point of an outside observer who does not seem, quite, to have witnessed the violence in person, except in the moments of overlap I note in "Nineteen." The difference in this violence does not mean that "The Second Coming" must be about the pandemic, but it does highlight how the poem registers violence that Yeats had seen firsthand and that his wife had experienced, captured from within the immediacy of that trauma and allowing little distance from the unfolding events. The reader is within the violated body, within the delirious mind, within the hallucination, within the grief and terror, and within the anarchy and blood and drowning, without being able to see or understand its cause or its remedy or what might come next. The poem's terror additionally emerges from there being no raping swan or drunken soldiery—no source for the anarchy and blood that has been loosed upon the world—and thus no possible recourse or way to mount a defense. Something is coming for the innocent and the rest of the world, and something is both threatening the cradle and promising a grotesque new birth. This is indeed a second coming—a reference to the apocalypse, as I detail in the next section—but also the herald of a new threat: after the first coming of war and political upheaval, a second coming, this time of plague. The poem is certainly about a thousand other things, including the human-based violence that was tearing at the world, but it also distinctly registers—and does not name—a violence that produced part of its terror from that very anonymity.

TAKE TWO: A PUBLIC APOCALYPSE AND PANDEMIC-LEVEL VIOLENCE

"The Second Coming" reveals another terrain of illness-based violence that emerges when a lethal disease reaches pandemic levels: the widespread breakdown of social structures and institutions that may, in turn, produce disorder and human-initiated violence. The poem's depictions of chaos and unrest have been difficult to see as expressions of such violence because these conditions were so profoundly entangled with those of war and revolution. We need to recover the particular forms of societal violence that a pandemic may produce to recognize the ways "The Second Coming" speaks to these forms. To initiate this recovery, I turn to two classic literary accounts of pandemics where the widespread disruption was not intertwined with (and thus not obscured by) global war: Giovanni Boccaccio's *The Decameron* (c. 1353) and Daniel Defoe's *A Journal of the Plague Year* (1722). These works remain the iconic literary depictions of plague (with Albert Camus's *The Plague* added in 1947), and Yeats had close ties to both. He was reading Boccaccio as early as 1904 and likely before; *The Decameron* was part of his personal library, and he drew on the work when writing *A Vision* in 1925.[63] Defoe's work was likewise familiar; Yeats's father had done the illustrations for an edition of *A Journal of the Plague Year* in 1895, with Yeats's sister serving as his model, and Yeats held a biography of the author in his library.[64] Both visually and linguistically, then, such plague accounts would have been part of Yeats's imaginative wellspring. They also epitomize the ways a pandemic may produce a breakdown of social norms, laws, and communities and grant eerie parallels to scenes from the influenza pandemic, both in Dublin and elsewhere (with some instructive differences). The parallels bring into sharp relief the way Yeats's images of "mere anarchy" capture a pandemic-level violence and disruption.

Things fall apart; the centre cannot hold

Boccaccio and Defoe depict communities ravaged by pandemic illness and breaking apart. Boccaccio's *Decameron* recounts the bubonic plague of Florence in 1348, using the outbreak as a frame tale: the description of the plague-ridden city is offered in vivid detail at the start of the story, the outbreak prompting a group of ten people to flee to the countryside, where they distract themselves by telling the one hundred stories that make up the bulk of the work. Defoe's *Journal* remains focused on the plague throughout the narrative, describing the terrible epidemic in London in 1665 from the perspective of a saddler who stays in the city after many have fled. Both authors explore how pandemics break the structures that tie together a community. As one Boccaccio scholar notes, in a description that summarizes Defoe's account as well, in these plague-ridden cities, "the social, political, and religious institutions and hierarchies that served to organize and direct people's life have all broken down ... the structures that maintain society all seem to have crumbled."[65] In descriptions that might be taken from the influenza accounts I recount in my introduction, Boccaccio writes how the plague "spread[] ever-greater misery as it moved relentlessly from place to place," leaving deserted neighborhoods in its wake.[66] Burial practices were disrupted in both London and Florence: "the city was overwhelmed with corpses," Boccaccio writes, and Defoe's narrator notes how carts were pulled through the streets with calls for people to "*Bring out your Dead.*"[67] Defoe summarizes the situation in scenes familiar from this study:

After the Funerals became so many, that People could not Toll the Bell, Mourn, or Weep, or wear Black for one another, as they did before; no, nor so much as make Coffins for those that died ... all the Remedies ... had been used till they were found fruitless, and ... the Plague spread itself with an irresistible Fury ... it came at last to such Violence that the People sat still looking at one another, and seem'd quite abandon'd to Despair; whole Streets seem'd to be desolated, and not to be shut up only, but to be emptied of their Inhabitants; Doors were left open, Windows stood shattering with the Wind in empty Houses.... In a Word, People began to give up themselves to their Fears, and to think that all regulations and Methods were in vain, and that there was nothing to be hoped for, but an universal Desolation.[68]

Defoe's language captures the cascading breakdown a pandemic brings. Streets are empty, stores shut up, and in imagery that parallels Eliot's windblown empty chapel with its "tumbled graves" and Yeats's "levelling wind," the wind is the only occupant of the empty houses with their shattered windows.[69] Boccaccio likewise notes the "baleful wind blowing through" the emptying city.[70] As with the influenza pandemic, the tolling of bells is halted, the coffins are in short supply, and mass graves are prepared, with "trenches ... dug in the cemeteries" in Florence and corpses "all huddled together" in a "Pit, or Trench" throughout London.[71] Yeats's father represents this chaotic atmosphere in one of his illustrations for Defoe's work (figure 6.1), one that anticipates the scene in the photograph of the 1918 mass grave I discussed in the previous chapter (figure 5.2). Set in Defoe's plague

"He cried out aloud unable
to contain himself."

FIGURE 6.1. "He cried out aloud unable to contain himself." *Source*: Illustration by J.B. Yeats for Daniel Defoe's *A Journal of a Plague Year*, vol. 9, ed. George A. Aitken (London: J.M. Dent & Co., 1895), 70. Public domain.

graveyard, John Yeats's image depicts an isolated figure turning away from an open pit in despair, his whole family having succumbed. Two yawning mass graves dominate the image, ready to receive the ambiguous, undifferentiated tumble of bodies denoted by the white haze at the right. As in the influenza photograph, a cluster of gravediggers in masks stand uncertainly around one pit, their figures blurring with both the grave and the surroundings. The center of these communities indeed cannot hold, replaced, as in the images, by emptiness, chaos, and the open grave.

Dublin, and Ireland more generally, experienced a similar sense of chaos and a widespread breakdown of social structures during the influenza pandemic, which was frequently referred to as "the plague" or the "black flu."[72] As the register general, Sir William J. Thompson, observed in 1919, since the Great Famine, "no disease of an epidemic nature created so much havoc in any one year in Ireland as Influenza in 1918."[73] Dublin in particular, he noted, "paid a heavy toll to the great epidemic."[74] One doctor reported in the *Journal of the Irish Medical Association* that "it was truly a plague, a Black Death . . . [and] not influenza as we know it today . . . terrible fear . . . was everywhere."[75] In Dublin, "hundreds lay awaiting burial," and "observers noted the seemingly incessant funeral processions to Glasnevin cemetery in Dublin."[76] One witness described the "towering barricades" of coffins outside the undertakers.[77] In all three waves, schools, business, libraries, and even courts were closed. Hospitals and mortuaries were overwhelmed, and many of those tasked with helping maintain structure and order—from doctors and nurses to the police force and priests—were hit hard by the outbreak.[78] In Dublin, "business-owners complained of a 'trade paralysis,' as many people were reluctant or simply unable to leave their homes." The Abbey Theatre, launched by Yeats and Lady Gregory, took a heavy financial hit during the pandemic.[79] Transit shut down in many places, and especially in the counties, food and fuel shortages were widespread, the outbreak "incapacitat[ing] urban and rural communities across the island."[80] As the Irish flu historian Caitriona Foley summarizes, "the flu's intrusion on Irish society was sharp and far-reaching, causing disruptions across virtually all facets of daily life. Politics, religion, economics, education, agriculture, law and order, were all subject to its troublesome effects," and while these effects were not as disruptive or as long lasting as in the bubonic plague accounts, the disability and grief that followed the flu were.[81]

Mere anarchy is loosed upon the world, / The blood-red tide is loosed

The erosion of all these social structures, as Defoe and Boccaccio detail and as Yeats's poem evokes, is intimately tied to an illness-based, pandemic-level violence. In the long passage quoted in the previous section, Defoe offers a vivid portrait of how the plague's "irresistible Fury" brings the city "at last to such Violence" that residents are "abandon'd to Despair."[82] He uses similar language throughout the work, describing the "Violence of the Plague," the "Violence of the Contagion," "the Violence of the Distemper," and the "Violence of their Pain" as well as the way the outbreak "rage[d] with great Violence" and "spread its utmost Rage and violence."[83] Alongside this powerful, atmospheric force, the violence also moves internally, a blood-red tide that streams through bodies: victims, Defoe notes repeatedly, "had the Plague in their very Blood," "the Poison in their Blood" and "the penetrating Poison insinuating itself into their Blood in a Manner which it is impossible to describe, or indeed conceive."[84] Both authors observe how this bodily violence, coupled with the "fury" of the plague, in turn produced human-initiated violence and lawlessness. One character in *The Decameron* laments how people who had been exiled for their crimes now "mock[] that law as they rampage through the city committing acts of violence," while "the dregs of our city . . . thirst[] for our blood."[85] Defoe talks about the "Violence" committed against the watchmen who enforced the quarantines as well as the violent rages of those with fever (parallel to those from the influenza accounts in chapter 4) who, "Delirious and Distracted," ran "up and down the Streets . . . and offer'd all sorts of Violence to those they met."[86]

In Ireland, the influenza pandemic was described in similar violent terms. As Dr. Kathleen Lynn reported at a Sinn Féin convention at the time, "'the October and February outbreaks were of a violence almost unparalleled in the history of medicine.'"[87] Another doctor, Sir John Moore, who worked at Dublin's Adelaide Hospital during the pandemic, observed that no epidemic he had seen "'equaled the present outbreak in extent, virulence, or treacherous course.'"[88] Caitriona Foley notes how frequently the word "rage" was used in describing the Irish outbreak:

One verb frequently chosen for portrayals of the epidemic was "rage"—the flu was "raging" in winter 1918, it "raged so violently," "the flu epidemic now raged," "I now developed the flu which was raging at the time." . . . Witnesses retained a common sense of the omnipresence, speed, and uncontrollable spread of the flu waves, while the expressive, dramatic language which they selected to portray their experiences suggests that the epidemic had the ability to leave a deeply ingrained memory on those who witnessed its worst effects.[89]

The local government board spoke of "the virulence of the outbreaks," both the education commissioners and the registrar-general of the "ravages of influenza," and school inspectors of "the widespread and virulent outbreak of Influenza which raged throughout the entire world."[90] In language that echoes Defoe's account, the *Irish News* noted in an editorial in 1918 that the influenza was a "virulent infectious 'poison.' "[91]

In Dublin and Ireland, the sense of the flu's widespread virulence and the chaos it brought, however, often blended inextricably with the war and political conflict, making it palpable but hard to see. The historian Patricia Marsh, who has studied the newspaper coverage of the pandemic in Ireland, reports that political conflict continued to dominate the news even during the pandemic; articles certainly appeared on the outbreak, but they tended to emphasize the high casualty rates from the pandemic in enemy countries like Germany. Many in Ireland saw the outbreak as an extension of the war, with some newspapers reporting that the disease was trench fever brought over by the troops.[92] Imprisoned political activists were often hit hard by the virus, and Sinn Féin used the deaths to expose the cruel conditions imposed by England, furthering the way the outbreak was framed in political terms.[93] Some imprisoned activists who were also doctors were let out of prison to tend to the overwhelming numbers of patients.[94] One doctor, Vincent White, reported that he "had scarcely finished [his] battle against the 'flu" when he had "to move into another battle zone" and enter politics, noting ironically that the very patients he had treated during the pandemic now screamed political slurs at him as he walked by.[95] At an emergency station for flu victims, set up in Dublin on Harcourt Street, an angry mob stormed the building on November 11, 1918, during the Armistice celebrations. One activist, Eilis, Bean Ui Chonaill, was helping at the station that night and reported that they "suddenly realised that a hostile mob were attacking the building":

They immediately started to barricade the front door and windows with chairs and other furniture. Soon we found ourselves hauling chairs, etc., and stacking them up against the windows and helping the Volunteers generally. Shots rang out, mingled with vile language and shouts of "God save the King!" A state of terror reigned over the whole neighbourhood until a late hour when the crowds dispersed.[96]

The description neatly captures how the unsettled conditions produced by the pandemic overlapped and—here literally—ran into both the war and the political conflicts roiling Ireland, creating a sense of terror and siege and indeed an ambiguous sense of "mere anarchy." While the disruptions caused by the pandemic in Dublin were of shorter duration than what the earlier plague narratives expose, and while they were blended into the political disruptions in ways that are hard to untangle, Dublin's atmosphere of chaos and violence nevertheless echoes the earlier narratives, highlighting how the pandemic was a hidden but vital player in producing these conditions.

And everywhere / The ceremony of innocence is drowned

Part of the dissolving order in all the pandemic accounts lay in the profound defenselessness of the victims from the onslaught. As Boccaccio notes, the illness lay outside "all human wisdom and foresight," with remedies "all to no avail."[97] The bubonic plague, Defoe writes, "defy'd all the Application of Remedies," and "the very Physicians were seized with it."[98] Families were particularly vulnerable. Boccaccio relates that "fathers and mothers refused to tend to their children and take care of them," and Defoe recounts scene after scene of dead or dying mothers and children, his narrator declaring in despair that if such a scourge ever returned, "all Women that are with Child" should leave to spare them the untold "Misery" of these scenes.[99] Yeats's father captures this vulnerability in the frontispiece illustration for Defoe's *Journal* (figure 6.2). A watchman set to guard a plague house peeks in a window to discover the family has fled, leaving behind a young woman victim in her shift, stretched out on the floor. The young woman's face is that of Yeats's sister, Lily, who served as her father's model. The spilled container near the window, her scattered shoes, and the general sense of disarray, coupled with the figure's youth, suggest both violence and vulnerability.

Swirling around Yeats in 1918 were similar scenes, which were reported frequently in the newspapers. No effective cure was forthcoming—though

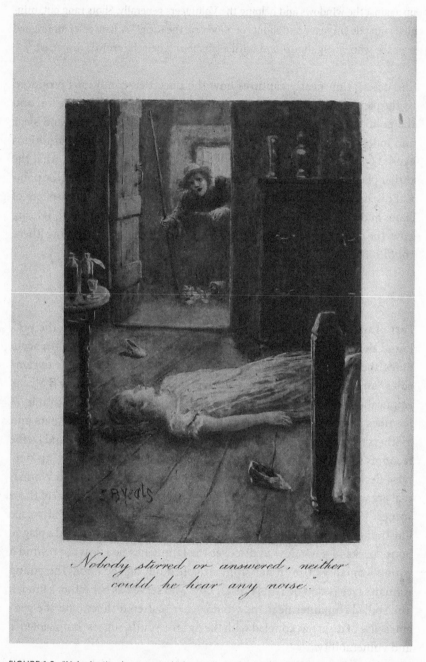

"Nobody stirred or answered, neither
could he hear any noise."

FIGURE 6.2. "Nobody stirred or answered." *Source*: Illustration by J.B. Yeats for Daniel Defoe's *A Journal of a Plague Year*, vol. 9, ed. George A. Aitken (London: J.M. Dent & Co., 1895), frontispiece. Public domain.

the newspapers were full of fake remedies—and the sense of vulnerability and fear was widespread.[100] One doctor's report, appearing in the *Connacht Tribune*, stressed that it was hard to convey how "bad things were" and relates a story that echoes John Yeats's illustration: he had gone "into one house at half past three in the morning" to find "a woman lying dead on the kitchen floor. Two children were staggering about hardly able to stand, and two more children were dead."[101] One Dublin activist noted that "it was not unusual for whole families to be stricken down together."[102] Another echoed the same sentiment, observing that "most families were stricken down and many lost three or four," with "thousands of unburied bodies."[103] "In Dublin," one witness observed, "one died in every house."[104] While the war and political news at first dominated Irish newspapers, during the second wave—when George Yeats caught the virus—newspapers across Ireland started "recounting the human tragedy of the disease." Articles told of suffering families: parents dying and leaving young children behind, parents losing all their young adult children in a week, young wives and husbands suddenly bereft of their spouses.[105] And unlike much of the political conflict, always rife with blame and recrimination, these deaths were more overtly those of innocent victims, with little sense that someone or some group could be blamed directly. This atmosphere, together with Yeats's grim vigil at the side of his pregnant wife, fueled the sense that family structures were vulnerable and breaking, producing a world in which "everywhere / The ceremony of innocence is drowned."

Despite the overlap among the pandemic experiences, Boccaccio and Defoe offer a far more overt and structured portrait than Yeats, reflecting some key differences among the outbreaks. The two earlier accounts treat pandemics that were more visible not only because they did not coincide with a world war but also because they killed a higher percentage of the population, even if they infected and killed far fewer people than the 1918 virus. There was also a significant emotional difference between the bubonic plague—which had a well-known fatality rate and produced terror even when simply rumored—and influenza, which while certainly dangerous did not at first generate a sense of widespread panic and fear. Perhaps for all these reasons, even at the influenza pandemic's height, it didn't seem to cause the same level of all-consuming disruption and breakdown described in the earlier accounts. Given the many destabilizing forces at work in 1918, it was difficult for many to acknowledge the pandemic for what it, in fact, was: a threat on a Black Plague–like scale. For Boccaccio and Defoe, a more direct treatment of a pandemic made sense. For Yeats, writing just after the war, amid ongoing civil violence, the pandemic understandably registers more indirectly.

For many in 1918, the influenza pandemic also lacked a key explanatory narrative that was more available to the authors of the earlier accounts: a belief that the outbreaks reflected a divine judgment or punishment and were thus part of a larger order. While Boccaccio and Defoe do, in part, question this explanation, they still frame the outbreaks according to this structure. Boccaccio's narrator wonders whether it was "the influence of the heavenly bodies or was sent down by God in His righteous anger to chastise us because of our wickedness."[106] Defoe's narrator declares repeatedly that the plague was part of God's judgment, though he rejects the idea that God might be "strik[ing] this and that particular Person."[107] By the time Yeats writes his poem, the idea that disease was sent as a punishment from God was far less widely accepted, even if, as Caitriona Foley points out, many in Ireland saw pandemic deaths as "God's will" and believed God might send healing.[108] The idea, however, that the *cause* of disease was divine punishment had faded; indeed, the prevailing attitude was one of bewilderment at the senselessness of the death. The divine-justice model for illness, while cruel and scientifically wrong, had ironically offered a potentially comforting structure of meaning amid the anarchy the plague inflicted: the suffering had a purpose—punishment—and was not simply random. Those still alive in 1919 who could no longer believe in such a structure had to find other ways to manage the vast sense of meaningless death the pandemic delivered. "The Second Coming" not only references this older Christian model of divine justice but also advances Yeats's own spiritual models as potential ways to understand and to cope with the societal collapse.

STRUCTURING THE APOCALYPSE

"The Second Coming" both evokes and resists the crisis of meaning the pandemic suggested. Yeats plays with explanatory biblical structures—the apocalypse (in which plague is a defining feature) and the story of the Second Coming. Critics frequently note the poem's climate of apocalyptic terror, one that centers on the destruction part of the end-of-the-world

Christian narrative.[109] In the biblical account, the first half of the end stage is an apocalypse involving war, earthquakes, plagues, and famine; as Matthew 24:7 summarizes, "nation shall rise against nation, and kingdom against kingdom: and there shall be famines, and pestilences, and earthquakes, in divers places."[110] In Revelation, one of the four horsemen of the apocalypse is the pale rider who represents plague, an image Katherine Ann Porter develops in her novella. After this destruction, the second phase begins, when Christ comes again, trumpets sounding, to raise the dead and usher in a new world. As Defoe and Boccaccio evoke, the story has the potential—grim though it is—to grant plot and meaning to a pandemic, seeing a deadly outbreak as a harbinger of an eventual glorious end. Yeats's poem references this narrative, but as the Yeats scholar David Rudrum points out, "The Second Coming" pushes against the salvation finale, when Christ comes in triumph to raise the dead.[111] Despite its title, the poem's opening stanza is drenched in first-phase apocalyptic destruction, when things fall apart, all is mere anarchy, the sea fills with blood, and innocents are lost.

The poem's second stanza narrates both the frantic search for meaning amid this destruction and the underlying fear that no meaning can be found. The delirious voice vacillates between a crazed certainty ("Surely the Second Coming is at hand") and an abiding sense of ambiguity: this certainty may just be delirious ravings.[112] The atmosphere casts doubt on whether the destruction fits into any larger structure. Yeats may reference the "second coming" part of the story, but like Eliot's use of both pagan and Christian stories of salvation, Yeats exposes the emptiness of these resurrection tropes for the modern moment. The poem, in effect, rejects central Christian ideas of sacrificial violence that indeed were already challenged at the time, first from the war and then from the pandemic. In the model at the heart of the Christian tradition, Jesus is tortured, disfigured, and killed in an act of human-based violence; this suffering and death, though, hold great meaning, framed as a sacrifice that redeems the world. And in the apocalypse, when Jesus is supposed to come again, the terrible destructive forces of war, plague, and natural disaster make possible—the narrative suggests—a better, cleaner world. In both cases, the violence is framed as redemptive; to borrow Yeats's formulation, a "terrible beauty is born."[113] As the war ground on, these Christian frames fell under fire, with many war writers exposing how the parallels between soldiers and Jesus could highlight and yet obscure the pointlessness of the modern slaughter.[114] In the pandemic's more extreme, nihilistic reality, death could not be constructed as saving any nation, ideal, or person. And no one could easily be blamed or demonized.[115] For many, of course, a viral death might be preferable—*because* no one could be blamed and because it cast less doubt on human behavior. The question, though, wasn't one of preference (as if anyone had the option) but the way the pandemic dissolved the stakes and expanded the targets.

"The Second Coming" suggests the collapse of Christian models of redemptive violence and the arrival of a modern formulation. In this new model, resurrection no longer signals salvation but a deathly renewal that ripples throughout the pandemic literature that follows. In Yeats's own spiritual system, the gyre that started with Jesus's birth is finishing, and whatever the "rough beast" might be, it certainly isn't Christ coming to purify the world. The violence within the poem promises no salvation, speaking to Yeats's grim sense of the political violence around him and, more poignantly if more invisibly, to the unbearable costs of the pandemic. On a personal level for Yeats, the pandemic virus also directly threatened his own dreams of a redemptive, Christ-like birth. As their spirit guides had informed Yeats and George, each new historical cycle was initiated by a messiah's arrival; when the Christian cycle reached its close, a new messiah or avatar would be born. The guides had told the couple that they would bear a son who might be this figure, and they thought their unborn daughter was a boy who would fulfill this prophecy (underscoring the dynamics of which gender "counts" more).[116] As Yeats watched, the virus threatened to drown this dream, both literally and figuratively, as the promised birth and salvation is "rocked to nightmare" by the pandemic, and the new messiah's birth seems imaginatively and nightmarishly replaced by the birth of the "rough beast." From a broader perspective, the poem alters the apocalypse narrative, turning the second phase into a perverted, viral resurrection, a plague that turns birth into a sign of death.

Yeats does create two other possible structures, two additional ways to find meaning within the chaos of his current moment. First, as critics have exhaustively studied, the poem reflects his elaborate spiritual systems. The poem reads, as Rudrum observes, like a "traditional dream vision or revelation."[117] Yeats had long experienced mystical visions and revelations, summarizing many of them—and codifying them into a system—in

A Vision in 1925. The poem is indebted to these visions and structured in part around Yeats's various theories I've touched on.[118] Some critics even question if the poem is really apocalyptic, arguing that the "rough beast" headed toward Bethlehem might be a more positive image than first imagined, ushering in, potentially, a new age that would bring change but not necessarily darkness.[119] Read in this way, the poem becomes a possible effort by Yeats to grant structure and hope to the uncertainty and violence of his time. Even if the Beast is not a positive image, Yeats's belief that history could be mapped, that the upheaval of the moment could be explained based on his elaborate systems, brought some measure of structure to the chaos. Within the poem, though, these beliefs are nevertheless caught in the confusion and turmoil of his own situation and the radical uncertainty of his apocalyptic moment.

Far more powerfully and successfully, though, Yeats offers poetry as a way to structure—and to represent—this chaos. On the one hand, the poem's form at least gestures toward structure: unrhymed, with an irregular but roughly blank-verse meter, and, in its second stanza of fourteen lines, a ghost of a sonnet. The amorphous threat of the first stanza materializes (sort of) in the second with the vision of the beast. On the other hand, though, the poem pushes away from structure in classically modernist ways: the language and thoughts are fragmented; agency is at first diffuse and hidden and then ambiguous; the voice is despairing, alienated, possibly mad. The style allows Yeats to frame a new (for him) form of violence, one that could be felt viscerally—as delirium, disintegration, madness, and terror—but not confronted, a way to depict a threat that perhaps not even the poet could think about directly.

"A poem," writes Michael Wood in *Yeats and Violence*, "can refer to history in more than one way, and to more than one history."[120] I have worked in this chapter to excavate one untold history of "The Second Coming," tracing a central element of the poem's context. The pandemic lens is meant to complement rather than to contradict the many other histories that the poem represents. The poem's connections to an illness-based violence reveal a history of personal anguish that was widespread at the time and an element of Yeatsean violence set apart—even when registered with—the political violence upon which he so often brooded. In a broader way, I have aimed in part 2 to excavate how these authors tell a history of the body at a particular moment and grant a record of its suffering. Such bodily experiences largely make their impact in moments of private grief, in nightmares, in scattered thoughts, in internal pains and terrors. And even though the pandemic's effects on communities were everywhere, those communities were already so burdened by the political chaos that had preceded it that this history, too, became difficult to represent. Such shifts, as Woolf, Eliot, and Yeats knew, were best registered as atmospheres, as something everywhere felt yet not fully seen.

PART III

Pandemic Cultures

Chapter Seven

SPIRITUALISM, ZOMBIES, AND THE RETURN OF THE DEAD

In this final chapter, I extend my discussion of the pandemic into popular culture, investigating the outbreak's surprising presence within two traditions centrally concerned with resurrection: spiritualism and zombies. Both traditions reflect a profound cultural grappling with loss and mass death, and both offer quasi-secular and pseudoscientific models of resurrection for a modern age. Scholars have read spiritualism and zombies as reflecting various widespread traumas, from war to slavery, but have largely overlooked how each one responded to and was shaped by the era's viral disaster. In the pandemic's wake, spiritualism and zombies offered two distinct ways to reframe its losses within clear narrative structures, granting alternatives to the grim ambiguity of the literary accounts discussed in parts 1 and 2. Those accounts express the stark realities of the pandemic and its aftermath; the images of resurrection they employ—from Miranda's visions, to Ben's visitation, to the ghostly mother in Maxwell, to Woolf's, Eliot's, and Yeats's spirit-haunted landscapes—primarily signal grief and ongoing danger and reflect the elements of viral resurrection I have traced: bodily states from delirium to hallucinations; a sense of living death; emotional representations of loss, fear, and guilt; and the biological realities of viral replication. Rarely were such images sources of consolation. Spiritualism (during its 1920s resurgence) and early Anglophone zombie figures differed from these starker representations, transforming the outbreak's most difficult realities in ways that granted unexpected avenues of consolation, in part through their insistence on the materiality of their resurrections. These resurrections were presented not as deliriums or hallucinations or expressions of loss but as ectoplasmic entities or flesh-based monsters. This materiality fell onto opposite ends of what we might term a consolation spectrum: At one end, the revival of spiritualism—with its intense interest in ectoplasm, spirit photography, and the scientific proof of the dead's return—granted a reassuring consolation, providing material evidence of a loved one's presence in ways that helped negate the pandemic's unique burdens of helplessness, especially for doctors and scientists. At the other end of the spectrum, the early zombie figures offered a threatening consolation, embodying a materialized viral enemy and a visceral expression of ravenous guilt and anger that are then securely reburied.

I first analyze how post-pandemic spiritualism provided the perfect medium (if you will) for reimagining the pandemic. I focus on the 1920s work of the most well-known spokesman for spiritualism in both the United States and Britain: Arthur Conan Doyle. Creator of the famous Sherlock Holmes detective stories, Doyle had long been interested in spiritualism but became its most enthusiastic public promoter in the aftermath of 1918. While Doyle, who lost several family members on the front lines, often framed his public lectures on spiritualism around the war, his work explicitly and implicitly reflected his own grief and guilt over his son's death in the pandemic and spoke to widespread experiences of the outbreak's aftermath. In his fiction—particularly the pandemic/spiritualist novel *The Land of Mist*— his lectures, and his work in spirit photography, Doyle offered both literary and material ways to reframe pandemic losses that granted comfort to his grieving followers. The era's larger interest in ectoplasm and the renewed popularity of spirit photography dovetailed with Doyle's work and granted potent ways to reimagine pandemic bodies and the sense of ever-present death.

In my second set of examples, I investigate the menacing protozombie figures that emerged alongside Doyle's more benevolent returns, analyzing first the most famous scene of Abel Gance's war film *J'accuse*, in which dead soldiers rise up and lurch into a local village. While understandably read almost entirely through a war lens, these figures link to Gance's and his assistant director's graphic exposure to the pandemic's aftermath and reflect iconic pandemic experiences. Gance's film has the dead return quietly to their graves, but the work of the popular horror writer H. P. Lovecraft features scarier zombie manifestations. In a related set of short stories from the 1920s, Lovecraft's early zombies embody widespread fears of contagion and negate images of the dead returning with hopeful messages. Far from spiritualism's reassuring resurrections, these zombie figures offer terrifying material embodiments of the rage and horror left over from the viral tragedy. They become the ultimate form of viral resurrection, intent on reproducing their deathly vitality and bringing ideas of contagion to the center of the zombie mythos.

The post-pandemic examples of spiritualism and zombie culture I investigate also functioned as understandable contagion narratives for popular audiences—at a moment when such accounts were lacking but desperately needed. Only later, in the second half of the twentieth century, as the scholar Priscilla Wald has detailed, did the ubiquitous "contagion narrative" take form in literature and film, but in the 1920s, such models had yet to emerge. Wald details the similar pattern of these narratives: an infectious threat arrives and is identified, the danger spreads widely and threatens growing numbers of victims, teams of doctors and scientists work to map the threat and fight it, and the danger is safely contained.[1] The 1918 pandemic lay outside this framework (and indeed may have inspired some of the narrative's popularity): the threat could not be mapped, doctors and scientists were largely powerless, and it was never contained, though it did disappear. While the ambiguity and fluidity of modernist narratives could represent these very qualities, people also hungered to escape them. Post-pandemic spiritualism and zombie tales offered multiple, workable narratives to explain the threat's rise and disappearance. Both created their own type of "mapping," making visible and material the penetration of the dead into the spaces of the living: the dead arrived in drawing rooms, stood just behind the shoulders of family members, marched from battlefields into villages, rose from graveyards to enter domestic spaces. Spiritualism framed this penetration as good news, while zombies served to figure it as a threat, but both added structure to what seemed (and was) uncontainable. Both approaches likewise reimagined the roles of physicians and scientists as well as metaphors of contagion: spiritualism crafted life-giving doctor figures who countered the anguish of those unable to stop the virus's spread, and zombies provided an outlet for a repressed fury toward doctors who failed to contain the destruction. Finally, both traditions created ways to safely combat the threat of the pandemic at a moment when the virus's continued disappearance was anything but certain: one negated the threat by declaring that its victims lived on happily; the other materialized an invisible threat but then securely reburied it. These narratives—and their characters—did not represent the pandemic so much as reimagine it in life-giving and monstrous forms.

SPIRITUALISM AND THE PANDEMIC

The spiritualist movement emerged well before the pandemic, starting in mid-nineteenth-century America and quickly developing across Europe. Intrepid readers with extra time on their hands can read Arthur Conan Doyle's exhaustive, two-volume work *The History of Spiritualism*, and recent critics have offered additional histories.[2] Briefly, the movement had its origins at a remote farmhouse in Hydesville, New York, in 1848, when the young Fox sisters claimed to be communicating through taps with an invisible spirit.[3] The sisters quickly became celebrities, with the famous showman P. T. Barnum bringing them on tour, letting people ask them questions while the spirit rapped out the answers.[4] Interest in spiritualism grew rapidly, and by the early twentieth century, its standard special effects were well established. In séances in Europe and the United States, spirits were tilting tables, tapping shoulders, and playing musical instruments, and the phenomena of spirit writing (when spirits would channel messages through a human writer), spirit photography (where ghostly images appeared in photos), and ectoplasmic manifestations had started. Celebrity mediums emerged who could allegedly transmit messages from the dead. Despite its seemingly fringe nature and spectacle quality, spiritualism attracted some of the most accomplished scientific minds of the late nineteenth and early twentieth century, and central to its mission was to bring scientific methods to bear on psychic phenomena. Societies were formed to investigate spirit communication, with well-respected scientists like William James and Alfred Russel Wallace (a leading researcher in evolution) taking an avid interest.[5]

As with any widespread movement, spiritualism was fueled by changing needs and forces. Its sudden rise in the United States stemmed in part, as Drew Gilpin Faust has detailed, from the terrible losses of the Civil War, a conflict that produced on a smaller scale many of the same conditions we find in 1918: an astonishing number of damaged and missing corpses and a population crippled by grief.[6] While by the early twentieth century interest had started to wane, after the war and the pandemic, spiritualism saw a widespread resurgence. In the United States and Britain, people flocked to mediums and séances, and thousands came to hear discussions by researchers investigating psychic phenomena. Arthur Conan Doyle packed auditoriums across two continents with his lectures on afterlife communication in 1922 and 1923, and his many works on spiritualism saw multiple reprintings.[7] In the early 1920s, scientists were studying ectoplasm, and *Scientific American* was publishing serious investigations into both ectoplasm and mediums.[8] Scholars often frame this surge in interest as a response to the massive losses in the war, as indeed it was. The historian Jay Winter, for example, notes that "during and after the Great War, interest in the paranormal and the after-life naturally deepened."[9] Mary Roach observes that the interest in spiritualism peaked after the war, "which left millions of American and European families grieving for lost sons and sadly vulnerable to the promise of contacting them in the afterlife."[10] Jenny Hazelgrove, a researcher who has done an extensive study of spiritualism in Britain between the wars and who explores additional reasons for the interest, still observes that as bereavement after the war became "a national experience . . . stories of the return of the dead were common."[11] Indeed, accounts of soldier's returns sold briskly, including the researcher Hereward Carrington's popular 1918 book *Psychical Phenomena and the War* and the bestselling memoir *Raymond, or Life After Death*, by the renowned physicist Sir Oliver Lodge, who wrote of his dead soldier son's afterlife communications.[12]

The pandemic played its own distinct role in spiritualism's resurgence, however. As the scholar Esyllt Jones notes, "the interwar spiritualist revival is generally described in social and cultural histories of the era without reference to the influenza pandemic," but the outbreak was a critical player in fueling its popularity.[13] As one witness from Virginia recalled, "The flu deaths (combined with the war deaths) brought on a wave of spiritualism and I had cousins in Richmond who lost several members, of flu, and became convinced that they were receiving messages from the dead and went in for a sort of automatic writing. . . . Others used ouiji [sic] boards, which I had never seen until this time."[14] Spiritualism offered ways to address (and not simply represent) some of the pandemic's most traumatic elements, reinventing—and in many cases establishing—new characters and narratives. In part, the pandemic fed the interest in spiritualism by augmenting the conditions already in place after the war, including the mass deaths and the insecure burials. Spiritualism also expressed the pandemic's peculiar cultural position as a spectral trauma to the war; its losses, its suffering, and its grief haunted the culture and were both ever present and shaded from view. Post-trauma moments are typically spectral in this way—memories lurk beneath a present moment, but in the pandemic, the spectral quality was enhanced by the lack of material memorialization and by its cultural erasure. Spiritualism's central tasks—to turn silence into voices and to make what is invisible appear—served as both emblems of the pandemic's subordinate cultural position and a powerful tool with which to combat it.

Spiritualism also offered ways to structure the pandemic within understandable narratives, granting more positive versions of viral resurrection. If the dead could be reached, it didn't matter as much how they had died; the haunting meaninglessness of the pandemic death mattered less, as we'll see, if that death might in turn show that death itself is meaningless (but in a good way). Likewise, the haunting sense of living death is recast in spiritualism into an exciting threshold for investigation. Interest in spiritualism was not simply tied to getting messages from the dead but also about exploring the *threshold* between the living and the dead, illuminating the movement, as it were, between the two states in ways that might bring consolation rather than despair at death's omnipresence. Spiritualism also translated many of the pandemic's seemingly immaterial qualities into comforting material form: the hallucinatory experiences of seeing the dead walk again that weave throughout the pandemic accounts become actual narratives of return, complete with bodies that might be touched and seen. Ectoplasm could reform into the bodies of loved ones and potentially erase more troubling memories of pandemic bodies oozing fluids in the final stage of dissolution.

More specifically, spiritualism featured an appealing doctor/scientist figure who could counter the unique anguish of many medical professionals after the pandemic. Before the outbreak, doctors and researchers were making huge advances in treatments, with many believing that disease might soon be a thing of the past. The pandemic dashed these hopes, introducing a common illness that they were powerless to stop. Doctors and nurses in the war had often fought losing battles—but they had also saved soldiers and made important advances in surgical techniques. With the pandemic, the best doctors and the most advanced treatments were usually ineffectual, though medical professionals fought on nevertheless. Adding to the burden, doctors and nurses, after failing to cure their patients, could bring the virus home to their families and often succumbed themselves. Spiritualism provided an intriguing figure who could help counter these experiences, one I'll call the "afterlife doctor." Usually male, though not exclusively, such figures used all the emerging tools of science to investigate psychic phenomena, developing diagnostic instruments to record, photograph, measure, and test the reality of spiritual bodies.[15] Particularly appealing in the wake of the pandemic, such research circumvented the need to find a cure and save the patient, allowing "science" a way to provide hope and establish life even after a patient had died.

Some of the best known afterlife doctors in the wake of the pandemic were actual medical doctors. Esyllt Jones, who traces the popularity of spiritualism in Canada after 1918, notes the way the movement tended to "attract[] the well educated and professionals, many of them . . . physicians." One of the most popular séance circles, for example, was run by Dr. Thomas Hamilton and his wife, Lillian (who was a nurse), in Winnipeg. The couple had lost one of their twin boys to the flu, and Thomas—who had treated scores of patients during the pandemic—possibly transmitted the virus to his family. Haunted by grief and guilt, the couple threw themselves into psychical research, convinced that their son was quite literally reaching out to them from beyond the grave. Not surprisingly, the Hamiltons befriended the most famous afterlife detective at the time—Arthur Conan Doyle.[16]

Doyle was known for his interest in spiritualism even before the war and the pandemic, but he became its most vocal advocate in their wake. Doyle, though—and thus often scholars—frequently framed his spiritualism work around the war. Critics note that Doyle's own losses in the war were heavy: Chris Willis reports that "his son, brother, and brother-in-law all had been killed in the war,"[17] and Martyn Jolly agrees that Doyle's son Kingsley died "as a result of wounds received in the war."[18] In the only known film recording of Doyle, made in the late 1920s, he describes his own increased involvement in spiritualism as stemming from the deaths of young soldiers:

It was only in the time of the war, when all these splendid young fellows were disappearing from our view, and the whole world was saying, well, what's become of them, where are they, what are they doing now, have they dissipated into nothing, or are they still the grand fellows that we used to know? It was only at that time that I realized the overpowering importance to the human race of knowing more about this matter. Then it was that I flung myself more earnestly into it, and that I felt the highest purpose that I could possibly devote the remainder of my life to, was trying to bring across to other people, something of that knowledge and assurance which I had acquired myself. Certainly the results have justified me. I am quite sure I could fill a room of my house with the letters that I have received from people, telling me of the consolation which my writings on this subject, and my lectures on this subject, have given to them. How they have once more heard the sound of a vanished voice and felt the touch of a vanished hand.[19]

His work, Doyle claims, is done in the memory of these young fellows—like his own family members—who were lost in the war. We can see in his language the agony of the missing body and the thought that it might simply have "dissipated into nothing." Doyle sees his central mission as one of "bringing across" both the message of spiritualism but also the actual presence of the dead, allowing mourners to hear the voice and feel the touch of what is paradoxically both vanished and materially present.

Despite the public focus on the war—and the frequent critical assumption that Doyle's particular grief stems from the war—Doyle's son in fact died in the pandemic. Kingsley Doyle was wounded in the war, but he was in London recovering when he was struck down by the influenza virus and killed by the pneumonia that was the flu's deadly second act.[20] And as Jones reports, "four months later, Doyle's younger brother, Inness, to whom he had long been close, died of pneumonia following influenza."[21] We can see in Kingsley's often inaccurately reported death the ways the pandemic was overshadowed, with war losses easier to frame and linking the dead to a clearer cause.

Doyle, however, pushed against this erasure in his fascinating 1926 novel *The Land of Mist*, a work that highlights the unique pressures the pandemic losses could produce. Primarily a mouthpiece for Doyle's ideas on spiritualism, the novel offers a window into the grief surrounding the pandemic and the ensuing guilt both of doctors and family members who were powerless to stop it. Part of Doyle's Professor Challenger series, the novel features three central characters: the irritable and skeptical professor in the later years of his life, his daughter Enid, and her suitor and friend, the journalist Edward Malone. Most of the book recounts the experiences of Enid and Edward as they investigate spiritualism and move gradually from skepticism to belief. The biggest skeptic, and the biggest convert by the end of the novel, is the professor himself.

From the start of the novel, the accounts of séances and hauntings are framed by influenza, a tragedy that receives more attention than the war. The narrator notes that Edward has been hardened into manhood by the war (though there's no account of his possible role in the conflict), but in the opening chapter, Doyle establishes how the professor remains shattered by the death of his wife, who died as Doyle's son did: "suddenly from virulent pneumonia following influenza."[22] After the loss, "the man staggered and went down," and his body continues to register the effect of his grief: he was "losing something of his fire. Those huge shoulders were a little bowed"; his beard "showed tangles of grey amid the black." It's the pandemic, not the war, that makes him "not the same man."[23] He refuses, naturally, to be comforted by any of what he feels are the outrageous claims of spiritualism.

Just before Enid and Edward go off on their first foray into spiritualism, Dr. Challenger recounts a curious story, and within this anecdote, Doyle introduces two competing narratives of what might happen to the body after death. Challenger offers his account, he says, to warn how even the best minds might be fooled at a moment of grief. Speaking directly to Edward Malone, he notes that the event took place at a particularly difficult moment: "It was after my wife's death. You knew her, Malone. You can guess what it meant to me. It was the night after the cremation. Horrible, Malone, horrible! I saw the dear little body slide down, down . . . and then the glare of the flame and the door clanged to."[24] Challenger dwells on the haunting image that pervaded the popular consciousness at the time: a well-loved material body dissipating and turning into nothing. The perspective also reflects the larger vantage point of doctors like Doyle who had to watch helplessly during the pandemic as their patient's bodies slid into oblivion. That night, though, another narrative emerges that presses against the sense of loss and silence. He had been sitting in his living room, he recounts, when he had heard a sudden noise—a rapping, but of a particular kind. His wife had "had a peculiar way of knocking at a door," and the rapping took on this same rhythm and "was repeated a dozen times at least." It gave him a turn, but he quickly came to see the incident as mere folly on his part: "when that dear body dissolved into its elements—when its gases went into the air and its residue of solids sank into a grey dust—it was the end. There was no more.... Death ends all."[25] The professor not only insists on the narrative of dissolution; he also defines death as the dissolution of narrative. Doyle registers in the professor a widespread loss while hinting that an alternative narrative might be possible.

The novel offers several striking "conversion" moments that expand on such alternative narratives and specifically transform the role of doctors. In the first conversion, Challenger goes to visit one of his former medical students, Dr. Ross Scotton, an accomplished doctor who is now in the final stages of an incurable illness. Wracked with pain, Scotton tells his friend what "a fearful thing [it is] to lie awake at night and feel these cursed microbes nibbling away at the very roots of your life."[26] While both Challenger and his official doctors declare nothing can be done, Scotton—while skeptical and resistant—agrees to talk to a "spirit" doctor who channels his treatment through a human control. The new doctor effects a miraculous cure, and Scotton becomes a convert. The spirit doctor tells Challenger (through his control) that while during life he was an "undistinguished practitioner," when he "passed over [he] continued [his] studies and was permitted ... to do something to help humanity."[27] His eyes now work as X-rays, allowing him to see the body's map of nerves and to dictate the exact treatment necessary. Two doctors are transformed here: the spirit doctor shifts from an ineffectual physician to a superhero healer made more powerful by death, and Dr. Scotton shifts from a skeptical dying man to a healthy practitioner ready to return to his life-saving research. Dr. Challenger, however, angrily denounces the whole experience, refusing to believe in these transformations—until he himself is transformed.

At the end of the novel, Doyle offers us Challenger's dramatic conversion and an emblematic story of a flu doctor redeemed—this time, from terrible guilt. Challenger is dragged to a séance by his daughter and future son-in-law, where he accuses the medium of fraud and disrupts the proceedings at every stage. As the séance is ending, he discovers Enid has entered a trance and cannot be moved. Everyone turns their attention to her. She first reports a message from her mother, telling Challenger that it was, indeed, she who had done the knocking. The professor flies into a rage, claiming his daughter is being used to trick him. Then, though, another message comes through; Enid tells him that two men are trying to communicate, and the name of the first is "Aldridge." At the name, Challenger staggers backward, a "look of absolute wonder" crossing his face.[28] At the next name, "Ware," he starts to resemble a corpse himself, turning "deadly pale" and falling back in his chair. The two men want to talk about "a grey powder," and they relate their central message:

"The message that men want me to say is: 'You did not kill us.'"

"Ask them then—ask them—how did they die?" His voice was broken and his great frame was quivering with his emotion.

"They die disease."

"What disease?"

"New—new. What that? Pneumonia."

Challenger sank back in his chair with an immense sigh of relief. "My God!" he cried, wiping his brow.[29]

Challenger will go on to explain his reaction, but here already we can see the intense guilt surrounding this story and his relief when the men reveal that he was not responsible for their deaths. While the men's deaths predated the pandemic, in the stutter of the medium, we can read the "new pneumonia" reference, a link to the genuinely new virulence of the influenza-induced pneumonia of 1918. The message has an immediate effect on Challenger, who apologizes to the medium and states that "no living person upon this earth was in a position to give" such evidence, making it "incontrovertible" that the dead have returned.[30]

Once Challenger is home, he provides an explanation that highlights the lingering guilt of doctors at the time. As he explains, he had had in the past an experience that had "cast a cloud over [his] life—a cloud which has only been raised to-night." He had given a new, experimental drug to two of his gravely ill patients in a public hospital "in what [he] thought was a safe dose." The drug was from "the durata family which supplies deadly poisons as well as powerful medicines." Both patients were dead by morning, and his own complicity haunts him for years: "I had given [the drug] secretly. None knew of it. There was no scandal for they were both very ill, and their death seemed natural. But in my own heart I had fears. I believed that I had killed them. It has always been a dark background to my life. You heard yourselves to-night that it was from the disease, and not from the drug that they died."[31]

Challenger's story echoes the struggles of doctors during the pandemic. As the flu historian John M. Barry points out, "physicians attempted everything—*everything*—to save lives." They tried experimental drugs; they tried existing vaccines; they even tried the poison and stimulant strychnine (said to have cured Katherine Anne Porter).[32] Sometimes the patients died; sometimes they survived, though it was difficult to tell what might have governed the difference. For physicians, who were overworked and vulnerable themselves, the pandemic was a lesson in helplessness. As Esyllt Jones summarizes, "many physicians experienced influenza as a highly disempowering disease, because medical treatment was largely ineffectual and failed to save so many of the ill."[33] Challenger reveals his keen wish to be on the forefront of a saving technique, "desir[ing his] name to be associated with the first exploration" of the drug, a wish that instead resulted in lifelong guilt. Not only had he not been able to treat them for pneumonia, but he had potentially killed them outright. He knows he "worked for science" and tells them that "Science must take risks. I do not know that I am to blame. And yet—and yet—my heart is very light to-night."[34] He has not entirely forgiven himself, given the ambiguous assignment of blame in his language, but a weight has been removed. Doyle imagines a narrative antidote that treats multiple layers of hidden fears, particularly when doctors were also mourners, absolving them from their haunted worry over being the possible means of exposure, their anguish at not saving the victims, and the guilt of being alive at all after 1918.

Ectoplasm and Spirit Photography

Doyle offered his followers not simply literary forms of post-pandemic comfort but tangible, scientific "proof" of health-after-death through that versatile signifier ectoplasm. Indeed, one of the most remarkable phenomena of the early 1920s was the culture's sudden obsession with this sometimes gelatinous, sometimes vaporish, and sometimes more solid substance. Scientists in both Europe and the United States studied ectoplasm carefully, and it became, as the writer Mary Roach notes, a "subject of elaborate and stone-serious scientific inquiry for more than two decades," including a research study at Paris's Sorbonne University in 1922.[35] The *New York Times* reported frequently on the substance, with ninety-one mentions of ectoplasm between 1920 and 1929 (compared to one mention between 1910 and

1919 and fifteen mentions between 1930 and 1939). In 1923, *Scientific American* announced a well-publicized contest that offered a prize to anyone who could, under scientific conditions, produce a paranormal phenomenon like ectoplasm.[36]

Ectoplasm was seen as the critical material link between the world of the dead and the world of the living. As grieving minds dwelled obsessively on the threshold between life and death, and those with debilitated bodies often felt half alive and half dead, ectoplasm became a physical manifestation of this in-between space. Doyle and many others believed it to be "the connecting link between the material and spiritual worlds."[37] The substance would emerge from the medium, generally through the nose, mouth, or ears, but it could also materialize spontaneously, as seen in spirit photographs. Once in the world, it could perform all manner of comforting acts that pushed against many of the worst experiences of the previous years. A writer named Horace Green reported on these acts in an article appearing in the *New York Times* in 1922, entitled "Is the Supernatural Natural?":

Decidedly, the most interesting [experiments] concern the substance known as ectoplasm, which has been seen to issue from the bodies of certain mediums, take human shape, levitate chairs, tables, and other objects; which has been touched, weighed, photographed, whose sounds have been recorded on the phonograph and whose contents have been chemically analyzed. To the ordinary intelligence, there was something quite tangible in this reduction to the realm of photography and pounds of forces hitherto called mysterious. It gave the layman something to take hold of, some known and comprehensible analogy from which to reason.[38]

Doyle's spirit photographs, Green continues, "reconstructed for the widow and the sonless father" the "faces of persons who have passed beyond the grave."[39] Ectoplasm was an appealing, tangible contrast to the layers of intangibility and loss produced by both the pandemic and the war. It could be studied and measured, giving people "something to take hold of" that was "known and comprehensible" yet provided a kind of religious consolation. It took what had been beyond the realm of scientific inquiry and (purported to) grant doctors and others a narrative of discovery that served as a powerful counter to the recent failures of the medical establishment. Most alluringly, it could appear to take the shape of a deceased loved one. In another article in the *Times*, the writer reports on Doyle's (rather confusing) description of how this process took place: ectoplasm "is a vapor and creates an atmosphere that makes the spirit, passing through it, visible. The emanation becomes putty like...when the spirit passes through it, giving the spirit the appearance it had when inside a living body."[40] Ectoplasm could function on multiple layers as the ultimate cure for a viral threat: in this formulation, an ominous "vapor" and "atmosphere" passes into a body not as contagion but as a sign of life and continuity. The miasmic threat of the pathogen gives way to the visible materiality of the lost loved one, solid enough to grasp a hand or stroke a cheek or appear in a photograph. And ectoplasm coming from the ear, nose, and mouth of the medium offered a compelling re-visioning of one of the most traumatic memories from the pandemic, when blood and fluid emerged in the same way but prefigured death. Ectoplasm meant not disintegration but re-formation. Consider, for example, the photograph in figure 7.1, taken in 1932 by Dr. Hamilton. Ectoplasm streams from the nose of the medium, part of it forming, in this case, an image of their now deceased friend Arthur Conan Doyle. While to the modern eye such a photo is an obvious fraud, it also demonstrates the way the body's fluid might be reimagined, might be translated from a symptom of disease or injury into an image of the healed body.

Indeed, ectoplasm's most famous manifestation was in spirit photography. In these photographs, ghostly "extras" would appear that were allegedly the ectoplasmic representations of the dead, typically a deceased person known to the sitter. While certainly existing before 1918, spirit photography rapidly gained in popularity in the 1920s, much to the delight of many "enterprising" photographers. As the scholar Martyn Jolly notes, the renewed interest in spiritualism and its photography followed "the immense combined death toll of the war and the influenza epidemic."[41] While many people were rightly skeptical, such pictures were also a source of profound comfort. Spirit photographs filled an emptiness, meeting the "ardent desire to see and touch a lost loved-one once more."[42] Doyle—who appeared to be a genuine believer—knew the power of these images. In his first American tour, speaking to a packed audience at Carnegie Hall in April 1922, he showed ghostly pictures of his son, dead of influenza, as well as, according to the *Times*, "men killed in the war, one showing the bullet hole in the temple."[43] As Doyle told the audience, "You may realize...how consoling it was to me...to see my son again." The audience was friendly,

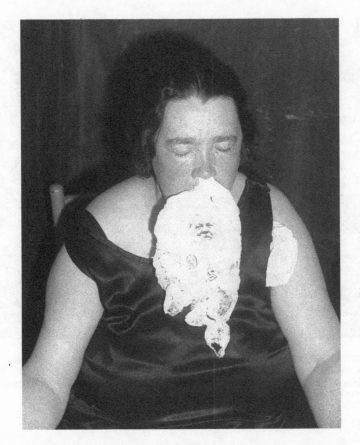

FIGURE 7.1. Ectoplasm showing face of Arthur Conan Doyle. *Source*: Photo taken by T.G. Hamilton, 1932. University of Manitoba Library and Special Collections, Hamilton Family fonds, PC12 (A.79-41); T.G. Hamilton Spirit Photography Archive, Group XIII, #48.

the reporter notes, and waited with an air of "awesome expectancy" as Doyle showed them pictures and reassured them that people were not "disfigured in the next world."

On his next American tour, in April 1923, Doyle revealed two of the most famous spirit photographs of all time. Taken by the well-known medium and spirit photographer Ada Dean, the photos showed the Armistice memorial ceremony at the London Cenotaph in 1922, during the two minutes of silence. The first depicted the people in prayer at the start of the silence, with "a faint luminous patch" above the crowd (figure 7.2) that Doyle called

FIGURE 7.2. Spirit photograph of 1922 Cenotaph Memorial Ceremony, London: start of moment of silence. *Source:* Photo by Ada Deane. Held at the British Library, London: A Collection of Psychic Photographs, Fred Barlow, Secretary of the Society for the Study of Supernormal Pictures. Cup.407.a.1. UIN: BLL01000202744. Image provided by kind permission of the British Library.

ectoplasm.[44] The second photo, though, caused a sensation, for—as the *Times* reported—over the crowd in the picture "floated countless heads of men with strained, grim expressions," all wearing "the fixed, stern look of men who might have been killed in battle" (figure 7.3). The audience was amazed, as "voices and sobs of women" broke out amid the "hysterical cry: 'don't you see them?'"; even the skeptical reporter admitted "there was something about this picture and the conditions under which it was shown that was so eerie, so weird, so supernatural that it impressed even the scoffers." Doyle felt it was "no wonder that this picture moves people's emotions," as it was "the greatest spirit photograph ever taken."

What's spectral in these photographs is not just the war dead. In setting and subject, the photographs are overtly about the war, but as we've seen, a crowded Armistice ceremony held a palimpsestic double, linked in the

FIGURE 7.3. Spirit photograph of 1922 Cenotaph Memorial Ceremony, London: two minutes later.
Source: Photo by Ada Deane. Held at the British Library, London: A Collection of Psychic Photographs,
Fred Barlow, Secretary of the Society for the Study of Supernormal Pictures. Cup.407.a.1. UIN:
BLL01000202744. Image provided by kind permission of the British Library.

minds of so many to the pandemic that was raging as the first Armistice
ceremonies were unfolding. The ectoplasmic mist over the heads in the
photo is "luminous," but it also hints at—and even memorializes—the airborne contagion that everyone now knew had hovered over such crowds in
1918, making people, as one survivor remembered, "afraid to breathe the
outside air."[45] Such memories are transformed by the next photo, when the
mist re-forms into the dead—bringing the men back, rather than causing
more death. And while the heads are men, and while they "might have been
killed in battle," they also suggest the return of all the dead from that era.
Framed by the war, the photos allowed viewers to see the pandemic dead
through a metaphorically resonant vehicle, one that registers the pandemic's
spectral presence yet makes it visible. Counter to the pervasive sense in the
1920s of existing in a haunted, living-death state, such photos suggested a

more enticing threshold, not one that was haunted by the dead but one tangible and crossable, one that could provide solace to those left behind, and most importantly, one that might bring meaning to unimaginable loss. As Doyle poignantly remarked, "This is all I live for now."[46]

DREADFUL RETURNS: ZOMBIES, GUILT, AND ANGER

The same nexus of conditions that made spiritualist resurrections so urgent and so popular could also be channeled another way, producing an abiding horror of more dreadful returns, when the deceased would come back bearing malice rather than comfort for the living. I turn now to examples of such angry dead in Abel Gance's film *J'accuse* and in short stories by H. P. Lovecraft. Their figures share some of the traits we have seen in pandemic victims and survivors: Like Miranda, Ben and his family, Clarissa, Septimus, and Eliot's walking dead, they are caught between life and death and are living diminished versions of their previous lives. Gance's and Lovecraft's living dead, though, are far from quietly enervated. They appear as eruptions of rage and horror, bearing a striking resemblance to the now prolific zombie figure in popular culture: They are uncontrolled, reanimated corpses that hunt humans and are hungry for their flesh; they bear marks of contagion and disease; they are bloody and disheveled and crash about looking for prey; and something essential is missing from their past human selves.[47]

Zombies and their characteristics have shifted over the last century, reflecting the historical contingency of this figure.[48] Much as spiritualism responded over time to changing cultural needs, the zombie is a lurching signifier that functions, the scholar Peter Dendle notes, as a "barometer" of various anxieties felt at different moments.[49] If, as researchers have argued, the popularity of the modern version of the zombie—an "unstoppable, flesh-eating automaton"—arises in part from "our fear of contagion," it's unsurprising that an early form of the viral zombie would emerge in the post-pandemic moment.[50] The examples I trace link to the particular conditions of both minds and bodies at the time and unleash elements far more repressed in my earlier examples: explosions of anger and guilt, a paralyzing fear of contagion, and the terror and destruction of a flesh-eating monster. These protozombies emerge as material emblems of the physical and mental damage suffered not only by the dead but also by those who survived, providing a way to "see" pandemic suffering and to shape it into a more understandable—if terrifying—narrative.

In addition to what they meant when Gance was filming and Lovecraft was writing, these 1920s protozombies are also missing links in a long zombie tradition, and they predate the more traditional understanding of when zombies "arrive" in European and American culture. Scholars trace the Anglophone introduction of the vodou term "zombie" to W. B. Seabrook's 1929 work *The Magic Island*. Seabrook, a white American war veteran, traveled to Haiti in the mid-1920s to study vodou, often writing in starkly racist terms about the traditions he observed. He devotes one section of his work to the zombie figure, noting, "The *zombie*, they say, is a soulless human corpse, still dead, but taken from the grave and endowed by sorcery with a mechanical semblance of life," forced into an enslaved position by a controlling master figure who revived the body. The resulting zombie, Seabrook reports, is occasionally commanded into "the commission of some crime" but is "more often simply [used] as a drudge" and beaten "like a dumb beast if it slackens."[51] As critics such as Chera Kee and Franck Degoul have observed, this zombie tradition reflects the history of slavery, oppression, and rebellion in Haiti and elsewhere as well as the exploitation of labor more generally. Critics have focused considerable attention on the manipulation of this tradition and its influence on early zombie movies such as *White Zombies* (1932) and *Ouanga* (1936).[52]

The "vodou zombie" tradition later gave way to what Stephanie Boluk and Wylie Lenz have termed the "viral" or "plague" zombie. This figure, they argue, was introduced by Romero's 1968 movie *Night of the Living Dead*.[53] Romero's film indeed helped popularize the infectious, cannibalistic qualities of so many contemporary zombie figures. In works like Max Brooks's *World War Z*, Colson Whitehead's *Zone One*, and the show *The Walking Dead*, zombies become the ultimate form of viral resurrection. Produced by a virus, they also swarm like monstrous, visible microbes: infecting and consuming the body and replicating with a deathly fecundity. These viral zombies, though, have their origins in figures that predate Romero's movies, germinating from an infectious 1920s atmosphere and a plague-ravaged populace. In their lurching, bloody states, their flesh-consuming attributes, and their powers of contagion, the protozombies in Gance and Lovecraft not only embody pandemic elements but suggest key historical influences for now classic expressions of modern zombies.

The Return of the Dead in *J'accuse*

The final scene of Abel Gance's film *J'accuse* depicts a dramatic mass resurrection, one that serves as a powerful antiwar message but critically also
narrates the pandemic's traumatic arrival. The scene was shot in the final
weeks of the war and in the midst of the pandemic. The film's central character, Jean Diaz—a shell-shocked and delusional soldier-poet just returned
from the war—calls a group of French villagers together with a promise that
their war dead will return that evening. The bewildered civilians flock to
Jean's house, and Jean tells them a story that the camera then brings to life.
The scene moves by a series of cuts between the astonished audience—who,
like the viewers in the theater, seem to be seeing Jean's story as he tells it—
and the battlefield he describes. He relates that one night during the war,
he was on guard duty, standing on a battlefield with "their dead" (figure 7.4).[54] The camera shows a desolate Jean, his head bent over his rifle,
while stretching all around him are haphazard crosses marking the graves
of soldiers. A dark mountain range, with storm clouds or smoke rising from
the top, looms in the distance, an ominous reminder that more death may
be coming. The camera cuts back to the Jean telling the story. He is surrounded by his audience, who are illuminated by the fire hidden behind
Jean; the spectators, sitting or standing in rows, look like movie viewers,
their faces lit by the central light in front of them (figure 7.5). Those watching
the film, Gance hints, should see themselves as aligned with the villagers.

As the camera returns to the battlefield, the crosses suddenly morph into
dead bodies. One of the dead wakes up and stumbles to his feet. He declares
he wants to see if their deaths have done any good, to return to the village
and discover if those at home have been worthy of the sacrifice. He calls
out to the dead, "Awaken!" and the remaining men all rise up.[55] The walking dead, wounded still and covered in blood, lurch and limp together down
the road. They stare blindly ahead with their arms outstretched as they
make their way to the village (and the audience), a crowd of protozombies
returning (figure 7.6). The camera then cuts to a quick series of short scenes
that show villagers misbehaving in various ways (wives flirting with soldiers, sons squandering money, and so on), all of which end with one of
the dead men suddenly appearing to stare in disbelief at the unfolding sor-
didness. After these scenes, the camera returns to the audience by the fire,
and at this point, the villagers have jumped to their feet and turned to the

FIGURE 7.4. *J'accuse*: at the battlefield. *Source: J'accuse*, dir. Abel Gance, France (1919–1921): Pathé Frères and United Artists. Public Domain Film Archive: https://www.youtube.com/watch ?v=T8VeawLoNm4.

FIGURE 7.5. *J'accuse*: the audience at home. *Source: J'accuse*, dir. Abel Gance, France (1919–1921): Pathé Frères and United Artists. Public Domain Film Archive: https://www.youtube.com/watch ?v=T8VeawLoNm4.

FIGURE 7.6. *J'accuse*: the dead return. *Source*: *J'accuse*, dir. Abel Gance, France (1919–1921): Pathé Frères and United Artists. Public Domain Film Archive: https://www.youtube.com/watch?v=T8VeawLoNm4.

window, as the story that Jean is telling collapses into the time and place of the fireside scene. Jean accuses the villagers of forgetting and betraying their dead, just as the dead in fact crowd around the windows and doors of the house (figure 7.7). As the dead approach in ever larger numbers, the living seem to grow increasingly zombified, as if infected by the same living-death state of the soldiers. Over the course of the scene, their eyes widen, their mouths drop open, and almost as if in a trance, they move to the windows and doors. The villagers plead for forgiveness (figure 7.8) as the dead gradually retreat, finally dissolving into a single image of a cross and once again sinking out of sight. The camera returns to the villagers, who feel as if they themselves are waking up, and one villager wonders if it was a dream or a possession.

The Return of the Dead scene would seem to have everything to do with the war and little to do with the influenza pandemic; Jay Winter, in his oft-quoted and magisterial reading of the scene in *Sites of Memory, Sites of Mourning*, focuses on the way the moment exemplifies elements of postwar

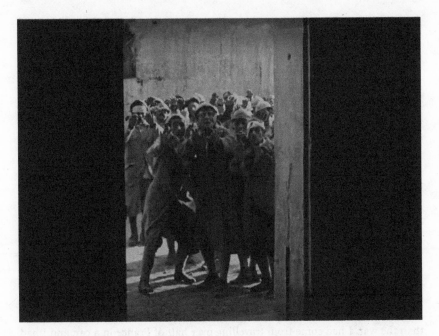

FIGURE 7.7. *J'accuse*: back at the village. *Source*: *J'accuse*, dir. Abel Gance, France (1919–1921): Pathé Frères and United Artists. Public Domain Film Archive: https://www.youtube.com/watch?v=T8VeawLoNm4.

FIGURE 7.8. *J'accuse*: seeing the dead. *Source*: *J'accuse*, dir. Abel Gance, France (1919–1921): Pathé Frères and United Artists. Public Domain Film Archive: https://www.youtube.com/watch?v=T8VeawLoNm4.

mourning.[56] In fact, though, when we add the experiences that surrounded its filming into the critical frame, the scene emerges as a powerful and even explanatory narrative of the pandemic's arrival, its protozombies shadowed yet materialized expressions of the flu's domestic horrors.[57] Much of this background is described in the memoirs of Gance's assistant director, the modernist writer Blaise Cendrars, which detail both Gance's and his own grim encounters with the pandemic.[58] In early November 1918, shortly before the scene was shot, Cendrars writes that he had left the film set to gather various things he needed for his work. He ran into his friend, the famous modernist poet Guillaume Apollinaire, in Paris, and over lunch, they talked of the flu and the nightmarish sights Cendrars had seen on his trip across France:

We talked of . . . the epidemic of Spanish influenza that was creating more victims than the war. I had come from travelling over half of France in a car, and I had witnessed in the suburbs of Lyon the burning of the plague victims that had been piled up in the streets and that had been splashed with petrol, the city lacking coffins, and the tableau was made all the more tragic as, on the side by the freight yard, the factories were burning in the aftermath of an air raid.[59]

Here, Cendrars paints an apocalyptic landscape and notes in his visual picture how the damage of one conflict deepened and also blended into the damage of the other. He positions, though, the pandemic, rather than the war, as the central tragedy—the two men knew that the flu was claiming more victims than the war, and it is the existing viral devastation that is made "all the more tragic" by the air raid. The grisly image of corpses piled up in the city streets, with the coffin shortage requiring burning rather than burial, suggests an unsettling picture of uncontained death.

Cendrars's sense of spreading danger and the pandemic's encroachment on the war quickly intensified. A few days after the lunch, Apollinaire lay dying of the flu. Like Cendrars, Apollinaire had been seriously wounded in the war, surviving terrible injuries and even the trepanning of his skull.[60] Despite making it through the battles, he succumbed quickly to the virus. When Cendrars visited him on November 8, he was shocked to discover the poet's body had turned dark as Apollinaire struggled through the final stages of the flu-induced pneumonia. The poet's wife, Jacqueline—who also was ill—cautioned him about getting too close to the infected couple. Cendrars frantically arranged for medical care, but the poet was dead by the next evening.[61] Four days later, he was buried with full military honors. Gance and Cendrars attended the ceremony, and Cendrars notes that all the important writers, artists, and journalists of Paris, including Picasso and Max Jacob, were in attendance.[62] In an experience that made a deep impression on the two filmmakers, the funeral cortege literally ran into the ecstatic crowds celebrating the Armistice: "The funeral procession was attacked . . . by the raging crowd of demonstrators who were celebrating the Armistice, men and women, with arms linked, sang, danced, embraced each other, and bawled as in a delirium. . . . It was exceedingly hard."[63] The two tragedies mingle here on multiple levels: in language—the demonstrators are raging and delirious and attack the mourners; in action—the groups become physically entangled; and in biologic foreshadowing—the linked arms and embraces of the Armistice crowd cast a sense of spreading contagion over the scene. The overlap of life and death suggested separately by both groups (the funeral mourners with the dead body, the war crowd signifying both celebration and loss) becomes further blurred by the literal blend of the funeral and victory parades.

This atmosphere of mingled tragedies, widespread death, and disrupted burial deepened and took an eerier turn when, after the funeral, Cendrars went with his girlfriend Raymone Duchâteau and the artist Fernand Léger to the graveyard to pay his respects to his friend. They stopped first for a hot drink in the hopes of protecting their own bodies from infection.[64] They were right to be worried. When they reached the graveyard, they immediately ran into a common difficulty for the time: there were so many new graves that they could not find the one they wanted. They finally stopped to ask some gravediggers, who could offer little direction, given the number of dead. As one digger told him,

"You have to understand, with the flu, with the war, they don't tell us the names of the dead that we bury. There are too many. Ask at the front office. We don't have the time and are too exhausted." "But," I said, "it's a lieutenant, the lieutenant Guillaume Apollinaire. . . . There must have been a salvo at the tomb." "My poor sir," answered the team leader, "there were two salvos. There are two lieutenants. We don't know which one you want. Look for yourselves!"[65]

They continued to wander around the tombs, seeing graves half-filled but nothing to identify them. They started to leave when Cendrars spotted a mound of dirt at the bottom of an open grave that, he thought, looked like the head of Apollinaire, and he suddenly felt as if he had seen his friend return:

I pointed out a clod of earth with a bit of turf at the bottom of one of the two tombs. "Look," I said to Raymone and Fernand Léger, "look, it is wonderful! You would think it was Apollinaire's head." The clod of frozen earth at the bottom of the hole had exactly the form of Apollinaire's head and the turf was planted like his hair when he was alive, and around the scar of the trepanation.[66]

The friends could not believe their eyes, and as they left the cemetery, Cendrars noted that a glacial fog was enveloping the tombs as if to say "It was definitely him. We saw him. Apollinaire did not die. Soon he will appear. Do not forget what I tell you all."[67] After this experience, as Jay Winter observes, Cendrars traveled back to the movie set to film the Return of the Dead scene.[68]

Analyzed within the frame of these pandemic stories, the final scene and its protozombies shift in meaning, not simply expressing the agonies of the war but also granting a visual representation of spreading death, a powerful narration of the war-to-flu chronology, and an early breeding ground for the viral zombie. At the start of the scene, the piles of unburied bodies laid out on the battlefield, with the dark, smoky mountain rising behind, reflect familiar war images but also hint of the deaths to come, like the stacked pandemic bodies burning amid the war's destruction that Cendrars had described. The dead then bring this destruction from the battlefields straight into the domestic space, capturing several key elements. First, both the visual of the march and the protozombies themselves grant a sense of widening, unbounded death; the dead—and death itself—will not stay buried, echoing the brooding realization that despite the war's end, the killing had overflowed the battlefields and morphed into a new viral threat. The zombies likewise suggest a lethal, emotional uncontainability, an explosion of horror, rage, and suffering that spills from the grave. The burial problems in the war and exemplified in Cendrars's pandemic accounts suggest a fertile atmosphere for believing that the dead might not be resting quietly. Second, the march grants a visual timeline, showcasing how mass death moved from the front lines into the home front. Third, the scene hints at the climate of contagion Cendrars describes; as the zombie soldiers lurch toward the village, their bodies damaged, their sense of self emptied, their existence trapped into a living death, the villagers' bodies take on the same traits, like a spreading infection of death and horror—which was what indeed occurred. Such a climate not only narrates how the pandemic brought its own form of living death but also anticipates the viral quality of the modern zombie.[69] Finally, the scene rewrites the complicated, sacrificial narratives of both the war and the pandemic. The dead soldiers both feel and express the anger that their war sacrifice is unappreciated and potentially not meaningful. Their threatening invasion of the village hints that the pandemic is a kind of punishment, a vengeful viral scourge delivered on civilians for not appreciating (or stopping) the sacrifice of so many in the war. And this very structure even allows a recasting of viral mass death, granting it a still horrifying but at least understandable presence and offering a reason behind its otherwise meaningless destruction. And in the end, all of these threats are reburied: the villagers recover, and the dead return to their graves. The scene first embodies the threat—giving it contours and visual qualities—and then, at the end, covers it more securely.

A few years later, in 1922, Abel Gance added footage to the scene that encapsulated these elements and deepened the film's connection to the pandemic. Gance and his girlfriend Ida Danis had both caught the flu in Paris just after the war. Ida never fully recovered, her lungs turning consumptive, and she died in 1921 from its complications.[70] The loss was devastating, and it would have been in Gance's mind as he edited a memorable split-screen shot into the final scene, one that also explicitly evoked, as Winter observes, Cendrars's account of the funeral of Apollinaire, creating on multiple levels a silent memorial to the pandemic's ravages.[71] Gance took the moment when the protozombie dead are lurching down the road toward the village, and he split the screen with actual footage taken from a 1919 war victory parade on the Champs Elysées.[72] The visual at the top of the screen was of the dead returning, with the bottom of the screen showing the living, if damaged, survivors celebrating the end of the war (figure 7.9). This split scene narrates an entangled atmosphere. Both groups of the dead link to the war—the war dead on top, as if in a heavenly afterlife, and the survivors on the bottom—but the two crowds also represent the era's two distinct tragedies: the protozombies above echo the mourners for Apollinaire's

FIGURE 7.9. *J'accuse*: split-screen shot of the dead's return (above) and victory parade (below). *Source*: *J'accuse*, dir. Abel Gance, France (1919–1921): Pathé Frères and United Artists. Public Domain Film Archive: https://www.youtube.com/watch?v=T8VeawLoNm4.

funeral and by extension the pandemic victims themselves as they blur with the war survivors below. Despite the war's end (represented by the group at the bottom), death continues to stream into villages from above—dominating and even threatening the war survivors. The protozombies suggest the widespread physical suffering, embodying both the living-death state and death itself—and the emotional suffering of the mourners, grief-stricken and shocked by being literally and figuratively caught in the midst of another disaster while war celebrations surge around them. We have seen versions of this scene throughout this study, most recently in Doyle's spirit photograph, where the cloud of the dead hovers over the crowds marking the Armistice.

Implicit in both the film and in Cendrars's stories are the bifurcated desires surrounding resurrection in the post-1918 moment. As Jay Winter observes, a return of the dead was "longed for, dreamed of, [and] dreaded" in these years.[73] On the one hand, the desire to experience a bodily manifestation of the departed is poignantly represented in the villagers' initial excitement about seeing the war dead and in Cendrars's sense that Apollinaire's head has re-formed from the very dirt of his grave. Even years later, Cendrars would recount that "I have a hard time believing that he is dead."[74] The hint of hope this experience might suggest has its parallel in resurrection moments from Porter to Maxwell to Wolfe to Woolf to Doyle. On the other hand, the protozombies reflect the most damaging elements of viral resurrection and warn of the terrors embedded in the dead's return. These menacing dead become rich material metaphors, physical manifestations of guilt, revenge, and the lurking fear of a viral threat that has not been effectively contained. When the protozombies are reburied at the end of the scene, the large cross that hovers over the graves signals both memorial and warning.

H. P. Lovecraft and the Ravenous Dead

As Gance's dead lurched toward villages, a far more vicious strain of protozombies was emerging in the work of H. P. Lovecraft. In a cluster of stories written in the 1920s, Lovecraft crafts a pandemic-era zombie figure and a newly imagined contagion narrative. The horror genre—with its classic links to dead bodies returning, insidious infections, and flesh-hungry monsters[75]—aligned well with post-pandemic anxieties, and Lovecraft drew on and shaped these tropes into new zombie creations. Like deadly microbes gone wild, Lovecraft's reanimated dead are ravenous for the flesh of those still living, pushing against any sense of a happy or restorative resurrection. Despite their horror, Lovecraft's figures do grant a brutal post-pandemic comfort on several levels: they serve as an understandable and embodied explanation of pandemic violence, they are potential weapons to wreak revenge on the origins of that violence, they are reifications of the fears surrounding burial, and they are horrors far worse (Lovecraft's narrators assure us) than the pandemic or the war. Lovecraft's stories also offer clearly defined origins for this terrifying new threat: primarily doctor-scientist figures who, rather than cure their patients, turn them into zombies and often become zombies themselves. Doyle had recast doctors as helpful afterlife detectives in ways that pushed against the burdens of guilt the pandemic produced, both in terms of the lack of cures and in the way doctors could spread the virus. Lovecraft, in contrast, positions his doctors as enthusiastic supporters of deadly cures and horrific resurrections, creating monsters hungry to spread death from house to house. He grants his readers a terrifying, exaggerated expression of both doctors and contagion and a potentially powerful channel for the rage and helplessness so many experienced. The stories also reveal how anxieties over viral contagion could all too easily blend into xenophobic images of infecting hordes of outsiders. Lovecraft's racist and homophobic fears of contamination by anyone not straight or of European-Caucasian descent helped fuel his zombie creations and suggest how the influenza pandemic in turn helped fuel the larger prejudicial implications of invading viral zombies.

In 1920, Lovecraft was at the start of his writing career, and he was becoming a leading figure in the world of amateur journalism.[76] The preceding years, however, had been difficult. An avid supporter of the war, Lovecraft could not get the army to accept him given his poor health,[77] and by 1918, the pandemic was tearing through Rhode Island, where Lovecraft lived. All public facilities in Providence shut down in early October, as the virus swept through the city, overwhelming hospitals and doctors. At Rhode Island Hospital, "half the nursing staff fell ill," and flu accounts from the city and the surrounding areas speak of the grim conditions, with "whole families being stricken, and mass funerals being held."[78] The virus quite possibly killed Lovecraft's uncle, Edwin Phillips, in November. While Lovecraft did not appear close to his uncle, following the death of her brother, Lovecraft's mother, Susie, experienced a steep physical and mental decline. In March 1919, she entered the Butler Hospital for the Insane, the same institution where Lovecraft's father had died, and she passed away there two years later.[79] Lovecraft himself was in poor physical and mental shape during these years, writing that his "nervous strain" was causing him headaches and dizziness; he felt that "existence seem[ed] of little value" and wished "it might be terminated."[80]

Lovecraft channeled this grim public and private atmosphere into his hallucinatory prose-poem "Nyarlathotep," published by *United Amateur* in November 1920.[81] While not a zombie tale, the story suggests the conditions from which his zombies emerged, a nightmarish world saturated in disease, corpses, and anxiety. Reminiscent of works by French decadent writers,[82] the tale also parallels the hallucinatory-delirium mode I've traced in Wolfe, Eliot, Woolf, and Yeats; indeed, Lovecraft claimed the story came to him in a nightmare and was written while still in a dream state.[83] The story opens with a fevered encapsulation of the 1918 environment:

The general tension was horrible. To a season of political and social upheaval was added a strange and brooding apprehension of hideous physical danger; a danger widespread and all-embracing, such a danger as may be imagined only in the most terrible phantasms of the night. I recall that the people went about with pale and worried faces, and whispered warnings and prophecies which no one dared consciously repeat or acknowledge to himself that he had heard. A sense of monstrous guilt was upon the land, and out of the abysses between the stars swept chill currents that made men shiver in dark and lonely places. There was a demoniac alteration in the sequence of the seasons[;] the autumn heat lingered fearsomely, and everyone felt that the world and perhaps the universe had passed from the control of known gods or forces to that of gods or forces which were unknown.[84]

The narrator traces here the emotional taxonomy of the period. The central horror is a pandemic-like specter, a "hideous physical danger" set apart from the political threats of war and violence. This "phantasm" is "widespread and all-embracing," its fearfulness tied up in its intangibility. The threat produces a brooding apprehension, and people are too scared to speak or hear about it consciously. Guilt abounds and bodies are threatened—pale, shivering, and yet overwhelmed by a fever-like "autumn heat." Adding to the anxiety is the sense of vulnerability—the warnings, the prophecies, and the gods grant no defense against this danger. The language registers the vast, invasive quality of both the menace and the emotions it produces, seeming to spread everywhere and dissolve barriers of time, space, and bodies.[85]

The atmosphere in turn breeds an all-encompassing sense of living death, one that invades both people and landscapes in an exaggerated and anticipatory form of Eliot's wasteland. Entire geographic areas are sentient corpses, dead yet somehow still animate. The world, the narrator tells us, is a "rotting creation" full of "sores that were cities," which trap hapless and only half-alive citizens. The narrator describes himself—and seemingly the universe as well—as "a sickened, sensitive shadow writhing in hands that are not hands, and whirled blindly past ghastly midnights." Bodies have become diseased shadows, caught in a hallucinatory temporal confusion.

The narrator notes that wherever he goes, sleep has been disrupted, adding another layer of half-awake existence: "rest vanished; for the small hours were rent with the screams of nightmare. Never before had the screams of nightmare been such a public problem; . . . the shrieks of cities . . . disturb[ed] the pale, pitying moon as it glimmered on green waters gliding under bridges, and old steeples crumbling against a sickly sky."[86] The Lovecraft scholar David Haden links the screams to shell-shocked soldiers,[87] and they also recall the pandemic accounts of the pervasive nightmares of flu victims, trapped in hallucinatory rages.[88] These nightmares have seeped into public, and even the cities shriek, the "green waters" and "sickly sky" applying equally to bodies and the landscape. Anticipating Thomas Wolfe's apocalyptic pandemic vision of "the million bones of cities,"[89] the whole universe appears to have become a "revolting graveyard" that nevertheless lurches on.[90]

Arising from these conditions is the shadowy but powerful figure of Nyarlathotep, who appears to be both bred from and an agent of the world's infection. A combination of evil scientist, spiritualist showman, foreign invader, and ancient god, Nyarlathotep captures many of the forces that Lovecraft felt were producing and preying on his culture's diseased state. Nyarlathotep travels to various cities, enticing the fevered denizens of crowded urban spaces with mesmerizing spectacles.[91] In a seeming deliberate swipe at figures like Doyle, Lovecraft—who was an outspoken critic of spiritualism and its promoters—shows Nyarlathotep deluding vulnerable crowds using quasi-scientific instruments "of glass and metal" and giving "exhibitions of power which sent his spectators away speechless."[92] Nyarlathotep also anticipates Lovecraft's later depictions of evil scientists bent on reanimating corpses; here, though, the villain seems more interested in leading astray the living-dead masses already produced by the infectious atmosphere. Alongside his jabs at scientists and spiritualists, Lovecraft displays how a fear of disease may morph into racist fears of "foreign" invaders. He gives Nyarlathotep a seemingly Egyptian-styled name, calls him "swarthy . . . and sinister," and says he comes from "the blackness of twenty-seven centuries." Nyarlathotep in turn fuels racist fears by showing his followers flickering screens where "yellow evil faces" threaten to stream into cities.[93] Reflected is both Lovecraft's paranoia that hordes of immigrants were infecting Anglo-Saxon genetic lines and the grotesque, prejudicial ways disease metaphors may be harnessed to justify racism.[94]

A deeply problematic foci of post- (and pre-)1918 white fears, the figure of Nyarlathotep offers Lovecraft's (white) readers a terrifying but potentially appealing instantiation of the more nebulous threat of the tale's opening, a target and an insidious explanation for the world's sickly condition. At the end of the story, Lovecraft hints that what will arise from this contagious, zombie-fertile atmosphere are "blind, voiceless, mindless gargoyles"— creatures that he endows with greater life in subsequent stories.[95]

Lovecraft develops his zombie-like figures—and their emergence out of an infectious 1918 climate—in his central story of resurrection, "Herbert West: Reanimator." He wrote the tale in 1922, and it appeared in the new magazine *Home Brew* in six installments.[96] The story concerns the ghoul-ish experiments of a Dr. West, who seeks scientific ways to bring the dead back to life. His methods prove disastrous, turning the dead into violent, lurching, nonspeaking (except for the screams and moans), soulless versions of their former selves, with a hunger for human flesh. While in part evocative of earlier horror tales of reanimated corpses, like Mary Shelley's *Franken-stein* (1818), Edgar Allan Poe's "The Fall of the House of Usher" (1839), or Ambrose Bierce's "Chickamauga" (1889), the dead in "Herbert West" embody the horror of their particular historical moment and anticipate the flesh-eating, infectious quality of more recent zombie manifestations. These walking dead lurch out of a Nyarlathotep-like atmosphere of contagion, vio-lence, and racist paranoia, with the most destructive protozombie arising in the midst of a massive epidemic. Lovecraft unleashes in his story elements that other pandemic accounts sought to record or ameliorate, taking the survivor's guilt, the physical suffering, the contagion anxiety, the burial fears, and the pain of an invisible enemy and animating them all into exces-sive, monstrous forms. Far from Doyle's gentle reframing of medical guilt, the story places doctors at the center of the horror, both the source of infec-tion and of the protozombies themselves. Lovecraft shapes a narrative where healers become villains, cures become curses, and death becomes consoling.

The story's first episode offers a preview of the terrors to come. Herbert West and his friend, the unnamed narrator/sidekick, are both training to be doctors. West has already begun his grisly trials in reanimation on a series of unfortunate animals, but he hungers to experiment on fresh human corpses, which during the episode's pre-pandemic/prewar moment are hard to find. They finally discover a promising specimen in a young man who has just drowned (anticipatorily evocative of pandemic and war corpses), and they dig up the body and bring it back to their lab. West injects the corpse with his cocktail of reanimation drugs, to no effect, and they leave their subject on his slab; later that night, the narrator relates, they hear "the most appalling and daemoniac succession of cries," a sound of "supernal terror and unnatural despair." They run away in horror, returning the next morning to find the house burned down, the grave disturbed as if someone had tried to dig back in, and no sign of the body, leading West to "look frequently over his shoulder" for the next seventeen years.[97]

While the episode, with its dead young man and ineffectual doctors, its anguished screams, and its insecure burial, sketch a familiar atmosphere, the next episode, entitled "The Plague-Daemon," seems lifted right from newspaper accounts of the pandemic. West and the narrator have just completed their medical studies when a terrible plague breaks out in the fictional town of Arkham. While the outbreak is one of typhoid, the descriptions would have immediately recalled scenes from 1918 to the readers' minds:

I shall never forget that hideous summer sixteen years ago, when like a noxious afrite from the halls of Eblis typhoid stalked leeringly through Arkham. It is by that satanic scourge that most recall the year, for truly terror brooded with batwings over the piles of coffins in the tombs of Christchurch Cemetery ... the scourge, grinning and lethal, from the nightmare caverns of Tartarus ... broke with full daemoniac fury upon the town. Though not as yet licensed physicians, we now had our degrees, and were pressed frantically into public service as the numbers of the stricken grew. The situation was almost past management, and deaths ensued too frequently for the local undertakers fully to handle. Burials without embalming were made in rapid succession, and even the Christchurch Cemetery receiving tomb was crammed with coffins of the unembalmed dead. ...

We were frightfully overworked, and the terrific mental and nervous strain made my friend brood morbidly.[98]

The stacks of coffins, the chaotic atmosphere, the besieged undertakers, and the exhausted doctors reflect widespread influenza conditions including those in Lovecraft's Providence, where, as one Rhode Island undertaker summarized, "people died so fast there was barely time to bury them," so they were "buried all hours of the day and *night* without even having services for them."[99] Lovecraft's imagery suggests the infectious threat had already taken on classic, horror-like forms—it stalks, it leers, it grins, it's an afrite—and its origins are cast in demonic terms, emerging from Hell, Eblis, and Tartarus. For the two young doctors, the spooky atmosphere produced by the unburied, unembalmed bodies is augmented by their fear that the corpse from their last experiment remains somewhere half-animated; "it would have been better," the narrator notes, "if we could have known it was underground."[100]

Lovecraft then adds to the horror, starting with the seemingly sympathetic, overworked doctors. The man in charge of the hospital, Dr. Allan Halsey (and our next zombie-to-be), may heroically tend victims, but he suffers from "the chronic mental limitations of the 'professor-doctor' type," his kindly exterior hiding the way, the narrator claims, that such figures are "always narrow, intolerant, custom-ridden, and lacking in perspective." When he dies in the outbreak, the two more overtly ghoulish doctors, West and the narrator, waste no time in bringing his body back to their apartment for reanimation. Their "cure" creates a fully monstrous version of Dr. Halsey, who escapes through an open window after leaving behind a common if extreme version of the pandemic sickroom: a bloody bedroom, a sense of violent derangement in the broken bottles and instruments that scatter the floor (the failed "cures"), and a set of empty garments that, West tells the police, were "specimens collected for bacteriological analysis in the course of investigations on the transmission of germ diseases" and should be "burnt as soon as possible."[101]

The doctors, though, have unleashed—and become—a materialized contagion. A nightmarish creature that "eclipsed the plague itself" begins to stalk the town. In Christchurch Cemetery, a watchman is "clawed to death," and the killings continue the next night, but with more ferocity:

Through the fevered town had crept a curse which some said was greater than the plague, and which some whispered was the embodied daemon-soul of the plague itself. Eight houses were entered by a nameless thing which strewed red death in its wake—in all, seventeen maimed and shapeless remnants of bodies were left behind by the voiceless, sadistic monster that crept abroad. . . . It had not left behind quite all that it had attacked, for sometimes it had been hungry.[102]

The doctor has morphed into a walking plague, a figure of destruction that parallels the pandemic virus: a voiceless, nameless threat that enters houses in fevered towns, eating away at the body's flesh and leaving bloody and distorted corpses in its wake. The former doctor becomes a horrifying manifestation of the fear (and the reality) of spreading contagion—infected with a virus he caught treating patients, his reanimated corpse brings death rather than cures into other homes, his "house calls" an exaggerated expression of what contagion produced. And while this zombie is created by Dr. West in a Frankenstein-like reanimation, so he doesn't technically pass his zombie status on to others, he nevertheless anticipates the infectious quality of zombie production in the way he emerges from an epidemic and the way the destruction passes from Dr. West to Dr. Halsey and finally to the village. While delivering similar results as the flu (with a far lower body count), this protozombie figure also offers several potentially cathartic advantages for readers: it turns an unseen threat into an animated monster capable of being captured and contained, as indeed the figure is in the story, and it positions doctors as the source of the problem, channeling the simmering frustration and rage at the medical establishment toward an identified and clear target.

The pandemic doctor is by far the most dangerous protozombie in the story, though West continues to reanimate the dead with grisly results. As the episodes unfold, the atmosphere of contagion from the plague episode morphs into the racist vision of infection Lovecraft introduced in "Nyarlathotep," this time in much starker terms and with homophobic fears added to the mix. West increasingly emerges as an example of what Lovecraft believed was Anglo-Saxon degeneracy caused by the contamination of "pure" bloodlines. Marked repeatedly as Aryan (Lovecraft mentions his blond hair and blue eyes ad nauseam), West is also "a small, slender, spectacled youth with delicate features," "pale" eyes, and "a soft voice." His effeminate qualities and macabre pursuits hint of thinly veiled homophobic fears (or desires): with his devoted male companion at his side, West constantly searches out young, healthy, male bodies to inject. Lovecraft blends these signs of "degenerate" infection with his anxiety over racial and foreign contamination in West's third zombie creation. In a grotesquely racist episode, the doctor and his sidekick bring back to life an African American boxer killed in a fight, whom the narrator describes as "a loathsome, gorilla-like thing." Reanimated, the former boxer runs off into the night, only to appear later with the severed hand of an immigrant child.[103] The episode highlights how fears of infection within a pandemic could turn into, feed, or falsely justify (or all three) existing prejudices—and also suggests that zombies have been deployed in racist ways even before Seabrook introduced the vodou zombie to Anglo-American audiences.

To these multifaceted fears of contagion, Lovecraft adds an additional thread in an episode from the war that deepens the dark portrait of doctors in the story. With its abundant supply of dead male bodies, the war delights West. He is supposed to be reattaching limbs and treating "hitherto hopeless cases of maiming" but instead works near the front to reanimate severed body parts. His key specimen is a decapitated soldier who is both a celebrated surgeon and an army major; West succeeds in reanimating both head and body, and his final zombie figure is born. As with the plague episode, the horror of West's experiments eclipse even the surrounding mass death; as the narrator tells us, the Great War held "hideous things," but "the most hideous thing of all" was "the shocking, the unnatural, the unbelievable horror from the shadows" embodied in West's experiments.[104]

Lovecraft offers here his own peculiar brand of consolation, insisting in the story that West's creations are far worse than war or plague. Much of this hype is hackneyed exaggeration done for cheap thrills, but Lovecraft also gives voice to the possibility that there might be something more unnatural and more disturbing than the worst things people saw or imagined in these years: a person for whom such things were no longer horrifying, a Herbert West figure who, like zombies, relished rather than reviled such sights. The reader's invited shock thus becomes a comforting sign that she or he has not yet sunk to that degree of depravity. And since, after all, the dead were not returning, it might bring relief to imagine that even if they did, it would be terrible.

At the story's end, a final zombie eruption maps multiple elements of post-1918 anxiety and paranoia. West, in later years, has become an example of both an irreparably scarred witness and the original and continued source of the terror. As the narrator relates, his experiments have left him "with a soul calloused and seared, and a hardened eye which sometimes glanced with a kind of hideous and calculating appraisal at men of especially sensitive brain and especially vigorous physique." There's an embedded homophobic slur here, and West also targets the very age group most at risk in both the war and the pandemic, becoming an instantiation of a continued threat and still eying fresh specimens. He is, in many ways, zombie-like himself, a "scientific automaton" on the hunt for fresh victims. At the same time, West suggests a paranoid survivor continuously haunted by the aftermath of plague and war and fears of their return. Such fears are literally embodied in the two remaining zombie doctors: the plague doctor "was still alive—a frightful carnivorous thing" locked away but ever capable of coming back, and the decapitated war doctor who, in addition to representing the war's grisly aftermath, was "a fellow-physician who knew about [West's] experiments and could have duplicated them."[105]

The zombies, of course, return. One evening, West is startled to read in the newspaper that "a body of silent men" had attacked Sefton Asylum, where the plague doctor still resided, seeking the release of the "cannibal monster." The newspaper accounts of the individual members of the group suggest both pandemic and racist fears (one has a "bluish face" that "seemed half eaten way by some unknown malady") and the aftermath of the war (the "wax face" of the leader suggests the reconstructed facial masks of the war injured).[106] The group riots in the asylum, "beat[ing], trampl[ing], and bit[ing] every attendant." Not surprisingly, they soon arrive at West's house, moving with "a jerky tread," and while they had been uncontrolled and unguided in their individual manifestations, they are now "unthinkable automata" directed by the headless leader. They break through the plastered walls into West's subterranean laboratory, "a horde of silent toiling things," and making "no sound," they proceed to tear West to pieces and drag him away.[107]

This grisly denouement offers partial recontainment. A nebulous sense of threat has again been transferred onto visible zombie figures, including the unfeeling Dr. West, and the whole group mercifully disappears into the vault, which detectives discover the next morning now sports an "unbroken plaster wall." A rough zombie justice is delivered, and Lovecraft retombs the horrors he has unleashed, a move poignantly unavailable in real life. The narrator, though, remains haunted and unable to relate the full tale: "Detectives have questioned me," he says, "but what can I say?" They don't believe his story, so he "[tells] them no more." He is probably mad, he concedes, but he "might not be mad if those accursed tomb-legions had not been so silent."[108] Laced into these final moments is a sense of untold stories, of bodies covered up and forgotten, and of the madness—both in terms of mental suffering and in terms of anger—that remains. Lovecraft grants a voice to these horrors and imagines a new monster figure embodying both a numbness to human and nonhuman violence and an instantiation of corrosive anger.

"Cool Air" (1928), a somewhat later Lovecraft story, offers a more benevolent but still unsettling doctor who has turned himself into a zombie-like figure with ties to the pandemic.[109] Here, Lovecraft recasts the zombie not as a raging, cannibalistic automaton but as a monstrous form of enervated living death, one that emerges from "the great illness" that had struck eighteen years before.[110] Told by a sickly man living in an apartment building run by a Spanish landlady, the story recalls the pandemic both in the vague references to a great illness, noted as something the reader would certainly remember, and in Lovecraft's careful designation of the landlady and the central doctor in the story as Spanish (the pandemic was widely known as the "Spanish Influenza").[111] Such a designation suggests Lovecraft's continued associations between contagion and "foreign" influences as well as the nationalist prejudices implicit in the name of the flu.

At the start of the story, the narrator himself embodies a mild version of post-survivor enervation. He has, he tells the reader, been drifting about, eventually finding in the boarding house "at least a bearable place to hibernate till one might really live again."[112] Plagued by continued heart troubles (another link to the flu's aftermath), the narrator appears troubled both mentally and physically. His need to stay in suspended animation is reflected in exaggerated ways in the odd Dr. Muñoz, who lives above him. The narrator consults with the doctor about his heart, growing gradually more horrified as he learns more about the doctor's habits. The doctor suffers from many bodily ailments that extend from his illness in the earlier outbreak, when he had nearly died. He had, he tells the narrator, been saved by another doctor, who later succumbed to the disease. Described repeatedly as "hollow" and living in a state of "nervous animation," Dr. Muñoz never leaves his rooms, obsessed with pursuing scientific enhancements that might preserve a body's animation "despite the most serious impairments." His health depends on having no strong emotions, and he hints to the narrator that it is even possible "to possess some kind of conscious existence—without any heart at all!" This state of living death requires an unnatural coldness that the narrator dwells on obsessively, describing the "abnormal" chilliness, the alienation of the "singular cold," and the "icy air" that continues to haunt him even years later.[113] The doctor's state—and by extension the narrator's—has a metaphoric resonance, suggesting the sense of ongoing damage in those still alive in 1923, when the story takes place, and also the costs of trying to keep the past at bay. The image of a man terrified to leave his apartment, seeking to stay so cold he might freeze time at one moment, shunning strong emotions, and trying to live on without a heart all offer a bleak picture of the traumatized survivor, one echoed in the narrator's own poor health and the way the cold now triggers memories of his nightmarish experiences.

As the doctor grows sicker, he turns more zombie-like, becoming a monstrous creature of animated soullessness that horrifies those around him. His voice takes on a "lifeless, rattling hollowness," and his "muscular motions" are less coordinated. When an electrician who visits his apartment takes an "unexpected glimpse" at the man, he suffers an epileptic fit, even though he "had been through the terrors of the Great War without having incurred any fright so thorough." By the middle of October, the doctor is frantically engaged in efforts to keep his rooms colder, and while he tries to keep his emotions dead, his "rage and fear" now "swell[ed] to grotesque proportions."[114] At the end of the story, when his cooling mechanism breaks down, he melts away into a dark puddle, though not before leaving the narrator a note confessing that he had actually died in that great illness and had been preserved since through a vague mix of modern science and quasi-sorcery. The final scene magnifies the sights, sounds, and locations of the influenza pandemic—it's mid-October, the body turns to fluids, and the horror is worse than the war and arrives at home in the midst of a crowded city. Horror, the narrator reminds us, does not just come in "darkness, silence, and solitude" or in the Great War but "in the glare of mid-afternoon, in the clangour of a metropolis, and in the teeming midst of a shabby and commonplace rooming-house."[115] Doctors are no help with this domestic threat—indeed, they produce it in monstrous form, with Dr. Muñoz emerging as a new zombie subtype that embodies an exaggerated and horrifying post-pandemic enervation. Like Dr. West, Dr. Muñoz becomes a perverse version of the doctors in Wald's later 1950s contagion narratives who race to find a cure. Lovecraft's tale nevertheless grants its own comfort, explaining and recontaining the threat as the doctor grossly but harmlessly melts away.

Lovecraft combines both strains of proto-zombies—the angry, carnivorous type and the extreme enervation type—in his story "In the Vault," which shifts the target of rage from doctors to another figure of lingering post-1918 horror: the gravedigger/undertaker.[116] By the very nature of their jobs, of course, such figures are standard gothic tropes, but after the widespread domestic burial problems in the pandemic, they became the source both of anger and continued grief. Chaotic scenes like the one Cendrars describes at Apollinaire's grave were commonplace, and pandemic accounts return repeatedly to the overtaxed gravediggers, who often "were sick or refused to bury influenza victims,"[117] and to the horrors of seeing loved ones haphazardly buried. As Nancy Bristow notes, in America, "even in the best scenarios, families often did not feel that they had been able to put their loved ones to rest in a fashion that met their expectations."[118] Cemetery workers spoke with horror of the pandemic; at St. Ann Cemetery in Cranston, Rhode Island, just seventeen miles from where Lovecraft lived, one witness summarized the grisly pandemic atmosphere:

I will try to give you my version of the Black Plague as many called it at that time. . . . All around me people were dying. . . . Funeral directors worked with fear and lived with the same. Men digging graves showed fear of this form of death. Many graves were fashioned by long trenches, bodies were placed side by side. . . . As it came so it went, leaving in its wake countless dead, and the living stunned at their loss. . . . Later on . . . I worked at St. Annes [sic] Cemetery in Cranston[;] . . . those that lie in death from the Black Plague and the graves marked by small 2–6 markers projected fear in our selves, never to remove [sic] or agree by any order for reburial else where, no order ever came. The trench of bodies lie[s] today in mute evidence of this the black Plague. . . . I saw [the trench], I fear it today after all these years.[119]

Lovecraft offers a target for the fear and anger produced by such burials in the figure of George Birch, the indifferent cemetery caretaker of "In the Vault." Birch, the doctor-narrator informs us at the start of the tale, is not to be mistaken for the comic figure of the "bungling . . . village undertaker" who offers humorous antics with his "careless mishap in a tomb." His story, in fact, has "aspects beside which some of our darkest tragedies are light." Birch has, in the past, mixed up bodies and caskets, to the horror of family members, and is a "very calloused and primitive specimen even as such specimens go."[120] At the start of the story, bodies have piled up in his holding vault, unable to be buried because of the frozen December ground, and while the tale is set before the pandemic or the war, the scene was a familiar one to Lovecraft's readers. Lovecraft imagines a fitting, zombified revenge for Birch's professional sins. On—ominously—Good Friday, the ground has started to thaw enough that Birch decides to begin the burial process. He goes out to the vault that holds the bodies in their coffins and inadvertently becomes locked inside. Echoing the indifference of Dr. West, Birch is untroubled amid this scene of horror, with the narrator repeatedly noting that he lacks the imagination and the caring to register the ghastliness. Birch knows he has sloppily made some of the coffins, like the one that holds a deceased vindictive farmer, Asaph Sawyer, so he selects what he thinks are the sturdiest coffins and stacks them on top of each other to reach a small opening. Yet again mixing up his wares, though, Birch inadvertently puts the "flimsy" Sawyer coffin on top; his foot breaks through the rotten lid to land on the body beneath—and the evening's first zombie figure emerges.[121]

The corpse from the coffin animates, and Birch finds his feet are held "in relentless captivity," jerking him out of his cool indifference.[122] As the doctor who treats Birch's injuries later discovers, the body of Asaph Sawyer had risen from the dead to exact his revenge, biting Birch's ankles and severing his tendons. Sawyer was an ideal specimen for producing a revengeful pandemic zombie: dead of "a malignant fever," in life he had had an "almost inhuman vindictiveness and tenacious memory for wrongs real or fancied."[123] The doctor who had treated Sawyer in his last illness recognizes the man's distinctive teeth marks on Birch's legs.[124] This doctor—another example of a medical professional who, the narrator tells us, had become indifferent to death and bodies—is nevertheless horrified by what he sees in the vault after treating Birch's injuries. He finds Sawyer's decayed body has spilled from the coffin onto the floor, cracking the skull and revealing the source of the corpse's anger: "The skull turned my stomach," the doctor tells Birch, "but the other was worse—*those ankles cut neatly off to fit* [the] ... *cast-aside coffin!*" The doctor declares Birch "got what [he] deserved," Birch's own almost severed feet a fitting "eye for an eye" revenge for what he had done to make Sawyer's body fit the subpar coffin.[125] Lovecraft creates an inflated picture of undertaker malfeasance and then imagines a grisly payback. Sawyer's ravenous viciousness against such treatment reflects a pandemic-driven source of rage, one that produces a viral resurrection that, on this Good Friday, fuels destruction rather than salvation.

The attack creates a second zombie-like figure in the form of Birch, but of the enervated variety. Immediately after the bite, he crawls out of the vault like a resurrected corpse himself, his ankles covered in blood and his "fingers clawing the black mold in brainless haste." The bites end up infecting his whole being, rendering him physically lame, but "the greatest lameness was in his soul." His "thinking processes," the narrator tells us, "had become ineffaceably scarred," and he remains a half-living shell. His existence bears witness to his past misdeeds, a figure of the guilt-ridden, living-dead survivor, "preyed upon" by fears and a "belated sort of remorse."[126] In Sawyer's bites, Lovecraft creates an early infectious zombie figure, a materialized contagion that produces a new monster. The story seems less a morality tale on the dangers of wishing for resurrection—Birch has no interest in the dead returning—and more a satisfying tale of rough justice, combined with a sense of guilt that lives on well past death.

Zombies may play different cultural roles in each decade, but as with all monsters, the origin story matters. The protozombies of Gance and Lovecraft arise at a moment of crisis and haunting fear, granting a material representation of the influenza virus's most haunting traits—its infectious quality, its disfigurement, its eating away at bodies and minds, its proliferation, its monstrous familiarity, its uncontrollability, and its manifestation of walking death. These monsters made viral resurrection literal, the returning dead the conduit for deathly fecundity. They were taunting mockeries of spiritualism and horror-movie versions of Eliot's cruel April. Resurrection was not even necessary: the still living could also be turned, as we see in Gance's zombified audience and in the transformation of Lovecraft's undertaker. The characteristics of these pandemic zombies swarm out of the outbreak and morph into the wildly proliferating modern monster figure zombies have become. A genetic family line stretches from these early viral, flesh-eating creatures, to works like Richard Matheson's infectious zombie-vampires in *I Am Legend* (1954), to the Romero's films, to *The Walking Dead*, with many stops in between. This line bypasses Seabrook, bearing little resemblance to the Anglo-American, vodou-inspired zombie. While zombies may signal a range of modern anxieties, from radiation poisoning to consumerism, this figure continues to embody, in its very manifestation, the buried but still lurking terror of a monstrous, disfiguring contagion.

Spiritualism and protozombie narratives granted two versions of the resurrected dead, both of which spoke to—and were shaped by—postpandemic anguish. Alongside the distinctions I've traced between the comfort each one offered lies another instructive variance. Spiritualism was *meant* to be believed, the presence of its resurrected dead a matter of scientific proof; by contrast, the protozombie tales were *meant* to be seen as illusion, the comfort of their reanimations arising from their fictional quality. For those grieving the pandemic dead, spiritualism's insistence on the literal truth of continued life granted a heady combination of religiously tinged and scientifically based consolation. Without changing the facts of the pandemic, spiritualism allowed the narrative to be extended beyond death in such a way that the experience itself could be transformed; if the dead lived on in health and safety, the guilt, plotlessness, and meaninglessness of the pandemic death could also be rewritten. The narrative, though, required belief for its solace. The protozombie tales, however, relied on illusion for their comfort. From their worldview, *believing* the dead might return is a disaster—these dead are angry and vengeful, which might also lessen the blow over the fact that the dead were not, in fact, returning. *Imagining* the dead (or doctors or undertakers) as zombies, though, provided a new storyline and an outlet for anger and guilt that might otherwise be unexpressed. Evaluating the pandemic as a spectral trauma requires we make a parallel move, at once believing in its tangible and continued cultural presence and acknowledging its persistently illusory position.

THE STRUCTURE OF ILLNESS,
THE SHAPE OF LOSS

A lethal pandemic leaves few tangible reminders behind. No buildings collapse. No battlefields or crash sites are preserved. Rarely do memorials mark its passing. Its effects are felt everywhere but located in no particular place, except perhaps in the bodies and memories of the living who remain. As I researched this book, caught up in the details and the close readings, I would at times be brought short by a particular story or statistic, and the breadth of the loss would catch me unawares: the number of orphans the pandemic produced and all the large and small losses even one of those stories entailed, the men who returned from war to find their families gone, mothers and babies buried together. The pandemic produced so many layers of loss—the loss of life, the loss those deaths produced for loved ones, the loss of health for many survivors, and the loss of the event itself in so many of our histories. We can account for the impact of the pandemic, but how do we represent the loss? The scope challenges the very possibility of adequate representation.

In mapping the pandemic's presence in interwar literature and culture, I have focused on recovering stories and tracing the way losses reverberate. I have analyzed how these stories reveal gaps and silences in our own critical accounts of the era. Elements that had been hidden have come to the surface, subtly shifting the contours of modernism. The ill or recovering body emerges as more central to the era's literature. The war's mass deaths become twinned, taking on a grim spectral parallel. Patterns of imagery carry new resonance, from miasmic atmospheres to the walking dead to bells to corpses to uncertain burial to linguistic fragments that read as delirium. These images do not always reflect the pandemic or only reflect the pandemic, but knowing the outbreak's sensory and affective history changes our sense of the wellspring from which interwar literature arose. Works outside of the ones I explore change their shape. James Joyce did not have a personal encounter with the pandemic, but the ghosts and corpses and coffins in *Ulysses* (1922), the ill and ravaged body of Mary Dedalus that haunts Stephen, and the many references to drowning would all have spoken to readers still in the grips of the pandemic's miasmic aftermath. The book-long effort to bury Addie Bundren in William Faulkner's *As I Lay Dying* (1930) may not reference the pandemic but nevertheless memorializes the protracted sense of dying and insecure burial the era encompassed. As we've seen, even the way the pandemic is dismissed or left out of a particular text may reshape our understanding of the work's central concerns. In *To Have and Have Not* (1937), Ernest Hemingway uses the pandemic to kill off the wife of the washed-up, alcoholic Professor MacWalsey, a device that underscores the deflating, less masculine elements of the professor. Nella Larsen nursed patients throughout the pandemic, but the experience does not seem present in her fiction; might the absence underscore how many threats already faced African American communities, so that the flu, as grim as it was, didn't register as distinct?[1] And other cultural impacts remain to be explored. The Anglican Church in England and the United States, as well as the Mormon Church, shaped new doctrines and services in the wake of flu and war losses. The most popular magic trick of all time—sawing a woman in half—came to stages everywhere starting in 1921, where night after night a woman was disfigured and resurrected whole once more, rising from her coffin-like box.[2] How might the pandemic weave its way into these stories?

I end, though, not with presence but with absence, focusing on the idea of loss and the challenge of representing an emptiness. At the same time, I offer an experiment in reading, a longer application than the short examples in the previous paragraph of how this study has shifted the modernist terrain. I turn to the "Time Passes" section of Virginia Woolf's *To the Lighthouse* (1927), one of the era's most profound reflections on loss and grief. Structurally, it serves as the connecting bridge between the Victorian era of the novel's first part and the post-1918 moment at its end, "a corridor," as Woolf wrote in her notebook, joining "two blocks."[3] Taking place, like the rest of the novel, entirely at a summer home in the Hebrides, the section is a prose poem on mortality and meaning. The language is saturated in grief; the very air of the domestic space is marked by loss. Woolf shapes an aesthetics of ineffability, built from images of absence, silence, emptiness, darkness, and nothingness. She encompasses the war within this loss—the section is peppered with subtle military language—as well as the pandemic, evoking both the overt destruction and darkness of these years and also the subtle shifts in mood and thought wrought by death on such a massive scale.[4]

I propose playing with a category shift, asking how the landscape alters if we read the fundamental structure and images of "Time Passes" as shaped by the contours of illness—and illness on a vast scale. I do not claim that the section is "really" about the pandemic, only that Woolf uses elements closely aligned to illness to express the scope and scale of the era's losses. In this coda, at least for a moment, I pursue what happens when we flip the era's central metaphor, as it were, and read the pandemic and illness as providing an enabling vehicle to which the war may be compared and in which the war imagery resides. I deliberately push the envelope not to prove that the pandemic matters more—it doesn't, and it's not a contest anyway—but as an experiment, as a way to startle us out of more familiar narratives and patterns of reading. Not only does history look different, but what we thought was history in the first place, what we assumed counted as context, changes when we see as foundational a structure that is made of the body's private, internal experiences exponentially repeated. As Woolf observes in "On Being Ill," we need a new language to convey such histories. We may say, she writes, " 'I am in bed with influenza'—but what does that convey of the great experience; how the world has changed its shape"?[5]

Woolf builds "Time Passes" around an empty domestic space, rather than a trench or a barracks. Even as she uses this space to exemplify the era's destruction and loss, she registers the shock that such a space would be so ravaged. From the section's opening moments, she reminds her readers how fundamentally perceptions will shift in these years. As the characters come in from the outdoors, they find familiar territories and structures dissolving; the land and sea can no longer be distinguished, and "it's almost too dark to see."[6] An ominous darkness falls, and invisible forces enter through the house and move toward the bedrooms. The narrative voice expresses bewilderment that these forces would penetrate the domestic areas: "But here surely, they must cease. Whatever else may perish and disappear, what lies here is steadfast . . . here you can neither touch nor destroy." The surprise attaches to location, reflected in the astonished repetition of "here" three times.[7] Her vehicle for depicting these experiences is a domestic one, the location shaped from images of home, the action at pandemic ground zero. The locations and narrative encompass an experience repeated everywhere in the preceding years, the horror and dawning realization that mass death had moved from the battlefields to the bedrooms. Woolf uses this vehicle to capture the much broader and deeply human shock of realizing that places that seem safe and fundamental may be violated or lost.

The constitutive qualities of the threats in "Time Passes"—built from nothing yet omnipresent, indifferent yet relentless—likewise encompass the war but are structured like a pathogenic threat. Woolf uses three key clusters of images: darkness, air or wind, and water. Each conceptualizes in different ways the ineffability and spreading quality of this danger. The first depiction combines images of darkness with water:

Nothing, it seemed, could survive the flood, the profusion of darkness which, creeping in at keyhole and crevices, stole round window blinds, came into bedrooms, swallowed up here a jug and basin, there a bowl of red and yellow dahlias, there the sharp edges and firm bulk of a chest of drawers. Not only was furniture confounded; there was scarcely anything left of body or mind by which one could say, "This is he" or "This is she."[8]

The darkness moves everywhere; it seems nothing can survive it. Capable of passing through cracks and keyholes, it is unstoppable by doors or windows. The darkness swallows the comforting, everyday elements of the bedroom—jug and basin, flowers and furniture; it dissolves bodies and minds, irrespective of gender. The darkness holds elements of war, but the structural metaphor on which a larger sense of loss is built seems far more viral in nature, moving everywhere, breaching borders of both countries and bodies. The passage echoes the perspective of Clarissa Dalloway, who feels "it was her punishment to see sink and disappear here a man, there a woman, in this profound darkness," imagery that, like the "he" and "she" of the *Lighthouse* passage, makes the gendered expansion of mass death fundamental.[9] And this darkness is not simply extensive but seemingly endless, with no armistice that might mark its close.

Alongside these images of an all-encompassing darkness lies a second conceptualization of destruction, built from the literal medium through which contagion so often spreads: the air. Like the darkness, the air can sneak through small spaces, invading the indoors and introducing a sense of impending defeat. At first seemingly innocent, different "airs" enter "through the rusty hinges and swollen sea-moistened woodwork," creeping "round corners and ventur[ing] indoors." They initially seem merely to introduce questions about endurance; as the narrator says, "one might imagine [these airs], as they entered the drawing-room questioning and wondering, toying with the flap of hanging wall-paper, asking, would it hang much longer?" The airs then question "the torn letters in the waste-paper basket, the flowers, the books, all of which were now open to them and asking, Were they allies? Were they enemies? How long would they endure?"[10] The blurred syntax makes it unclear if it's the airs or the objects that are doing the asking, as if the questions themselves are unspoken but in the air, as it were. Like the syntax, the lines between allies and enemies are ambiguous, and identification becomes difficult. The words suggest the language of the war but describe the particular uncertainty of an airborne death that takes no account of sides; the air is both necessary ally and pathogenically loaded enemy.

As the airs breach the bedrooms, they take on a more ominous quasi-incarnation, like an invisible molester come at night: "Here one might say to those sliding lights, those fumbling airs that breathe and bend over the bed itself, here you can neither touch nor destroy. Upon which, wearily, ghostlily, as if they had feather-light fingers and the light persistency of feathers, they would look, once, on the shut eyes, and the loosely clasping fingers, and fold their garments wearily and disappear." The figure in the bed appears to be asleep or dead, and the airs themselves—as if tired out by all their destruction—wearily take their insubstantial selves away and disappear. And yet, they don't; they continue on to the servants' bedrooms, to the attics, to the dining room, to the gardens, before "at length, desisting, all ceased together, gathered together, all sighed together; all together gave off an aimless gust of lamentation to which some door in the kitchen replied; swung wide; admitted nothing; and slammed to."[11] The language embodies the pervasiveness of this threat as well as its insubstantial quality. It is aimless, it brings lamentation, it takes over an unconsenting body, it acts in the world, yet is "nothing" and produces nothing and brings about a nothingness—a loss, an absence—that in turn produces the gust of lamentation. The threat is not defeated so much as stops from a weary disinterest. The imagery allows the reader to "see" this threat and also the way it is not there—and the terrible emptiness it leaves in its wake.

And these stray airs, the narrator tells us in a passage right after the death of Mrs. Ramsay, continue to stalk the house; they are "advance guards of great armies" that "blustered in . . . [and] met nothing in bedroom or drawing-room that wholly resisted them."[12] The language acknowledges that the militarism of the war would not cease with its end, yet the airs, the evocation of wind in "bluster," the location, and the lack of any possible resistance suggest an invisible, airborne army. Woolf had used similar military language to encode the wages of illness in "On Being Ill." As she observes in her essay, literature is so often silent about "those great wars which [the body] wages by itself, with the mind a slave to it, in the solitude of the bedroom against the assault of fever."[13] In "Time Passes," this war has been lost, and this assault so successful as to be irresistible and unresisted.

Woolf ramps up the scope of destruction in her third formulation of the threat, drawing on meteorological imagery—storms, wind, rough water—and sea monsters in a vision of Yeatsean "mere anarchy"[14] that exemplifies the inhuman quality of this violence:

Listening (had there been any one to listen) from the upper rooms of the empty house only gigantic chaos streaked with lightning could have been heard tumbling and tossing, as the winds and waves disported themselves like the amorphous bulks of leviathans whose brows are pierced by no light of reason, and mounted one on top of another, and lunged and plunged in the darkness or the daylight (for night and day, month and year ran shapelessly together) in idiot games, until it seems as if the universe were battling and tumbling, in brute confusion and wanton lust aimlessly by itself.[15]

Like Yeats's "The Second Coming," the language evokes both an individual, delirious nightmare as well as a more global sense of purposeless destruction. Seen from within the landscape of a single body, the language makes monstrous the spreading chaos and proliferation of internal threat—as well as its hallucinatory results. From a broader perspective, the language evokes the chaos and amorality of an intangible, nonhuman destruction. The monsters are based in nature in both viewpoints—wind and waves and amorphous beasts that are guided by no reason, bringing aimlessness and confusion. All this destruction seems both to linger and to be forgotten the following spring: the funereal "garden urns" are full of flowers, and "the stillness and the brightness of the day" seems as unsettling "as the chaos and tumult of night." The destruction lives on even when no longer seen; indeed, the trees and flowers, like shocked mourners, "stand[] there, looking before them . . . yet beholding nothing, eyeless, and so terrible."[16]

The victims of all this destruction are hidden and in plain sight, their deaths more centrally structured around illness, though they contain the war as well. Woolf's famous brackets, which announce the deaths of Mrs. Ramsay, the pregnant Prue, and Andrew, narrate the stark facts of their passing. As critics note, the deaths parallel Woolf's own sudden losses of her mother, her sister Stella, and her brother Thoby (all from disease).[17] Two of the three deal with women, a surprising ratio at a moment focused on the deaths of young men, but one that brings female victims into focus. The death of Andrew, who is killed in the war, would have been anticipated at the time; the deaths of Mrs. Ramsay and Prue come as a brutal shock both for readers and the family—these were not the expected victims. Like the air's invasion of the domestic space, this shock speaks to the unexpectedness and horror with which death so often strikes, an experience that took on brutal new extremes in the pandemic, when more died in a shorter period—mostly healthy adults—than at any time in history. The section builds a universal experience from a structure with deep resonances to the pandemic's losses. Both female deaths also seem to reflect illness—the reader is only told that Mrs. Ramsay died "rather suddenly the night before" and that Prue dies from "some illness connected with childbirth."[18] The female deaths arise from a nonhuman cause and a hidden agent. Woolf's mother, on whom Mrs. Ramsay is based, likely died of complications from influenza—though not in the 1918 outbreak—granting an additional viral link to this death.[19] William Maxwell connects the pandemic to Mrs. Ramsay, crafting *They Came Like Swallows* around a similar sudden death of a mother who had anchored the family and structured its reality.[20] And the death of the pregnant Prue embodies the most vulnerable population during the pandemic, as we saw both in Maxwell's novel and in Yeats's "The Second Coming." Woolf places Andrew's death last, the narrator starkly informing the reader that he dies from a shell explosion that kills "twenty or thirty" others, the language evocative of war's senselessness.[21] The positioning makes the war echo illness, the female deaths setting the models and standards for reading the war death, rather than the reverse. And even with Andrew's death, illness lurks: he is based on Woolf's brother Thoby, who died not in the war but of typhoid fever.[22] While the two female deaths represent illness more broadly, the very way these deaths seem generalized rather than from a specific cause encodes, but also fights against, the gendered way war registers as a recognized tragedy while illness becomes swallowed within the larger atmosphere of loss.

Alongside this reallocation of the section's—and the era's—individual deaths, "Time Passes" flips one of the war's central tropes of mass death into an illness-infused image. While the shell that kills Andrew and the others expresses the unsettling anonymity of the war's slaughter, another image offers a more abstract and anonymous sense of vast annihilation: "The nights now are full of wind and destruction; the trees plunge and bend and their leaves fly helter skelter until the lawn is plastered with them and they lie packed in gutters and choke rain-pipes and scatter damp paths."[23] Such images immediately call to mind war deaths—Hemingway and others draw on images of packed leaves to suggest the countless bodies of soldiers.[24] Woolf, though, in "On Being Ill," specifically uses such language to describe illness—and indeed the ill as deserters from war. When ill, she writes, "we cease to be soldiers in the army of the upright; we become deserters. They march to battle. We float with the sticks on the stream; helter skelter with the dead leaves on the lawn."[25] If we read the "helter skelter" leaves as linked to ill bodies—as Woolf does in her essay— the "Time Passes" imagery emerges as an echo of a pandemic landscape: death litters the domestic space (the lawn, the gutters) rather than the battlefields, the imagery appearing not before Andrew's death but before Mrs. Ramsay's. The critical instinct to associate such imagery with the war's mass death repeats a reflex in play at the time, but the image allows us to register other bodies that are scattered right before our eyes.

The empty house and the sea become ersatz bodies of victims—material yet empty or insubstantial. The house is infected from within by the darkness and creeping airs, barely able to withstand the onslaught. The sea displays an eerie resemblance to a flu body without an actual body, showing "a purplish stain upon the bland surface . . . as if something had boiled and bled, invisibly, beneath. . . . It was difficult blandly to overlook [these signs]; to abolish their significance in the landscape."[26] The stain suggests that the carnage marks nature itself and links to war deaths at sea—though such deaths were hardly overlooked or invisible. Woolf emphasizes hidden internal damage and also something overlooked because of its "bland surface" (even as she notes the difficulty in keeping up this indifference). The sea's blood recalls Yeats's "blood-dimmed tide," and the visual of a "purplish stain" was familiar across the globe; as the British flu historian Niall Johnson observes, the flu's *heliotrope cyanosis*, which granted a "purple-blue" color to the body, was "one of the most commonly remarked features of this pandemic,"[27] a microbial violence that boiled and bled beneath the skin. Woolf's image is not a coded reference to the pandemic so much as an evocative example of how she builds on widespread emotions and experiences from the preceding years to express a vast sense of unseen pain and loss.

The victims and the threats have their parallel in the emptiness of the section's narrative structure. The bare bones of linear plot exist: a house is ruined, and then saved, barely; we are offered tiny bracketed stories, mostly of death. The section's telos, though, is not one of sacrifice or structure but the negation of both. The words "aimless" and "nothing" echo everywhere. The famous sleeper, who goes to the beach to seek an answer from nature, is left without answers. The passage on his search, which is another set before the death of Mrs. Ramsay, reflects two scenes simultaneously: a larger, more generalizable moment of a vast, indifferent nature and a deathbed-like moment when the hand of the dying, held by another, goes limp:

Should any sleeper fancying that he might find on the beach an answer to his doubts, a sharer of his solitude, throw off his bedclothes and go down by himself to walk on the sand, no image with semblance of serving and divine promptitude comes readily to hand bringing the night to order and making the world reflect the compass of the soul. The hand dwindles in his hand; the voice bellows in his ear. Almost it would appear that it is useless in such confusion to ask the night those questions as to what, and why, and wherefore, which tempt the sleeper from his bed to seek an answer.[28]

The war's carnage had challenged so many structures of meaning—the nature of death, ideas of "divine promptitude" or "the compass of the soul," a belief in an affinity between the natural world and human endeavor. As we've seen, illness—and in particular pandemic illness—offers even less structure, a death enfolded in such confusion that it can indeed seem useless to ask "what, and why, and wherefore." The hand dwindles, the voice bellows, but no framework for understanding this death (faced by "any sleeper") arises—and to punctuate this sense, the reader immediately faces the shocking and unexplained bracket announcing Mrs. Ramsay's death. Nature is not simply indifferent here, as it was called so often in the war; it is deadly. When the narrative voice asks in a later section, "Did Nature supplement what man advanced? Did she complete what he began?"[29] we can read the questions as being about a possible affinity between nature and humans, but these questions are also more menacing, as Nature becomes a force that may complete the mass destruction already advanced by "man."

By the end of "Time Passes," what arrives is silence and forgetting:

At last, in the evening, one after another the sounds die out, and the harmony falters, and silence falls. With the sunset sharpness was lost, and like mist rising, quiet rose, quiet spread, the wind settled; loosely the world shook itself down to sleep, darkly here without a light to it, save what came green suffused through leaves, or pale on the white flowers in the bed by the window.[30]

The passage moves from the present to the past tense, as if the reader is watching as the tragedies of the section move out of view. And yet, the language suggests the way trauma remains, just under the surface even when unspoken or pushed away. Something ominous lurks: the sounds dying, the harmony faltering, the silence falling, the world shaken to sleep, and the darkness without light, except what falls on a seemingly empty bed. Surrounding all these grim images is a contagious quietness that "rose" and "spread," with the darkness and the mist providing—almost—additional cover. The language captures the pandemic's disappearance from cultural memory and a post-traumatic moment more generally: the memory quieted, obscured, shaken into sleep, yet infusing every sentence. The temptation is to forget, especially, as Woolf suggests, when guests start to arrive again at the house and a sense of "normal" life resumes. At the very end of the section, peace descends, the voice of beauty lulling the sleepers, "as the curtains of dark wrapped themselves over the house, over Mrs. Beckwith, Mr. Carmichael, and Lily Briscoe so that they lay with several folds of blackness on their eyes, why not accept this, be content with this, acquiesce and resign?" Here again, something seems ominous; there is something dangerous about a darkness that requires both acquiescence and resignation. The war is here—with the "never forget" fears that the peace produced—but the more hidden danger is the one already forgotten, folded in the blackness of covered eyes and curtained rooms hiding the bodies within. Woolf, like her artist figure Lily, however, does not forget. In the section's final moments, Lily jolts out of this acquiescence, bolting up from a nightmare about falling off a cliff. Woolf finishes the section with a resurrection of sorts, a sudden return of the memory and a warning against forgetting; she ends with a single-word sentence that functions as a way to describe Lily's state; as a plea or prayer for resurrection, however hopeless; and as an imperative to the reader: "Awake."[31]

"Time Passes" is a virtuoso performance of the ways literature may register a vast hidden trauma like the influenza pandemic. The section achieves the seemingly impossible, granting form to loss and emptiness, making visible what is invisible. It offers in concentrated form the atmospheres I have traced throughout this study. It makes linguistically tangible the ineffable quality of a viral threat, shaping it into darkness, air, wind, mist, and water. It creates a structure for what has no structure, finding ways to grant form to loss and grief—which by definition are made by emptiness, by what is not there. This form is supplemented through constant images of emptiness—jugs, urns, beds, rooms, houses, and most poignantly, the clothes that "in the[ir] emptiness indicated how once they were filled and animated"[32]—and in successions of "nothingness" that are repeated so often as to create a structure built of nothing. We have seen how Porter, Cather, Wolfe, and Maxwell strove to make visible such an atmosphere; how Eliot, Yeats, and Woolf herself captured the pandemic's intangible presence and offered readers new ways to see it; and how popular works granted new narratives of materialized resurrections to push against this emptiness. In its very structure, "Time Passes" embodies the shape of this loss—the loss of the pandemic memory itself but, more critically, the vast and catastrophic losses that a lethal pandemic leaves behind.

As scientists and researchers continually remind us, we are not ready for the next severe global pandemic, which—as they also remind us—is most assuredly coming.[33] On the one hand, the last one hundred years have seen dramatic advances in disease treatments, and efforts are made every day to monitor and prevent outbreaks and to develop new vaccines. On the other hand, as I write this coda, dramatic cuts are proposed in the United States to some of the very programs that might prevent or respond to future global pandemics.[34] Public support for such programs tends to peak during outbreaks, like the swine flu in 2009 and Ebola in 2014, but then wanes in their aftermath.[35] And in the United States, as budgets for health care programs are reduced, funds for military spending have increased. The willingness to tolerate this discrepancy echoes the difference I have traced throughout this study between the attention the war received and the attention the pandemic received. For all the reasons I have analyzed, military threats, political conflict, and human-based violence are typically treated, represented, and seen far more clearly than threats posed by disease; the pandemic killed more people, but it's the war we remember. It would be more than possible to build and augment effective global response systems that would greatly reduce the impact of a deadly pandemic—but first far more people have to see the threat and be willing to act. The works I investigate remind us that even a modern catastrophic pandemic *that has already happened* can be hidden, unless we learn to read for its presence.

NOTES

ABBREVIATIONS

PIS   Pandemic Influenza Storybook. A collection of stories about the flu in the United States, gathered by the Centers for Disease Control and Prevention, updated 2014. https://www.cdc.gov/publications/panflu/. Cited as *PIS*, subject, storyteller, and location.

RC   Archive of letters written by pandemic survivors to the researcher Richard Collier in the 1970s. Collier placed advertisements asking for letters in newspapers throughout the United States, Canada, and Europe. Letters held at the Imperial War Museum Archives in London, England, collection #18909, Boxes 63/5/1–9. Collected 1972–1973. Letters arranged in boxes by country, and then in alphabetical order by last name of letter writer (maiden name if applicable). Letters cited as *RC*, author, and country.

1. INTRODUCING THE PANDEMIC

1. Pandemic death statistics vary widely: records were spotty and communities overwhelmed. Recent accounts put the global death rate as at least 50 million and likely 100 million or more. See John M. Barry, *The Great Influenza: The Story of the Deadliest Pandemic in History* (New York: Penguin, 2004), 396–98, for a summary of the studies; and Niall P. A. S. Johnson and Juergen Mueller, "Updating the Accounts: Global Mortality of the 1918–1920 'Spanish' Influenza Pandemic," *Bulletin of the History of Medicine* 76, no. 1 (Spring 2002): 105–15. Alfred W. Crosby observes that the United States lost more in the pandemic than "in World War I, World War II, and the Korean and Vietnamese conflicts," and I have added American casualties in Afghanistan and Iraq; see Alfred W. Crosby, *America's Forgotten*

Pandemic: The Influenza of 1918, 2nd ed. (Cambridge: Cambridge University Press, 2003), 207.

2. Mark Honigsbaum, *Living with Enza: The Forgotten Story of Britain and the Great Flu Pandemic of 1918* (London: Macmillan, 2009), xiii, 5 (infection statistics). British colonies were also devastated; in areas of India controlled by Britain, studies suggest that 13.88 million people died; see Siddharth Chandra, Goran Kuljanin, and Jennifer Wray, "Mortality from the Influenza Pandemic of 1918–1919: The Case of India," *Demography* 49, no. 3 (August 2012): 857–65. South Africa and Nigeria saw overwhelming death tolls; see Howard Phillips, "South Africa's Worst Demographic Disaster: The Spanish Influenza Epidemic of 1918," *South African Historical Journal* 20 (1988): 57–73; and Marc Matera, Misty L. Bastian, and Susan Kingsley Kent, *The Women's War of 1929: Gender and Violence in Colonial Nigeria* (New York: Palgrave Macmillan, 2012), 78–107. Death rates were high across the globe, and while here, too, statistics are difficult to assess, one state in Mexico, Chiapas, lost 10 percent of its population; a third of Japanese residents contracted the flu; Russia and Iran lost as much as 7 percent of their populations; China lost a tremendous but unknown number of people; in Buenos Aires, Argentina, 55 percent of the population contracted the virus; in Fiji, 14 percent of the population died in just sixteen days; Barry, *The Great Influenza*, 363–65.

3. See John Dorney, "Ireland and the Great Flu Epidemic of 1918," *The Irish Story*, May 16, 2013, http://www.theirishstory.com/2013/05/16/ireland-and-the-great-flu-epidemic-of-1918/. Dorney also notes that 800,000 people in Ireland likely caught the flu. While Ireland loses far more people in the pandemic than in the civic political violence, Ireland, like Britain, does lose more men in the war than to the flu, though the exact ratio is difficult to determine; Irish death rates in the war range from 27,405 to 49,000; see Myles Dungan, "Counting the Irish Dead," *Irish Times*, October 22, 2014, https://www.irishtimes.com/culture/heritage/counting-the-irish-dead-1.1951023.

4. George Hutchinson, *In Search of Nella Larsen: A Biography of the Color Line* (Cambridge, MA: Harvard University Press, 2006), 119. The pandemic experience does not seem to make its way into the artistic works of Larsen, Lawrence, and H.D. in a pervasive way. Biographical details on Porter, Yeats, Wolfe, Eliot, and Woolf are offered in later chapters.

5. Jane Elizabeth Fisher, *Envisioning Disease, Gender, and War: Women's Narratives of the 1918 Influenza Pandemic* (New York: Palgrave Macmillan, 2012), is one exception, exploring modernist works and the flu in its first four chapters. I return to Fisher's work at the end of the introduction.

6. Judith Butler, *Frames of War: When Is Life Grievable?* (London: Verso, 2009); I discuss Butler's work at length later in the chapter.

7. The war and the pandemic overlapped in multiple ways; see Crosby, *America's Forgotten Pandemic*, 26–27, 172–96; and Barry, *The Great Influenza*, 383–88, for its effects on the war's end and the Treaty of Versailles.

8. Death rates in the pandemic for men versus women are difficult to determine and vary by country. The United States, Australia, New Zealand, Norway, and South Africa had higher death rates for men; in England and Wales, more women seem to have died: Niall Johnson, *Britain and the 1918–1919 Influenza Pandemic: A Dark Epilogue* (London: Routledge, 2006), 91–92. Pregnant women faced the highest death rates; see Barry, *The Great Influenza*, 239–40.

9. Glenn R. Schiraldi, *The Post-Traumatic Stress Disorder Sourcebook*, 2nd ed. (New York: McGraw-Hill, 2009), chap. 1.

10. Anne Whitehead, *Trauma Fiction* (Edinburgh: Edinburgh University Press, 2004), considers how contemporary literature conveys trauma through narrative disruption, intertextuality, repetition, and the recovery of silenced voices. She also notes how ghosts are a recurring theme, a trait I explore in the pandemic literature.

11. Richard Collier wrote one of the first books on the pandemic, *The Plague of the Spanish Lady: The Influenza Pandemic of 1918-1919* (London: Macmillan, 1974). For citation information on the two archives, see the list of abbreviations that opens the notes section.

12. I construct the flu's history from my own research in newspapers and from survivor accounts, as well as from the work of flu historians cited. For the timing of the pandemic's waves, which varied, see Barry, *The Great Influenza*, 180-81, 407-8; Crosby, *America's Forgotten Pandemic*, 17, 45; and Honigsbaum, *Living with Enza*, 35-36, 65ff., 107ff.

13. Crosby, *America's Forgotten Pandemic*, 26.

14. Barry, *The Great Influenza*, 98; Honigsbaum, *Living with Enza*, 41. Fisher offers a summary of the latest and, at times, contradictory scientific theories on the flu's origin in *Envisioning Disease*, 11-12.

15. Crosby, *America's Forgotten Pandemic*, 28; Honigsbaum, *Living with Enza*, 49.

16. "The Spanish Influenza: A Sufferer's Symptoms," *Times* (London), June 25, 1918, 9.

17. Doctor's letter reprinted in Dr. Norman Roy Grist, "Pandemic Influenza 1918," *British Medical Journal* (December 22-29, 1979): 1632-33. Letter dated September 29, 1918, from Camp Devens, Massachusetts; letter found in a trunk in 1959 and given to Grist.

18. Barry, *The Great Influenza*, 182-83.

19. Honigsbaum, *Living with Enza*, 19-20.

20. Grist, "Pandemic Influenza 1918," 1632-33.

21. Barry, *The Great Influenza*, 4-5 (for plague in 1300s), 397.

22. See Nancy K. Bristow, *American Pandemic: The Lost Worlds of the 1918 Influenza Epidemic* (New York: Oxford University Press, 2012) 4; Crosby, *America's Forgotten Pandemic*, 21-24, 222; Barry, *The Great Influenza*, 238-39, 249-50.

23. *RC*, C. J. Barrow, UK; Horace R. Belcher, UK.

24. Bristow, *American Pandemic*, 50, 60; Barry, *The Great Influenza*, 391. Mary McCarthy, in *Memories of a Catholic Girlhood* (New York: Harcourt Brace Jovanovich, 1946), describes losing both her parents. The narratives in *PIS* frequently recount how the flu created orphans, single parents, and broken families; see Marcella Bobzien, storyteller Marilynn Sutherland, North Dakota; Thomas Langan, storyteller Barbara Reynolds, Nebraska; Arthur and Julienne Scoltic-Valley and Loretta Carmel Crowley, storyteller Kathy Parker, New York.

25. George Newman, "Chief Medical Officer's Introduction," in Ministry of Health, "Report on the Pandemic of Influenza, 1918-1919," *Reports on Public Health and Medical Subjects*, no. 4 (London: His Majesty's Stationery Office, 1920), iv.

26. Descriptions of symptoms have been drawn from survivor letters, medical literature, and flu histories. For the symptoms noted here, see *RC*, letters from Horace Allen, Betty Boath (now Barr), and A. Forbes, all UK; Newman,

"Report on the Pandemic," vii–ix; Barry, *The Great Influenza*, 2, 224, 232–41; Honigsbaum, *Living with Enza*, xii–xiii, 4, 15–16, 25, 50, 53; Crosby, *America's Forgotten Pandemic*, 5–9.

27. *RC*, Gilberte Boulanger, France.

28. Barry, *The Great Influenza*, 241.

29. Karl A. Menninger, "Psychoses Associated with Influenza," *Journal of the American Medical Association* 72, no. 4 (January 25, 1919): 235–41. Researchers still debate the mental-health effects of the pandemic; for a summary, see Narayana Manjunatha et al., "The Neuropsychiatric Aspects of Influenza/Swine Flu: A Selective Review," *Industrial Psychiatry Journal* (July–December 2011): 83–90. Barry discusses the anecdotal evidence in *The Great Influenza*, 378–81; I examine the influenza/mental-instability link in chapter 4.

30. For suicide study, see I. M. Wasserman, "The Impact of Epidemic, War, Prohibition and Media on Suicide: United States, 1910–1920," *Suicidal & Life-Threatening Behavior* 22, no. 2 (Summer 1992): 240–54.

31. *RC*, Frederick Bebbington, UK.

32. See, for example, "Triple Murder and Suicide: An Attack of Influenza," *Times* (London), November 6, 1918, 3. See also *PIS*, Ethel Hubble Harter, Virginia.

33. See, for example, the accounts in Nancy Tomes, *The Gospel of Germs: Men, Women, and the Microbe in American Life* (Cambridge, MA: Harvard University Press, 1998); and in Allen Conrad Christensen, *Nineteenth-Century Narratives of Contagion: "Our Feverish Contact"* (London: Routledge, 2005).

34. It wasn't until the 1930s that scientists isolated the influenza virus. For a history, see Jeffery K. Taubenberger, Johan V. Hultin, and David M. Morens, "Discovery and Characterization of the 1918 Pandemic Influenza Virus in Historical Context," *Antiviral Therapy* 12, no. 4 (2007): 581–91.

35. Crosby, *America's Forgotten Pandemic*, 101.

36. I examine contagion guilt in chapters 2 and 3 and the particular guilt of doctors in chapter 7.

37. See "1,895 Deaths Last Week from Influenza: Many Victims in Large Centres," *Times* (London) October 24, 1918, 3; "'Influenza' Mystery. Situation Still Serious," *Times* (London) November 5, 1918, 3.

38. *RC*, Francis King, UK; Matthew, UK; Bernard Wilson, UK.

39. Barry, *The Great Influenza*, 242.

40. Quotations from interviews with Lee Reay, Daniel Tonkel, and William Maxwell, *Influenza 1918*, dir. Robert Kenner (1998; Alexandria, VA: American Experience, WGBH Educational Foundation, VIVA PBS Streaming, 2005).

41. *RC*, Cairns; Winifred Dainty, now Mason, UK.

42. Barry, *The Great Influenza*, 5.

43. See, for example, *RC*, Dilks; Gladys Hanson, now Bowden; Hilda Toone, UK.

44. *RC*, Ellen Monahan, UK; Luigia Ceccarelli, now Candoli, Italy.

45. Interview with Priscilla Reyna Jojola, Taos Peublo, New Mexico. *We Heard the Bells: The Influenza of 1918*, dir. Lisa Laden (U.S. Department of Health and Human Services, 2010), https://www.youtube.com/watch?v=XbEefT_M6xY.

46. *RC*, Maria del Monaco (now Gioitti), Italy; Einar Ekman, Sweden; Erik Johansson, Sweden.

47. *RC*, Elide Anette Forfod (now Dugstad), Norway; Gunhild Åkesson (now Härde-lin), Sweden.

48. *RC*, Gunnar Hegardt, Sweden.

49. *RC*, E. Bishop, UK.

50. *RC*, Philip Learoyd, UK.

51. See note 45.

52. Crosby, *America's Forgotten Pandemic*, 7; Barry, *The Great Influenza*, 202.

53. *RC*, Sydney Thomas Durrance, UK.

54. *RC*, David Jenkins, UK.

55. *PIS*, Amos Brownell and Mary Palmer Hensley, storyteller Dave Brownell, Missouri.

56. *RC*, Ellen Garrett (now Kendall), UK.

57. *RC*, Francis King, UK. The Collier letters frequently mention the lack of coffins and the piles of bodies, and newspaper accounts constantly note the shutting down of services. Narratives in the *PIS* tell of coffins stacked at train stations and the frequent sight of the hearse bringing bodies to the graveyards.

58. Barry, *The Great Influenza*, 242–49, 392.

59. Dorothy Ann Pettit and Janice Bailie, *A Cruel Wind: Pandemic Flu in America, 1918–1920* (Murfreesboro, TN: Timberlane, 2008), 228.

60. *RC*, F. M. Brown; Evelyn Hardwick, UK. For hair examples, Daisy Hazell; Elsie Buchan, UK.

61. Red Cross General Manager to division managers, March 1, 1919 (Washington, DC: Record Group 200, National Archives), qtd. in Barry, *The Great Influenza*, 392.

62. Cincinnati Health Commissioner Dr. William H. Peters, America Public Health Association meeting, 1919, qtd. in Barry, *The Great Influenza*, 392.

63. *PIS*, Dr. Otto Wernecke, storyteller Caroline Wernecke Pharris, Wisconsin.

64. Bristow, *American Pandemic*, 50.

65. Red Cross General Manager to division managers, March 1, 1919; qtd. in Barry, *The Great Influenza*, 392.

66. McCarthy, *Memories of a Catholic Girlhood*, 5.

67. *PIS*, Marcella Bobzien, storyteller Marilynn Sutherland, North Dakota; Amos Brownell and Mary Palmer Hensley, storyteller Dave Brownell, Missouri.

68. *PIS*, Geneva Searcy Thompson, storyteller Nancy Lybarger, Missouri; Lloyd Nelson, storyteller Dwight Nelson, Iowa.

69. *RC*, F. M. Brown, UK; Hannah Denham (now Gow), UK.

70. *RC*, Dorothy E. Jack, UK.

71. *RC*, Claude Todd, UK; Robert Swan, UK.

72. Crosby, *America's Forgotten Pandemic*; Bristow, *American Pandemic*; Johnson, *Britain and the 1918–1919 Influenza Pandemic*; Honigsbaum, *Living with Enza*; Barry, *The Great Influenza*; Laura Spinney, *Pale Rider: The Spanish Flu of 1918 and How It Changed the World* (London: Jonathan Cape, 2017). Gina Kolata offers a popular account in *Flu: The Story of the Great Influenza Pandemic of 1918 and the Search for the Virus That Caused It* (New York: Touchstone, 2001). Two recent works look at the pandemic's history from a global perspective: Susan K. Kent, *The Influenza Pandemic of 1918–1919* (New York: Bedford/St. Martin's, 2012); and Howard Philips and David Killingray, eds., *The Spanish Influenza Pandemic of 1918–1919: New Perspectives* (London: Routledge, 2011). For the Iberian

Peninsula, see María-Isabel Porras-Gallo and Ryan A. Davis, eds., *The Spanish Influenza Pandemic of 1918–1919: Perspectives from the Iberian Peninsula and the Americas* (New York: University of Rochester Press, 2014). For Canada, see Magda Fahrni and Esyllt W. Jones, eds., *Epidemic Encounters: Influenza, Society, and Culture in Canada, 1918–1920* (Vancouver: University of British Columbia Press, 2012); for South Africa, see Howard Phillips, *"Black October": The Impact of the Spanish Influenza Epidemic of 1918 on South Africa* (Pretoria: The Government Printer, 1990); for New Zealand, Geoffrey W. Rice, *Black November: The 1918 Influenza Pandemic in New Zealand* (Christchurch: Canterbury University Press, 2005). Carol R. Byerly writes on the army and the flu in *Fever of War: The Influenza Epidemic in the U.S. Army During World War I* (New York: New York University Press, 2005). See footnote 2 for additional works.

73. Thomas Mullen, *The Last Town on Earth* (New York: Random House, 2006); Stephenie Meyer, *Twilight* (New York: Little Brown, 2005). The pandemic also appears in Horton Foote's play *1918* (1998); Alice Munro's short story "Carried Away," in *Open Secrets* (1994); Ellen Bryant Voigt's poetry sequence *Kyrie: Poems* (1995); Myla Goldberg's novel *Wickett's Remedy* (2005); and Kaye Gibbon's novel *Drowning Ruth* (2004), among others. Two earlier works, Elechi Amadi's *The Great Ponds* (1969) and Buchi Emecheta's *The Slave Girl* (1977), explore the impact of the pandemic in Nigeria, where World War I did not subsume its tragedy. Jane Fisher explores Munro, Voigt, Amadi, and Emecheta, along with Virginia Woolf, Willa Cather, and Katherine Anne Porter, in *Envisioning Disease*.

74. In this well-worn debate in literary studies, Cathy Caruth, Bessel van der Kolk, and others are linked to the first camp, with Ruth Leys providing the most vocal dismissal of this approach in the second; see Cathy Caruth, ed., *Trauma: Explorations in Memory* (Baltimore, MD: Johns Hopkins University Press, 1995); and Ruth Leys, *Trauma: A Genealogy* (Chicago: University of Chicago Press, 2000). Mieke Verfaellie and Jennifer J. Vasterling offer an overview of the controversies in "Memory in PTSD: A Neurocognitive Approach," in *Post–Traumatic Stress Disorder: Basic Science and Clinical Practice*, ed. Priyattam Shiromani, Terrence Keane, and Joseph LeDoux (New York: Humana, 2009), 105–32.

75. The *Diagnostic and Statistical Manual of Mental Disorders (DSM-5)* offers the official criteria for Trauma- and Stressor-Related Disorders. Mark Greenberg and Bessel A. van der Kolk argue that the forgetting linked to PTSD can "paradoxically coexist with the opposite: intruding memories and unbidden repetitive images of traumatic events"; see "Retrieval and Integration of Traumatic Memories with the 'Painting Cure,'" in *Psychological Trauma*, ed. Bessel A. van der Kolk (Washington, DC: American Psychiatric Press, 1987), 191; qtd. in Cathy Caruth, *Trauma: Explorations in Memory*, 152.

76. Robert Graves, *Good-Bye to All That* (1929; New York: Doubleday, 1985), 285.

77. *RC*, Seacombe, now Adams, UK.

78. *RC*, Courtenay, UK.

79. *RC*, Dr. Walter Schröder, Germany.

80. Barry, *The Great Influenza*, 335.

81. *RC*, Gladys Fussell, UK.

82. "The Great Death," *Times* (London), February 2, 1921, 11.

83. Ruth Winchester Ware, "Thomas Wolfe's 1918 Flu Story: The Death of Ben in the Context of Other Literary Narratives of the Pandemic," *The Thomas Wolfe Review* 33 (2009): 69–70.

84. Ware, "Thomas Wolfe's 1918 Flu Story," 71.

85. Drew Gilpin Faust, *This Republic of Suffering: Death and the American Civil War* (New York: Vintage, 2008), 4. Half of the American troops who died in World War I died of disease, while Britain's much larger force, at war for far longer, lost roughly one soldier to disease for every ten in battle: Byerly, *Fever of War*, 132.

86. Crosby, *America's Forgotten Pandemic*, 320.

87. *RC*, Margaret Woodhouse (now Jones), UK.

88. *RC*, Dorothy E. Jack, UK.

89. *RC*, F. M. Brown, UK.

90. The Collier letters and newspapers frequently cite wartime deprivations as contributing to the pandemic's lethality. See, for example, "The Spanish Influenza: A Sufferer's Symptoms," *Times* (London) June 25, 1918, 9; and "Mystery of Influenza: The Epidemic of 1918–1919," *Times* (London) February 2, 1921, 7.

91. Priscilla Wald, *Contagious: Cultures, Carriers, and the Outbreak Narrative* (Durham, NC: Duke University Press, 2008); Rita Charon, *Narrative Medicine: Honoring the Stories of Illness* (New York: Oxford University Press, 2008).

92. Charon, *Narrative Medicine*, 4, 17, 20.

93. Wald, *Contagious*, 33.

94. Elaine Scarry's magisterial study *The Body in Pain: The Making and Unmaking of the World* (1985; Oxford: Oxford University Press, 2008) investigates the way pain unmakes language and poses unique challenges to representation. I discuss Scarry's work at greater length in subsequent chapters.

95. Kathlyn Conway, *Beyond Words: Illness and the Limits of Expression* (Albuquerque: University of New Mexico Press, 2007), 42.

96. Conway, *Beyond Words*, 42.

97. Charon, *Narrative Medicine*, 31.

98. Fisher, *Envisioning Disease*, 12; Patricia J. Fanning explores how the immigrant population was blamed in Massachusetts in *Influenza and Inequality: One Town's Tragic Response to the Great Epidemic of 1918* (Amherst: University of Massachusetts Press, 2010). Barry, *The Great Influenza*, 394–95, argues that the pandemic produced far less scapegoating than other outbreaks.

99. Wald, *Contagious*, 42.

100. Wald, *Contagious*, 16.

101. See Fisher's summary, *Envisioning Disease*, 11–12.

102. Interview with Dr. Shirley Fannin, *Influenza 1918* documentary.

103. Wald, *Contagion*, 36.

104. Paul de Kruif, *Microbe Hunters* (New York: Harcourt Brace, 1926).

105. Barry, *The Great Influenza*, 11–87, 401–27, offers a lengthy discussion of the medical establishment before and after the pandemic.

106. Geddes Smith, *Plague on Us* (New York: Commonwealth Fund, 1941), 1, 2.

107. Barry, *The Great Influenza*, 394.

108. While the flu killed across ages, genders, races, classes, and nations, many of the higher death rates occurred in vulnerable populations, like poorer communities

where overcrowding allowed infection to spread more easily. The dangers faced by different populations, though, was at times unpredictable; the unevenness of prior immunity and the fact that the virus was often most fatal to the healthiest bodies meant that some urban areas fared better than some rural areas, and some vulnerable populations may have had some modest protections, having been exposed to a larger range of viruses. Barry observes the "correlation between population density and hence class and deaths" but notes "the disease still struck down everyone" (*The Great Influenza*, 395). Fanning, in *Influenza and Inequality*, challenges the idea that the flu was a democratic killer, at least in Norwood, Massachusetts, where the immigrant population was hardest hit. See, too, Vanessa Northington Gamble, "'There Wasn't a Lot of Comforts in Those Days': African Americans, Public Health, and the 1918 Influenza Epidemic," *Public Health Report* 125, no. 3 (2010): 114–22. For the rural-versus-urban divide, see Svenn-Erik Mamelund, "Geography May Explain Adult Mortality from the 1918–20 Influenza Pandemic," *Epidemics* 3, no. 1 (March 2011): 46–60.

109. Wald, *Contagious*, 264. Timothy Mitchell traces, in his brilliant piece "Can the Mosquito Speak?," how complex networks of environmental and political actions produced the conditions that made possible the spread of a deadly form of malaria in Egypt: see his *Rule of Experts: Egypt, Techno-Politics, Modernity* (Berkeley: University of California Press, 2002), 19–53.

110. Butler, *Frames of War*, 18.

111. Charon, *Narrative Medicine*, 39.

112. Virginia Woolf, "On Being Ill," originally published in *The New Criterion*, January 1926; reprinted in *The Essays of Virginia Woolf*, vol. 4: *1925–1928*, ed. Andrew McNeillie (New York: Harvest/Harcourt, 1994), 317, 318.

113. Charon, *Narrative Medicine*, 43, 44, vii, 48, 49. Susan Sontag famously cautions against, though, the drive to build metaphors around illness—and she notes the influenza pandemic as an example of an outbreak immune to such metaphors. I discuss Sontag at greater length in chapter 3. Susan Sontag, *Illness as Metaphor* (1977), in *Illness as Metaphor and AIDS and Its Metaphors* (New York: Picador, 1990), 71.

114. Wald, *Contagious*, 2, 39.

115. The pandemic did not fit other models for illness narratives, such as what Kathlyn Conway has termed the "narrative of triumph" and Arthur W. Frank has called restitution narratives and quest narratives, which shape illness into a story where the malady is overcome and the patient healed. See Conway, *Beyond Words*, 5; and Arthur W. Frank, *The Wounded Storyteller: Body, Illness, and Ethics*, 2nd ed. (Chicago: University of Chicago Press, 2013).

116. Crosby, *America's Forgotten Pandemic*, 319.

117. Fisher, *Envisioning Disease*. Charles De Paolo recently published *Pandemic Influenza in Fiction: A Critical Study* (Jefferson, NC: McFarland, 2014); De Paolo's study looks broadly at pandemic influenza in literature from 1892 to 2014.

118. Patricia Rae, ed., *Modernism and Mourning* (Lewisburg, PA: Bucknell University Press, 2007); Tammy Clewell, *Mourning, Modernism, Postmodernism* (New York: Palgrave Macmillan, 2009).

119. Allyson Booth, *Postcards from the Trenches: Negotiating the Space Between Modernism and the First World War* (New York: Oxford University Press, 1996), 50.

120. See, for example, Ezekiel Black, "Mouthlessness and Ineffability in World War I Poetry and *The Waste Land*," *War, Literature & the Arts: An International Journal of the Humanities* 25 (2013): 1–17.

121. David Sherman, *In a Strange Room: Modernism's Corpses and Mortal Obligation* (New York: Oxford University Press, 2014), 44, 43–107.

122. Sarah Cole, *At the Violet Hour: Modernism and Violence in England and Ireland* (New York: Oxford University Press, 2012), 5–6, 42.

123. Paul K. Saint-Amour, *Tense Future: Modernism, Total War, Encyclopedic Form* (New York: Oxford University Press, 2015), 93, 305, 179.

124. Mao and Walkowitz, "The New Modernist Studies," *PMLA* 123, no. 3 (2008): 738.

125. Fisher, *Envisioning Disease*, 177–95.

126. Butler, *Frames of War*, xiii.

127. See Vincent Sherry's terrific account of the sacrificial paradigms during the war in "Imbalances: Mass Death and the Economy of 'Sacrifice' in the Great War," in Santanu Das and Kate McLoughlin, eds., *The First World War: Literature, Culture, Modernity* (Oxford: Oxford University Press, 2018).

128. Marianne Hirsch and Leo Spitzer, "Vulnerable Lives: Secrets, Noise, Dust," *Profession* 17 (2011): 55. Hirsh and Spitzer draw on Carolyn Steedman's idea of archival dust as a residue of past beliefs; see Carolyn Steedman, *Dust: The Archive and Cultural History* (New Brunswick, NJ: Rutgers University Press, 2002).

PART I. PANDEMIC REALISM: MAKING AN
ATMOSPHERE VISIBLE

1. One other American author from the interwar era offers an account of the pandemic: John O'Hara, in his short story "The Doctor's Son," in *The Doctor's Son and Other Stories* (New York: Harcourt, Brace, 1935). O'Hara chronicles the experiences of an overworked medical student and the teenager who drives him to see influenza patients. The story captures the chronic stress of doctors during the pandemic but does not add significantly to the experiences traced by the authors I discuss here. Wallace Stegner also has two novels that touch on the pandemic, *On a Darkling Plain* (New York: Harcourt Brace, 1940) and *The Big Rock Candy Mountain* (New York: Penguin, 1943), but both are published later than my interwar focus, and the pandemic is not structurally as central to either work.

2. UNTANGLING WAR AND PLAGUE: WILLA CATHER
AND KATHERINE ANNE PORTER

1. Most early reviewers praised the Nebraska sections but criticized the depictions of war as inauthentic and romanticized, with many taking sexist swipes at a woman writing of war; see note 97 in this chapter. More recent critics distinguish between Claude's idealism and Cather's own satiric stance toward the conflict; Joshua Doležal summarizes these debates and observes how the novel continues to be misconstrued as "a celebration of the war" in "'Waste in a Great Enterprise': Influenza, Modernism, and *One of Ours*," *Literature and Medicine* 28, no. 1 (Spring

2009): 86. James Woodress and Janis P. Stout argue Cather both shares and resists Claude's views on the war: James Woodress, *Willa Cather: A Literary Life* (Lincoln: University of Nebraska Press, 1987), 303; Janis P. Stout, *Willa Cather: The Writer and Her World* (Charlottesville: University Press of Virginia, 2000), 176–81.

2. Jane Elizabeth Fisher explores the fluidity of gender roles in Porter's and Cather's pandemic works, arguing that the outbreak grants the characters new perceptions and roles within an atmosphere of war, producing a sense of liberation and, for Porter's Miranda, new creative power: Jane Elizabeth Fisher, *Envisioning Disease, Gender, and War: Women's Narratives of the 1918 Influenza Pandemic* (New York: Palgrave Macmillan, 2012). I read the pandemic as far less liberating though certainly revealing about shifting gender dynamics. More broadly, critical work on gender and the war is plentiful, though it rarely considers the pandemic. A few highlights: Sandra Gilbert, in her well-known article "Soldier's Heart: Literary Men, Literary Women, and the Great War," *Signs* 8, no. 3 (Spring 1983): 422–50, argues that guilt over the war infuses women's fiction. Miriam Cooke and Angela Woollacott's edited collection *Gendering War Talk* (Princeton, NJ: Princeton University Press, 1993) looks at gender issues across multiple military conflicts, including World War I. The essays in *Women's Fiction and the Great War*, ed. Suzanne Raitt and Trudi Tate (Oxford: Oxford University Press, 1997), emphasize the vast range of experiences women had in the war. Robert von Hallberg and Cassandra Laity coedited a special issue focused on both genders and the war: "Men, Women, and World War I," *Modernism/modernity* 9, no. 1 (January 2002). Agnès Cardinal, Dorothy Goldman, and Judith Hattaway's anthology *Women's Writing on the First World War* (Oxford: Oxford University Press, 2002) captures the range of war writing women produced. More recently, Susan R. Grayzel and Tammy M. Proctor's *Gender and the Great War* (Oxford: Oxford University Press, 2017) offers a fresh collection of essays on both masculinity and femininity during the war.

3. Grayzel and Proctor, "Introduction," in *Gender and the Great War*, 5, 7.

4. See endnote 97 in this chapter.

5. Letter from Cather to Frances Smith Cather, November 11, 1918, in *The Selected Letters of Willa Cather*, ed. Andrew Jewell and Janis Stout (New York: Knopf, 2013), 260–61.

6. Letter from Cather to Elizabeth Shepley Sergeant, December 3, 1918, in *Selected Letters*, 264.

7. Cather's partner, Edith Lewis, may have contracted the flu during the pandemic, but the case was likely mild; see the editorial note in *Selected Letters*, 273. Lewis recounts Cather's exchanges with Dr. Frederick Sweeney in *Willa Cather Living: A Personal Record* (New York: Knopf, 1953), 118–19.

8. Quoted in Sharon O'Brien, "Combat Envy and Survivor Guilt: Willa Cather's 'Manly Battle Yarn,'" in *Arms and the Woman: War, Gender, and Literary Representation*, ed. Helen M. Cooper, Adrienne Auslander Munich, and Susan Merrill Squier (Chapel Hill: University of North Carolina Press, 1989), 184; from Willa Cather, *The Kingdom of Art*, ed. Bernice Slote (Lincoln: University of Nebraska Press, 1966), 409.

9. O'Brien, "Combat Envy," 184, 185.

10. See Dr. Frederick C. Sweeney, *Diary of Dr. Frederick C. Sweeney, Captain in the United States Army Medical Corps*, 1918–1919, typewritten copy presented to the

University of California-Davis Library, prepared by Margaret C. Bean, October 1990. Original diary held at the Jaffrey-Gilmore Foundation in Jaffrey, NH.

11. Letter from Cather to Dorothy Canfield Fisher, probably late March 1922, discussing the novel's sources, in *Selected Letters*, 316.

12. As I detail, Jane Fisher and Joshua Doležal are notable exceptions. Early critics focused on the war's depiction though praised the pandemic episode if mentioned; Sinclair Lewis found it the only authentic war section: "A Hamlet of the Plains," *New York Evening Post, The Literary Review* 16 (September 1922): 23; reprinted in *Willa Cather: The Contemporary Reviews*, ed. Margaret Anne O'Connor (Cambridge: Cambridge University Press, 2001), 129. Sharon O'Brien discusses Cather and illness but not the pandemic in "Willa Cather in the Country of the Ill," 146–56; and Joseph R. Urgo reads the section as a metaphor for the illness of war in "The Cather Thesis: The American Empire of Migration," 47; both essays in *The Cambridge Companion to Willa Cather*, ed. Marilee Lindemann (Cambridge: Cambridge University Press, 2005). Steven Trout also reads the pandemic as part of the war's tragedy in *Memorial Fictions: Willa Cather and the First World War* (Lincoln: University of Nebraska Press, 2002), 59, 155.

13. Willa Cather, *One of Ours* (New York: Knopf, 1922), 273. Hereafter cited by page numbers in endnotes in clusters, if multiple quotations.

14. Cather, *One of Ours*, 285, 297, 296.

15. Cather, *One of Ours*, 299.

16. Wilfred Owen, "Dulce et Decorum Est" (1920; written 1917), in *The Penguin Book of First World War Poetry*, ed. George Walter (New York: Penguin, 2004), 141–42, ll. 19, 16, 20–21.

17. John M. Barry, *The Great Influenza: The Story of the Deadliest Pandemic in History* (New York: Penguin, 2004), 241.

18. Cather, *One of Ours*, 292.

19. Doležal, "'Waste in a Great Enterprise,'" 92.

20. Cather, *One of Ours*, 268, 294, 310.

21. Susan Sontag, *Illness as Metaphor* (1977), in *Illness as Metaphor and AIDS and Its Metaphors* (New York: Picador, 1990).

22. Cather, *One of Ours*, 311.

23. Cather, *One of Ours*, 301.

24. Cather, *One of Ours*, 292, 293.

25. Cather, *One of Ours*, 319, 319, 318.

26. Cather, *One of Ours*, 358. Cather notes this timing change in a footnote: "The actual outbreak of influenza on transports carrying United States troops is here anticipated by several months." *One of Ours*, 292.

27. Cather, *One of Ours*, 358, 335, 335.

28. Cather, *One of Ours*, 453.

29. O'Brien, in "Combat Envy," analyzes Cather's embedded critique of the war as well as her admiration, noting how Cather displays both "combat envy" and "survivor guilt" in her story of Claude.

30. See Joan Givner, *Katherine Anne Porter: A Life*, rev. ed. (Athens: University of Georgia, 1991), 124–26; and Janis P. Stout, *Katherine Anne Porter: A Sense of the Times* (Charlottesville: University Press of Virginia, 1995), 9. Kitty Barry Crawford, a friend of Porter, recounts her memories of the pandemic and Porter's

illness in Darlene Harbour Unrue, *Katherine Anne Porter Remembered* (Tuscaloosa: University of Alabama Press, 2010), 32–34.

31. Critical discussion unsurprisingly focuses on the pandemic. David Davis explores trauma, memory, and the flu's shadowy status in "The Forgotten Apocalypse: Katherine Anne Porter's 'Pale Horse, Pale Rider,' Traumatic Memory, and the Influenza Pandemic of 1918," *Southern Literary Journal* 43, no. 2 (Spring 2011): 55–74. See, too, the work of Catherine Belling, Jane Fisher, and Caroline Hovanec, quoted later.

32. Katherine Anne Porter, *Pale Horse, Pale Rider*, in *The Collected Stories of Katherine Anne Porter* (1939; New York: Harcourt, 1979), 300. Hereafter cited as *PHPR* and by page numbers in endnotes in clusters, if multiple quotations. I italicize the novella's title, though it was originally published with two other short novels in 1939.

33. Porter claimed Adam was based on a boyfriend—or even fiancé—but these stories seem fictional. See Givner's thoughtful summary in *Katherine Anne Porter: A Life*, 127–29. Darlene Harbour Unrue links Adam to Porter's various husbands in *Katherine Anne Porter: The Life of an Artist* (Jackson: University Press of Mississippi, 2005), 57, 169.

34. Porter, *PHPR*, 269.

35. See Rita Charon, *Narrative Medicine: Honoring the Stories of Illness* (New York: Oxford University Press, 2008). I discuss Charon at length in my introduction.

36. Porter, *PHPR*, 270, 269, 269, 269.

37. Porter, *PHPR*, 269, 270, 270, 270.

38. Porter, *PHPR*, all from 270.

39. *The Bible*, New International Version.

40. Porter, *PHPR*, 281.

41. Porter, *PHPR*, 270.

42. Porter, *PHPR*, 271, 272, 287, 286.

43. Allyson Booth, *Postcards from the Trenches: Negotiating the Space Between Modernism and the First World War* (New York: Oxford University Press, 1996), 21–49.

44. Porter, *PHPR*, 276, 277, 277.

45. Porter, *PHPR*, 280, 279–80.

46. Paul K. Saint-Amour, *Tense Future: Modernism, Total War, Encyclopedic Form* (New York: Oxford University Press, 2015).

47. Porter, *PHPR*, 279.

48. Porter, *PHPR*, 282, 284.

49. Porter, *PHPR*, 295.

50. Porter, *PHPR*, 273.

51. Porter, *PHPR*, 295.

52. Porter, *PHPR*, 280–81.

53. Porter, *PHPR*, 273.

54. Porter, *PHPR*, 293, 293.

55. Porter, *PHPR*, 294.

56. Porter, *PHPR*, 279.

57. Porter, *PHPR*, 280–81.

58. Porter, *PHPR*, 284, 284.

59. See Nancy K. Bristow, *American Pandemic: The Lost Worlds of the 1918 Influenza Epidemic* (New York: Oxford University Press, 2012), 77.

60. Porter, *PHPR*, 274.

61. Porter, *PHPR*, 282.

62. Porter, *PHPR*, 296. Caroline Hovanec, in her terrific article "Of Bodies, Families, and Communities: Refiguring the 1918 Influenza Pandemic," *Literature and Medicine* 29, no. 1 (Spring 2011): 164, argues that the flu "defamiliarizes and fragments the human body."

63. Porter, *PHPR*, 300.

64. Porter, *PHPR*, 299.

65. Porter, *PHPR*, 304.

66. Porter, *PHPR*, 304–5.

67. See Jane Fisher, *Envisioning Disease, Gender, and War*, 128–37, for a fascinating discussion of the arrow's symbolism, the links to the horsemen of the Apocalypse and Apollo, and the gender dynamics of the St. Sebastian figure. Sarah Youngblood explores the link to Apollo and his association with plagues delivered through arrows in "Structure and Imagery in Katherine Anne Porter's 'Pale Horse, Pale Rider,'" in *Critical Essays on Katherine Anne Porter*, ed. Darlene Harbour Unrue (New York: G. K. Hall & Co., 1997), 197.

68. *RC*, Gunter Hanssen, Germany.

69. *RC*, Erna Krukenberg (born Wäsche), Germany.

70. *RC*, Lucia Dallari Gnutti, Italy.

71. Hovanec, "Of Bodies, Families, and Communities," 167, argues that Miranda's dream suggests she is not responsible for Adam's death. I find that the arrows passing through Miranda suggest she metaphorically contaminates them.

72. Porter, *PHPR*, 305.

73. Porter, *PHPR*, 308, 308.

74. Porter, *PHPR*, 308–9.

75. Porter, *PHPR*, 309.

76. Porter, *PHPR*, 309.

77. Sontag, *Illness as Metaphor*, 71.

78. Catherine Belling argues that Porter's modernist style allowed her to convey both the flu's delirium and the challenges trauma may pose to memory and narrative structure: Catherine Belling, "Overwhelming the Medium: Fiction and the Trauma of Pandemic Influenza in 1918," *Literature and Medicine* 28, no. 1 (Spring 2009): 55–81.

79. Porter, *PHPR*, all from 310.

80. Porter, *PHPR*, 311.

81. Katherine Anne Porter, "Interview with Barbara Thompson," in *Katherine Anne Porter: Conversations*, ed. Joan Givner (Jackson: University Press of Mississippi, 1987), 85.

82. Porter, *PHPR*, 311–12.

83. Porter, *PHPR*, 312.

84. Porter, *PHPR*, 312.

85. Elaine Scarry, *The Body in Pain: The Making and Unmaking of the World* (1985; Oxford University Press, 2008), 4, 161–80.

86. Scarry, *The Body in Pain*, 21, 35.

87. Porter, *PHPR*, 312.

88. Porter, *PHPR*, all from 313.

89. Porter, *PHPR*, 314.

90. Fisher, *Envisioning Disease*, 105–47, offers an alternative reading, focusing on how Miranda's illness offers her a potentially empowering vision.
91. Porter, *PHPR*, 314.
92. Letter from Porter to Margaret Harvey, September 15, 1964, in *Selected Letters of Katherine Anne Porter: Chronicles of a Modern Woman*, ed. Darlene Harbour Unrue (Jackson: University Press of Mississippi, 2012), 302.
93. Porter, *PHPR*, 316.
94. Hovanec, "Of Bodies, Families, and Communities," 168; Porter, *PHPR*, 316.
95. Porter, *PHPR*, 316–17.
96. Porter, "Interview with Barbara Thompson," 85.
97. H. L. Mencken, "Portrait of an American Citizen," *Smart Set* 69 (October 1922): 140–42, reprinted in *Willa Cather: The Contemporary Reviews*, ed. Margaret Anne O'Connor (Cambridge: Cambridge University Press, 2001), 141. Sidney Howard noted that the book showed him "what a woman can write supremely and what she cannot write at all": "Miss Cather Goes to War," *Bookman* 56 (October 1922): 217–18, in *Willa Cather: The Contemporary Reviews*, 137. Sinclair Lewis declared that "except for the arousing scenes on the army transport, with influenza stalking, her whole view of the war seems second-hand": "A Hamlet of the Plains," 23, in *Willa Cather: The Contemporary Reviews*, 129.
98. Margaret R. Higonnet summarizes the difficulties women had when writing about World War I—and the ways they push against those difficulties—in "Not So Quiet in No-Woman's-Land," in Cooke and Woollacott, eds., *Gendering War Talk*, 205–26.

3. DOMESTIC PANDEMIC: THOMAS WOLFE AND WILLIAM MAXWELL

1. See chapter 1 for mortality rates by gender.
2. Elizabeth Nowell, *Thomas Wolfe: A Biography* (New York: Doubleday, 1960), 42–43.
3. Richard S. Kennedy, *The Window of Memory: The Literary Career of Thomas Wolfe* (Chapel Hill: University of North Carolina Press, 1962), 53–54.
4. Paula Gallant Eckard, "'A flash of fire': Illness and the Body in *Look Homeward, Angel*," *The Thomas Wolfe Review* 34, no. 1/2 (2010): 6. Eckard explores how illness is pervasive in Wolfe's work. Nowell, *Thomas Wolfe: A Biography*, 44, notes that "Wolfe always referred to Ben's death as the most tragic experience of his entire life."
5. Letter from Wolfe to Mabel Wolfe Wheaton, May 1929, in *The Letters of Thomas Wolfe*, ed. Elizabeth Nowell (New York: Charles Scribner's Sons, 1946), 178. Ruth Winchester Ware explores the biographical details surrounding Ben's death and summarizes how other authors responded to the flu in "Thomas Wolfe's 1918 Flu Story: The Death of Ben in the Context of Other Literary Narratives of the Pandemic," *The Thomas Wolfe Review* 33 (2009): 67–82.
6. Letter from Wolfe to Norman H. Pearson, December 18, 1936, in *The Letters of Thomas Wolfe*, 566.
7. Letter from Wolfe to Julia Wolfe, May 1923, in *The Letters of Thomas Wolfe to His Mother*, ed. C. Hugh Holman and Sue Fields Ross (Chapel Hill: University of North Carolina Press, 1968), 43–44.

8. Thomas Wolfe, "The Story of a Novel," in *The Thomas Wolfe Reader*, ed. C. Hugh Holman (1936; New York: Charles Scribner's Sons, 1962), 16.

9. Gérald Préher, "A Cosmos of His Own: Loss, Ghosts, and Loneliness in Thomas Wolfe's Fiction," *The Thomas Wolfe Review* 35, no. 112 (2011): 25.

10. Eckard, "'A flash of fire,'" 8.

11. Thomas Wolfe, *Look Homeward, Angel: A Story of the Buried Life* (1929; New York: Charles Scribner's Sons, 1957), 228; hereafter cited as *LHA* and by page numbers in endnotes in clusters, if multiple quotations.

12. Wolfe, *LHA*, 275.

13. Terry Roberts and Elizabeth Spencer both discuss the possible identity of the ghost, including Ben and Wolfe himself, and Roberts analyzes the novel's 143-word proem, which ends in the "O lost" phrase, as Wolfe's way to capture subconscious thoughts; Terry Roberts, "'By the Wind Grieved': The Proem of *Look Homeward, Angel*," *The Southern Literary Journal* 29, no. 1 (Fall 1996): 81–92; Elizabeth Spencer, "*Look Homeward, Angel*: Of Ghosts, Angels, and Lostness," *North Carolina Literary Review* 12 (2003): 78–86.

14. Wolfe, *LHA*, 423.

15. Wolfe, *LHA*, 447, 447.

16. Wolfe, *LHA*, 451, 451, 454.

17. Wolfe, *LHA*, 452.

18. Wolfe, *LHA*, 452, 454, 453.

19. Wolfe, *LHA*, 451, 452.

20. Wolfe, *LHA*, 451, 457, 459.

21. Wolfe, *LHA*, 504.

22. Wolfe, *LHA*, 451, 453, 452.

23. Wolfe, *LHA*, 457, 461.

24. Wolfe, *LHA*, 458.

25. Wolfe, *LHA*, 456.

26. Wolfe, *LHA*, 457, 458.

27. Wilfred Owen, "Dulce et Decorum Est," in *The Penguin Book of First World War Poetry*, ed. George Walter (New York: Penguin, 2004), 141–42, ll. 14–16.

28. I am not, of course, suggesting that Owen references the pandemic in his poem—he composed his work in 1917 before the outbreak—only that by the time the poem is published in 1920, the soldier's strangulation echoed pandemic deaths that had just erupted everywhere. The pandemic context changes not the poem but our reading of the poem, revealing the hidden deaths that were unfolding alongside the deaths that Owen's poem helped make visible and iconic. Owen later saw the ravages of the virus but dismissed the pandemic as trivial compared to the war, a viewpoint we should push against. For Owen's views on the pandemic, see Mark Honigsbaum, *Living with Enza: The Forgotten Story of Britain and the Great Flu Pandemic of 1918* (London: Macmillan, 2009), 3–4.

29. Wolfe, *LHA*, 465.

30. Wolfe, *LHA*, 514, 514.

31. Wolfe, *LHA*, 516, 516.

32. Wolfe, *LHA*, 515.

33. Kennedy, *The Window of Memory*, 141. Abbey Zink places Wolfe in the "nativist modernism" tradition proposed by Walter Benn Michaels: Abbey Zink, "Is Blood

Thicker Than Artistry? Nativist Modernism and Eugene Gant's Initiation Into Blood Politics in *Look Homeward, Angel*," *The Thomas Wolfe Review* 25, no. 1–2 (2001): 44–52.

34. See Jimmie Carol Still Durr, "*Look Homeward, Angel*, Thomas Wolfe's *Ulysses*," *Southern Studies* 24, no. 1 (Spring 1985): 56.

35. See Vernon Hyles, "Ben, Rudy, and the Fantastic: Wolfe's Journey to Nighttown," *The Thomas Wolfe Review* 13, no. 2 (Fall 1989): 48. Claire Culleton also links Joyce's Wandering Rocks chapter and Wolfe's chapter 14 in "Joycean Synchronicity in Wolfe's *Look Homeward, Angel*," *The Thomas Wolfe Review* 13, no. 2 (1989): 49–52.

36. Wolfe, *LHA*, all "legions of dead" quotations from 518.

37. Wolfe, *LHA*, 519, 520, 520.

38. Wolfe, *LHA*, all quotations in paragraph from 517.

39. See Barbara Burkhardt's excellent summary of Maxwell's pandemic experiences in *William Maxwell: A Literary Life* (Urbana: University of Illinois Press, 2005), 19–22; quotations from 22.

40. Nancy K. Bristow, *American Pandemic: The Lost Worlds of the 1918 Influenza Epidemic* (New York: Oxford University Press, 2012), 50, 60.

41. William Maxwell, *They Came Like Swallows* (New York: Harper & Brothers, 1937), 15; hereafter cited as *Swallows* and by page numbers in endnotes in clusters, if multiple quotations.

42. Maxwell, *Swallows*, 87.

43. Maxwell, *Swallows*, 94, 94.

44. Maxwell, *Swallows*, 97, 105.

45. Maxwell, *Swallows*, 128.

46. Maxwell, *Swallows*, 20; ellipses in original.

47. Maxwell, *Swallows*, 20–21.

48. Maxwell, *Swallows*, 89–95.

49. Maxwell, *Swallows*, 24.

50. Maxwell, *Swallows*, 251.

51. Maxwell, *Swallows*, 207.

52. Nancy Tomes, *The Gospel of Germs: Men, Women, and the Microbe in American Life* (Cambridge, MA: Harvard University Press, 1998); Allen Conrad Christensen, *Nineteenth-Century Narratives of Contagion: "Our Feverish Contact"* (New York: Routledge, 2005).

53. Tomes, *The Gospel of Germs*, 246.

54. Maxwell, *Swallows*, 107.

55. Maxwell, *Swallows*, 108–9.

56. Maxwell, *Swallows*, 211.

57. Maxwell, *Swallows*, 226, 227.

58. Maxwell, *Swallows*, 174–75.

59. Maxwell, *Swallows*, 198, 246.

60. Maxwell, *Swallows*, 10, 14.

61. Maxwell, *Swallows*, 249.

62. Maxwell, *Swallows*, 254, 255.

63. Maxwell, *Swallows*, 267.

64. Quoted by Dale Hrebik, "William (Keepers) Maxwell, (Jr.)," in *Dictionary of Literary Biography*, vol. 218: *American Short-Story Writers Since World War II*:

Second Series, ed. Patrick Meanor and Gwen Crane (Detroit: Gale, 2000), online at *Literature Resource Center*.

65. Maxwell, *Swallows*, 200, 201.

66. Maxwell, *Swallows*, 260.

67. Maxwell, *Swallows*, 237.

68. Judith Butler, *Frames of War: When Is Life Grievable?* (London: Verso, 2009), xiii.

4. ON SEEING ILLNESS: VIRGINIA WOOLF'S *MRS. DALLOWAY*

1. Virginia Woolf, *The Diary of Virginia Woolf*, vol. 1: *1915–1919*, ed. Anne Olivier Bell (New York: Harvest/Harcourt, 1977), 163. Hereafter cited as *D1* and by page numbers in endnotes in clusters, if multiple quotations.

2. Woolf, *D1*, 165, 209, 229.

3. Woolf's mother, Julia Stephen, died May 5, 1895, probably from rheumatic fever; the family believed, with justification, that her death stemmed in part from her attack of influenza in February and March. Her nephew Quentin Bell describes her death as from the *"sequelae"* of her influenza case: *Virginia Woolf: A Biography* (New York: Harvest/HBJ, 1972), 39. Douglas Orr argues Julia's "earlier influenza" included an infection that aggravated her condition and led to her death: *Virginia Woolf's Illnesses*, ed. Wayne K. Chapman (Clemson, SC: Clemson University Digital Press, 2004), 27. The family was blindsided by her death: the Stephen children had recorded in their family newspaper in March that their mother was recovering from her influenza (Bell, *Virginia Woolf*, 37–38), and Leslie Stephen, Woolf's father, notes he thought "she had fully recovered from her influenza" and is shocked by her death; see *Sir Leslie Stephen's Mausoleum Book*, ed. Alan Bell (Oxford: Clarendon, 1977), 96. Both medically and emotionally, Julia's sudden death was linked to influenza.

4. Letter from Woolf to Janet Case, January 26, 1915, in *The Letters of Virginia Woolf*, vol. 2: *1912–1922*, ed. Nigel Nicolson and Joanne Trautmann (New York: Harvest/Harcourt, 1976), 59. Hereafter cited as *L2*.

5. Letter from Woolf to Vanessa Bell, April 14, 1916, *L2*, 88.

6. Woolf, *D1*, 119.

7. Letter from Woolf to Vanessa Bell, February 23, 1918, *L2*, 218.

8. Letters from Woolf to Vanessa Bell: December 24, 1919, *L2*, 407; January 2, 1920, *L2*, 411.

9. See diary entry for February 14, 1922, *D2*, 160; she also laments in her letters about influenza's effects on her heart and her work: *L2*, 500–12; for the specialist, see Orr, *Virginia Woolf's Illnesses*, 96.

10. Orr summarizes her illnesses during this period in *Virginia Woolf's Illnesses*, 93–101.

11. Letter from Woolf to Janet Case, January 5, 1920, *L2*, 415.

12. Virginia Woolf, "On Being Ill," *New Criterion*, January 1926; reprinted in *The Essays of Virginia Woolf*, vol. 4: *1925–1928*, ed. Andrew McNeillie (New York: Harvest/Harcourt, 1994), 317. Hereafter cited as *OBI*.

13. Jane Elizabeth Fisher represents a key exception in her interesting discussion of the pandemic in relationship to both *Mrs. Dalloway* and "On Being Ill" in

Envisioning Disease, Gender, and War: Women's Narratives of the 1918 Influenza Pandemic (New York: Palgrave Macmillan, 2012). Fisher takes a different approach than I do, focusing on how illness offers Woolf and her characters creative vision that "becomes one of the compensatory gains a patient can receive from the otherwise disorienting and destructive experience of illness" (73). Fisher explores the postwar landscape, specifically the airplane and motorcar scene, through Clarissa's visions of illness and Septimus's post-traumatic war vision. I consider the consolation Woolf imagines, but I focus far more on the costs of the pandemic, on how it shifts our understanding of the novel's structure, and on how Clarissa and Septimus remap London through the pandemic.

14. The Paris Press issued a tenth-anniversary edition of their reprint of "On Being Ill," together with Julia Stephen's *Notes from Sick Rooms*, with introductions by Hermione Lee and Mark Hussey and an afterword by Rita Charon. Lee summarizes Woolf's illnesses in these years (xiv–xvii) and notes Woolf's fainting (xvi): Virginia Woolf and Julia Stephen, *On Being Ill with Notes from Sick Rooms* (Ashfield, MA: Paris Press, 2012).

15. Susan Sontag, *Illness as Metaphor* (1977), in *Illness as Metaphor and AIDS and Its Metaphors* (New York: Picador, 1990).

16. Critics have refocused on Woolf's writings on illness. In addition to Fisher, *Envisioning Disease*, see "Virginia Woolf and Illness," a special issue of *Virginia Woolf Miscellany* 90 (Fall 2016), guest edited by Cheryl Hindrichs. Hindrichs notes that while modernists do discuss illness, "our critical discussion about the modernist body has focused on sexuality, the war, and psychology" (44), with insufficient attention paid to illness itself or to the 1918 pandemic. Kimberly Engdahl Coates, "Phantoms, Fancy (and) Symptoms: Virginia Woolf and 'The Art of Being Ill,'" *Woolf Studies Annual* 18 (2012): 1–28, examines how Woolf turns illness into an aesthetic strategy; Madelyn Detloff investigates the link between Woolf's work and disability/queer studies in "Woolf and Crip Theory," in *A Companion to Virginia Woolf*, ed. Jessica Berman (New York: Wiley-Blackwell, 2016), 277–89. Lorraine Sim, in *Virginia Woolf: The Patterns of Ordinary Experience* (Farnham: Ashgate, 2010), focuses on how "On Being Ill" is a meditation on mild and ordinary illnesses like the cold and (regular) influenza. Janine Utell, "View from the Sickroom: Virginia Woolf, Dorothy Wordsworth, and Writing Women's Lives of Illness," *Life Writing* 13, no. 1 (2016): 27–45, explores "how the lines of a writing life are shaped by illness" (29) for both Wordsworth and Woolf.

17. Woolf, *OBI*, 317.

18. John McCrae's "In Flanders Field" (1915) helped popularize the poppy as a symbol of the war and soldiers' bodies. Samuel Hynes, *A War Imagined: The First World War and English Culture* (New York: Atheneum, 1991), 3, notes the oft-quoted quality of Grey's comment and the difficulties in finding the original source.

19. Woolf, *D1*, 70.

20. Woolf, *OBI*, 318.

21. Woolf, *OBI*, 317. For Woolf's experiences with gas, tooth extraction, and influenza, see David Eberly, "Gassed: Virginia Woolf and Dentistry," *Virginia Woolf Miscellany* 90 (2016): 53–55.

22. Woolf, *OBI*, 317.

23. Woolf, *OBI*, 318.

24. Woolf, *OBI*, 318–19.

25. Elaine Scarry, *The Body in Pain: The Making and Unmaking of the World* (1985; Oxford University Press, 2008), 4. Scarry directly links her description of pain to Woolf's essay.

26. Woolf, *OBI*, 319, 319.

27. "The Great Death," *Times* (London), February 2, 1921, 11.

28. Woolf, *OBI*, 319.

29. Fisher, *Envisioning Disease*, 73–79. Janine Utell, "View from the Sickroom," and Kimberly Coates, "Phantoms, Fancy (and) Symptoms," also explore Woolf, illness, and creativity.

30. Lee, introduction to Virginia Woolf and Julia Stephen, *On Being Ill with Notes from Sick Rooms*, xxvii.

31. Woolf, *OBI*, 321, 324.

32. Woolf, *OBI*, 321–22.

33. Virginia Woolf, *Mrs. Dalloway*, annotated and introduced by Bonnie Kime Scott, general ed. Mark Hussey (1925; New York: Harvest/Harcourt, 2005), 4–5. Hereafter cited as *MD* and by page numbers in endnotes in clusters, if multiple quotations.

34. The links between Septimus Smith and Siegfried Sassoon, who met Woolf in 1924, are well documented. See Elaine Showalter, *The Female Malady: Women, Madness, and English Culture, 1830–1980* (New York: Penguin, 1987), 192; Sarah Cole, "Siegfried Sassoon," in *The Cambridge Companion to the Poetry of the First World War*, ed. Santanu Das (Cambridge: Cambridge University Press, 2013), 94; and Peter Leese, *Shell Shock: Traumatic Neurosis and the British Soldiers of the First World War* (New York: Palgrave, 2002), 166. Karen L. Levenback, in *Virginia Woolf and the Great War* (Syracuse, NY: Syracuse University Press, 1999), 57, proposes Leonard's brother, Philip Sidney, as a closer parallel to Septimus than Sassoon.

35. Sandra M. Gilbert and Susan Gubar, *No Man's Land: The Place of the Woman Writer in the Twentieth Century*, vol. 2: *Sexchanges* (New Haven, CT: Yale University Press, 1991), 315. Levenback, in *Virginia Woolf and the Great War*, 44–82, discusses the war atmosphere of *Mrs. Dalloway* at length. See too Mark Hussey, ed., *Virginia Woolf and War: Fiction, Reality, and Myth* (Syracuse, NY: Syracuse University Press, 1991); Karen DeMeester, "Trauma and Recovery in Virginia Woolf's *Mrs. Dalloway*," *Modern Fiction Studies* 44, no. 3 (Fall 1998): 649–73; and Christine Froula, "Mrs. Dalloway's Postwar Elegy: Women, War, and the Art of Mourning," *Modernism/modernity* 9, no. 1 (January 2002): 125–63. Paul K. Saint-Amour explores the sense of total war in *Mrs. Dalloway* in *Tense Future: Modernism, Total War, Encyclopedic Form* (Oxford: Oxford University Press, 2015), 110–20; Sarah Cole investigates Septimus as a "repository" of war violence in *At the Violet Hour: Modernism and Violence in England and Ireland* (New York: Oxford University Press, 2012), 247–52. Vara S. Neverow considers Septimus as a World War I poet in "Septimus Warren Smith, Modernist War Poet," *South Carolina Review* 48, no. 2 (Spring 2016): 58–65.

36. Woolf, *MD*, 4.

37. Woolf, *MD*, 36.

38. For more on the recurring image of the sickroom in Woolf's work, see Janine Utell, "View from the Sickroom"; and Mark Hussey, "Introduction," *On Being Ill with Notes from Sick Rooms*.

39. See Mark Honigsbaum, *Living with Enza: The Forgotten Story of Britain and the Great Flu Pandemic of 1918* (London: Macmillan, 2009), xiii, 5.

40. Woolf, *MD*, 28, 30, 46, 46.

41. Woolf, *MD*, 46, 10, 10, 103.

42. Woolf, *MD*, 12, 12.

43. Woolf, *MD*, 4.

44. Woolf, *MD*, 4.

45. Woolf, *MD*, 49.

46. Woolf, *MD*, 9.

47. Shakespeare quotation from *Cymbeline*, 4.2.

48. *RC*, Mary Stevenson, now Lincoln, UK.

49. Woolf observed in her diary the discordant quality of the Armistice celebration: "so far neither bells nor flags, but the wailing of sirens & intermittent guns," while wheeling rooks "performing some ceremony, partly of thanksgiving, partly of valediction over the grave," *D1*, 216.

50. Woolf, *MD*, 133.

51. Woolf, *MD*, 135.

52. Woolf, *OBI*, 319.

53. Woolf, *MD*, 17.

54. Woolf, *MD*, 109–10.

55. Woolf, *OBI*, 326.

56. Woolf, *OBI*, 322.

57. Woolf, *OBI*, 9.

58. Sir William Osler, with Thomas McCrae, *The Principles and Practices of Medicine*, 8th ed. (New York and London: D. Appleton, 1915), 118. Osler notes depression following influenza is "one of its most unpleasant and obstinate features" (119).

59. Edwin O. Jordan, *Epidemic Influenza: A Survey* (Chicago: American Medical Association, 1927), 278.

60. George H. Savage, "The Psychosis of Influenza," *Practitioner* 52 (January–June 1919): 36–46; qtd. in Jordan, *Epidemic Influenza*, 280.

61. David Thomson and Robert Thomson, "Influenza," in *Annals of the Pickett-Thomson Research Laboratory* (London: Baillière, Tindall & Cox, 1934), 10:768. John Barry quotes Jordan and Thomson as well and summarizes the connection between the 1918 pandemic and psychiatric disorders in *The Great Influenza: The Story of the Deadliest Pandemic in History* (New York: Penguin, 2004), 378–81.

62. Karl A. Menninger, "Psychoses Associated with Influenza," *Journal of the American Medical Association* 72, no. 4 (January 25, 1919): 236–40.

63. Thomson and Thomson, in "Influenza," 772, for example, note that in the pandemic, depression was found to be "common" after the virus had struck.

64. I. M. Wasserman, "The Impact of Epidemic, War, Prohibition and Media on Suicide: United States, 1910–1920," *Suicidal & Life-Threatening Behavior* 22, no. 2 (Summer 1992): 240.

65. Narayana Manjunatha, Suresh Bada Math, Girish Baburao Kulkarni, and Santosh Kumar Chaturvedi summarize the research on the influenza-psychiatric connection in "The Neuropsychiatric Aspects of Influenza/Swine Flu: A Selective Review," *Industrial Psychiatry Journal* (July–December 2011): 83–90.

66. Barry, *The Great Influenza*, 378–81. The 1918 virus may be linked to the deadly encephalitis lethargica, or sleeping sickness, that affected millions in the 1920s, though the link is unclear. It could cause a catatonic sleep state but also violent mental disturbances. See Molly Caldwell Crosby, *Asleep: The Forgotten Epidemic That Remains One of Medicine's Greatest Mysteries* (New York: Berkley Books, 2010), and Oliver Sacks, *Awakenings* (1973; New York: Vintage, 1999).

67. "Triple Murder and Suicide: An Attack of Influenza," *Times* (London), November 6, 1918, 3.

68. *RC*, W. F. Eaton, UK.

69. *PIS*, Ethel Hubble Harter, Virginia.

70. *RC*, Dr. Walter Schröder, Germany.

71. *RC*, Dorothy E. Jack, UK.

72. *RC*, Eric Newell, UK.

73. *RC*, Hilda Toone, now Ford, UK.

74. *RC*, A. M. Spark, now Clarihew, UK.

75. Katherine Anne Porter, *Pale Horse, Pale Rider* (1939), in *The Collected Stories of Katherine Anne Porter* (New York: Harcourt, 1979), 305.

76. *RC*, Frederick Bebbington, UK.

77. *RC*, Philip Learoyd, UK.

78. *RC*, E. Philips Cole, UK.

79. *RC*, Marie Svenningsen, Norway.

80. Dr. James C. Harris, "Self-Portrait After Spanish Flu," *Archives of General Psychiatry* 63 (April 2006): 354–55. Harris analyzes Munch's two influenza paintings and Norway's pandemic experiences, noting Munch lost a close friend in the outbreak.

81. Harris, "Self-Portrait," 354. Harris also connects the red color to fever.

82. Hermione Lee, *Virginia Woolf* (New York: Knopf, 1997), 171–96, summarizes the overlaps among influenza, illness more generally, and Woolf's mental health.

83. Letter from Woolf to Vanessa Bell, February 23, 1918, *L2*, 218.

84. Woolf, *D2*, 160.

85. Lee, *Virginia Woolf*, 182.

86. Letter from Woolf to Ethel Smyth, February 27, 1930, in *The Letters of Virginia Woolf*, vol. 4: *1929–1931*, ed. Nigel Nicolson and Joanne Trautmann (New York: Harcourt Brace, 1978): 144–45.

87. Lee, *Virginia Woolf*, 181.

88. Critics have considered Septimus's mental health from many angles, though not as linked to the pandemic: DeMeester examines the links to shell shock in "Trauma and Recovery in Virginia Woolf's *Mrs. Dalloway*"; Suzette Henke investigates disrupted language in "Virginia Woolf's Septimus Smith: An Analysis of 'Paraphrenia' and Schizophrenic Use of Language," *Literature and Psychology* 31, no. 4 (1981): 13–23. Henke and David Eberly explore trauma in *Virginia Woolf and Trauma: Embodied Texts* (New York: Pace University Press, 2007). Jane Fisher,

Envisioning Disease, 81, notes the link between mental health and the pandemic but primarily reads Septimus as a complicated embodiment of war trauma. I investigate war trauma and metaphor in "Dead Men, Walking: Actors, Networks, and Actualized Metaphors in *Mrs. Dalloway* and *Raymond*," *NOVEL: A Forum on Fiction* 46, no. 2 (2013): 253–74.

89. Woolf, *MD*, 67.

90. Woolf, *OBI*, 319.

91. Woolf, *MD*, 67, 15, 66.

92. Rivers discusses these nightmares in "An Address on the Repression of War Experience," delivered on December 4, 1917, at "Section of Psychiatry," Royal Society of Medicine, 1–20. Reprinted in *The Lancet* 191, no. 4927 (February 2, 1918): 173–77.

93. For Sassoon and Owen at Craiglockhart, see *Poetry of the First World War: An Anthology*, ed. Tim Kendall (Oxford: Oxford University Press, 2014), 86. Poems quoted from Kendall edition; Sassoon's "Repression of War Experience," 97–98, l. 27.

94. Wilfred Owen, "Mental Cases," written 1917–1918, reprinted in Kendall, *Poetry of the First World War*, 170–71.

95. Jay Winter, *Sites of Memory, Sites of Mourning: The Great War in European Cultural History* (Cambridge: Cambridge University Press, 1995), 204.

96. Woolf, *MD*, 68.

97. In her memoir essay "Old Bloomsbury," Woolf recounts how during one episode, she thought "the birds were singing Greek choruses." In *Moments of Being*, 2nd ed., ed. Jeanne Schulkind (New York: Harvest/Harcourt: 1985), 184.

98. Woolf, *MD*, 69.

99. Woolf, *MD*, 136.

100. Woolf, *MD*, 139.

101. Woolf, *OBI*, 319.

102. Woolf, *MD*, 137.

103. Woolf, *MD*, 142.

104. Hermione Lee, *Virginia Woolf*, 178–82, discusses the rest cure and Woolf's doctors. Molly Hite notes the unusually critical portrait of the doctors in "Tonal Cues and Uncertain Values: Affect and Ethics in *Mrs. Dalloway*," *Narrative* 18, no. 3 (October 2010): 255.

105. Woolf, *MD*, 179, 179.

106. Woolf, *MD*, 181.

107. The Collier letters (*RC*) from the United Kingdom frequently note the blinds as a sign of flu deaths: Gladys Hanson (now Bowden) describes how "many times I called at houses, one day, and the next found the blinds down, knowing one or more had died." Hilda Toone (now Ford) notes the constant presence of "drawn blinds and black boards up at windows" and how people would run "past houses with drawn blinds" for fear of germs. See also Edith Dilks (now How).

108. Woolf, *MD*, 181.

109. In *The Female Malady*, Elaine Showalter explores how World War I created a crisis of masculinity when shell-shocked men like Septimus exhibited a female-associated "hysteria." Other critics question Showalter's conclusions; see Laurinda Stryker, "British Shell-Shock and the Politics of Interpretation," in *Evidence, History, and the Great War: Historians and the Impact of 1914–1918*, ed. Gail Braybon (New York: Berghahn, 2003), 154–71.

5. A WASTELAND OF INFLUENZA: T. S. ELIOT'S
THE WASTE LAND

1. Letter from Eliot to his mother, Charlotte Stearns Eliot, December 8, 1918, in *The Letters of T. S. Eliot*, ed. Valerie Eliot and Hugh Haughton, 2 vols. (New Haven, CT: Yale University Press, 2009–2011), 306.

2. Letter from Eliot to his mother, December 8, 1918, *Letters*, 1:306.

3. Letter from Vivien Eliot to Charlotte Eliot, December 15, 1918, *Letters*, 1:309.

4. Letter from Eliot to Graham Wallas, December 14, 1918, *Letters*, 1:308.

5. For more on these years, see Robert Crawford, *Young Eliot: From St. Louis to* The Waste Land (New York: Farrar, Straus and Giroux, 2015), 309–17, 384–99; and Peter Ackroyd, *T. S. Eliot: A Life* (New York: Simon and Schuster, 1984), 87–144.

6. Letter from Eliot to his brother, February 27, 1919, *Letters*, 1:323.

7. Letter from Eliot to his mother, February 27, 1919, *Letters*, 1:324.

8. See February 27, 1919, letters to Henry and his mother, *Letters*, 1:322–25.

9. T. S. Eliot, "London Letter," *The Dial* 71 (New York: Dial Publishing Company, July–December 1921): 213, https://hdl.handle.net/2027/uc1.b2924815.

10. Criticism on Eliot's poem is, of course, plentiful. Two excellent recent collections are *A Companion to T. S. Eliot*, ed. David E. Chinitz (New York: Wiley Blackwell, 2014); and *The Cambridge Companion to "The Waste Land,"* ed. Gabrielle McIntire (Cambridge: Cambridge University Press, 2015). For Eliot and the war, see Carl Krockel, *War Trauma and English Modernism: T. S. Eliot and D. H. Lawrence* (New York: Palgrave Macmillan, 2011); and Jean-Michel Rabaté, "'The World Has Seen Strange Revolutions Since I Died': *The Waste Land* and the Great War" in *The Cambridge Companion*, 9–23. Crawford's *Young Eliot* considers the early years and Eliot's marriage. For more on Eliot's sexuality, see Patrick Query, "'The pleasures of higher vices': Sexuality in Eliot's Work," in *Companion to T. S. Eliot*, 350–62.

11. Peter's original article, "A New Interpretation of *The Waste Land*," was to be published in 1952 but was blocked by Eliot's lawyers; it appeared after Eliot's death, in 1969, in *Essays in Criticism* 19 (April 1969): 140–75. Peter's exploration of Verdenal was extended by James E. Miller Jr., *T. S. Eliot's Personal Waste Land: Exorcism of the Demons* (University Park: Pennsylvania State University Press, 1977).

12. For example, Leon Surette explores Weston, Eliot, and the occult in "*The Waste Land* and Jessie Weston: A Reassessment," *Twentieth Century Literature* 34, no. 2 (Summer 1988): 223–44. Gregory Jay examines the Fisher King myths in "Eliot's Poetics and the Fisher King," *Yeats Eliot Review* 7, no. 2 (June 1982): 28–35. For Eliot and Buddhism, see Christina Hauck, "Not One, Not Two: Eliot and Buddhism," in *A Companion to T. S. Eliot*, 40–52; and for Eliot and popular culture, see Chinitz, "A Vast Wasteland? Eliot and Popular Culture," 66–78, in the same collection. For an ecocritical perspective, see Gabrielle McIntire, "*The Waste Land* as Ecocritique" in *The Cambridge Companion*, 178–93.

13. See T. S. Eliot, *The Waste Land: A Facsimile and Transcript of the Original Drafts Including the Annotations of Ezra Pound*, ed. Valerie Eliot (London: Faber and Faber, 1971): 1; epigraph cited as "Quoted by the late Professor Theodore Spencer during a lecture at Harvard University, and recorded by the late Henry Ware Eliot, Jr., the poet's brother" (1).

14. *The Waste Land*, l. 139. Quotations from *The Waste Land* (1922) are from *Collected Poems: 1909–1962* (London: Faber and Faber, 1963). Hereafter cited as *WL* and by line number, sometimes in clusters.

15. Samuel Hynes, *A War Imagined: The First World War and English Culture* (New York: Atheneum, 1991), 342.

16. See Ezekiel Black, "Mouthlessness and Ineffability in World War I Poetry and *The Waste Land*," *War, Literature & the Arts: An International Journal of the Humanities* 25 (2013): 1–17.

17. T. S. Eliot, "A Note on War Poetry," in *Collected Poems, 1909–1962* (New York: Harcourt, 1991), 215–16, ll. 22–24. I am indebted to Black, "Mouthlessness and Ineffability," 3, for calling my attention to these lines.

18. T. S. Eliot, "Tradition and the Individual Talent," 43. Essay first published in two parts in *The Egoist* 6, no. 4 and 6, no. 5 (September and December 1919): 54–55, 72–73. Reprinted in *Selected Prose of T. S. Eliot*, ed. Frank Kermode (New York: Harcourt Brace, 1975), 37–44.

19. In *Middlemarch* (1883), George Eliot's character Edward Casaubon is writing a key to all mythologies.

20. Michael Levenson, *A Genealogy of Modernism: A Study of English Literary Doctrine, 1908–1922* (Cambridge: Cambridge University Press, 1986), 172.

21. Eliot, *WL*, 308–11.

22. *RC*, Anonymous, USA. Letter from Ashton, Illinois, filed with the "A" letters.

23. Hynes, *A War Imagined*, 343.

24. Eliot, *WL*, 105–10.

25. Eliot, *WL*, 377–86.

26. Katherine Anne Porter, *Pale Horse, Pale Rider* (1939), in *The Collected Stories of Katherine Anne Porter* (New York: Harcourt, 1979), 310, 305, 312.

27. Eliot, "London Letter," 213.

28. Eliot, *WL*, 335–39.

29. Eliot, *WL*, 384.

30. Eliot, *WL*, 346–49, 353–56, 357–58.

31. Eliot, *WL*, 55, 47, 321.

32. Emily Breidbart, "The Forgotten Influenza of 1918: When a Strong Immune System Becomes a Weakness," *Clinical Correlations: The NYU Langone Online Journal of Medicine* (September 23, 2009), https://www.clinicalcorrelations.org/?p=1862.

33. Krockell, *War Trauma and English Modernism*, 95, notes this fear. Black, "Mouthlessness and Ineffability," 10, observes that Eliot's friend Jean Verdenal "drowned at Gallipoli."

34. Sarah Cole, *At the Violet Hour: Modernism and Violence in England and Ireland* (New York: Oxford University Press, 2012), 67.

35. Eliot, *WL*, 313, 317.

36. Eliot, *WL*, 76, 320–21.

37. Eliot, *WL*, 61.

38. Eliot, *WL*, 87, 89, 89–90.

39. Eliot, *WL*, 118, 119–20.

40. Eliot, *WL*, 208, 174–75.

41. Eliot, *WL*, 185–86, 286–88.

42. Eliot, *WL*, 388, 387, 393.

43. Eliot, *WL*, 67–68.

44. Eliot, *WL*, 288, 383, 379, 384.

45. Eliot, *WL*, 116, 186, 193–94.

46. Eliot, *WL*, 316, 390.

47. Eliot, *WL*, 2, 23, 68.

48. David Sherman, *In a Strange Room: Modernism's Corpses and Mortal Obligation* (New York: Oxford University Press, 2014), 156, 162.

49. Paul Fussell, *The Great War and Modern Memory* (Oxford: Oxford University Press, 1977), 325–26; Cole, *At the Violet Hour*, 66.

50. Allyson Booth details the lack of corpses on the home front in *Postcards from the Trenches: Negotiating the Space Between Modernism and the First World War* (Oxford: Oxford University Press, 1996).

51. Eliot, *WL*, 115–16.

52. Eliot, *WL*, 187–88, 193–95.

53. Paul Fussell, *The Great War*, 23, for example, consistently links *The Waste Land* and the war, with "its rats' alleys, dull canals, and dead men who have lost their bones." Cole, *At the Violet Hour*, 72, notes "the Great War's bones and rats."

54. For example, the *Times* reports on November 4, 1918, that a doctor had isolated the germ and noted it was like "the bubonic plague": "The Influenza Germ Isolated. A Spanish Doctor's Claim," 7. The Collier letters repeatedly link the pandemic to the bubonic plague: E. Johnson notes "It really was like a plague"; Ellen Monahan writes "Some called it a Plague. . . . many bodies turned blue-black"; and Hilda Toone (now Ford) says it was "like the plague of London" (all *RC*, UK).

55. John M. Barry, *The Great Influenza: The Story of the Deadliest Pandemic in History* (New York: Penguin, 2004), 223; see 190 for bodies stacked like "cord wood."

56. Joanna Bourke, for example, looks at the war's burial practices in *Dismembering the Male: Men's Bodies, Britain, and the Great War* (London: Reaktion, 1996), esp. 221–28; as does Peter E. Hodgkinson, "Clearing the Dead," *Centre for First World War Studies* 3, no. 1 (September 2007); and Joanna Legg, Graham Parker, and David Legg, "War Graves for the WWI Dead on the Western Front," in *The Great War, 1914–1918: A Guide to World War 1 Battlefields and History of the First World War*, website, http://www.greatwar.co.uk/war-graves/ww1-war-graves.htm.

57. Eliot, *WL*, 193.

58. Daniel Defoe, *A Journal of the Plague Year*, ed. Paula R. Backscheider (1722; New York: Norton, 1992), 55.

59. Eliot, *WL*, 69–75.

60. Letter from Eliot to Graham Wallas, December 14, 1918, *Letters*, 1:308.

61. Letter from Eliot to Lytton Strachey, February 17, 1920, *Letters*, 1:445.

62. Letter from Eliot to John Middleton Murry, mid-April? 1925, *Letters*, 2:627.

63. Background information and translation from the Norton critical edition of *The Waste Land*, ed. Michael North (New York: Norton, 2001), 3n1.

64. See, for example, book 5, chapter 14, when her books are consulted during a terrible plague: Titus Livius, *Roman History*, trans. William Gordon (Aberdeen: J. Chalmers, 1805), 429. Eric M. Orlin investigates the Sibylline books in *Temples, Religion, and Politics in the Roman Republic* (Boston: Brill, 2002), chap. 3. He notes how frequently the books were consulted "to control a pestilence which was

devastating the city," with Livy noting such consultations eleven different times (87). Another classical link between Eliot's poem and plague lies in the figure of Tiresias, who narrates "The Fire Sermon" section. At the start of Sophocles's *Oedipus Rex*, a virulent plague has descended on Thebes, and Tiresias helps Oedipus identify the bad man who—according to the oracle at Delphi—had caused the plague.

65. Levenson, *A Genealogy of Modernism*, 172–73. Levenson goes on to discuss recurring tropes of resurrection in the poem.

66. Eliot, *WL*, 2, 4, 7.

67. Eliot, *WL*, 1, 2, 3, 5, 6.

68. Simon Hay investigates the poem's gothic elements and the living-death quality of the poem: "Modernist Ghosts, Transatlantic Apparitions: *The Waste Land*," *Journal X: A Journal of Culture and Criticism* 7, no. 2 (Spring 2003): esp. 132–35.

69. Eliot, *WL*, 6.

70. *Times Literary Supplement* 1, no. 1 (October 26, 1922): 690. Reprinted in the Norton edition of *The Waste Land*, 137.

71. Eliot, *WL*, 62–66.

72. Eliot, *WL*, 38–40.

73. Eliot, *WL*, 121–26.

74. Eliot, *WL*, 322–30.

75. The Norton edition of *The Waste Land* notes these lines are likely "a description of the betrayal, arrest, interrogation, and crucifixion of Christ": 16n6.

76. Headnote to Eliot's footnotes, *The Waste Land*, 21. Jessie L. Weston, *From Ritual to Romance* (Cambridge: Cambridge University Press, 1920), excerpted in the Norton edition of *The Waste Land*, 35–40; quotations from 36.

77. James Frazer, *The Golden Bough: A Study in Magic and Religion*, abr. ed. (London: Macmillan, 1922), excerpted in the Norton edition of *The Waste Land*, 29–34; quotation from 33.

78. Rupert Brooke, "The Soldier" (1914), in *The Penguin Book of First World War Poetry*, ed. George Walter (New York: Penguin, 2004), 108.

79. The flu's violence typically fell into what Cole terms "disenchanted violence," one that offers no sense of renewal or redemption; see *At the Violet Hour*.

80. Barry Spurr, *Anglo-Catholic in Religion: T. S. Eliot and Christianity* (Cambridge: Lutterworth, 2010), 38.

81. Eliot, *WL*, 363.

82. See the Norton edition of *The Waste Land*, Eliot's note, 25.

83. See, for example, Black, "Mouthlessness and Ineffability."

84. Sarah Cole, *Modernism, Male Friendship, and the First World War* (Cambridge: Cambridge University Press, 2003), 143.

85. Black, "Mouthlessness and Ineffability," 1.

86. Eliot, *WL*, 6, 5–6.

87. Eliot, *WL*, 48, 125.

88. Eliot, *WL*, 39, 122, 81.

89. Eliot, *WL*, 54, 52, 53.

90. Eliot, *WL*, 38–39, 112, 184.

91. Eliot, *WL*, 204.

92. Eliot, *WL*, 24, 68, 174–75, 106, 175, 323.

6. APOCALYPTIC PANDEMIC: W. B. YEATS'S "THE SECOND COMING"

1. Caitriona Foley, who offers the most comprehensive account of the pandemic in Ireland, notes the flu "claimed more than 20,000 lives" and "infected as many as 600–800,000": *The Last Irish Plague: The Great Flu Epidemic in Ireland, 1918–19* (Dublin: Irish Academic Press, 2011), 8. John Dorney places Ireland's death rate at 23,000 and notes the flu far outstrips the 4,000 to 5,000 deaths between 1916 to 1923 from the country's internal political violence: "Ireland and the Great Flu Epidemic of 1918," *The Irish Story*, May 16, 2013, http://www.theirishstory.com/2013 /05/16/ireland-and-the-great-flu-epidemic-of-1918. Ireland does lose more men in the war—statistics range from a few thousand more to roughly twice as many; see chapter 1 for more statistics.

2. John M. Barry, *The Great Influenza: The Story of the Deadliest Pandemic in History* (New York: Penguin, 2004), 239–40.

3. Most broad theories of violence likewise focus on the human-initiated variety and rarely consider the violence of illness. Slavoj Žižek, for example, describes the division between subjective violence, or "violence performed by a clearly identifiable agent," and objective (but still human-initiated) forms such as hate speech that is more systematic, like an invisible "dark matter": *Violence: Six Sideways Reflections* (New York: Picador, 2008), 1–2. Žižek does touch on "The Second Coming" but entirely in relation to human-based violence (85). Roland Barthes contrasts the violence of noncorporal restraints on an individual by the larger group with the violence inflicted on bodies by other humans (like imprisonment, wounds, assassination, murders, war, and so on): Roland Barthes, "On the Subject of Violence," in *The Grain of the Voice: Interviews, 1962–1980*, trans. Linda Coverdale (Evanston, IL: Northwestern University Press, 2009), 307–8. Rob Nixon offers his penetrating theory of "slow violence" to describe the often hidden quality of violence that happens over time, as human actions damage the environment incrementally, rather than the more spectacular violence presented by war. Rob Nixon, *Slow Violence and the Environmentalism of the Poor* (Cambridge, MA: Harvard University Press, 2011); Nixon discusses illness briefly, but in relationship to Gulf War illness, clearly arising from human-based violence (210).

4. Michael Wood, *Yeats and Violence* (Oxford: Oxford University Press, 2010), 7. Helen Vendler repeatedly remarks on "the enigma" of human violence in her analysis of the poet: *Our Secret Discipline: Yeats and Lyric Form* (Cambridge, MA: Harvard University Press, 2007), 64, 77, 79.

5. See, for example, Simona Vannini, "The Genesis of 'The Second Coming': A Textual Analysis of the Manuscript-Draft," *Yeats: An Annual of Critical and Textual Studies* 16 (1998): 103; and Seamus Deane, " 'The Second Coming': Coming Second; Coming in a Second," *Irish University Review* 22, no. 1 (Spring–Summer, 1992): 93. Vannini notes that George linked the poem to politics, telling the critic Donald Torchiana in the 1960s that "The Second Coming" grew out of Yeats's worry about European and Russian revolutions (119).

6. A. R. Ammons, "Triphammer Bridge," in *The Selected Poems*, exp. ed. (New York: Norton, 1986), 88. Appropriately, Ammons finds "sanctuary" not in his

outer world but in the sound of the word itself, the sound becoming "the one place to dwell."

7. I am indebted to Ann Saddlemyer's meticulous account of George's illness in *Becoming George: The Life of Mrs. W. B. Yeats* (Oxford: Oxford University Press, 2002), which she dates as starting on November 18, 1918 (195). While the birthday of Yeats's daughter, Anne, is listed on Wikipedia (and thus infiltrating elsewhere) as May 9, 1919, she was born on February 26, 1919, as many biographers and accounts agree, making George about six months pregnant during her illness. For the February birth date, see Saddlemyer, *Becoming George*, 205; A. Norman Jeffares, *W. B. Yeats: A New Biography* (New York: Continuum, 2001), 211; and David A. Ross, *A Critical Companion to William Butler Yeats: A Literary Reference to His Life and Work* (New York: Facts on File, 2009), 203.

8. Saddlemyer, *Becoming George*, 195.

9. Qtd. in Saddlemyer, *Becoming George*, 195; from November 26, 1918, letter from Yeats to Gregory in Berg Collection, New York Public Library.

10. Barry, *The Great Influenza*, 239–40.

11. Qtd. in Saddlemyer, *Becoming George*, 195; from November 29, 1918, letter from Yeats to Gregory, William Butler Yeats Microfilmed Manuscripts Collection, Special Collections Department, State University of New York at Stony Brook.

12. Qtd. in Saddlemyer, *Becoming George*, 195; from November 27, 1918, letter from Gregory to Yeats, in the Stony Brook collection.

13. Saddlemyer, *Becoming George*, 198.

14. Saddlemyer, *Becoming George*, 196.

15. Saddlemyer describes Maud Gonne's visit in *Becoming George*, 196–97.

16. William Butler Yeats, "The Second Coming," originally published in *The Dial* in November 1920 and then in *Michael Robartes and the Dancer* (1921). Version quoted here from *The Variorum Edition of the Poems of W. B. Yeats*, ed. Peter Allt and Russell K. Alspach (New York: Macmillian, 1957), 401–2, l. 1. Poem hereafter cited as *TSC* and by line number.

17. In his notes on "The Second Coming," Yeats links the poem to his theory of the gyres, which I discuss later in the chapter. *Variorum*, 823–25.

18. Yeats, *TSC*, 3, 9, 11.

19. Yeats, *TSC*, 13, 14, 18.

20. Yeats, *TSC*, 19, 20, 21.

21. Simona Vannini, "The Genesis of 'The Second Coming,'" 103.

22. Saddlemyer, *Becoming George*, 198–99.

23. Yeats, *TSC*, 9–13.

24. For more on George's automatic writing and her role in Yeats's spiritual theories and his poetic processes, see Margaret Mills Harper, *Wisdom of Two: The Spiritual and Literary Collaboration of George and W. B. Yeats* (Oxford: Oxford University Press, 2006); and Bette London, *Writing Double: Women's Literary Partnerships* (Ithaca, NY: Cornell University Press, 1999), 179–209. Brenda Maddox explores spirit writing and the Yeats's marriage in *Yeats's Ghosts: The Secret Life of W. B. Yeats* (New York: Harper Collins, 2000).

25. Yeats, *TSC*, 18, 19, 20.

26. In the 1960s, Jon Stallworthy and Curtis B. Bradford started analyzing Yeats's revision process: Jon Stallworthy, *Between the Lines: Yeats's Poetry in the Making*

(Oxford: Clarendon, 1963); Curtis B. Bradford, *Yeats at Work* (Carbondale: Southern Illinois University Press, 1965). The publication of Yeats's manuscript materials by Cornell University (the Cornell Yeats Project) beginning in the 1980s has made tracking his revisions easier; see *Michael Robartes and the Dancer: Manuscript Materials*, ed. Thomas Parkinson and Anne Brannen, Cornell Yeats Project, general ed. Phillip L. Marcus, J. C. C. Mays, Ann Saddlemyer, and Jon Stallworthy (Ithaca, NY: Cornell University Press, 1994). See too Vannini's "The Genesis of 'The Second Coming.'"

27. Yeats, *Michael Robartes and the Dancer: Manuscript Materials*, 151.
28. Yeats, *Michael Robartes and the Dancer: Manuscript Materials*, 153.
29. Yeats, *Michael Robartes and the Dancer: Manuscript Materials*, 147.
30. Vannini, "The Genesis of 'The Second Coming,'" 122.
31. Yeats, *TSC*, 4, 5, 6.
32. Yeats, *TSC*, 12, 13, 14, 18, 15.
33. Yeats, *TSC*, 21. The significance of the "rough beast" is controversial; A. Raghu summarizes the debates in "Yeats's 'The Second Coming,'" *Explicator* 50, no. 4 (Summer 1992): 224–25. Don McDermott explores the debates over whether the beast is bad or good in "The Last Judgment on 'The Second Coming,'" *Yeats Eliot Review* 10, no. 3 (Spring 1990): 70–73. Robert O'Driscoll argues for a positive reading in "'The Second Coming' and Yeats's Vision of History," in *A Festschrift for Edgar Ronald Seary: Essays in English Language and Literature* (Newfoundland: Memorial University of Newfoundland, 1975): 170–81; as does Russell E. Murphy, "The 'Rough Beast' and Historical Necessity: A New Consideration of Yeats's 'The Second Coming,'" *Studies in the Literary Imagination* 14, no. 1 (Spring 1981): 101–10.
34. "The Great Death," *Times* (London), February 2, 1921, 11.
35. Yeats, *TSC*, 6.
36. Yeats, *TSC*, 6, 5.
37. Barry, *The Great Influenza*, 236–37.
38. "Easter, 1916" was written in 1916 and published in *Michael Robartes and the Dancer* (1921); version quoted here from *Variorum*, 391–94. Yeats wrote "Leda and the Swan" in 1923; it was published in *The Dial* and in *The Cat and the Moon and Certain Poems* in 1924 and again in *The Tower* in 1928; version quoted here is from *Variorum*, 441. Yeats published an early version of "Nineteen Hundred and Nineteen" in September 1921 in *The Dial* as "Thoughts Upon the Present State of the World"; published a new version in *The Tower* in 1928. Version quoted here from *Variorum*, 428–33; Woods, *Yeats and Violence*, 30–31, recounts the poem's publication history. Poems hereafter cited by abbreviated titles and line numbers.
39. As Sarah Cole observes in *At the Violet Hour: Modernism and Violence in England and Ireland* (New York: Oxford University Press, 2012), 148, the poem "expresses the promise, as well as the limits, of enchanted violence."
40. Yeats, "Easter," 57–58.
41. Yeats, "Easter," 68.
42. Yeats, *TSC*, 4.
43. Yeats, "Easter," 16, 40, 80.
44. Yeats, "Nineteen," 1.
45. Yeats, "Nineteen," 35, 36.

46. Yeats, "Nineteen," 108.

47. Yeats, "Nineteen," 84–88.

48. Yeats, "Nineteen," 97, 107, 119, 121. In *At the Violet Hour,* Cole finds the violence of "Nineteen" disenchanted, the poem functioning as a revision of the more generative violence of "Easter, 1916" (176). The images of wind build this sense of violent disenchantment, signifying "wild movement that is troubling and chaotic, even brutal" (175), and later sees both Virginia Woolf and Yeats as using wind "to signify force itself, the very limit of human value, individuation, and meaning" (239).

49. Yeats, "Nineteen," 25–29.

50. Many critics discuss Quinn's murder and its link to the poem, including Vendler, *Our Secret Discipline,* 64; and Ross, *A Critical Companion,* 176. Wood, *Yeats and Violence,* 27–28, notes how the critical confusion over whether Quinn is named "Ellen" or "Eileen" suggests how this death is both particular and allegorical.

51. See, for example, Vendler, *Our Secret Discipline,* 76; Cole, *At the Violet Hour,* 173.

52. Yeats, "Nineteen," 113, 117, 119–21, 125–30.

53. Yeats, *Variorum,* 433.

54. Michael Ragussis, *The Subterfuge of Art: Language and the Romantic Tradition* (Baltimore, MD: Johns Hopkins University Press, 1978), 102. Woods, *Yeats and Violence,* 138–39.

55. Rob Doggett, "Writing out (of) Chaos: Constructions of History in Yeats's 'Nineteen Hundred and Nineteen' and 'Meditations in the Time of Civil War,'" *Twentieth Century Literature* 47, no. 2 (Summer 2001): 150–51. In his smart reading of "Nineteen," Doggett suggests Yeats unsettles "nationalist narratives of history" to focus instead on the "rupture and the chaos of the present" (139).

56. Ross, *A Critical Companion,* 140–42, positions the poem amid both myth and Yeats's historical eras.

57. From Yeats's notes on the poem, *Variorum,* 828.

58. Yeats, "Leda," 1.

59. Yeats, "Leda," 10–11.

60. See, for example, Edward W. Said's classic "Yeats and Decolonization," in *Nationalism, Colonialism, and Literature,* by Terry Eagleton, Fredric Jameson, and Edward W. Said (Minneapolis: University of Minnesota Press, 1990), 69–96. For a feminist postcolonial response to Said and Yeats's poem, see Sabina Sharkey, "Gendering Inequalities: The Case of Irish Women," *Paragraph* 16, no. 1 (March 1993): 5–22.

61. Yeats, "Leda," 13.

62. Yeats, "Leda," 12.

63. A 1903 edition of *The Decameron,* as well as a folder of eight illustrations by Louis Chalon, are listed as part of the Yeatses' personal library: Wayne K. Chapman, "The W. B. and George Yeats Library: A Short-Title Catalogue," Clemson University Digital Press (2006), item 238 and 238a (YL231 and 231a): 16, https://tigerprints .clemson.edu/cgi/viewcontent.cgi?article=1001&context=cudp_bibliography. Robin Barrow notes that "Yeats was undoubtedly familiar with the *Decameron*" and explores Yeats's references to the work in "An Identification in Yeats's *A Vision (B),*" *Notes and Queries* 51, no. 2 (June 2004): 162.

64. John Butler Yeats illustrated the sixteen-volume edition of Defoe's works, *Romances and Narratives,* ed. George A. Aitken (London: J. M. Dent & Co., 1895). *A Journal*

of the Plague Year is volume 9. William Michael Murphy describes how Lily, Yeats's sister, "served as a model" for all the Defoe illustrations except for Friday in *Robinson Crusoe*; Lily writes to her father in 1910 reminding him how someone had recognized her face in the illustration of the plague victim in Defoe's work: see *Prodigal Father: The Life of John Butler Yeats (1839–1922)* (Syracuse, NY: Syracuse University Press, 2001), 182, 579n42. Wayne K. Chapman, "The W. B. and George Yeats Library," lists Thomas Wright's *The Life of Daniel Defoe* (London: Cassell, 1894): item 2316 (YL 2296), 158, as part of the Yeatses' library.

65. Wayne A. Rebhorn, introduction to Giovanni Boccaccio, *The Decameron*, ed. and trans. Wayne A. Rebhorn (New York: Norton, 2016), xxiv. Quotations from *The Decameron* (c. 1353) are taken from this edition, hereafter cited as *TD*. Quotations from Defoe's *A Journal of the Plague Year*, ed. Paula R. Backscheider (1722; New York: Norton, 1992), hereafter cited as *Journal*.

66. Boccaccio, *TD*, 6.

67. Boccaccio, *TD*, 10; Defoe, *Journal*, 45.

68. Defoe, *Journal*, 136.

69. T. S. Eliot, *The Waste Land*, Norton critical ed., ed. Michael North (New York: Norton, 2001), l. 387; Yeats, "Nineteen," 97.

70. Boccaccio, *TD*, 10.

71. Boccaccio, *TD*, 10; Defoe, *Journal*, 83.

72. Patricia Marsh, "'Mysterious Malady Spreading': Press Coverage of the 1918–19 Influenza Pandemic in Ireland," *Quest Proceedings of the QUB AHSS Conference* 6 (Autumn 2008): 170, https://www.qub.ac.uk/sites/QUEST/FileStore/Issue6/Filetoupload,146247,en.pdf. For "black flu" references, see Dorney, "Ireland and the Great Flu."

73. William J. Thompson, MD, "Mortality from Influenza in Ireland," *Journal of the Statistical and Social Inquiry Society of Ireland* 14, no. 1 (1919/1920): 1.

74. Thompson, "Mortality from Influenza in Ireland," 10, notes that the death rates in Dublin are even higher if the spike in pneumonia deaths in 1918 is attributed to influenza.

75. D. W. Macnamara, "Memories of 1918 and 'the 'Flu,'" *Journal of the Irish Medical Association* 35, no. 208 (1954): 306.

76. Foley, *The Last Irish Plague*, 48, 134.

77. Seán O'Casey, in Peter Somerville-Large, *Irish Voices: Fifty Years of Irish Life, 1916–1966* (London: Chatto and Windus, 1999), 20; qtd. in Foley, *Last Irish Plague*, 141.

78. Foley, in *Last Irish Plague*, explores the variable responses of Irish medical professionals and government officials; all were overwhelmed and many succumbed to the flu, but many kept attempting to provide help; for medical responses, see 85–102; for government responses, see 103–18. For church, court, and transit responses, see Guy Beiner, Patricia Marsh, and Ida Milne, "Greatest Killer of the Twentieth Century: The Great Flu of 1918–1919," *Twentieth Century Social Perspectives* 17, no. 2 (March–April 2009), History Ireland, https://www.historyireland.com/20th-century-contemporary-history/greatest-killer-of-the-twentieth-century-the-great-flu-of-1918-19/.

79. Foley, *The Last Irish Plague*, 69, 63.

80. Beiner, "Greatest Killer of the Twentieth Century."

81. Foley, *The Last Irish Plague*, 161.

82. Defoe, *Journal*, 136.
83. Defoe, *Journal*, 92, 92, 34, 130, 135, 16.
84. Defoe, *Journal*, 159, 138, 158.
85. Boccaccio, *TD*, 12.
86. Defoe, *Journal*, 47, 129.
87. Dr. Kathleen Lynn, "Report on Influenza Epidemic. March 1919," *Ard-Fheis Sinn Féin, 8th April 1919 Reports*, 104; qtd. in Foley, *Last Irish Plague*, 134.
88. Sir John Moore, "Influenza from a Clinical Standpoint," *The Practitioner*, 102, no. 1 (1919): 29; qtd. in Foley, *Last Irish Plague*, 133.
89. Foley, *Last Irish Plague*, 141.
90. Foley, *Last Irish Plague*, 48–49.
91. *Irish News*, July 12, 1918; qtd. in Patricia Marsh, "'Mysterious Malady Spreading,'" 170.
92. Marsh, "'Mysterious Malady Spreading,'" 167–76, 169–70.
93. Foley, *Last Irish Plague*, 55–59.
94. Dorney, "Ireland and the Great Flu."
95. Vincent White, Bureau of Military History, 1913–1921, Collection of Military History and National Archives, Ireland, WS 1764, http://www.bureauofmilitaryhistory .ie/reels/bmh/BMH.WS1764.pdf, 11; also qtd. in Dorney, "Ireland and the Great Flu."
96. Eilis, Bean Ui Chonaill, Bureau of Military History, WS 568, 28; also qtd. in Dorney, "Ireland and the Great Flu."
97. Boccaccio, *TD*, 6.
98. Defoe, *Journal*, 34.
99. Boccaccio, *TD*, 8; Defoe, *Journal*, 97.
100. See Marsh, "'Mysterious Malady Spreading,'" 174–75, on remedy advertisements. Foley discusses the widespread fear the pandemic brought to Ireland, *Last Irish Plague*, 67–84.
101. *Connacht Tribune*, April 26, 1919; qtd. in Foley, *Last Irish Plague*, 96.
102. Eilis, Bean Ui Chonaill, Bureau of Military History, WS 598, 27; also qtd. in John Dorney, "Ireland and the Great Flu."
103. Seamus Babington, Bureau of Military History, WS 1595, 16.
104. Kathleen Behan, in Brian Behan, *Mother of All the Behans: The Story of Kathleen Behan as Told to Brian Behan* (London: Hutchinson, 1984), 43; qtd. in Foley, *Last Irish Plague*, 141.
105. Marsh, "'Mysterious Malady Spreading,'" 173–74; Foley, *Last Irish Plague*, 141, discusses the "repeated references to the way in which the disease felled entire households and to the inescapable presence of death."
106. Boccaccio, *TD*, 6.
107. Defoe, *Journal*, 64.
108. Foley, *Last Irish Plague*, 126–28. In the Anglican Book of Common Prayer, the service for illness in 1919 still attributed disease to divine judgment, but the service generally went unused; during the revisions to the prayer book in the 1920s, which were in part shaped by the pandemic experience, the service was rewritten to emphasize the comfort God might offer without attributing blame for the illness to the sins of the sufferer; see E. Clowes Chorley, *The New American Prayer Book: Its History and Contents* (New York: Macmillan, 1929), 100, 114.

109. See, for example, David Rudrum, "Slouching Towards Bethlehem: Yeats, Eliot, and the Modernist Apocalypse," in *Ecstasy and Understanding: Religious Awareness of English Poetry from the Late Victorian to the Modern Period*, ed. Adrian Grafe (New York: Continuum, 2008), 58–70. Don McDermott analyzes the debates around the Christian imagery in "The Last Judgment on 'The Second Coming,'" *Yeats Eliot Review* 10, no. 3 (Spring 1990): 70–73. Nathan Cervo reads the poem as not prophetic or Christian but satiric: "Yeats's 'The Second Coming,'" *The Explicator* 59, no. 2 (2001): 93–95. Most critics agree that the occult influences are more prominent than the Christian ones: see Jane Lindskold, "The Autobiographical Occult in Yeats's 'The Second Coming,'" *Eire-Ireland: A Journal of Irish Studies* 26, no. 4 (1991): 38–44. Several authors offer longer discussions of Yeats's mysticism; see, for example, Leon Surrette, *The Birth of Modernism: Ezra Pound, T. S. Eliot, W. B. Yeats, and the Occult* (Montreal: McGill-Queen's University Press, 1993).
110. King James Version.
111. See Rudrum, "Slouching Towards Bethlehem," 59–60. Rudrum is one of the only critics to mention the pandemic as part of the poem's general apocalyptic postwar landscape, though he doesn't link specific details of the poem to Yeats's experiences in the pandemic.
112. Yeats, *TSC*, 10.
113. Yeats, "Easter," 16, 40, 80.
114. Vincent Sherry offers an incisive account of the changes in sacrificial paradigms during the war in "Imbalances: Mass Death and the Economy of 'Sacrifice' in the Great War," in *The First World War: Literature, Culture, Modernity*, ed. Santanu Das and Kate McLoughlin (Oxford: Oxford University Press, 2018).
115. As I analyze in chapter 7, though, fears of flu contagion could at times insidiously morph into virulent racism.
116. See George Mills Harper and his readings of the December 21, 1917–January 30, 1918, guide sessions in *The Making of Yeats's* A Vision, vol. 1: *A Study of the Automatic Script* (London: Palgrave UK, 1987), 106, 154, 170. See also Saddlemyer, *Becoming George*, 200, 206–7.
117. Rudrum, "Slouching Towards Bethlehem," 60.
118. Yeats explicitly links the poem to his visions in his footnote on the gyres: *Variorum*, 824–25. For more on links between "The Second Coming" and *A Vision*, see Allen, "What Rough Beast."
119. See chapter 6, note 33.
120. Wood, *Yeats and Violence*, 212.

7. SPIRITUALISM, ZOMBIES, AND THE RETURN OF THE DEAD

1. Priscilla Wald, *Contagious: Cultures, Carriers, and the Outbreak Narrative* (Durham, NC: Duke University Press, 2008), 2–3.
2. Arthur Conan Doyle, *The History of Spiritualism*, 2 vols. (London: Cassell and Co., 1926). I quote from vol. 1, online at http://www.archive.org/details/history ofspiritu015638mbp. Many critics discuss spiritualism, often noting the role of the female medium: see Alex Owen, *The Darkened Room: Women, Power, and Spiritualism in Late Victorian England* (Chicago: University of Chicago Press,

1989); and Karen Beckman, *Vanishing Women: Magic, Film, and Feminism* (Durham, NC: Duke University Press, 2003). For two popular accounts, see Deborah Blum, *Ghost Hunters: William James and the Search for Scientific Proof of Life After Death* (New York: Penguin, 2006); and Mary Roach, *Spook: Science Tackles the Afterlife* (New York: Norton, 2005). Helen Sword's excellent *Ghostwriting Modernism* (Ithaca, NY: Cornell University Press, 2002) explores modernism and spiritualism. Jenny Hazelgrove, *Spiritualism and British Society Between the Wars* (Manchester: Manchester University Press, 2000), examines postwar spiritualism in Britain.

3. Doyle, *History*, 56–69; Blum, *Ghost Hunters*, 16–17.
4. Blum, *Ghost Hunters*, 18.
5. Blum, *Ghost Hunters*, 6, 72–73.
6. For spiritualism and the Civil War, see Drew Gilpin Faust, *This Republic of Suffering: Death and the American Civil War* (New York: Vintage, 2008), 180–85.
7. See Hazelgrove, *Spiritualism and British Society*, 14–16, on the popularity of spiritualism after 1918. For more on Doyle and spiritualism, see Andrew Lycett, *The Man Who Created Sherlock Holmes: The Life and Times of Sir Arthur Conan Doyle* (New York: Free Press, 2007); John Dickson Carr, *The Life of Sir Arthur Conan Doyle* (New York: Carroll & Graf, 2003); and Martin Booth, *The Doctor and the Detective: A Biography of Sir Arthur Conan Doyle* (1997; New York: St. Martin's, 2013).
8. On ectoplasm's heyday, see Roach, *Spook*, 123–48.
9. Jay Winter, *Sites of Memory, Sites of Mourning: The Great War in European Cultural History* (Cambridge: Cambridge University Press, 1995), 57–58.
10. Roach, *Spook*, 125.
11. Hazelgrove, *Spiritualism and British Society*, 13. Hazelgrove explores other reasons why interwar spiritualism was so popular, including its ability to unite religious, scientific, medical, and spiritual beliefs.
12. See Hereward Carrington, *Psychical Phenomena and the War* (New York: Dodd, Mead, & Co., 1918); and Sir Oliver Lodge, *Raymond, or Life After Death* (New York: George H. Doran Co., 1916). I examine Lodge's work in "Dead Men, Walking: Actors, Networks, and Actualized Metaphors in *Mrs. Dalloway* and *Raymond*," *NOVEL: A Forum on Fiction* 46, no. 2 (2013): 253–74.
13. Esyllt W. Jones, "Spectral Influenza: Winnipeg's Hamilton Family, Interwar Spiritualism, and Pandemic Disease," in *Epidemic Encounters: Influenza, Society, and Culture in Canada, 1918–20*, ed. Magda Fahrni and Esyllt W. Jones (Vancouver: UBC Press, 2012), 201. Jones details the experiences of the Hamilton family during the pandemic in Canada.
14. *RC*, Janet Coleman, now Dr. Janet Kimbrough, USA.
15. Like all of spiritualism, such figures predate the pandemic but fulfilled different cultural functions at different moments; in the nineteenth century, the occult detective was a popular literary figure; for a history, see Srdjan Smajić, *Ghost-Seers, Detectives, and Spiritualists: Theories of Vision in Victorian Literature and Science* (Cambridge: Cambridge University Press, 2010).
16. Jones, "Spectral Influenza," 203, 195, 198–99, 202.
17. Chris Willis, "Making the Dead Speak: Spiritualism and Detective Fiction," in *The Art of Detective Fiction*, ed. Warren Chernaik, Martin Swales, and Robert Vilain (New York: Palgrave Macmillan, 2000), 62.

18. Martyn Jolly, *Faces of the Living Dead: The Belief in Spirit Photography* (New York: Mark Batty, 2006), 92.

19. In the summer of 1927, a film crew led by William Fox filmed Doyle discussing spiritualism; the Doyle quotation is from this film, the only visual recording of Doyle known; interview at https://www.youtube.com/watch?v=XWjgt9PzYEM.

20. Booth, *The Doctor and the Detective*, 311; Jones, "Spectral Influenza," 201.

21. Jones, "Spectral Influenza," 201.

22. Doyle, *The Land of Mist* (1926), chap. 1; quotations from Project Gutenberg of Australia eBook, produced by Richard Scott (Urbana, Illinois: June 2006), http://gutenberg.net.au/ebooks06/0601351h.html, no page numbers; hereafter cited by chapter.

23. Doyle, *The Land of Mist*, chap. 1.

24. Doyle, *The Land of Mist*, chap. 1.

25. Doyle, *The Land of Mist*, chap. 1.

26. Doyle, *The Land of Mist*, chap. 14.

27. Doyle, *The Land of Mist*, chap. 14.

28. Doyle, *The Land of Mist*, chap. 16.

29. Doyle, *The Land of Mist*, chap. 16.

30. Doyle, *The Land of Mist*, chap. 16.

31. Doyle, *The Land of Mist*, chap. 16.

32. John M. Barry, *The Great Influenza: The Story of the Deadliest Pandemic in History* (New York: Penguin, 2004), 352. For Porter, see David A. Davis, "The Forgotten Apocalypse: Katherine Anne Porter's 'Pale Horse, Pale Rider,' Traumatic Memory, and the Influenza Pandemic of 1918," *Southern Literary Journal* 43, no. 2 (Spring 2011): 57.

33. Jones, "Spectral Influenza," 197.

34. Doyle, *The Land of Mist*, chap. 16.

35. Roach, *Spook*, 126.

36. The associate editor of *Scientific American*, J. Malcolm Bird, announced the contest in 1923: "Our Psychic Investigation," 128, no. 1 (January 1923): 6–7, 61, 67. The journal gathered scientists and others (including Harry Houdini) to study the medium Mina Crandon, reporting on the experiments in 1923 and 1924. Bird had attended séances with Doyle; see "Acid Test of Spiritualism," *New York Times* magazine section, April 22, 1923. The judges disagreed as to the outcome of the contest, with some finding proof and others fraud; see E. E. Free, "Our Psychic Investigation," *Scientific American* 131, no. 5 (November 1924): 304.

37. "Doyle Reaffirms Ectoplasm Belief," *New York Times*, October 1, 1922, 46.

38. Horace Green, "Is the Supernatural Natural?" *New York Times*, July 2, 1922, 37.

39. Green, "Is the Supernatural Natural?"

40. "Suicide Not an End of Ills, Says Doyle," *New York Times*, April 11, 1922, 11.

41. Jolly, *Faces*, 90.

42. Jolly, *Faces*, 8. Jolly offers a complete history of spirit photography from its nineteenth-century origins in *Faces of the Living Dead*.

43. "Doyle Shows Spirit Pictures of the Dead," *New York Times*, April 22, 1922, 13.

44. "Spirit Picture Stirs Spectators to Sobs," *New York Times*, April 7, 1923, 18. Subsequent quotations of event also from this article.

45. *RC*, Dora Almond, now Ferro, USA.

46. "Conan Doyle Back to Prove Spiritism," *New York Times*, April 5, 1923, 1.

47. Kevin Boon argues the defining feature of all zombies is "a loss of something essential that previous to zombification defined it as human": "And the Dead Shall Rise," in *Better Off Dead: The Evolution of the Zombie as Post-Human*, ed. Deborah Christie and Sarah Juliet Lauro (New York: Fordham University Press, 2011), 7.

48. George A. Romero's zombie films, in particular *Night of the Living Dead* (1968; Pittsburgh, PA: Image Ten) and *Dawn of the Dead* (1978; Pittsburgh and Monroeville, PA: Laurel Group Inc.), helped popularize the zombie. See, too, Max Brooks, *World War Z: An Oral History of the Zombie War* (New York: Three Rivers, 2006); Max Brooks, *The Zombie Survival Guide: Complete Protection from the Living Dead* (New York: Three Rivers, 2003); Colson Whitehead, *Zone One* (New York: Doubleday, 2011); and the TV series *The Walking Dead*, developed by Frank Darabont and produced by Robert Kirkman et al. (2010; Georgia: AMC).

49. See Peter Dendle, "The Zombie as Barometer of Cultural Anxiety," in *Monsters and the Monstrous: Myths and Metaphors of Enduring Evil*, ed. Niall Scott (New York: Rodopi, 2007), 48–57. Zombie criticism has proliferated almost as fast as zombies themselves. For a history, see John Cussans, *Undead Uprising: Haiti, Horror, and the Zombie Complex* (London: Strange Attractor, 2017); Greg Garrett argues for the zombie's therapeutic relevance in *Living with the Living Dead: The Wisdom of Zombie Apocalypse* (New York: Oxford University Press, 2017). Edited volumes include Sarah Juliet Lauro's recent *Zombie Theory: A Reader* (Minneapolis: Minnesota University Press, 2017); *Zombies Are Us: Essays on the Humanity of the Walking Dead*, ed. Christopher M. Moreman and Cory James Rushton (Jefferson, NC: McFarland, 2011); *Better Off Dead: The Evolution of the Zombie as Post-Human*, ed. Deborah Christie and Sarah Juliet Lauro; and *Generation Zombie: Essays on the Living Dead in Modern Culture*, ed. Stephanie Boluk and Wylie Lenz (Jefferson, NC: McFarland, 2011).

50. "The Lure of Horror," *The Psychologist* 24, no. 11 (November 2011): 813.

51. W. B. Seabrook, *The Magic Island* (New York: Harcourt, Brace: 1929), 93.

52. For more on the Haitian strain of zombies and links to slavery and exploitation, see Chera Kee, "'They are not men . . . they are dead bodies!': From Cannibal to Zombie and Back Again," 9–23; and Franck Dougoul, "'We are the mirror of your fears': Haitian Identity and Zombification," trans. Elisabeth M. Lore, 24–38, both in *Better off Dead*, ed. Christie and Lauro. See, too, Edward P. Comentale, "Zombie Race," in *The Year's Work at the Zombie Research Center*, ed. Edward P. Comentale and Aarron Jaffe (Bloomington: Indiana University Press, 2014), 276–314. Christopher M. Moreman and Cory James Rushton's collection *Race, Oppression, and the Zombie: Essays on Cross-Cultural Appropriations of the Caribbean Tradition* (Jefferson, NC: McFarland, 2011) offers a book-length treatment. For more on links to Seabrook, see Gyllian Phillips, "White Zombie and the Creole: William Seabrook's *The Magic Island* and American Imperialism in Haiti," in *Generation Zombie*, ed. Boluk and Lenz, 27–40.

53. See Stephanie Boluk and Wylie Lenz, "Infection, Media, and Capitalism: From Early Modern Plagues to Postmodern Zombies," *Journal for Early Modern Cultural Studies* 10, no. 2 (Fall/Winter 2010): 135.

54. *J'accuse* appeared in a 1919 version in France, a 1920 version in the United Kingdom, a 1921 version in the United States, and a later version in 1938; original movie

filmed on location in France and distributed by Pathé Frères and United Artists. Quotations from the restored and rereleased version of original film by Turner Classic Movies and Flicker Alley Digital from Lobster Film Studios, 2008.

55. The figure who awakens the dead may anticipate the controlling master figure from zombie movies of the 1930s and 1940s, but he is not enslaving them.

56. Jay Winter, *Sites of Memory, Sites of Mourning: The Great War in European Cultural History* (Cambridge: Cambridge University Press, 1995), 15–22.

57. Some limited critical work has been done on the links between zombies and plague. Boluk and Lenz, for example, in "Infection, Media, and Capitalism," explore how images of the plague in Ben Jonson, Daniel Defoe, and more recent zombie movies link to anxieties surrounding capitalism and technology.

58. Blaise Cendrars's full account can be found in his *Oeuvres complètes* (Paris: Éditions Denoël, 1965), 8:662–73. I have translated the original account into English here, with special thanks to Ray Hilliard for translation checks. I am also indebted to Jay Winter's account of the scene and for first introducing me to parts of Cendrars's descriptions of the death and funeral for Apollinaire: see *Sites of Memory*, 15–22. Winters nevertheless reads Apollinaire's pandemic death as part of the larger narrative of the war and the mourning for the war dead.

59. Cendrars, *Oeuvres complètes*, 8:668–69; author's translation.

60. See Peter Read, *Picasso and Apollinaire: The Persistence of Memory* (Berkeley: University of California Press, 2008), 113; and Jay Winter, *Sites of Memory*, 18–20, on Apollinaire's war injuries; see Winter, *Sites of Memory*, 15, for Cendrars's injuries.

61. Cendrars, *Oeuvres complètes*, 8:670–71; Read, *Picasso and Apollinaire*, 133–35, recounts other details of the deathbed scene and the mythologies that rose up around the death.

62. Cendrars, *Oeuvres complètes*, 8:663.

63. Cendrars, *Oeuvres complètes*, 8:663; author's translation.

64. Cendrars, *Oeuvres complètes*, 8:663.

65. Cendrars, *Oeuvres complètes*, 8:664; author's translation.

66. Cendrars, *Oeuvres complètes*, 8:664; author's translation.

67. Cendrars, *Oeuvres complètes*, 8:664; author's translation.

68. The timing for filming the Return of the Dead scene is somewhat unclear. Jay Winter, *Sites of Memory*, 21, notes that after the funeral, Cendrars goes back to Nice and films the scene, in which Cendrars himself appears; this account places the scene's shooting after the war's end, which conflicts with Abel Gance's claim, recorded by Kevin Brownlow, that he had recruited two thousand soldiers "to shoot the sequence of the Return of the Dead" and that "within a few weeks of their return [to the front], eighty per cent had been killed": *The Parade's Gone By* (New York: Knopf, 1968), 533. Both accounts may well be true, as different parts of the scene may have been shot at different times, or Gance may have been thinking of earlier scenes using soldiers; as Winter observes, "many of the soldiers in earlier scenes of Gance's film . . . had been killed" (15).

69. Gance published a synopsis of the movie, along with images, in 1922. His selection of four stills from the end of the film reinforces the narrative I suggest here: In the first, the dead are rising up; the second shows the parade of dead stumbling back to the village, with the third showing the dead outside the door. The final

image shows Edith—the film's central female character—and Jean Diaz, their arms stretched out, their faces half in shadow, mimicking the stances of the dead. See Gance, *J'accuse: d'après le film* (Paris: La Lampe Merveilleuse, 1922), 116–17.

70. See Brownlow's account in *The Parade's Gone By*, 537–38.

71. Winter, *Sites of Memory*, 21–22, notes the way Cendrars's experiences with Apollinaire are captured in the new split-screen scene.

72. Winter, *Sites of Memory*, 22.

73. Winter, *Sites of Memory*, 18.

74. Cendrars, *Oeuvres complètes*, 8:662; author's translation.

75. Christian Jarrett identifies the fear of being eaten, the fear of infection, and the fear of figures who are almost human (such as the undead) as central themes in horror literature; see "The Lure of Horror," 812–15.

76. I rely on Lovecraft's two principal biographers, S. T. Joshi and L. Sprague de Camp, for background information; see Joshi's two-volume work *I Am Providence: The Life and Times of H. P. Lovecraft* (New York: Hippocampus, 2010); and L. Sprague de Camp, *Lovecraft: A Biography* (New York: Doubleday, 1975); all quotations from Joshi from vol. 1. For Lovecraft's start at journalism, see Joshi, *I Am Providence*, 281.

77. Joshi, *I Am Providence*, 277, 300.

78. The Collier archive materials from Rhode Island recount the grim conditions: for the hospital, see in the collection Joseph E. Garland, *To Meet These Wants: The Story of the Rhode Island Hospital, 1863–1963* (Providence: Rhode Island Hospital, 1963); quotation on mass graves from *RC*, Anna Manna, now Goufas, RI, USA. See, too, Rhode Island letters from *RC*, Russell Booth, Catherine Dunphy, Elizabeth Baker (now Sullivan), Elsie D'Itri, Frances Hopkins, and Evander F. Hawes, all USA, and entry for Providence, RI, on the webpage *Influenza Encyclopedia: The American Influenza Epidemic of 1918–1919*, ed. J. Alex Navarro, Alexandra Stern, and Howard Markel, produced by the University of Michigan Center for the History of Medicine and Michigan Publishing, University of Michigan Library, 2016, http://www.influenzaarchive.org.

79. de Camp, *Lovecraft: A Biography*, 134; Joshi, *I Am Providence*, 301.

80. Qtd. in de Camp, *Lovecraft: A Biography*, 134, from March 30, 1919, letter from Lovecraft to R. Kleiner.

81. Joshi, *I Am Providence*, 369.

82. Peter Cannon links stories like "Nyarlathotep" to the French decadents in *H. P. Lovecraft* (Boston: Twayne, 1989), 31.

83. Joshi, *I Am Providence*, 370.

84. Quotations from "Nyarlathotep" from Project Gutenberg of Australia eBook, produced by Roy Glashan, May 2015, http://gutenberg.net.au/ebooks15/1500481h .html. David Haden offered an annotated version of the story on August 19, 2011, on his Lovecraft blog, http://www.tentaclii.wordpress.com, to mark Lovecraft's 121st birthday. Original story published in *The United Amateur* (November 1920).

85. The Lovecraft scholar David Haden also notes the link between the story's atmosphere and the pandemic; see note 8 of his online, annotated version of "Nyarlathotep." Haden argues Lovecraft may be critiquing here spiritualism's ideas of an invisible ether filling interstellar space through which the dead communicated with the living; see note 11 of Haden's annotated "Nyarlathotep" as well as his essay

"Lovecraft's 'Nyarlathotep': Science, Sound, and the Chaos of the Other," *Lovecraft in Historical Context: Essays*, Online Originals (Lulu, 2011), 44–49.

86. Lovecraft, "Nyarlathotep."

87. See note 25 of Haden's annotated "Nyarlathotep."

88. The Collier letters describe the screams and nightmares of influenza patients; Dorothy E. Jack, for example, remembers, "we were all delirious, having terrible nightmares," *RC*, UK.

89. Thomas Wolfe, *Look Homeward, Angel: A Story of the Buried Life* (1929; New York: Charles Scribner's Sons, 1957), 520.

90. Lovecraft, "Nyarlathotep."

91. Note 23 of Haden's annotated "Nyarlathotep"; Joshi, *I Am Providence*, 370.

92. Lovecraft, "Nyarlathotep." Lovecraft disliked spiritualism and in 1925 was in the early stages of writing a book with the magician Harry Houdini to expose séance tricks. The book was never finished, as Houdini died in 1926; de Camp, *H. P. Lovecraft*, 214.

93. Lovecraft, "Nyarlathotep."

94. Many scholars have explored Lovecraft's racism; see, for example, Joshi, *I Am Providence*, 110–14, 137–39, 212–18, 280–81; Leif Sorensen, "A Weird Modernist Archive: Pulp Fiction, Pseudobiblia, H. P. Lovecraft," *Modernism/modernity* 17, no. 3 (September 2010): 501–22; Tracy Bealer, in "'The Innsmouth Look': H. P. Lovecraft's Ambivalent Modernism," *Journal of Philosophy: A Cross-Disciplinary Inquiry* 6, no. 14 (Winter 2011): 44–50; and Michael Saler, "Modern Enchantments: The Canny Wonders and Uncanny Others of H. P. Lovecraft," *The Space Between* 2, no. 1 (2006): 11–32.

95. Lovecraft, "Nyarlathotep."

96. Joshi, *I Am Providence*, 411.

97. H. P. Lovecraft, "Herbert West—Reanimator," reprinted in *Tales*, ed. Peter Straub (New York: Library of America, 2005), 28, 29, hereafter cited as *HW* and by page numbers in endnotes in clusters, if multiple quotations.

98. Lovecraft, *HW*, 29, 31.

99. *RC*, Mary S. McGrath, USA, recounting her father's words.

100. Lovecraft, *HW*, 30.

101. Lovecraft, *HW*, 30, 32–33.

102. Lovecraft, *HW*, 33, 33.

103. Lovecraft, *HW*, 25, 37, 38.

104. Lovecraft, *HW*, 47, 44.

105. Lovecraft, *HW*, 50, 36, 51.

106. Lovecraft, *HW*, 52–53. Soldiers with disfigured faces were sometimes provided masks that mimicked their original facial shape; one of the best known makers of these masks was the Boston sculptor Anna Coleman Watts, who worked in France and frequently gave interviews about her work after her return; see Caroline Alexander, "Faces of War," *Smithsonian Magazine* (February 2007), https://www.smithsonianmag.com/arts-culture/faces-of-war-145799854/.

107. Lovecraft, *HW*, 53–54.

108. Lovecraft, *HW*, all 54.

109. "Cool Air" was written in 1926 and published first in *Tales of Magic and Mystery* 1, no. 4 (March 1928). Reprinted in Lovecraft, *Tales*, 158–66; publication information in *Tales*, 823.

110. Lovecraft, "Cool," 162.
111. The story takes place in 1923, so Dr. Munoz's illness eighteen years before predates the pandemic. The reference would nevertheless have recalled the recent outbreak to the readers, and the selection of "18" may hint of the grim marker of 1918.
112. Lovecraft, "Cool," 158.
113. Lovecraft, "Cool," 161, 161, 161, 163.
114. Lovecraft, "Cool," 164, 162, 164, 164.
115. Lovecraft, "Cool," 158.
116. Lovecraft, "In the Vault," originally published in *Tryout* in November 1925; reprinted in *The Dunwich Horror and Others: The Best Supernatural Stories of H. P. Lovecraft*, ed. August Derleth (Sauk City, WI: Arkham House, 1963), 10–18.
117. John M. Barry, *The Great Influenza*, 223.
118. Nancy K. Bristow, *American Pandemic: The Lost Worlds of the 1918 Influenza Epidemic* (New York: Oxford University Press, 2012), 52.
119. *RC*, Russell Booth, USA (Cranston, RI).
120. Lovecraft, "Vault," all 10.
121. Lovecraft, "Vault," 12.
122. Lovecraft, "Vault," 15.
123. Lovecraft, "Vault," 12.
124. Lovecraft, "Vault," 16.
125. Lovecraft, "Vault," 18, 12.
126. Lovecraft, "Vault," 16–17.

CODA: THE STRUCTURE OF ILLNESS, THE SHAPE OF LOSS

1. James Joyce, *Ulysses*, ed. Hans Walter Gabler (1922; New York: Vintage, 1986); William Faulkner, *As I Lay Dying* (1930; New York: Vintage, 1991); Ernest Hemingway, *To Have and Have Not* (1937; New York: Scribner, 1996).
2. I have completed research on both influences, but they did not fit within the scope of this project and will be published as separate articles. The controversial 1920s revisions of the Book of Common Prayer shifted services and their wording in response to the era's losses, and the Church of Latter Day Saints added Covenant 138, "A Vision of the Redemption of the Dead," after a vision by Joseph E. Smith. See E. Clowes Chorley, *The New American Prayer Book: Its History and Contents* (New York: Macmillan, 1929); George S. Tate, "'The Great World of the Spirits of the Dead': Death, the Great War, and the 1918 Influenza Pandemic as Context for Doctrine and Covenants 138," *Brigham Young University Studies Quarterly* 46, no. 1 (2007): 4–40. For a summary of Selbit's trick, see Jim Steinmeyer, *Hiding the Elephant: How Magicians Invented the Impossible and Learned to Disappear* (New York: Carroll & Graf, 2003).
3. Notebook reproduced in Virginia Woolf, *To the Lighthouse: The Original Holograph Draft*, ed. Susan Dick (Toronto: Toronto University Press, 1982), app. A, p. 11 in original notebook.
4. Critics have read "Time Passes" from many angles, investigating the section's abstract language and narrative voice, the experimental play of its temporal registers, the impact of Woolf's own early bereavements, and the ways it traces the

trauma of the war. For its abstraction yet also its lessons in empathy, see David Sherman, "A Plot Unraveling Into Ethics: Woolf, Levinas, and 'Time Passes,'" *Woolf Studies Annual* 13 (2007): 159–79. For its temporal philosophy and links to war dead, see Ann Banfield, "Time Passes: Virginia Woolf, Post-Impressionism, and Cambridge Time," *Poetics Today* 24, no. 3 (Fall 2003): 471–516. For links to Woolf's losses, see Jane de Gay, *Virginia Woolf's Novels and the Literary Past* (Edinburgh: Edinburgh University Press, 2006), 100; for its sense of mother loss, see Christine Froula, *Virginia Woolf and the Bloomsbury Avant-Garde: War, Civilization, Modernity* (New York: Columbia University Press, 2004), 152–58, 370n55. For the war and Woolf's push away from direct references to it, see James M. Haule (and Virginia Woolf and Charles Mauron), "'Le Temps Passe' and the Original Typescript: An Early Version of the 'Time Passes' Section of *To the Lighthouse*," *Twentieth Century Literature* 29, no. 3 (Autumn 1983): 267–311; and Haule's essay "*To the Lighthouse* and the Great War: The Evidence of Virginia Woolf's Revisions of 'Time Passes,'" in *Virginia Woolf and War: Fiction, Reality, Myth*, ed. Mark Hussey (Syracuse, NY: Syracuse University Press, 1992), 164–79.

5. Virginia Woolf, "On Being Ill," originally published in *New Criterion*, January 1926; reprinted in *The Essays of Virginia Woolf*, vol. 4: *1925–1928*, ed. Andrew McNeillie (New York: Harvest/Harcourt, 1994), 319. Hereafter cited as *OBI*.

6. Virginia Woolf, *To the Lighthouse*, intro. and annotated by Mark Hussey (1927; New York: Harvest/Harcourt, 2005), 129; hereafter cited as *TTL*.

7. Woolf, *TTL*, 130. Recall that Thomas Wolfe portrays a similar emotion at the end of *Look Homeward, Angel*, when the main character expresses his surprise that death had entered the town square, declaring over and over "But not here!" Thomas Wolfe, *Look Homeward, Angel: A Story of the Buried Life* (1929; New York: Charles Scribner's Sons, 1957), 517.

8. Woolf, *TTL*, 129–30.

9. Virginia Woolf, *Mrs. Dalloway* (1925; New York: Harvest/Harcourt, 2005), 181.

10. Woolf, *TTL*, 130, 130.

11. Woolf, *TTL*, 130, 131.

12. Woolf, *TTL*, 132.

13. Woolf, *OBI*, 318.

14. William Butler Yeats, "The Second Coming" (1920), in *The Variorum Edition of the Poems of W. B. Yeats*, ed. Peter Allt and Russell K. Alspach (New York: Macmillan, 1957), line 4.

15. Woolf, *TTL*, 138.

16. Woolf, *TTL*, 138–39.

17. See, for example, de Gay, *Virginia Woolf's Novels*, 100; and Froula, *Virginia Woolf and the Bloomsbury Avant-Garde*, 370n55.

18. Woolf, *TTL*, 132, 136.

19. See chapter 3; Quentin Bell, *Virginia Woolf: A Biography* (New York: Harvest/HBJ, 1972), 39; and Douglas Orr, *Virginia Woolf's Illnesses*, ed. Wayne K. Chapman (Clemson, SC: Clemson University Digital Press, 2004), 27.

20. See the interview with William Maxwell by John Seabrook, "The Art of Fiction No. 71," *Paris Review* 85 (Fall 1982): 112. Maxwell's biographer Barbara Burkhardt notes both the parallels and the differences between Mrs. Ramsay and the mother

in Maxwell's novel in *William Maxwell: A Literary Life* (Urbana: University of Illinois Press, 2005), 68–69.

21. Woolf, *TTL*, 137.

22. Hermione Lee, *Virginia Woolf* (New York: Knopf, 1997), 226; Froula, *Virginia Woolf and the Bloomsbury Avant-Garde*, 21.

23. Woolf, *TTL*, 132.

24. See, for example, the opening of *A Farewell to Arms* (1929; New York: Scribner, 2014), 3–4, where Hemingway repeatedly links soldiers to fallen leaves.

25. Woolf, *OBI*, 321.

26. Woolf, *TTL*, 137.

27. Niall Johnson, *Britain and the 1918–1919 Influenza Pandemic: A Dark Epilogue* (London: Routledge, 2006), 66.

28. Woolf, *TTL*, 132.

29. Woolf, *TTL*, 138.

30. Woolf, *TTL*, 145.

31. Woolf, *TTL*, 146, 146.

32. Woolf, *TTL*, 133.

33. See Ed Yong, "The Next Plague Is Coming: Is America Ready?" *The Atlantic* (July/August 2018), https://www.theatlantic.com/magazine/archive/2018/07/when-the-next-plague-hits/561734/.

34. See Lena H. Sun, "CDC to Cut by 80 Percent Efforts to Prevent Global Disease Outbreak," *Washington Post*, February 1, 2018. See too the proposed 2018 CDC budget, which includes a modest sum for influenza planning but slashes many other prevention programs both nationally and globally: "Overview of the CDC FY 2018 Budget Request," CDC, May 23, 2017, https://www.cdc.gov/budget/documents/fy2018/fy-2018-cdc-budget-overview.pdf. See also the proposed "FY 2019 President's Budget" on the CDC website, March 23, 2018, https://www.cdc.gov/budget/documents/fy2019/fy-2019-detail-table.pdf.

35. Yong, "The Next Plague Is Coming."

BIBLIOGRAPHY

"Acid Test of Spiritualism." *New York Times Magazine Section*, April 22, 1923.

Ackroyd, Peter. *T. S. Eliot: A Life*. New York: Simon and Schuster, 1984.

Alexander, Caroline. "Faces of War." *Smithsonian Magazine*. February 2007. https://www.smithsonianmag.com/arts-culture/faces-of-war-145799854/.

Allen, James Lovic. "What Rough Beast? Yeats's 'The Second Coming' and *A Vision*." *REAL: The Yearbook of Research in English and American Literature* 3 (1985): 223–63.

Ammons, A. R. "Triphammer Bridge." In *The Selected Poems*, expanded ed. New York: Norton: 1986.

Annals of the Pickett-Thomson Research Laboratory. Vol. 10. London: Baillière, Tindall & Cox, 1934.

Banfield, Ann. "Time Passes: Virginia Woolf, Post-Impressionism, and Cambridge Time." *Poetics Today* 24, no. 3 (Fall 2003): 471–516.

Barrow, Robin. "An Identification in Yeats's *A Vision (B)*." *Notes and Queries* 51, no. 2 (June 2004): 162–163.

Barry, John M. *The Great Influenza: The Story of the Deadliest Pandemic in History*. New York: Penguin, 2004.

Barthes, Roland. "On the Subject of Violence." In *The Grain of the Voice: Interviews, 1962–1980*, trans. Linda Coverdale, 306–11. Evanston, IL: Northwestern University Press, 2009.

Bealer, Tracy. "'The Innsmouth Look:' H. P. Lovecraft's Ambivalent Modernism." *Journal of Philosophy: A Cross-Disciplinary Inquiry* 6, no. 14 (Winter 2011): 44–50.

Beckman, Karen. *Vanishing Women: Magic, Film, and Feminism*. Durham, NC: Duke University Press, 2003.

Beiner, Guy, Patricia Marsh, and Ida Milne. "Greatest Killer of the Twentieth Century: The Great Flu of 1918–1919." *20th Century Social Perspectives* 17, no. 2 (March/April 2009). History Ireland webpage. https://www.historyireland.com/20th

-century-contemporary-history/greatest-killer-of-the-twentieth-century-the-great
-flu-of-1918-19/.

Bell, Quentin. *Virginia Woolf: A Biography*. New York: Harvest/HBJ, 1972.

Belling, Catherine. "Overwhelming the Medium: Fiction and the Trauma of the Pandemic Influenza in 1918." *Literature and Medicine* 28, no. 1 (Spring 2009): 55–81.

Benjamin, Walter. "Critique of Violence." In *Selected Writings*, vol. 1: *1913–1929*, ed. Marcus Bullock and Michael W. Jennings, 236–52. Cambridge, MA: Harvard University Press, 1996.

Bird, J. Malcolm. "Our Psychic Investigation." *Scientific American* 128, no. 1 (January 1923): 6–7, 61, 67.

Black, Ezekiel. "Mouthlessness and Ineffability in World War I Poetry and *The Waste Land*." *War, Literature, and the Arts: An International Journal of the Humanities* 25 (2013): 1–17.

Blum, Deborah. *Ghost Hunters: William James and the Search for Scientific Proof of Life After Death*. New York: Penguin, 2006.

Boccaccio, Giovanni. *The Decameron* [1353]. Trans. and ed. Wayne A. Rebhorn. New York: Norton, 2016.

Boluk, Stephanie, and Wylie Lenz, eds. *Generation Zombie: Essays on the Living Dead in Modern Culture*. Jefferson: McFarland, 2011.

——. "Infection, Media, and Capitalism: From Early Modern Plagues to Postmodern Zombies." *Journal for Early Modern Cultural Studies* 10, no. 2 (Fall/Winter 2010): 126–47.

Boon, Kevin. "And the Dead Shall Rise." In *Better Off Dead*, ed. Deborah Christie and Sarah Juliet Lauro, 5–8.

Booth, Allyson. *Postcards from the Trenches: Negotiating the Space Between Modernism and the First World War*. New York: Oxford University Press, 1996.

Booth, Martin. *The Doctor and the Detective: A Biography of Sir Arthur Conan Doyle* [1997]. New York: St. Martin's Press, 2013.

Bourke, Joanna. *Dismembering the Male: Men's Bodies, Britain, and the Great War*. London: Reaktion, 1996.

Bradford, Curtis B. *Yeats at Work*. Carbondale: Southern Illinois University Press, 1965.

Breidbart, Emily. "The Forgotten Influenza of 1918: When a Strong Immune System Becomes a Weakness." *Clinical Correlations: The NYU Langone Online Journal of Medicine*, September 23, 2009. https://www.clinicalcorrelations.org/?p=1862.

Bristow, Nancy K. *American Pandemic: The Lost Worlds of the 1918 Influenza Epidemic*. New York: Oxford University Press, 2012.

Brooke, Rupert. "The Soldier" [1914]. In *The Penguin Book of First World War Poetry*, ed. George Walter, 108. New York: Penguin, 2004.

Brooks, Max. *World War Z: An Oral History of the Zombie War*. New York: Three Rivers, 2006.

——. *The Zombie Survival Guide: Complete Protection from the Living Dead*. New York: Three Rivers, 2003.

Brownlow, Kevin. *The Parade's Gone By . . .* New York: Knopf, 1968.

Bureau of Military History. Collection of Military History and National Archives, Ireland, 1913–1921. https://www.bureauofmilitaryhistory.ie.

Burkhardt, Barbara. *William Maxwell: A Literary Life*. Urbana: University of Illinois Press, 2005.

Butler, Judith. *Frames of War: When Is Life Grievable?* London: Verso, 2009.

Byerly, Carol R. *Fever of War: The Influenza Epidemic in the U.S. Army During World War I.* New York: New York University Press, 2005.

Camus, Albert. *The Plague* [1947]. Trans. Stuart Gilbert. New York: Vintage, 1991.

Cannon, Peter. *H. P. Lovecraft.* Boston: Twayne, 1989.

Cardinal, Agnès, Dorothy Goldman, and Judith Hattaway, eds. *Women's Writing on the First World War.* Oxford: Oxford University Press, 2002.

Carel, Havi. *Phenomenology of Illness.* Oxford: Oxford University Press, 2016.

Carr, John Dickson. *The Life of Sir Arthur Conan Doyle.* New York: Carroll & Graf, 2003.

Carrington, Hereward. *Psychical Phenomena and the War.* New York: Dodd, Mead, & Co., 1918.

Caruth, Cathy, ed. *Trauma: Explorations in Memory.* Baltimore, MD: Johns Hopkins University Press, 1995.

——. *Unclaimed Experience: Trauma, Narrative, and History.* Baltimore, MD: Johns Hopkins University Press, 1996.

Cather, Willa. *The Kingdom of Art: Willa Cather's First Principles and Critical Statements, 1893–1896.* Ed. Bernice Slote. Lincoln: University of Nebraska Press, 1966.

——. *One of Ours.* New York: Knopf, 1922.

——. *The Selected Letters of Willa Cather.* Ed. Andrew Jewell and Janis Stout. New York: Knopf, 2013.

Cendrars, Blaise. *Oeuvre Complètes.* Vol. 8. Paris: Éditions Denoël, 1965.

Centers for Disease Control and Prevention. "Estimating Seasonal Influenza-Associated Deaths in the United States." CDC webpage. January 29, 2018. https://www.cdc.gov/flu/about/disease/us_flu-related_deaths.htm.

——. "FY 2019 President's Budget." CDC webpage. March 23, 2018. https://www.cdc.gov/budget/documents/fy2019/fy-2019-detail-table.pdf.

——. "Overview of the CDC FY 2018 Budget Request." CDC webpage. May 23, 2017. https://www.cdc.gov/budget/documents/fy2018/fy-2018-cdc-budget-overview.pdf.

Cervo, Nathan. "Yeats's 'The Second Coming.'" *Explicator* 59, no. 2 (2001): 93–95.

Chandra, Siddharth, Goran Kuljanin, and Jennifer Wray. "Mortality from the Influenza Pandemic of 1918–1919: The Case of India." *Demography* 49, no. 3 (August 2012): 857–65.

Chapman, Wayne K. "The W. B. and George Yeats Library: A Short-Title Catalogue." Clemson University Digital Press (2006). Item 238 and 238a (YL231 and 231a). https://tigerprints.clemson.edu/cgi/viewcontent.cgi?article=1001&context=cudp_bibliography.

Charon, Rita. *Narrative Medicine: Honoring the Stories of Illness.* New York: Oxford University Press, 2008.

Chinitz, David E, ed. *A Companion to T. S. Eliot.* New York: Wiley Blackwell, 2014.

——. "A Vast Wasteland? Eliot and Popular Culture." In *A Companion to T. S. Eliot,* ed. David E. Chinitz, 66–78.

Chorley, E. Clowes. *The New American Prayer Book: Its History and Contents.* New York: Macmillan, 1929.

Christensen, Allen Conrad. *Nineteenth-Century Narratives of Contagion: "Our Feverish Contact."* New York: Routledge, 2005.

Christie, Deborah, and Sarah Juliet Lauro, eds. *Better Off Dead: The Evolution of the Zombie as Post-Human.* New York: Fordham University Press, 2011.

Clewell, Tammy. *Mourning, Modernism, Postmodernism*. New York: Palgrave Macmillan, 2009.

Coates, Kimberly Engdahl. "Phantoms, Fancy (and) Symptoms: Virginia Woolf and the Art of Being Ill." *Woolf Studies Annual* 18 (2012): 1–28.

Cole, Sarah. *At the Violet Hour: Modernism and Violence in England and Ireland*. New York: Oxford University Press, 2012.

——. *Modernism, Male Friendship, and the First World War*. Cambridge: Cambridge University Press, 2003.

——. "Siegfried Sassoon." In *The Cambridge Companion to the Poetry of the First World War*, ed. Santanu Das, 94–104. Cambridge: Cambridge University Press, 2013.

Collier, Richard. *The Plague of the Spanish Lady: The Influenza Pandemic of 1918–1919*. London: Macmillan, 1974.

Comentale, Edward P. "Zombie Race." In *The Year's Work at the Zombie Research Center*, ed. Edward P. Comentale and Aarron Jaffe, 276–314. Bloomington: Indiana University Press, 2014.

"Conan Doyle Back to Prove Spiritualism." *New York Times*, April 5, 1923.

Conway, Kathlyn. *Beyond Words: Illness and the Limits of Expression*. Albuquerque: University of New Mexico Press, 2007.

Cooke, Miriam, and Angela Woollacott, eds. *Gendering War Talk*. Princeton, NJ: Princeton University Press, 1993.

Crawford, Robert. *Young Eliot: From St. Louis to* The Waste Land. New York: Farrar, Straus and Giroux, 2015.

Crosby, Alfred W. *America's Forgotten Pandemic: The Influenza of 1918*. 2nd ed. Cambridge: Cambridge University Press, 2003.

Crosby, Molly Caldwell. *Asleep: The Forgotten Epidemic That Remains One of Medicine's Greatest Mysteries*. New York: Berkley Books, 2010.

Culleton, Claire. "Joycean Synchronicity in Wolfe's *Look Homeward, Angel*." *The Thomas Wolfe Review* 13, no. 2 (1989): 49–52.

Cussans, John. *Undead Uprising: Haiti, Horror, and the Zombie Complex*. London: Strange Attractor, 2017.

Davis, David. "The Forgotten Apocalypse: Katherine Anne Porter's 'Pale Horse, Pale Rider,' Traumatic Memory, and the Influenza Pandemic of 1918." *Southern Literary Journal* 43, no. 2 (Spring 2011): 55–74.

de Camp, L. Sprague. *Lovecraft: A Biography*. New York: Doubleday, 1975.

de Gay, Jane. *Virginia Woolf's Novels and the Literary Past*. Edinburgh: Edinburgh University Press, 2006.

de Kruif, Paul. *Microbe Hunters*. New York: Harcourt Brace, 1926.

De Paolo, Charles. *Pandemic Influenza in Fiction: A Critical Study*. Jefferson, NC: McFarland, 2014.

Deane, Seamus. " 'The Second Coming': Coming Second; Coming in a Second." *Irish University Review* 22, no. 1 (Spring/Summer 1992): 92–100.

Defoe, Daniel. *A Journal of the Plague Year* [1722]. Ed. Paula R. Backscheider. New York: Norton, 1992.

——. *A Journal of the Plague Year*. In *Romances and Narratives*, 16 vols., vol. 9. Ed. George A. Aitken, ill. John Butler Yeats. London: J. M. Dent & Co., 1895.

Degoul, Franck. "'We are the mirror of your fears': Haitian Identity and Zombifica-tion." Trans. Elisabeth M. Lore. In *Better Off Dead*, ed. Deborah Christie and Sarah Juliet Lauro, 24–38.

DeMeester, Karen. "Trauma and Recovery in Virginia Woolf's *Mrs. Dalloway*." *Modern Fiction Studies* 44, no. 3 (Fall 1998): 649–73.

Dendle, Peter. "The Zombie as Barometer of Cultural Anxiety." In *Monsters and the Monstrous: Myths and Metaphors of Enduring Evil*, ed. Niall Scott, 45–57. New York: Rodopi, 2007.

Detloff, Madelyn. "Woolf and Crip Theory." In *A Companion to Virginia Woolf*, ed. Jessica Berman, 277–89. New York: Wiley-Blackwell, 2016.

Doggett, Rob. "Writing Out (of) Chaos: Constructions of History in Yeats's 'Nineteen Hundred and Nineteen' and 'Meditations in the Time of Civil War.'" *Twentieth Century Literature* 47, no. 2 (Summer, 2001): 137–68.

Doležal, Joshua. "'Waste in a Great Enterprise': Influenza, Modernism, and *One of Ours*." *Literature and Medicine* 28, no. 1 (Spring 2009): 82–101.

Dorney, John. "Ireland and the Great Flu Epidemic of 1918." *The Irish Story*. May 16, 2013. http://www.theirishstory.com/2013/05/16/ireland-and-the-great-flu-epidemic-of-1918/.

Downton Abbey. Season 2. Created by Julian Fellowes. Carnival Film & Television and Masterpiece Theatre, 2012. DVD.

Doyle, Arthur Conan. Film interview. Film crew led by William Fox. Summer 1927. https://www.youtube.com/watch?v=XWjgt9PzYEM.

——. *The History of Spiritualism*. Vol. 1. London: Cassell and Co., 1926. http://www.archive.org/details/historyofspiritu015638mbp.

——. *The Land of Mist* [1926]. Produced by Richard Scott. Project Gutenberg of Australia eBook. Urbana, Illinois: June 2006. http://gutenberg.net.au/ebooks06/0601351h.html.

"Doyle Reaffirms Ectoplasm Belief." *New York Times*, October 1, 1922, 46.

"Doyle Shows Spirit Pictures of the Dead." *New York Times*, April 22, 1922, 1.

Dungan, Myles. "Counting the Irish Dead." *Irish Times*, October 22, 2014. https://www.irishtimes.com/culture/heritage/counting-the-irish-dead-1.1951023.

Durr, Jimmie Carol Still. "*Look Homeward, Angel*, Thomas Wolfe's *Ulysses*." *Southern Studies* 24, no. 1 (Spring 1985): 54–68.

Eberly, David. "Gassed: Virginia Woolf and Dentistry." *Virginia Woolf Miscellany* 90 (2016), Special issue, "Virginia Woolf and Illness," ed. Cheryl Hindrichs, 53–55.

Eckard, Paula Gallant. "'A flash of fire': Illness and the Body in *Look Homeward, Angel*." *The Thomas Wolfe Review* 34, no. 1/2 (2010): 6–24.

Eliot, T. S. *The Letters of T. S. Eliot*. Vol. 1: *1898–1922*. Ed. Valerie Eliot and Hugh Haughton. New Haven, CT: Yale University Press, 2011.

——. *The Letters of T. S. Eliot*. Vol. 2: *1923–1925*. Ed. Valerie Eliot and Hugh Haughton. London: Faber and Faber, 2009.

——. "London Letter." *The Dial* 71 (July–December 1921): 213–17. Accessed at Hathi Trust Digital: https://hdl.handle.net/2027/uc1.b2924815.

——. "Tradition and the Individual Talent." First published in two parts in *The Egoist* 6, no. 4 (September 1919): 54–55; and 6, no. 5 (December 1919): 72–73. Reprinted in *Selected Prose of T. S. Eliot*, ed. Frank Kermode, 37–44. New York: Harcourt Brace, 1975.

——. *The Waste Land* [1922]. In *Collected Poems: 1909–1962*. London: Faber and Faber, 1963.

——. *The Waste Land* [1922]. Norton Critical ed. Ed. Michael North. New York: Norton, 2001.

——. *The Waste Land: A Facsimile and Transcript of the Original Drafts Including the Annotations of Ezra Pound*. Ed. Valerie Eliot. London: Faber and Faber, 1971.

Fahrni, Magda, and Esyllt W. Jones, eds. *Epidemic Encounters: Influenza, Society, and Culture in Canada, 1918–1920*. Vancouver: University of British Columbia Press, 2012.

Fanning, Patricia J. *Influenza and Inequality: One Town's Tragic Response to the Great Epidemic of 1918*. Amherst: University of Massachusetts Press, 2010.

Farmer, Paul. *Infections and Inequalities: The Modern Plagues*. Berkeley: University of California Press, 1999.

Faulkner, William. *As I Lay Dying* [1930]. New York: Vintage, 1991.

Faust, Drew Gilpin. *This Republic of Suffering: Death and the American Civil War*. New York: Vintage, 2008.

Fisher, Jane Elizabeth. *Envisioning Disease, Gender, and War: Women's Narratives of the 1918 Influenza Pandemic*. New York: Palgrave Macmillan, 2012.

Foley, Caitriona. *The Last Irish Plague: The Great Flu Epidemic in Ireland 1918–19*. Dublin: Irish Academic Press, 2011.

Frank, Arthur W. *The Wounded Storyteller: Body, Illness, and Ethics*. 2nd ed. Chicago: Chicago University Press, 2013.

Frazer, Sir James G. *The Golden Baugh: A Study in Magic and Religion*. Abridged ed. London: Macmillan, 1922.

Free, E. E. "Our Psychic Investigation." *Scientific American* 131, no. 5 (November 1924): 304.

Froula, Christine. "Mrs. Dalloway's Postwar Elegy: Women, War, and the Art of Mourning." *Modernism/modernity* 9, no. 1 (January 2002): 125–63.

——. *Virginia Woolf and the Bloomsbury Avant-Garde: War, Civilization, Modernity*. New York: Columbia University Press, 2004.

Fussell, Paul. *The Great War and Modern Memory*. Oxford: Oxford University Press, 1977.

Gamble, Vanessa Northington. "'There Wasn't a Lot of Comforts in Those Days': African Americans, Public Health, and the 1918 Influenza Epidemic." *Public Health Report* 125, no. 3 (2010): 114–22.

Gance, Abel, dir. *J'accuse* [1919–1921]. France: Pathé Frères and United Artists. Restored and rereleased in original version by Turner Classic Movies and Flicker Alley Digital from Lobster Film Studios, 2008. DVD.

——. *J'accuse. D'après le film*. Paris: La Lampe Merveilleuse, 1922.

Garland, Joseph E. *To Meet These Wants: The Story of the Rhode Island Hospital, 1863–1963*. Rhode Island Hospital, 1963. Accessed in the Collier Archive, United States Box.

Garettt, Greg. *Living with the Living Dead: The Wisdom of Zombie Apocalypse*. New York: Oxford University Press, 2017.

Gilbert, Sandra. "Soldier's Heart: Literary Men, Literary Women, and the Great War." *Signs* 8, no. 3 (Spring 1983): 422–50.

Gilbert, Sandra M., and Susan Gubar. *No Man's Land: The Place of the Woman Writer in the Twentieth Century*. Vol. 2: *Sexchanges*. New Haven, CT: Yale University Press, 1991.

Givner, Joan. *Katherine Anne Porter: A Life*. Rev. ed. Athens: University of Georgia Press, 1991.

Graves, Robert. *Good-Bye to All That* [1929]. New York: Doubleday, 1985.

Grayzel, Susan R., and Tammy M. Proctor, eds. *Gender and the Great War*. Oxford: Oxford University Press, 2017.

"The Great Death." *Times* (London), February 2, 1921, 11.

Green, Horace. "Is the Supernatural Natural?" *New York Times*, July 2, 1922, 37.

Grist, Norman Roy. "Pandemic Influenza 1918." *British Medical Journal* (December 22–29, 1979): 1632–33.

Haden, David, ed. "Annotated version of Lovecraft's 'Nyarlathotep.'" *Tentaclii: H. P. Lovecraft Blog*. August 19, 2011. http://www.tentaclii.wordpress.com.

——. "Lovecraft's 'Nyarlathotep': Science, Sound, and the Chaos of the Other." In *Lovecraft in Historical Context: Essays*, 44–49. Online Originals: Lulu Press, 2011.

Harper, George Mills. *The Making of Yeats's A Vision*. Vol. 1: *A Study of the Automatic Script*. London: Palgrave UK, 1987.

Harper, Margaret Mills. *Wisdom of Two: The Spiritual and Literary Collaboration of George and W. B. Yeats*. Oxford: Oxford University Press, 2006.

Harris, James C. "Self-Portrait After Spanish Flu." *Archives of General Psychiatry* 63 (April 2006): 354–55.

Hauck, Christina. "Not One, Not Two: Eliot and Buddhism." In *A Companion to T. S. Eliot*, ed. David E. Chinitz, 40–52.

Haule, James M. "*To the Lighthouse* and the Great War: The Evidence of Virginia Woolf's Revisions of 'Time Passes.'" In *Virginia Woolf and War: Fiction, Reality, Myth*, ed. Mark Hussey, 164–79. Syracuse, NY: Syracuse University Press, 1992.

Haule, James M., Virginia Woolf, and Charles Mauron. "'Le Temps Passe' and the Original Typescript: An Early Version of the 'Time Passes' Section of *To the Lighthouse*." *Twentieth Century Literature* 29, no. 3 (Autumn 1983): 267–311.

Hay, Simon. "Modernist Ghosts, Transatlantic Apparitions: *The Waste Land*." *Journal X: A Journal of Culture and Criticism* 7, no. 2 (Spring 2003): 129–54.

Hazelgrove, Jenny. *Spiritualism and British Society Between the Wars*. Manchester: Manchester University Press, 2000.

Hemingway, Ernest. *A Farewell to Arms* [1929]. New York: Scribner, 2014.

——. *To Have and Have Not* [1937]. New York: Scribner, 1996.

Henke, Suzette. "Virginia Woolf's Septimus Smith: An Analysis of 'Paraphrenia' and the Schizophrenic Use of Language." *Literature and Psychology* 31, no. 4 (1981): 13–23.

Henke, Suzette, and David Eberly, eds. *Virginia Woolf and Trauma: Embodied Texts*. New York: Pace University Press, 2007.

Higonnet, Margaret R. "Not So Quiet in No-Woman's-Land." In *Gendering War Talk*, ed. Miriam Cooke and Angela Woollacott, 205–26.

Hindrichs, Cheryl. "Introduction." *Virginia Woolf Miscellany* 90 (Fall 2016), special issue, ed. Cheryl Hindrichs, 44–48.

Hirsch, Marianne, and Leo Spitzer. "Vulnerable Lives: Secrets, Noise, Dust." *Profession* 17 (2011): 51–67.

Hite, Molly. "Tonal Cues and Uncertain Values: Affect and Ethics in *Mrs. Dalloway*." *Narrative* 18, no. 3 (October 2010): 249–75.

Hodgkinson, Peter E. "Clearing the Dead." *Centre for First World War Studies* 3, no. 1 (September 2007).

Honigsbaum, Mark. *Living with Enza: The Forgotten Story of Britain and the Great Flu Pandemic of 1918*. London: Macmillan, 2009.

Hovanec, Caroline. "Of Bodies, Families, and Communities: Refiguring the 1918 Influenza Pandemic." *Literature and Medicine* 29, no. 1 (Spring 2011): 161–81.

Hrebik, Dale. "William (Keepers) Maxwell, (Jr.)." In *Dictionary of Literary Biography*, vol. 218: *American Short-Story Writers Since World War II: Second Series*, ed. Patrick Meanor and Gwen Crane, 205–13. Detroit, MA: Gale, 2000.

Hussey, Mark. "Introduction." In *On Being Ill with Notes from Sick Rooms*, by Virginia Woolf and Julia Stephen, 33–48. Ashfield, MA: Paris Press, 2012.

——, ed. *Virginia Woolf and War: Fiction, Reality, and Myth*. Syracuse, NY: Syracuse University Press, 1991.

Hutchinson, George. *In Search of Nella Larsen: A Biography of the Color Line*. Cambridge, MA: Harvard University Press, 2006.

Hyles, Vernon. "Ben, Rudy, and the Fantastic: Wolfe's Journey to Nighttown," *The Thomas Wolfe Review* 13, no. 2 (Fall 1989): 44–48.

Hynes, Samuel. *A War Imagined: The First World War and English Culture*. New York: Atheneum, 1991.

Influenza 1918. Dir. Robert Kenner. 1998. Alexandria, VA: American Experience: WGBH Educational Foundation, 2005. VIVA PBS streaming.

Influenza Encyclopedia: The American Influenza Epidemic of 1918–1919. Ed. J. Alex Navarro, Alexandra Stern, and Howard Markel. Ann Arbor: University of Michigan Center for the History of Medicine and Michigan Publishing, University of Michigan Library, 2016. http://www.influenzaarchive.org.

Jarrett, Christian. "The Lure of Horror." *The Psychologist: Publication of the British Psychological Society* 24, no. 11 (November 2011): 812–15.

Jay, Gregory. "Eliot's Poetics and the Fisher King." *Yeats Eliot Review* 7, no. 2 (June 1982): 28–35.

Jeffares, A. Norman. *W. B. Yeats: A New Biography*. New York: Continuum, 2001.

Johnson, Niall. *Britain and the 1918–1919 Influenza Pandemic: A Dark Epilogue*. London: Routledge, 2006.

Johnson, Niall P. A. S., and Juergen Mueller. "Updating the Accounts: Global Mortality of the 1918–1920 'Spanish' Influenza Pandemic." *Bulletin of the History of Medicine* 76, no. 1 (Spring 2002): 105–15.

Jolly, Martyn. *Faces of the Living Dead: The Belief in Spirit Photography*. New York: Mark Batty, 2006.

Jones, Esyllt. "Spectral Influenza: Winnipeg's Hamilton Family, Interwar Spiritualism, and Pandemic Disease." In *Epidemic Encounters: Influenza, Society, and Culture in Canada, 1918–20*, ed. Magda Fahrni and Esyllt W. Jones, 193–221. Vancouver: UBC Press, 2012.

Jordan, Edwin Oakes. *Epidemic Influenza: A Survey*. Chicago: American Medical Association, 1927.

Joshi, S. T. *I Am Providence: The Life and Times of H. P. Lovecraft*. Vol. 1. New York: Hippocampus, 2010.

Joyce, James. *Ulysses* [1922]. Ed. Hans Walter Gabler. New York: Vintage, 1986.

Kee, Chera. "'They are not men . . . they are dead bodies!': From Cannibal to Zombie and Back Again." In *Better Off Dead*, ed. Deborah Christie and Sarah Juliet Lauro, 9–23.

Kendall, Tim. *Poetry of the First World War: An Anthology*. Oxford: Oxford University Press, 2014.

Kennedy, Richard S. *The Window of Memory: The Literary Career of Thomas Wolfe*. Chapel Hill: University of North Carolina Press, 1962.

Kent, Susan K. *The Influenza Pandemic of 1918–1919*. New York: Bedford/St. Martin's, 2012.

Kolata, Gina. *Flu: The Story of the Great Influenza Pandemic of 1918 and the Search for the Virus That Caused It.* New York: Touchstone, 2001.

Krockel, Carl. "Legacies of War: The Reputations of Lawrence and T. S. Eliot in the Modernist Period." *D. H. Lawrence Review* 37, no.1 (2012): 1–17.

——. *War Trauma and English Modernism: T. S. Eliot and D. H. Lawrence.* New York: Palgrave Macmillan, 2011.

Lauro, Sarah Juliet, ed. *Zombie Theory: A Reader.* Minneapolis: University of Minnesota Press, 2017.

Lee, Hermione. "Introduction." In *On Being Ill with Notes from Sick Rooms,* by Virginia Woolf and Julia Stephen, xiii–xxxvi. Ashfield, MA: Paris Press, 2012.

——. *Virginia Woolf.* New York: Knopf, 1997.

Leese, Peter. *Shell Shock: Traumatic Neurosis and the British Soldiers of the First World War.* New York: Palgrave, 2002.

Legg, Joanna, Graham Parker, and David Legg. "War Graves for the WWI Dead on the Western Front." In *The Great War, 1914–1918: A Guide to World War 1 Battlefields and History of the First World War.* http://www.greatwar.co.uk/war-graves /ww1-war-graves.htm.

Levenback, Karen L. *Virginia Woolf and the Great War.* Syracuse, NY: Syracuse University Press, 1999.

Levenson, Michael. *A Genealogy of Modernism: A Study of English Literary Doctrine, 1908–1922.* Cambridge: Cambridge University Press, 1986.

Lewis, Edith. *Willa Cather Living: A Personal Record.* New York: Knopf, 1953.

Lewis, Sinclair. "A Hamlet of the Plains." *New York Evening Post, The Literary Review* 16 (September 1922): 23. Reprinted in *Willa Cather: The Contemporary Reviews,* ed. Margaret Anne O'Connor, 127–30. Cambridge: Cambridge University Press, 2001.

Leys, Ruth. *Trauma: A Genealogy.* Chicago: University of Chicago Press, 2000.

Lindemann, Marilee, ed. *The Cambridge Companion to Willa Cather.* Cambridge: Cambridge University Press, 2005.

Lindskold, Jane. "The Autobiographical Occult in Yeats's 'The Second Coming.'" *Eire-Ireland: A Journal of Irish Studies* 26, no. 4 (1991): 38–44.

Livius, Titus (Livy). *Roman History* [c. 28 BC]. Trans. William Gordon. Aberdeen: J. Chalmers, 1805.

Lodge, Sir Oliver. *Raymond, or Life After Death.* New York: George H. Doran Co., 1916.

London, Bette. *Writing Double: Women's Literary Partnerships.* Ithaca, NY: Cornell University Press, 1999.

Lovecraft, H. P. "Cool Air." *Tales of Magic and Mystery* 1, no. 4 (March 1928): 29–34. Reprinted in *Tales,* ed. Peter Straub, 158–66. New York: Library of America, 2005.

——. "Herbert West—Reanimator." *Home Brew* (1922), six installments. Reprinted in *Tales,* ed. Peter Straub, 24–54. New York: Library of America, 2005.

——. "In the Vault." *Tryout* (November 1925). Reprinted in *The Dunwich Horror and Others: The Best Supernatural Stories of H. P. Lovecraft,* ed. August Derleth, 10–18. Sauk City, WI: Arkham House, 1963.

——. "Nyarlathotep." *The United Amateur* (November 1920). Reproduced as Project Gutenberg of Australia eBook, produced by Roy Glashan, May 2015. http://gutenberg .net.au/ebooks15/1500481h.html.

Lycett, Andrew. *The Man Who Created Sherlock Holmes: The Life and Times of Sir Arthur Conan Doyle.* New York: Free Press, 2007.

Macnamara, D. W. "Memories of 1918 and 'the 'Flu.'" *Journal of the Irish Medical Association* 35, no. 208 (1954): 304–9.

Maddox, Brenda. *Yeats's Ghosts: The Secret Life of W. B. Yeats*. New York: Harper Collins, 2000.

Mamelund, Svenn-Erik. "Geography May Explain Adult Mortality from the 1918–20 Influenza Pandemic." *Epidemics* 3, no. 1 (March 2011): 46–60.

Manjunatha, Narayana, Suresh Bada Math, Girish Baburao Kulkarni, and Santosh Kumar Chaturvedi. "The Neuropsychiatric Aspects of Influenza/Swine Flu: A Selective Review." *Industrial Psychiatry Journal* (July–December 2011): 83–90.

Mao, Douglas, and Rebecca Walkowitz. "The New Modernist Studies." *PMLA* 123, no. 3 (2008): 738–48.

Marsh, Patricia. "'Mysterious Malady Spreading': Press Coverage of the 1918–19 Influenza Pandemic in Ireland." *Quest Proceedings of the QUB AHSS Conference* 6 (Autumn 2008): 167–76.

Matera, Marc, Misty L. Bastian, and Susan Kingsley Kent. *The Women's War of 1929: Gender and Violence in Colonial Nigeria*. New York: Palgrave Macmillan, 2012.

Maxwell, William. "The Art of Fiction No. 71." Interview by John Seabrook. *Paris Review* 85 (Fall 1982): 107–39.

——. *They Came Like Swallows*. New York: Harper & Brothers, 1937.

McCarthy, Mary. *Memories of a Catholic Girlhood*. New York: Harcourt Brace Jovanovich, 1946.

McDermott, Don. "The Last Judgment on 'The Second Coming.'" *Yeats Eliot Review* 10, no. 3 (Spring 1990): 70–73.

McIntire, Gabrielle, ed. *The Cambridge Companion to* The Waste Land. Cambridge: Cambridge University Press, 2015.

——. "*The Waste Land* as Ecocritique." See *The Cambridge Companion to* The Waste Land, ed. Gabrielle McIntire, 178–93.

Menninger, Karl A. "Psychoses Associated with Influenza." *Journal of the American Medical Association* 72, no. 4 (January 25, 1919): 235–41.

Miller, James E., Jr. *T. S. Eliot's Personal Waste Land: Exorcism of the Demons*. University Park: Pennsylvania State University Press, 1977.

Mitchell, Timothy. *Rule of Experts: Egypt, Techno-Politics, Modernity*. Berkeley: University of California Press, 2002.

Moreman, Christopher M., and Cory James Rushton, eds. *Race, Oppression, and the Zombie: Essays on Cross-Cultural Appropriations of the Caribbean Tradition*. Jefferson, NC: McFarland & Company, 2011.

——. *Zombies Are Us: Essays on the Humanity of the Walking Dead*. Jefferson, NC: McFarland & Company, 2011.

Murphy, Russell E. "The 'Rough Beast' and Historical Necessity: A New Consideration of Yeats's 'The Second Coming.'" *Studies in the Literary Imagination* 14, no. 1 (Spring 1981): 101–10.

Murphy, William Michael. *Prodigal Father: The Life of John Butler Yeats (1839–1922)*. Syracuse, NY: Syracuse University Press, 2001.

Neverow, Vara S. "Septimus Warren Smith, Modernist War Poet." *South Carolina Review* 48, no. 2 (Spring 2016): 58–65.

Newman, George. "Chief Medical Officer's Introduction." In Ministry of Health, "Report on the Pandemic of Influenza, 1918–1919," *Reports on Public Health and Medical Subjects*, no. 4. London: His Majesty's Stationery Office, 1920.

Nixon, Rob. *Slow Violence and the Environmentalism of the Poor*. Cambridge, MA: Harvard University Press, 2011.

Nowell, Elizabeth. *Thomas Wolfe: A Biography*. New York: Doubleday, 1960.

O'Brien, Sharon. "Combat Envy and Survivor Guilt: Willa Cather's 'Manly Battle Yarn.'" In *Arms and the Woman: War, Gender, and Literary Representation*, ed. Helen M. Cooper, Adrienne Auslander Munich, and Susan Merrill Squier, 184–204. Chapel Hill: University of North Carolina Press, 1989.

——. "Willa Cather in the Country of the Ill." In *The Cambridge Companion to Willa Cather*, ed. Marilee Lindemann, 146–56. Cambridge: Cambridge University Press, 2005.

O'Connor, Margaret Anne, ed. *Willa Cather: The Contemporary Reviews*. Cambridge: Cambridge University Press, 2001.

O'Driscoll, Robert. "'The Second Coming' and Yeats's Vision of History." In *A Festschrift for Edgar Ronald Seary: Essays in English Language and Literature*, ed. Alastair Macdonald et al., 170–81. Newfoundland: Memorial University of Newfoundland, 1975.

O'Hara, John. "The Doctor's Son." In *The Doctor's Son and Other Stories*. New York: Harcourt, Brace, 1935.

Orlin, Eric M. *Temples, Religion, and Politics in the Roman Republic*. Boston: Brill, 2002.

Orr, Douglas W. *Virginia Woolf's Illnesses*. Ed. Wayne K. Chapman. Clemson, SC: Clemson University Digital Press, 2004.

Osler, Sir William Osler, with Thomas McCrae. *The Principles and Practices of Medicine*. 8th ed. New York and London: D. Appleton, 1915.

Outka, Elizabeth. "Dead Men, Walking: Actors, Networks, and Actualized Metaphors in *Mrs. Dalloway* and *Raymond*." *NOVEL: A Forum on Fiction* 46, no. 2 (2013): 253–74.

——. "'Wood for the Coffins Ran Out': Modernism and the Shadowed Afterlife of the Influenza Pandemic." *Modernism/modernity* 21, no. 4 (November 2014) 937–60.

Owen, Alex. *The Darkened Room: Women, Power, and Spiritualism in Late Victorian England*. Chicago: University of Chicago Press, 1989.

Owen, Wilfred. "Dulce et Decorum Est." Written 1917, published 1920. In *The Penguin Book of First World War Poetry*, ed. George Walter, 141–42. New York: Penguin, 2004.

——. "Mental Cases." Written 1917–1918. In *Poetry of the First World War: An Anthology*, ed. Tim Kendall, 170–71. Oxford: Oxford University Press, 2014.

Pandemic Influenza Storybook. Centers for Disease Control and Prevention Digital Archive. https://www.cdc.gov/publications/panflu/.

Peter, John. "A New Interpretation of *The Waste Land*." *Essays in Criticism* 19 (April 1969): 140–75.

Pettit, Dorothy Ann, and Janice Bailie. *A Cruel Wind: Pandemic Flu in America, 1918–1920*. Murfreesboro, TN: Timberlane, 2008.

Phillips, Gyllian. "*White Zombie* and the Creole: William Seabrook's *The Magic Island* and American Imperialism in Haiti." In *Generation Zombie*, ed. Stephanie Boluk and Wylie Lenz, 27–40.

Phillips, Howard. *"Black October": The Impact of the Spanish Influenza Epidemic of 1918 on South Africa*. Pretoria: The Government Printer, 1990.

——. "South Africa's *Worst* Demographic Disaster: The Spanish Influenza Epidemic of 1918." *South African Historical Journal* 20 (1988): 57–73.

Philips, Howard, and Killingray, David, eds. *The Spanish Influenza Pandemic of 1918–1919: New Perspectives.* London: Routledge, 2011.

Porras-Gallo, María-Isabel, and Ryan A. Davis, eds. *The Spanish Influenza Pandemic of 1918–1919: Perspectives from the Iberian Peninsula and the Americas.* New York: University of Rochester Press, 2014.

Porter, Katherine Anne. "Interview with Barbara Thompson." In *Katherine Anne Porter: Conversations,* ed. Joan Givner, 78–98. Jackson: University Press of Mississippi, 1987.

——. *Pale Horse, Pale Rider* [1939]. In *The Collected Stories of Katherine Anne Porter,* 269–317. New York: Harcourt, 1979.

——. *Selected Letters of Katherine Anne Porter: Chronicles of a Modern Woman.* Ed. Darlene Harbour Unrue. Jackson: University Press of Mississippi, 2012.

Préher, Gérald. "A Cosmos of His Own: Loss, Ghosts, and Loneliness in Thomas Wolfe's Fiction." *The Thomas Wolfe Review* 35, no. 1–2 (2011): 22–39.

Query, Patrick. "'The pleasures of higher vices': Sexuality in Eliot's Work." In *A Companion to T. S. Eliot,* ed. David E. Chinitz, 350–62.

Rabaté, Jean-Michel. "'The World Has Seen Strange Revolutions Since I Died': The *Waste Land* and the Great War." In *The Cambridge Companion to* The Waste Land, ed. Gabrielle McIntire, 9–23.

Rae, Patricia, ed. *Modernism and Mourning.* Lewisburg, PA: Bucknell University Press, 2007.

Raghu, A. "Yeats's 'The Second Coming.'" *Explicator* 50, no. 4 (Summer 1992): 224–25.

Ragussis, Michael. *The Subterfuge of Art: Language and the Romantic Tradition.* Baltimore, MD: Johns Hopkins University Press, 1978.

Raitt, Suzanne, and Trudi Tate, eds. *Women's Fiction and the Great War.* Oxford: Oxford University Press, 1997.

Read, Peter. *Picasso and Apollinaire: The Persistence of Memory.* Berkeley: University of California Press, 2008.

Rebhorn, Wayne A. "Introduction." In *The Decameron,* by Giovanni Boccaccio, ed. and trans. Wayne A. Rebhorn, xv–xlvii. New York: Norton, 2016.

Rice, Geoffrey W. *Black November: The 1918 Influenza Pandemic in New Zealand.* Christchurch: Canterbury University Press, 2005.

Rivers, W. H. R. "An Address on the Repression of War Experience." Originally delivered on December 4, 1917, at "Section of Psychiatry" at the Royal Society of Medicine, 1–20. Reprinted in *The Lancet* 191, no. 4927 (February 2, 1918): 173–77.

Roach, Mary. *Spook: Science Tackles the Afterlife.* New York: Norton, 2005.

Roberts, Terry. "'By the Wind Grieved': The Proem of *Look Homeward, Angel.*" *The Southern Literary Journal* 29, no. 1 (Fall 1996): 81–92.

Romero, George A., dir. *Dawn of the Dead.* 1978; Pittsburgh and Monroeville, PA: Laurel Group Inc. Film.

——. *Night of the Living Dead.* 1968; Pittsburgh, PA: Image Ten. Film.

Ross, David A. *A Critical Companion to William Butler Yeats: A Literary Reference to His Life and Work.* New York: Facts on File, 2009.

Rudrum, David. "Slouching Towards Bethlehem: Yeats, Eliot, and the Modernist Apocalypse." In *Ecstasy and Understanding: Religious Awareness of English Poetry from the Late Victorian to the Modern Period*, ed. Adrian Grafe, 58–70. New York: Continuum, 2008.

Sacks, Oliver. *Awakenings* [1973]. New York: Vintage, 1999.

Saddlemyer, Ann. *Becoming George: The Life of Mrs. W. B. Yeats*. Oxford: Oxford University Press, 2002.

Said, Edward W. "Yeats and Decolonization." In *Nationalism, Colonialism, and Literature*, by Terry Eagleton, Fredric Jameson, and Edward W. Said, 69–96. Minneapolis: University of Minnesota Press, 1990.

Saint-Amour, Paul K. *Tense Future: Modernism, Total War, Encyclopedic Form*. New York: Oxford University Press, 2015.

Saler, Michael. "Modern Enchantments: The Canny Wonders and Uncanny Others of H. P. Lovecraft." *The Space Between* 2 no. 1 (2006): 11–32.

Sassoon, Siegfried. "Repression of War Experience" [1918]. Reprinted in *Poetry of the First World War: An Anthology*, ed. Tim Kendall, 97–98. Oxford: Oxford University Press, 2014.

Savage, George H. "The Psychosis of Influenza." *Practitioner* 52 (January–June 1919): 36–46.

Scarry, Elaine. *The Body in Pain: The Making and Unmaking of the World* [1985]. Oxford: Oxford University Press, 2008.

Schiraldi, Glenn R. *The Post-Traumatic Stress Disorder Sourcebook*. 2nd ed. New York: McGraw-Hill, 2009.

Seabrook, W. B. *The Magic Island*. New York: Harcourt, Brace, 1929.

Sharkey, Sabina. "Gendering Inequalities: The Case of Irish Women." *Paragraph* 16, no. 1 (March 1993): 5–22.

Sherman, David. "A Plot Unraveling Into Ethics: Woolf, Levinas, and 'Time Passes.'" *Woolf Studies Annual* 13 (2007): 159–79.

——. *In a Strange Room: Modernism's Corpses and Mortal Obligation*. New York: Oxford University Press, 2014.

Sherry, Vincent. "Imbalances: Mass Death and the Economy of 'Sacrifice' in the Great War." In *The First World War: Literature, Culture, Modernity*, ed. Santanu Das and Kate McLoughlin. Oxford: Oxford University Press, 2018.

Showalter, Elaine. *The Female Malady: Women, Madness, and English Culture, 1830–1980*. New York: Penguin, 1987.

Sim, Lorraine. *Virginia Woolf: The Patterns of Ordinary Experience*. Farnham: Ashgate, 2010.

Smajić, Srdjan. *Ghost-Seers, Detectives, and Spiritualists: Theories of Vision in Victorian Literature and Science*. Cambridge: Cambridge University Press, 2010.

Smith, Geddes. *Plague on Us*. New York: The Commonwealth Fund, 1941.

Sontag, Susan. *Illness as Metaphor* [1977]. In *Illness as Metaphor and AIDS and Its Metaphors*. New York: Picador, 1990.

Sorensen, Leif. "A Weird Modernist Archive: Pulp Fiction, Pseudobiblia, H. P. Lovecraft." *Modernism/modernity* 17, no. 3 (September 2010): 501–22.

"The Spanish Influenza: A Sufferer's Symptoms." *Times* (London), June 25, 1918, 9.

Spencer, Elizabeth. "*Look Homeward, Angel*: Of Ghosts, Angels, and Lostness." *North Carolina Literary Review* 12 (2003): 78–86.

Spinney, Laura. *Pale Rider: The Spanish Flu of 1918 and How It Changed the World*. London: Jonathan Cape, 2017.

"Spirit Picture Stirs Spectators to Sobs." *New York Times*, April 7, 1923, 1.

Spurr, Barry. *Anglo-Catholic in Religion: T. S. Eliot and Christianity*. Cambridge: Lutterworth, 2010.

Stallworthy, Jon. *Between the Lines: Yeats's Poetry in the Making*. Oxford: Clarendon, 1963.

Steedman, Carolyn. *Dust: The Archive and Cultural History*. New Brunswick, NJ: Rutgers University Press, 2002.

Stegner, Wallace. *On a Darkling Plain*. New York: Harcourt Brace, 1940.

——. *The Big Rock Candy Mountain*. New York: Duell, Sloan, and Pearce, 1943.

Steinmeyer, Jim. *Hiding the Elephant: How Magicians Invented the Impossible and Learned to Disappear*. New York: Carroll & Graf, 2003.

Stephen, Leslie. *Sir Leslie Stephen's Mausoleum Book*. Ed. Alan Bell. Oxford: Clarendon, 1977.

Stout, Janis P. *Katherine Anne Porter: A Sense of the Times*. Charlottesville: University Press of Virginia, 1995.

——. *Willa Cather: The Writer and Her World*. Charlottesville: University Press of Virginia, 2000.

Stryker, Laurinda. "British Shell-Shock and the Politics of Interpretation." In *Evidence, History, and the Great War: Historians and the Impact of 1914–1918*, ed. Gail Braybon, 154–71. New York: Berghahn, 2003.

"Suicide Not an End of Ills, Says Doyle." *New York Times*, April 11, 1922, 11.

Sun, Lena H. "CDC to Cut by 80 Percent Efforts to Prevent Global Disease Outbreak." *Washington Post*, February 1, 2018.

Surette, Leon. *The Birth of Modernism: Ezra Pound, T. S. Eliot, W. B. Yeats, and the Occult*. Montreal: McGill-Queen's University Press: 1993.

——. "*The Waste Land* and Jessie Weston: A Reassessment." *Twentieth Century Literature* 34, no. 2 (Summer 1988): 223–44.

Sweeney, Dr. Frederick C. *Diary of Dr. Frederick C. Sweeney, Captain in the United States Army Medical Corps*. 1918–1919. Typewritten copy presented to the University of California–Davis Library. Prepared by Margaret C. Bean, October 1990. Original diary held at Jaffrey-Gilmore Foundation in Jaffrey, NH.

Sword, Helen. *Ghostwriting Modernism*. Ithaca, NY: Cornell University Press, 2002.

Tate, George S. "'The Great World of the Spirits of the Dead': Death, the Great War, and the 1918 Influenza Pandemic as Context for Doctrine and Covenants 138," *Brigham Young University Studies Quarterly* 46, no. 1 (2007): 4–40.

Taubenberger, Jeffery K., Johan V. Hultin, and David M. Morens. "Discovery and Characterization of the 1918 Pandemic Influenza Virus in Historical Context." *Antiviral Therapy* 12, no. 4 (2007): 581–91.

Thomson, David, and Robert Thomson. "Influenza." In *Annals of the Pickett-Thomson Research Laboratory*, vol. 10. London: Baillière, Tindall & Cox, 1934.

Thompson, William J., MD. "Mortality from Influenza in Ireland." *Journal of the Statistical and Social Inquiry Society of Ireland* 14, no. 1 (1919/1920): 1–14.

Tomes, Nancy. *The Gospel of Germs: Men, Women, and the Microbe in American Life*. Cambridge, MA: Harvard University Press, 1998.

Trout, Steven. *Memorial Fictions: Willa Cather and the First World War*. Lincoln: University of Nebraska Press, 2002.

Unrue, Darlene Harbour. *Katherine Anne Porter: The Life of an Artist*. Jackson: University Press of Mississippi, 2005.

——. *Katherine Anne Porter Remembered*. Tuscaloosa: University of Alabama Press, 2010.

Urgo, Joseph R. "The Cather Thesis: The American Empire of Migration." In *The Cambridge Companion to Willa Cather*, ed. Marilee Lindemann, 35–50. Cambridge: Cambridge University Press, 2005.

Utell, Janine. "View from the Sickroom: Virginia Woolf, Dorothy Wordsworth, and Writing Women's Lives of Illness." *Life Writing* 13, no. 1 (2016): 27–45.

Vannini, Simona. "The Genesis of 'The Second Coming': A Textual Analysis of the Manuscript-Draft." *Yeats: An Annual of Critical and Textual Studies* 16 (1998): 100–32.

Vendler, Helen. *Our Secret Discipline: Yeats and Lyric Form*. Cambridge, MA: Harvard University Press, 2007.

Verfaellie, Mieke, and Jennifer J. Vasterling. "Memory in PTSD: A Neurocognitive Approach." In *Post-Traumatic Stress Disorder: Basic Science and Clinical Practice*, ed. Priyattam Shiromani, Terrence Keane, and Joseph LeDoux, 105–32. New York: Humana, 2009.

von Hallberg, Robert, and Cassandra Laity, eds. "Men, Women and World War I." Special issue, *Modernism/modernity* 9, no. 1 (January 2002).

Wald, Priscilla. *Contagious: Cultures, Carriers, and the Outbreak Narrative*. Durham, NC: Duke University Press, 2008.

The Walking Dead. Developed by Frank Darabont; produced by Robert Kirkman et al. 2010; Georgia: AMC. Television.

Ware, Ruth Winchester. "Thomas Wolfe's 1918 Flu Story: The Death of Ben in the Context of Other Literary Narratives of the Pandemic." *The Thomas Wolfe Review* 33 (2009): 67–82.

Wasserman, I. M. "The Impact of Epidemic, War, Prohibition and Media on Suicide: United States, 1910–1920." *Suicidal & Life-Threatening Behavior* 22, no. 2 (Summer 1992): 240–54.

We Heard the Bells: The Influenza of 1918. Dir. Lisa Laden. United States Department of Health and Human Services, 2010. https://www.youtube.com/watch?v=XbEefT_M6xY.

Weise, Matthew J. "How the Zombie Changed Videogames." In *Zombies Are Us*, ed. Christopher Moreman and Cory James Rushton, 151–68.

Weston, Jessie L. *From Ritual to Romance*. Cambridge: Cambridge University Press, 1920.

Whitehead, Anne. *Trauma Fiction*. Edinburgh: Edinburgh University Press, 2004.

Whitehead, Colson. *Zone One*. New York: Doubleday, 2011.

Willis, Chris. "Making the Dead Speak: Spiritualism and Detective Fiction." In *The Art of Detective Fiction*, ed. Warren Chernaik, Martin Swales, and Robert Vilain, 60–74. New York: Palgrave Macmillan, 2000.

Winter, Jay. *Sites of Memory, Sites of Mourning: The Great War in European Cultural History*. Cambridge: Cambridge University Press, 1995.

Wolfe, Thomas. *The Letters of Thomas Wolfe*. Ed. Elizabeth Nowell. New York: Charles Scribner's Sons, 1946.

——. *The Letters of Thomas Wolfe to His Mother*. Ed. C. Hugh Holman and Sue Fields Ross. Chapel Hill: University of North Carolina Press, 1968.

——. *Look Homeward, Angel: A Story of the Buried Life*. 1929. New York: Charles Scribner's Sons, 1957.

——. "The Story of a Novel" [1936]. In *The Thomas Wolfe Reader*, ed. C. Hugh Holman, 13–63. New York: Charles Scribner's Sons, 1962.

Wood, Michael. *Yeats and Violence*. Oxford: Oxford University Press, 2010.

Woodress, James. *Willa Cather: A Literary Life*. Lincoln: University of Nebraska Press, 1987.

Woolf, Virginia. *The Diary of Virginia Woolf*. Vol. 1: *1915–1919*. Ed. Anne Olivier Bell. New York: Harvest/Harcourt, 1977.

——. *The Diary of Virginia Woolf*. Vol. 2: *1920–1924*. Ed. Anne Olivier Bell with Andeew McNeville. New York: Harcourt Brace, 1978.

——. *The Letters of Virginia Woolf*. Vol. 2: *1912–1922*. Ed. Nigel Nicolson and Joanne Trautmann. New York: Harvest/Harcourt, 1976.

——. *The Letters of Virginia Woolf*. Vol. 4: *1929–1931*. Ed. Nigel Nicolson and Joanne Trautmann. New York: Harcourt Brace, 1978.

——. *Mrs. Dalloway* [1925]. Ed. Bonnie Kime Scott, gen. ed. Mark Hussey. New York: Harvest/Harcourt, 2005.

——. "Old Bloomsbury." Written 1921 or 1922. In *Moments of Being*, 2nd ed., ed. Jeanne Schulkind, 179–201. New York: Harvest/Harcourt, 1985.

——. "On Being Ill." *New Criterion*, January 1926. Reprinted in *The Essays of Virginia Woolf*, vol. 4: *1925–1928*, ed. Andrew McNeillie, 317–29. New York: Harvest/Harcourt, 1994.

——. *To the Lighthouse* [1927]. Ed. Mark Hussey. New York: Harvest/Harcourt, 2005.

——. *To the Lighthouse: The Original Holograph Draft*. Ed. Susan Dick. Toronto: Toronto University Press, 1982.

——. *The Voyage Out* [1915]. Ed. Jane Wheare. New York: Penguin, 1992.

Woolf, Virginia, and Julia Stephen. *On Being Ill with Notes from Sick Rooms*. Intro. by Hermione Lee and Mark Hussey, afterword by Rita Charon. Ashfield, MA: Paris Press, 2012.

Yeats, William Butler. *The Collected Poems of W. B. Yeats*. Rev. 2nd ed. Ed. Richard J. Finneran. New York: Scribner, 1996.

——. *Michael Robartes and the Dancer: Manuscript Materials*. Ed. Thomas Parkinson and Anne Brannen. Cornell Yeats Project. Ithaca, NY: Cornell University Press, 1994.

——. *The Variorum Edition of the Poems of W. B. Yeats*. Ed. Peter Allt and Russell K. Alspach. New York: Macmillan, 1957.

——. *A Vision* [1925]. New York: Macmillan, 1956.

Yong, Ed. "The Next Plague Is Coming. Is America Ready?" *Atlantic*, July/August 2018. https://www.theatlantic.com/magazine/archive/2018/07/when-the-next-plague -hits/561734/.

Youngblood, Sarah. "Structure and Imagery in Katherine Anne Porter's 'Pale Horse, Pale Rider.'" In *Critical Essays on Katherine Anne Porter*, ed. Darlene Harbour Unrue, 193–200. New York: G. K. Hall & Co., 1997.

Zink, Abbey. "Is Blood Thicker Than Artistry? Nativist Modernism and Eugene Gant's Initiation Into Blood Politics in *Look Homeward, Angel*." *The Thomas Wolfe Review* 25, no. 1–2 (2001): 44–52.

Žižek, Slavoj. *Violence: Six Sideways Reflections*. New York: Picador, 2008.

INDEX

"Mental Cases" (Owen), 134
mental health: delirium and, 12–13; of Eliot, 142–43; influenza pandemic and, 12–13, 115, 125–31; of Woolf, 130–31, 136
Meyer, Stephenie, 21
miasma, as trope, 5–6, 13, 24, 34, 40, 244; for Eliot, 145, 150, 157; for Porter, 55; in spiritualism, 212; for Wolfe, 75; for Woolf, 123; for Yeats, 169, 174, 177
Microbe Hunters (Kruif), 28
microbes, 91
military funerals, 48–49; of Apollinaire, 223
Miranda (fictional character), in *Pale Horse, Pale Rider* (Porter), 52–73, 119, 147–48
modernism, 1–3; corpse in, 32–33; encyclopedic, 34; miasmic, 5–6, 13; mourning and, 31–32; realism and, 4; reframing, 35–37; violence and, 33–34
modernist literature: character in, 100; influenza pandemic, in style of, 100–101; influenza pandemic in, 1–5, 34, 99–101, 243–45; miasma trope in, 5–6, 13; prose style, 124; techniques of, 100; viral resurrection in, 100. *See also specific authors*; *specific works*
modernist studies, influenza pandemic and, 31–37
mourning, 82, 93, 117–18, 138; by doctors, 210; language of, 132; Maxwell on, 32; and modernism, 31–32; for pandemic, incorporated into war mourning, 24–25; pandemics, 31–32
Mrs. Dalloway (Woolf): on afterlife, 122–23; Armistice in, 119–20, 139; bells ringing in, 116–18; body in, 113–15, 118–19, 121–24, 131–34, 137, 139; Clarissa Dalloway (fictional character) in, 105, 113–24, 131–33, 139–40, 247; contagion metaphors in, 121–24; corpses in, 113–14, 118–19; doctors in, 138–40; flashbacks in, 112, 133–34; hallucinatory-delirium mode of, 105–6, 131–39; illness in, 106, 111; influenza in, 101, 104–5, 109–10,

113–24, 131–41; on influenza pandemic and World War I, 105, 124–41; living death in, 114, 123; "On Being Ill" and, 111, 132, 140–41, 271n13; reframing of, 112–13, 124; resurrection in, 134–38; Sassoon and, 112, 135; Septimus Smith (fictional character) in, 105–6, 112–13, 124, 131–40, 147; Shakespeare quotation in, 118–19; sickroom, 114–15, 119–20, 132–33, 136–37; suicide in, 138–40; war parade in, 119–20; World War I in, 112–13, 124–31, 133–38
Mrs. Ramsay (fictional character), in *To the Lighthouse* (Woolf), 248–52
Mullen, Thomas, 21
Munch, Edvard, 128–29, *129, 130*
Munro, Alice, "Carried Away," 260n73
Murry, John Middleton, 157

narrative: contagion, 28, 30–31, 201, 227–28, 230–31, 234–35; cyclical, 63; of influenza pandemic, 49–50, 52; outbreak, 30–31; pandemic's disruption of, 25–26, 30–31, 40, 44–45, 53–54, 59–60, 62–63, 70, 72–73, 90, 115; structure, 72–73; of World War I, 44–45, 56, 59, 69–70, 90
Narrative Medicine (Charon), 25–27, 30
nature, indifference of, 111–12
Newell, Eric, 127
Newman, George, 11
New York Times, 210–12, 214
Nigeria, 35, 256n2, 260n73
Night of the Living Dead (1968), 217
"Nineteen Hundred and Nineteen" (Yeats), 177–80, 284n48
Nineteenth-Century Narratives of Contagion (Christensen), 91
Nixon, Rob, 281n3
"Note on War Poetry, A" (Eliot), 144
Notes from Sick Rooms (Stephen), 272n14
nothingness, 54–55, 245, 248, 253
"Nyarlathotep" (Lovecraft), 228–31, 292n85; contagion atmosphere of, 229–30; living death states in, 229–30; xenophobia of, 230

O'Brien, Sharon, 46
O'Hara, John, 263n1
"On Being Ill" (Woolf), 104–5, 120–22,
137; on illness and war, 106–7;
on illness's compensations, 111–12;
on influenza pandemic and World
War I, 106–8; on language, of illness,
109, 245, 248, 250; *Mrs. Dalloway*
and, 111, 132–33, 140–41, 271n13; on
sickroom, 114, 132; on sympathy, 110–11
One of Ours (Cather): Claude (fictional
character) in, 44, 47–52, 73; contagion
in, 47–49; death in, 48–52; doctors in,
48–50; influenza pandemic in, 43–52,
73–74; narrative structure of, 43–45,
47, 50–52, 72–73; Owen and, 48; *Pale
Horse, Pale Rider* and, 39, 43–45,
72–73; sexist reviews of, 73–74, 263n1;
story of, 47–51; World War I in,
45–46, 51–52; on World War I and
influenza pandemic, 43–47, 50–51,
72–74
Osler, William, 125
Ouanga (1936), 217
outbreak narratives, 30–31
Owen, Wilfred, 269n28; on death in war,
48, 52, 83–84; "Dulce et Decorum
Est" by, 48, 83–84; "Mental Cases" by,
134–35; Woolf and, 33

pain, 60–61, 64–65; body and, 48, 67–69,
116, 129, 134; female body and, 45, 68;
illness and, 26, 68–69; influenza,
67–69; language and, 67, 110; of war,
68–69
Pale Horse, Pale Rider (Porter): Adam
(fictional character) in, 57–62, 64,
70–72; Armistice in, 52–53, 69, 119;
bells ringing in, 69, 119; body in,
53–54, 56–61, 66–70; contagion in,
44, 55, 61, 66; death in, 54–55, 64–67,
70–72; on death and war, 57–58,
63–64; delirium in, 52–55, 59, 62,
64–67, 71; doctors and nurses in, 65,
67, 147; funerals in, 59–60, 69; gender
issues and, 44–45, 58, 61, 63–64,
68–69, 73–74; Grim Reaper/pale rider

in, 55; guilt in, 64–65; hallucinatory
prose of, 53–56, 65–66, 127, 147–48;
on influenza pain, 67–68; on
influenza pandemic and World War
I, 43–45, 56–72; influenza pandemic
in, 44, 52–72; influenza virus in,
61–64, 66–67; living death in, 69–71;
Miranda (fictional character) in,
52–73, 119, 147–48; narrative of,
influenza and, 59; narrative
disruption in, 44–45, 53–54, 59–60,
62–63, 70, 72–73; *One of Ours* and, 39,
43–45, 72–73; viral resurrection in,
62–64, 66–67, 70–72; *The Waste Land*
and, 147, 148; war imagery in, 65–66;
World War I in, 56–59
Pale Rider (Spinney), 21
pandemic death. *See* death, in influenza
pandemic
pandemic flashback, 7–8
Pandemic Influenza Storybook, 8
pandemics, mourning, 31–32
patient zero, 27–28
Pearson, Norman H., 77
Petronius Arbiter, 158
Pettit, Dorothy Ann, 18
Philadelphia, 16, 18, 19, 155
photography, spirit, 200, 202, 210–16, 213,
214, 215
plague, bubonic: Black Plague (1300s),
10; Boccaccio and Defoe on, 153,
183–84, 185, 186–87, 189, 190, 191–92;
burial and, 184; and comparisons
with influenza pandemic, 10, 60–61,
63, 103, 106, 152–53, 186–87, 191–92;
corpses in, 184; social breakdown
and, 183–84, 186–87
Plague on Us (Smith), 28–29
poison gas, 12, 48, 83–84
political violence, 167–70, 174–82,
188–89
Porter, Katherine Anne, 44–45, 193;
Cather and, 39, 41, 44–45, 68, 72–74,
75; influenza bout of, 39, 52, 66–67.
See also Pale Horse, Pale Rider (Porter)
post-pandemic body, 18, 105, 113–16, 157,
238